The Journals of the Lewis and Clark Expedition, Volume 8

June 10–September 26, 1806

Sponsored by the Center for
Great Plains Studies,
University of Nebraska–Lincoln
and the American
Philosophical Society, Philadelphia

A Project of the Center for
Great Plains Studies,
University of Nebraska–Lincoln
Gary E. Moulton, Editor

The Journals of
the Lewis & Clark
Expedition

June 10–September 26, 1806

University of Nebraska Press
Lincoln and London

Publication of this book has been assisted by a grant
from the National Endowment for the Humanities,
an independent federal agency.

The paper in this book meets the minimum require-
ments of American National Standard for Information Sciences – Permanence of Paper for Printed
Library Materials, ANSI Z39.48-1984.

Library of Congress Cataloging-in-Publication Data
(Revised for volume 8)

The Journals of the Lewis and Clark Expedition.
Vol. 2- Gary E. Moulton, editor; Thomas W. Dunlay,
Assistant editor.
Vol. 2- has title: The Journals of the Lewis & Clark
Expedition.
Sponsored by the Center for Great Plains Studies,
University of Nebraska – Lincoln, and the American
Philosophical Society, Philadelphia" – vol.1, t. p.
Includes bibliographies and indexes.
Contents: v.1. Atlas of the Lewis & Clark Expedi-
tion – v.2. August 30, 1803-August 24, 1804 – [etc.] –
v.8. June 10-September 26, 1806.
1. Lewis and Clark Expedition – (1804-1806).
2. West (U.S.) – Description and travel – To 1848.
3. United States – Exploring expeditions. 4. Lewis,
Meriwether, 1774-1809 – Diaries. 5. Clark,
William, 1770-1838 – Diaries. 6. Explorers – West
(U.S.) – Diaries. I. Lewis, Meriwether, 1774-
1809. II. Clark, William, 1770-1838. III. Moulton,
Gary E. IV. Dunlay, Thomas W., 1944- . V. Univer-
sity of Nebraska – Lincoln. Center for Great
Plains Studies. VI. American Philosophical
Society. VII. Journals of the Lewis & Clark
Expedition.
F592.4 1983 917.8'042 82-8510
ISBN 0-8032-2861-9 (v.1) ISBN 0-8032-2898-8 (v.7)

Contents

Preface

Again, this space provides a welcome opportunity to thank the many persons who helped to bring another volume to completion. Their aid, whether friendly advice, scholarly consultation, or financial assistance, made the task less demanding and the way more pleasant. Gladys Watkins Allen (Alton, Illinois), Emilie W. Betts (New York City), Samuel H. Douglas III (Whittier, California), William P. Sherman (Portland, Oregon), Nelson S. Weller (Piedmont, California), and Lyle S. Woodcock (St. Louis, Missouri) provided financial support to aid the editing of this volume. Financial aid also came from the National Endowment for the Humanities, an independent federal agency, and from the Lewis and Clark Trail Heritage Foundation, whose many members support this endeavor beyond their financial contributions.

A special friend of the project has died since publication of the last volume. Robert E. "Bob" Lange was a ceaseless laborer in the service of any cause connected with the Lewis and Clark expedition. He aided this project in countless ways; his unselfish assistance, ready encouragement, and great good will shall be sorely missed and never forgotten.

We again benefited from the expert service of librarians and archivists at repositories of the Lewis and Clark journals. Beth Carroll-Horrocks, Martin L. Levitt, Martha Harrison, Roy E. Goodman, Edward C. Carter II, and Randolph S. Klein, of the American Philosophical Society, Philadelphia, and Duane R. Sneddeker and Bryan Stephen Thomas of the Missouri Historical Society, St. Louis, were helpful and gracious during our work at their institutions. Staff, office, and administrative help came from the Center for Great Plains Studies and the project itself at the University of Nebraska–Lincoln. John R. Wunder, Lori L. Gourama, and Linda J. Ratcliffe of the Center, and Thomas W. Dunlay and Doris VanSchooten of the project performed valuable services.

The following scholars have been generous with their advice and assistance and have aided the project substantially in the areas of their expertise.

BOTANY: Margaret R. Bolick, University of Nebraska–Lincoln; Steven J. Brunsfeld, University of Idaho; A. T. Harrison, Westminster College, Salt Lake

City; and Kathleen Young, Lincoln. GEOLOGY: Robert N. Bergantino, Montana Bureau of Mines and Geology, Butte. LINGUISTICS: American Indian linguistic data in the notes were collected by Raymond J. DeMallie, Indiana University, and were provided by the following individuals: *Nez Perce*. Haruo Aoki, University of California–Berkeley. *Hidatsa*. A. Wesley Jones, Mary College, Bismarck, North Dakota. ZOOLOGY: Frederick P. Baxendale, University of Nebraska–Lincoln, and Lewis T. Nielson, University of Utah (retired) (insects); Patricia Freeman, University of Nebraska–Lincoln (mammals, taxonomy); Anthony Joern, University of Nebraska–Lincoln (grasshoppers); and John D. Lynch, University of Nebraska–Lincoln (fish).

For the Montana segment of the return route, especially for the portion of Lewis's reconnaissance of the Marias River and Clark's survey of the Yellowstone, we again (as in volume 4) used a set of United States Geological Survey (USGS) maps (1° × 2°, 1 : 250,000) supplied by Robert N. Bergantino of Butte, Montana. Bergantino carefully plotted the expedition's route, camps, and points of observation on these maps. He also read and commented on our reference notes to Montana identifications and gave us the benefit of his keen knowledge of Lewis and Clark's trip through his state.

Of course, none of these persons deserves blame for errors or inadequacies in this volume.

EDITORIAL SYMBOLS AND ABBREVIATIONS

[roman]   Word or phrase supplied or corrected.

[roman?]   Conjectural reading of the original.

[*italics*]   Editor's remarks within a document.

[*Ed: italics*]   Editor's remarks that might be confused with *EC, ML, NB, WC,* or *X.*

[*EC: italics*]   Elliott Coues's emendations or interlineations.

[*ML: italics*]   Meriwether Lewis's emendations or interlineations.

[*NB: italics*]   Nicholas Biddle's emendations or interlineations.

[*WC: italics*]   William Clark's emendations or interlineations.

[*X: italics*]   Emendations or interlineations of the unknown or an unidentified person.

⟨roman⟩   Word or phrase deleted by the writer and restored by the editor.

SPECIAL SYMBOLS OF LEWIS AND CLARK

α   Alpha

∠   Angle

☽   Moon symbol

☞   Pointing hand

★   Star

☉   Sun symbol

♍   Virgo

COMMON ABBREVIATIONS OF LEWIS AND CLARK

Altd., alds.	altitude, altitudes
Apt. T.	apparent time
d.	degree
do.	ditto
h.	hour
id., isd.	island
L. L.	lower limb
L., Larb., Lard., Lbd., or Ld. S.	larboard (or left) side
Lad., Latd.	latitude
Longtd.	longitude
m., mts.	minute, minutes
M. T.	mean time
mes., mls., ms.	miles
obstn.	observation
opsd.	opposite
pd., psd.	passed
pt.	point
qde., quadt., qudt.	quadrant
qtr., qutr.	quarter
s.	second
S., St., Star., Starbd., Stb., or Stbd. S.	starboard (or right) side
sext., sextn., sextt.	sextant
U. L.	upper limb

Note: abbreviations in weather entries are explained at the presentation of the first weather data, following the entry of January 31, 1804.

Introduction to Volume 8

Camp Chopunnish, Idaho, to St. Louis, Missouri

June 10–September 26, 1806

On June 10, 1806, the Corps of Discovery left Camp Chopunnish on the Clearwater River and moved up to higher ground on Weippe Prairie. They had waited over a month for the snow to melt in the Bitterroot Mountains so that they could proceed eastward on the Lolo Trail. They set out on the trail on June 15, but soon realized that they could not find their way in the deep snow. On June 17, after caching many of their goods in trees, they turned back. Lewis lamented, "this is the first time since we have been on this long tour that we have ever been compelled to retreat or make a retrograde march." To add discomfort to discouragement he also reported, "it rained on us most of this evening."

They returned to Weippe Prairie and sent to the Nez Perce camps to hire guides. Three young men offered to serve for the price of two guns. On June 24 the party set out again. The Indians found the trail easily and the party made their way to their old camp at Travelers' Rest, near present Missoula, Montana, taking only six days in contrast to the eleven days of the westbound trip. They spent a few days resting for the next stage of the journey. At Fort Clatsop the captains had decided to divide the party for an extended time to investigate previously unexplored territory. Lewis would head east across the mountains to the Great Falls of the Missouri, then explore the Marias River before returning to the Missouri. His purpose was to discover if the Marias drained northern reaches thus giving further territorial claims to the United States under the Louisiana Purchase. Clark would go southeast to the site of Camp Fortunate, then down the Beaverhead and Jefferson rivers to the Three Forks of the Missouri. Part of his party would then take canoes down the Missouri to the Great Falls to meet Lewis's party there, while Clark went east to the Yellowstone and down that river.

His object was to inspect the Yellowstone and perhaps make contact with additional Indian tribes. The two captains and their men would meet at the mouth of the Yellowstone.

On July 3 the two groups went their separate ways, Lewis admitting "I could not avoid feeling much concern on this occasion although I hoped this separation was only momentary." It was the first time during the expedition that they had separated for so great a distance and time. Lewis headed down the Bitterroot River, then up the Clark Fork and across the Continental Divide along a route suggested by the Shoshones and other Indians. By July 13 he and his nine men were at the Upper Portage Camp above the Great Falls, delighted after months of poor rations to be back in buffalo country. When Lewis's men dug up the cache at the camp they encountered problems with the host of grizzly bears in the vicinity. Hugh McNeal had a very close call with one beast in which he broke his musket over its head.

Several of their horses disappeared, probably stolen by Indians, so Lewis decided to take only his three best men—George Drouillard and Reubin and Joseph Field—on his exploration of the Marias. Sergeant Patrick Gass and the others remained at the Great Falls to await the canoe party from the Three Forks. Lewis and his companions set out on horseback on July 14, heading north to the Marias and then upriver to the stream's upper forks. On Cut Bank Creek, near the mountains, they camped from July 20 to 26, waiting for the clouds to clear so Lewis could take astronomical observations; Lewis was disappointed to discover the Marias did not extend so far north as he had hoped. On July 26 he gave up and set off for the mouth of the Marias, leaving what he named Camp Disappointment.

That afternoon they met eight Indians who proved to be Piegan Blackfeet, a tribe Lewis and his small party had wanted to avoid. They talked and all agreed to camp together that night on Two Medicine River. Lewis was awakened the next morning by sounds of a struggle as the Indians tried to make off with the expedition's guns and horses. Reubin Field stabbed one of the Indians to the heart, then the party pursued the others who were fleeing with the horses. Lewis was forced to shoot one of the Blackfeet in self-defense. It was the first and only instance of actual armed violence between the explorers and Indians in the whole expedition.

Lewis, Drouillard, and the Fields fled southeasterly as fast as they could. On July 28, near the mouth of the Marias River, they met the six men from the Great Falls, along with Sergeant John Ordway and nine others whom Clark had sent down from the Three Forks. They moved quickly on to the mouth of the Marias and retrieved cached goods and the white pirogue there. Then Lewis and his united group were able to travel down the Missouri with relative ease and speed.

At the mouth of the Yellowstone, which they reached on August 7, the remains of a note indicated that Clark had gone on down the Missouri. Lewis followed, taking time to hunt for food. On August 11 he was hunting on the banks of the river with Pierre Cruzatte when the Frenchman, thinking the captain was an elk, accidentally shot him in the thigh. The journey continued with Lewis in considerable pain, and on August 12, below the Little Knife River in North Dakota, the two captains and their parties were reunited.

Clark's party had had their difficulties, but their trip had been idyllic compared with Lewis's. Like Lewis, Clark had left Travelers' Rest on July 3, moving southeast over some new terrain across the mountains to their old Camp Fortunate at the forks of the Beaverhead River. There the party recovered cached goods and canoes and traveled down to the Three Forks by both canoe and horseback, arriving on July 13. From the forks Clark dispatched Ordway with the canoes down the Missouri to the Great Falls. Clark himself with twelve persons, including Charbonneau, Sacagawea, and their child, headed for the Yellowstone, which they reached on July 15.

They continued down the Yellowstone on horseback, but on July 18 George Gibson was injured and could not ride after his horse threw him, so Clark decided to make canoes and continue by water. On the twenty-fourth he set out again, sending Sergeant Nathaniel Pryor with three men and the horses to travel overland to the Mandan villages. Pryor was to make contact with trader Hugh Heney, going north into Canada if necessary, to secure Heney's services as an intermediary with the Sioux. Pryor's mission ended prematurely on the second night out when Indians, probably Crows, stole his party's horses. He and his men made Mandan-style "bull boats" of buffalo hides and floated down the Yellowstone and the Missouri pursuing Clark, whom they overtook on August 8.

Clark's trip down the Yellowstone was uneventful. He passed the landmark he named "Pompy's Tower"—after little Jean Baptiste Charbonneau—on July 25, near present Billings, Montana, and proceeded on, arriving at the mouth of the river on August 3. The original plan was for him to wait there for Lewis, but the mosquitoes were terrible and game was scarce so he left a note for Lewis and continued down the Missouri. On August 11 Clark's party met two trappers, Joseph Dickson and Forrest Hancock, the first whites they had seen since April 1805. These men could provide little information from the East, since they had been absent since the summer of 1804. They did, however, inform Clark that the Missouri River tribes were fighting one another again. The captain realized that his and Lewis's successes at peacemaking had been limited and of short duration. The next day the wounded Lewis and his contingent caught up with Clark.

The discomfort of his wound now caused Lewis to give up his journalizing, leaving Clark to continue the record to the end of the trip. Characteristically,

Lewis's last entry included the description of one last plant, the pin cherry. The Corps returned to the Mandan villages on August 14. They remained there only three days, trying to persuade Mandan and Hidatsa chiefs to go with them to see the president, but only Sheheke, the Mandan, and his family consented. Charbonneau, Sacagawea, and Jean Baptiste remained behind, and John Colter received a discharge so he could return to the mountains on a trapping venture with Dickson and Hancock.

As they headed downriver on August 17 their thoughts were all directed toward home. They stopped overnight on the twenty-first at the Arikara villages, where they found the Indians unhappy because a chief sent to Washington the previous year had not returned. No other chiefs would agree to go. On August 30 they gave some Teton Sioux the cold shoulder because of the troubles they had had with this tribe in 1804. They met with the Yankton Sioux near the mouth of the Niobrara on September 1, and held a friendly council. On September 4 they revisited Sergeant Charles Floyd's grave near the mouth of the Big Sioux River.

They were now meeting trading parties bound upriver, who gave them the news of over two years, including the fact that most people in the United States had given them up for lost, although "the President of the U. States had yet hopes of us." Lewis was recovering from his wound as they daily passed campsites and other familiar scenes of the toilsome upriver trip. In the last days of the journey the men were troubled by sore eyes, but they pushed on, eager to reach St. Louis. On September 20, near La Charette, they saw cows for the first time since leaving the settlements. Soon the inhabitants of the little settlement greeted them enthusiastically. The next day they reached St. Charles, meeting old friends, and on the twenty-second they saw a significant omen of change, the first American fort west of the Mississippi at Belle Fontaine a few miles above the mouth of the Missouri.

Emerging from the river's mouth on September 23, they briefly visited the camp at Wood River that they had left some twenty-eight months before, then sailed on and reached St. Louis at noon. The citizens, having received advance word, lined the riverfront and cheered. Two days later, at Christy's Tavern, they were treated to a lavish dinner, with eighteen toasts, ending with "Captains Lewis and Clark—Their perilous services endear them to every American heart." The next day Clark brought his journals to an end with a brief, anticlimactic entry: "a fine morning   we commenced wrighting &c."

The Journals of the Lewis and Clark Expedition, Volume 8

June 10–September 26, 1806

Chapter Thirty-Six

In the Bitterroot Mountains

June 10–July 2, 1806

[Lewis]   *Tuesday June 10th 1806.*

This morning we arrose early and had our horses collected except one
of Cruzatt's and one of Whitehouse's, which were not to be found; after a
surch of some hours Cruzatt's horse was obtained and the indians promised to find the other and bring it to us at the quawmash flatts[1] where we
purpose encamping a few days.   at 11 A. M. we set out with the party
each man being well mounted and a light load on a second horse, beside
which we have several supenemary [supernumerary] horses in case of accedent or the want of provision, we therefore feel ourselves perfectly
equiped for the mountains.   we ascended the river hills which are very
high and about three miles in extent our sourse being N. 22° E. thence
N. 15 W. 2 m to Collins's creek.[2]   thence due North 5 m. to the Eastern
border of the quawmash flatts where we encamped near the place we first
met with the Chopunnish last fall.[3]   the pass of Collins's Creek was deep
and extreemly difficult tho' we passed without sustaining further injury
than weting some of our roots and bread.[4]   the country through which
we passed is extreemly fertile and generally free of stone, is well timbered
with several speceis of fir, long leafed pine and larch.[5]   the undergrowth
is chooke cherry[6] near the water courses, black alder,[7] a large speceis of
redroot[8] now in blume, a growth[9] which resembles the pappaw in it's leaf
and which bears a burry with five valves of a deep perple colour, two

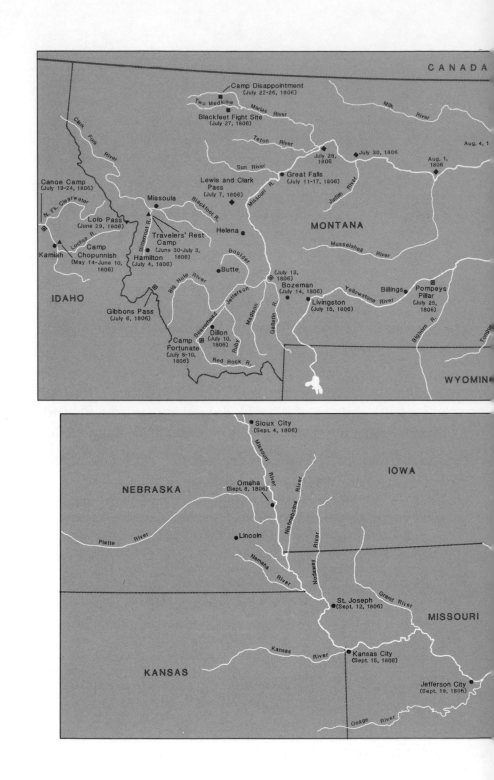

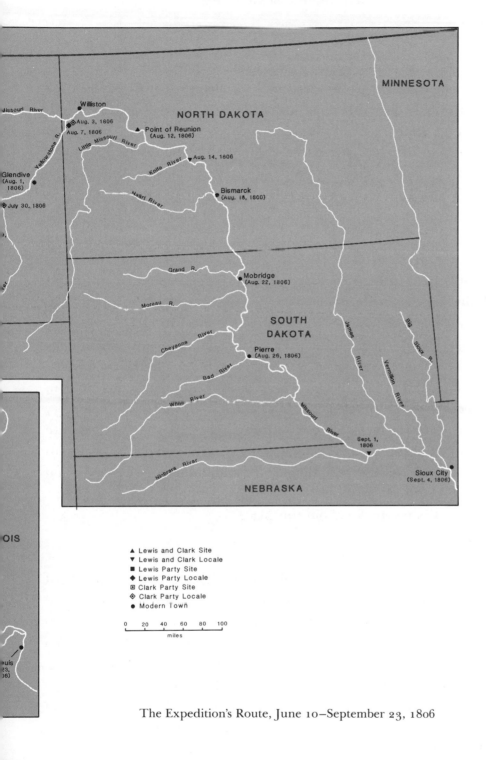

MINNESOTA

Missouri River

Williston
Aug. 3, 1806
Aug. 7, 1806

NORTH DAKOTA

▲ Point of Reunion
(Aug. 12, 1806)

Little Missouri River

Knife River

▼ Aug. 14, 1806

Glendive
(Aug. 1, 1806)

Yellowstone R.

Heart River

Bismarck
(Aug. 18, 1806)

July 30, 1806

Grand R.

Mobridge
(Aug. 22, 1806)

Moreau R.

SOUTH
DAKOTA

James River

Big Sioux R.

Cheyenne River

Pierre
(Aug. 26, 1806)

Vermilion River

Bad River

White River

Missouri River

Sept. 1,
1806
▼

Niobrara River

Sioux City
(Sept. 4, 1806)

NEBRASKA

OIS

▲ Lewis and Clark Site
▼ Lewis and Clark Locale
■ Lewis Party Site
◆ Lewis Party Locale
▣ Clark Party Site
◈ Clark Party Locale
● Modern Town

0   20   40   60   80   100
miles

uis
23,
06)

The Expedition's Route, June 10–September 23, 1806

speceis of shoemate[10] sevenbark,[11] perple haw,[12] service berry,[13] goos-
burry,[14] a wild rose honeysuckle[15] which bears a white berry, and a species
of dwarf pine[16] which grows about ten or twelve feet high. bears a
globular formed cone with small scales, the leaves are about the length
and much the appearance of the common pitch pine having it's leaves in
fassicles of two; in other rispects they would at a little distance be taken
for the young plants of the long leafed pine.   there are two speceis of the
wild rose[17] both quinqui petallous and of a damask red but the one is as
large as the common red rose of our gardens. I observed the apples of
this speceis last fall to be more than triple the size of those of the ordinary
wild rose; the stem of this rose is the same with the other tho' the leaf is
somewhat larger.   after we encamped this evening we sent out our hunters; Collins killed a doe on which we suped much to our satisfaction.   we
had scarcely reached Collins's Creek before we were overtaken by a party
of Indians who informed us that they were going to the quawmash flatts
to hunt; their object I beleive is the expectation of bing fed by us in which
how ever kind as they have been we must disappoint them at this moment
as it is necessary that we should use all frugallaty as well as employ every
exertion to provide meat for our journey.   they have encamped with
us.   we find a great number of burrowing squirels[18] about our camp of
which we killed several; I eat of them and found them quite as tender and
well flavored as our grey squirel.   saw many sand hill crains[19] and some
ducks in the slashey glades about this place.—

[Clark]   *Tuesday June 10th 1806.*

   rose early this morning and had all the horses Collected except one of
Whitehouses horses which could not be found, an Indian promised to
find the horse and bring him on to us at the quawmash fields at which
place we intend to delay a fiew days for the laying in Some meat by which
time we Calculate that the Snows will have melted more off the mountains and the grass raised to a sufficient hight for our horses to live.   we
packed up and Set out at 11 A M   we Set out with the party each man
being well mounted and a light load on a 2d horse, besides which we have
several supernumary horses in case of accident or the want of provisions,
we therefore feel ourselves perfectly equiped for the Mountains.   we as-

sended the hills which are very high and about three miles in extent our course being N. 22° E, thence N. 15° W 2 ms: to Collins Creek. Thence North 5 Miles to the Eastern boarders of the Quawmash flatts where we encamped near the place I first met with the Chopunnish Nation last fall. the pass of Collins Creek was deep and extreemly difficult tho' we passed without sustaining further injury than wetting some of our roots and bread. The Country through which we passed is extreemly fertile and generally free from Stone, is well timbered with several Species of fir, long leafed pine and Larch.[20] the undergrowth is choke cherry near the watercourses, black alder, a large species of red root now in blume, a Growth which resembles the poppaw in it's leaf and which bears a berry with five valves of a deep purple colour, two species of Shoemate, Seven bark, perple haw, Service berry, Goose berry, wildrose, honey suckle which bears a white berry, and a Species of dwarf pine which grows about 10 or 12 feet high, bears a globarlar formed cone with Small Scales, the leaf is about the length and much the appearance of the pitch pine haveing it's leaves in fassicles of two; in other respects they would at a little distance be taken for the young plants of the long leafed pine. There are two Species of the wild rose both quinque petallous and of a damask red, but the one is as large as the common red rose of our guardens. I observed the apples of these Species last fall to be more than triple the Size of those of the ordinary wild rose; the Stem of this rose is the Same with the other tho' the leaf is somewhat larger. after we encamped this evening we Sent out our hunters; Collins killed a doe on which we Suped much to our Satisfaction, we had not reached the top of the river hills before we were overtaken by a party of 8 Indians who informed me that they were gowing to the quawmash flatts to hunt; their object I belive is the expectation of being fed by us in which however *kind as they have been* we must disappoint them at this moment as it is necessary that we Should use all frugallaty as well as employ every exertion to provide meat for our journey. they have encamped with us. we find a great number of burrowing Squirels about our camp of which we killed Several; I eate of them and found them quit as tender and well flavd. as our grey squirel. Saw many Sand hill crains and Some ducks in the Slashey Glades about this place—.

1. On Weippe Prairie, in Clearwater County, Idaho, near the western bank of Jim Ford Creek ("Village Creek" on *Atlas* map 71) and about two miles southeast of present Weippe. Space, 30; Peebles (LT), map. The "quawmash" is camas, *Camassia quamash* (Pursh) Greene; see September 20, 1805, and the next entry, June 11, 1806.

2. Present Lolo Creek, in Clearwater County. *Atlas* map 71.

3. They were about a mile southeast of the first Indian village they had come to when meeting the Nez Perces on September 20, 1805. Space, 30; Peebles (LT), map; Appleman (LC), 284–85.

4. Probably meaning the roots of either camas or cous, *Lomatium cous* (Wats.) Coult. & Rose, and the bread made from these plants. Hitchcock et al., 3:548–49. On June 17 Lewis specifically mentions "roots and bread of cows [cous]."

5. The species of "fir" along the route include Douglas fir, *Pseudotsuga menziesii* (Mirb.) Franco, grand fir, *Abies grandis* (Dougl.) Lindl., and Engelmann spruce, *Picea engelmannii* Parry. See February 6, 1806. The pine with long leaves is Ponderosa pine, *Pinus ponderosa* Laws., and the larch is western, Montana, or mountain, larch, also called hackmatack, and tamarack, *Larix occidentalis* Nutt. Hitchcock et al., 1:131–32, 117, 122, 129, 121.

6. *Prunus virginiana* L.

7. The alder of this region is thinleaf alder, *Alnus incana* (L.) Moench. Hitchcock et al., 2:73–74. Lewis uses the common name of the closely related European species, *Alnus glutinosa* (L.) Gaertn. Bailey, 327.

8. Redroot is an eastern North American shrub also called New Jersey tea, *Ceanothus americanus* L., with reputed medicinal value as a blood coagulant. Lewis clearly realizes that he is seeing a different, "large" species, now called redstem ceanothus, buckbrush, or buckthorn, *C. sanguineus* Pursh. The species was new to science, but the captain did not collect the type specimen until possibly June 27. Uphof, 115; Hitchcock et al., 3:418; Cutright (LCPN), 306–7, 405–6.

9. The purple berry helps identify this as cascara, chittam bark, *Rhamnus purshiana* DC. Lewis wrote a similar description of the berry on the label of the type specimen he collected in the vicinity on May 29, 1806. Hitchcock et al., 3:420; Cutright (LCPN), 307–8, 416–17. He compares its leaves to the leaf of the pawpaw, *Asimina triloba* (L.) Dun. Bailey, 420; Barkley, 14. See references to pawpaw and its possible effects on September 11 and 19, 1806.

10. One species of the "shoemate" is probably smooth sumac, *Rhus glabra* L., which is common in the area. The second could be poison ivy, *R. radicans* L., which occurs at lower elevations around Camp Chopunnish. Since this plant was certainly known to the men, it is curious that it is not named specifically. Thus, Lewis could have been seeing Greene mountain ash, *Sorbus scopulina* Greene, which without flowers could be confused for sumac. See September 20, 1805, where he calls another mountain ash "shoemake." Hitchcock et al., 3:407, 189; Little (MWH), 193-W.

11. Identified previously as ninebark, *Physocarpus capitatus* (Pursh) Kuntze (see December 1, 1805), it now seems certain that Lewis's "sevenbark" is another plant. Sevenbark is an old common name for the eastern North American shrub, *Hydrangea arborescens* L., probably known to Lewis because of its importance as a medicinal. Lewis's syringa or

Lewis's mock orange, *Philadelphus lewisii* Pursh, is the only member of the Hydrangea family in the region, and it would have looked very similar to sevenbark (*Hydrangea arborescens*) at this time of year, prior to its midsummer flowering season. Syringa is common in the area, and Lewis had pressed a specimen of it four days earlier. He collected it again when he saw it in bloom on July 4, 1806. Based on these specimens, Frederick Pursh honored Lewis by attaching his name to it, one of the most attractive flowering shrubs in the Rocky Mountains, now the state flower of Idaho. Uphof, 274; Hitchcock et al., 3 : 86–87; Cutright (LCPN), 299, 363, 413–14.

12. Purple haw is black hawthorn, *Crataegus douglasii* Lindl. Hitchcock et al., 3 : 101; Cutright (LCPN), 288–89, 407.

13. Serviceberry, *Amelanchier alnifolia* Nutt. Hitchcock et al., 3 : 93–95.

14. Two species of gooseberry could have been seen on this day, snow gooseberry, *Ribes niveum* Lindl., which occurs at lower elevations in the vicinity of Camp Chopunnish, and Idaho gooseberry, *R. irriguum* Dougl., which could have been encountered at higher elevations as they ascended the slope. Ibid., 3 : 80, 75.

15. The honeysuckle with a white berry is common snowberry, *Symphoricarpos albus* (L.) Blake. Ibid., 4 : 464–65; see also August 13, 1805. Roses are discussed in detail a few lines below.

16. Lodgepole pine, *Pinus contorta* Dougl. ex Loud; not a dwarf pine, Lewis was simply observing young trees here. Ibid., 1 : 125–27. The species somewhat resembles the pitch pine (*P. rigida* Mill.) of eastern North America.

17. The wild rose with large flowers and "apples" (hips) is Nootka rose, *Rosa nutkana* Presl. The other species with smaller flowers but similar stems is western wild, or Wood's, rose, *R. woodsii* Lindl. Both were undescribed species at the time. Ibid., 3 : 169–71; Cutright (LCPN), 418. Lewis exhibits some of his botanical training by using the latin term "quinqui petallous," meaning that the two species, like most wild roses, have flowers with five petals, in contrast to cultivated forms that are bred to have many petals. It was probably Biddle who marked a red vertical line through this passage about roses.

18. Lewis and Clark commonly applied this term to the prairie dog, *Cynomys ludovicianus* (see September 7, 1804, and July 1, 1806); here he may be referring to the Columbian ground squirrel, *Spermophilus columbianus* (see May 23 and 27, 1806). The gray squirrel mentioned for comparison is *Sciurus carolinensis*. Burroughs, 99–101, 102–6; Cutright (LCPN), 308, 445.

19. Sandhill crane, *Grus canadensis* [AOU, 206].

20. Beginning with this sentence a light red vertical line runs through this botanical material, probably done by Biddle.

[Lewis] *Wednesday June 11th 1806.*

All our hunters were out this morning by daylight; Labuish and Gibson only proved successfull, the former killed a black bear of the brown speceis[1] and a very large buck, the latter also killed a fine fat buck. five of the Indians also turned out and hunted untill noon, when they returned without having killed anything; at three P. M. the left us on their return to ther villages.   previous to their departure one of our men exchanged an indifferent horse with one of them for a very good one.   in the evening our hunters resumed the chase; as game has become scarce and shye near our camp they were directed to hunt at a greater distance and therefore set out prepared to remain ⟨out⟩ all night and make a mornings hunt in grounds not recently frequented. Whitehouse returned this morning to our camp on the Kooskooske² in surch of his horse.—   As I have had frequent occasion to mention the plant which the Chopunnish call quawmash³ I shall here give a more particular discription of that plant and the mode of preparing it for food as practiced by the Chopunnish and others in the vicinity of the Rocky Mountains with whom it forms much the greatest portion of their subsistence.   we have never met with this plant but in or adjacent to a piny or fir timbered country, and there always in the open grounds and glades; in the Columbian vally and near the coast it is to be found in small quantities and inferior in size to that found in this neighbourhood and in the high rich flatts and vallees within the rocky mountains.   it delights in a black rich moist soil, and even grows most luxuriantly where the land remains from 6 to nine inches under water untill the seed are nearly perfect which in this neighbourhood or on these flats is about the last of this month. neare the river where I had an opportunity of observing it the seed were begining to ripen on the 9th inst. and the soil was nearly dry.   it seems devoted to it's particular soil and situation, and you will seldom find it more than a few feet from the inundated soil tho' within it's limits it grows very closely in short almost as much so as the bulbs will permit; the radix is a tunicated bulb, much the consistence shape and appearance of the onion, glutanous or somewhat ⟨slymy⟩ [*EC?: mucous*] when chewed and almost tasteless and without smell in it's unprepared state; it is white except the thin or outer tunicated scales which are few black and not succulent; this bulb is from the size of a nutmeg to that of a hens egg and most commonly of an intermediate size or about as large as an onion of one years growth from the seed.   the radicles are numerous, reather large, white, flexable, succulent and diverging.   the foliage consists of from one to four seldom five radicale, linear sessile and revolute pointed leaves; they are from 12 to 18 inches in length and from 1 to ¾ of an inch in widest part which is near the middle; the uper disk is somewhat groved of a pale green and marked it's whole length with a number of small longitudinal channels; the under disk is a deep glossy green and smooth. the leaves sheath the peduncle and each other as high as the surface of the earth or about 2 inches; they are more succulent than the grasses and less so than most of the lillies hyesinths &c.— the peduncle is soletary, proceeds from the root, is columner, smooth leafless and rises to the hight of 2 or 2½ feet. it supports from 10 to forty flowers which are each supported by seperate footstalk of ½ an inch in length scattered without order on the upper portion of the peduncle. the calix is a partial involucret situated at the base of the footstalk of each flower on the peduncle; it is long thin and begins to decline as soon as the corolla expands. the corolla consists of six long oval, obtusly pointed skye blue or water coloured petals, each about 1 inch in length; the corolla is regular as to the form and size of the petals but irregular as to their position, five of them are placed near ech other pointing upward while one stands horizantally or pointing downwards, they are inserted with a short claw on the extremity of the footstalk at the base of the germ; the corolla is of course inferior; it is also shriveling, and continues untill the seeds are perfect. The stamens are perfect, six in number; the filaments each elivate an anther, near their base are flat on the inside and rounded on the outer terminate in a subulate point, are bowed or bent upwards, inserted on the inner side and on the base of the claws of the petals, below the germ, are equal both with rispect to themselves and the corolla, smooth & membraneous. the Anther is oblong, obtusely pointed, 2 horned or forked at one end and furrowed longitudinally with four channels, the upper and lower of which seem almost to divide it into two loabs, incumbent patent, membranous, very short, naked, two valved and fertile with pollen, which last is of a yellow colour—. the anther in a few hours after the corolla unfoalds, bursts, discharges it's pollen and becomes very minute and shrivled; the above discription of the anther is therefore to be understood of it at the moment of it's first appearance. the pistillum is only one, of which, the germ is triangular reather swolen on the sides, smooth superior, sessile, pedicelled, short in proportion to the corolla atho' wide or bulky; the style is very long or longer than the stamens, simple, cilindrical, bowed or bent upwards, placed on the top of the germ, membranous shrivels and falls off when the pericarp has obtained its full size. the stigma is three cleft very minute, & pubescent. the pericarp is a capsule, triangular, oblong, obtuse, and trilocular with three longitudinal valves. the seed so far as I could judge are numerous not very minute and globelar.— soon after the seeds are mature the peduncle and foliage of this plant perishes, the grownd becomes dry or nearly so and the root encreases in size and shortly becomes fit for use; this happens about the middle of July when the natives begin to collect it for use which they continue untill the leaves of the plant attain some size in the spring of the year. when they have collected a considerable quantity of these roots or 20 30 bushels which they readily do by means of stick sharpened at one end, they dig away the surface of the earth forming a circular concavity of 2½ feet in the center and 10 feet in diameter; they next collect a parsel of split dry wood with which they cover this bason in the grown perhaps a foot thick, they next collect a large parsel of stones of about 4 or 6 lbs. weight which are placed on the dry wood; fire is then set to the wood which birning heats the stones; when the fire has subsided and the stones are sufficiently heated which are nearly a red heat, they are adjusted in such manner in the whole as to form as level a surface as pissible, a small quantity of earth is sprinkled over the stones and a layer of grass about an inch thick is put over the stones; the roots, which have been previously devested of the black or outer coat and radicles which rub off easily with the fingers, are now laid on in a conical pile, are then covered with a layer of grass about 2 or 3 inches thick; water is now thrown on the summit of the pile and passes through the roots and to the hot stones at bottom; some water is allso poared arround the edges of the hole and also finds its way to the hot stones; as soon as they discover from the quantity of steem which issues that the water has found its way generally to the hot stones, they cover the roots and grass over with earth to the debth of four inches and then build a fire of dry wood all over the connical mound which they continue to renew through the course of the night or for ten or 12 hours after which it is suffered to cool two or three hours when the earth and grass are removed and the roots thus sweated

and cooked with steam are taken out, and most commonly exposed to the
sun on scaffoalds untill they become dry, when they are black and of a
sweet agreeable flavor. these roots are fit for use when first taken from
the pitt, are soft of a sweetish tast and much the consistency of a roasted
onion; but if they are suffered to remain in bulk 24 hour after being
cooked they spoil. if the design is to make bread or cakes of these roots
they undergo a second process of baking being previously pounded after
the fist baking between two stones untill they are reduced to the consistency of dough and then rolled in grass in cakes of eight or ten lbs are
returned to the sweat intermixed with fresh roots in order that the steam
may get freely to these loaves of bread. when taken out the second time
the women make up this dough into cakes of various shapes and sizes
usually from ½ to ¾ of an inch thick and expose it on sticks to dry in the
sun, or place it over the smoke of their fires.— the bread this prepared
if kept free from moisture will keep sound for a great length of time.
this bread or the dryed roots are frequently eaten alone by the natives
without further preparation, and when they have them in abundance they
form an ingredient in almost every dish they prepare. this root is pal-
lateable but disagrees with me in every shape I have ever used it.—

[Clark]   *Wednesday June 11th 1806*

All of our hunters were out by daylight this Morning. Labeech and
Shann was the only Suckcessull hunters, Labeech killed a Black bear and
a large buck, and Gibson killed a very fat Buck. five of the indians also
turned out and hunted untill near Meridn. without having killed any
thing. at 3 P M they all packed up and returned to their village. one of
our men exchanged an indifferent horse for a verey good one with those
people before they left us. in the evening all our hunters turned out in
different directions with a view to find some probable Spot of killing deer
and were directed to lay out all night and hunt in the morning early.
Whitehouse returned this morning to our camp on the Kooskooske in
Serch of his horse.[4]

As I have had frequent occasion to mention the plant which the Chopunnish and other nations of the Columbia call Quawmash I Shall here
give a more particular discription of that plant and the mode of pre-

17

pareing it for food as practiced by the Chopinnish and others in the vicinity of the Rocky Mountains with whome it forms much the greatest portion of their Subsistence. we have never met with this plant but in or adjacent to a piney or fir timbered Country, and there always in the open grounds and glades; in the Columbian Vally and near the Coast it is to be found in small quantities and inferior in Size to that found in this neighbourhood or on those high rich flatts and vallies within the rocky mountains. it delights in a black rich moist Soil, and even grows most luxuriently where the lands remain from 6 to 9 inches under water untill the seed are nearly perfect, which in this neighbourhood or on those flatts is about the last of this month. near the river where I had an oppertunity of observing it, the Seed were beginning to ripen on the 9th inst. and the Soil was nearly dry. it seems devoted to it's particular Soil and Situation, and you will Seldom find more than a fiew feet from an inundated Soil tho' within it's limits it grows very closely. in short almost as much so as the bulbs will permit. the radix is a tumicated bulb, much the consistence Shape and appearance of the Onion, glutinous or somewhat Slymey when chewed and almost tasteless and without smell in it's unprepared state; it is white except the thin or outer tumicated scales which are fiew black and not Suculent; this bulb is from the Size of a nutmeg to that of a hen egg and most commonly of an intermediate size or about as large as a common onion of one years growth from the Seed. the radicles are noumerous, reather large, white, flexeable, Succulent and dividing the foliage consists of from one to four seldom five radicals, liner Sessile and revolute pointed leaves; they are from 12 to 18 inches in length and from 1 to ¾ of an inch in widest part which is nearest the middle; the upper disk is Somewhat groved of a pale green and marked it's whole length with a number of Small longitudinal channels; the under disk is of a deep glossy green and Smooth. the leaves sheath the peduncle and each other as high as the Surface of the earth or about 2 inches; they are more succulent than the grasses and less so than most of the lillies hyisinths &c.— the peduncle is soletary, proceeds from the root, is columner, smooth and leafless and rises to the hight of 2 or 2½ feet. it supports from 10 to 40 flowers which are each surported by a Seperate footstalk of ½ an inch in length scattered without order on the upper portion of the peduncle. the calix is a partial involucre or involucret Situated at the base of the footstalk of each flower on the peduncle; it is long thin and begins to decline as soon as the corrolla expands. the corolla consists of five long oval obtusely pointed Skye blue or water coloured petals, each about 1 inch in length; the Corolla is regular as to the form and size of the petals but irregular as to their position, five of them are placed near each other pointing upwards while one stands horozontially, or pointing downwards, they are inserted with a Short Claw on the extremity of the footstalk at the base of the germ; the corolla is of course inferior; it is also shriveling, and continues untill the Seed are perfect. The Stamens are perfect, Six in number; the falaments each elivate an anther, near their base are flat on the inner side and rounded on the outer, termonate in a subulate point, and bowed or bent upwards inserted on the inner Side and on the base of the Claws of the petals, below the germ, are equal both with respect to themselves and the Corolla, Smooth membranous. the Anther is oblong obtusely pointed, 2 horned or forked at one end and furrowed longitudinally with four channels, the upper and lower of which Seem almost to divide it into two loabs, incumbent, patent, membranous, very short, necked, two valved and fertile with pollen, which last is of a yellow colour. the Anther in a fiew hours after the Corolla unfoalds, bursts discharges it's pollen and becomes very manute and chrivled; the above discription of the Anther is therefore to be understood of it, at the moment of it's first appearance. the pistillum is only one, of which the Germ is triangular reather Swolen on the Sides, Smooth, Superior, Sessile, pedicelled, Short in proportion to the Corolla tho' wide or bulky; the Style is very long or longer than the stamens, simple, cilindrical, bowed or bent upwards, placed on the top of the germ, membranous shrivels and falls off when the pericarp has obtained it's full Size.

the Stigma is three clefts very manute and pubescent. the pericarp is a capsule, triangular, oblong, obtuse, and trilocular with three longitudinal valves. the Seed So far as I could judge are noumerous not very manute and globilar.— Soon after the seed are mature the peduncle and foliage of this plant perishes, the ground becoms dry or nearly so and the root increases in size and shortly become fit for use; this happens about the middle of July when the nativs begin to collect it[5] for use which they continue untill the leaves of the plant obtain Some Size in the Spring of the year. when they have Collected a considerable quantity of these roots or 20 or 30 bushels which they readily do by means of Sticks Sharpened at one end, they dig away the surface of the earth forming a cercular concavity of 2½ feet in the center and 10 feet in diameter; they next collect a parcel of dry split wood with which they cover this bason from the bottom perhaps a foot thick, they next collect a parcel of Stones from 4 to 6 lb. weight which are placed on the dry wood; fire is then Set to the wood which burning heats the Stones; when the fire has subsided and the Stones are sufficiently heated which are nearly a red heat, they are adjusted in such manner in the hole as to form as leavel a Surface as possible, a small quantity of earth is Sprinkled over the Stones, and a layer of grass about an inch thick is laid over the Stone; the roots which have been previously devested of the black or outer coat and radicles which rub off easily with the fingers, are now laid on in a circular pile, are then covered with a layer of grass about 2 or 3 inches thick; water is then thrown on the Summit of the pile and passes through the roots and to the hot Stones at bottom; Some water is also pored around the edges of the hole, and also find it's way to the hot Stones. they cover the roots and grass over with earth to the debth of four inches and then build a fire of dry wood all over the Connical mound which they Continue to renew through the course of the night or for 10 or 12 hours, after which it is Suffered to cool, 2 or three hours, when the earth and grass are removed. and the roots thus Sweated are cooled with Steam or taken out, and most commonly exposed to the Sun on Scaffolds untill they become dry. when they are black and of a Sweet agreeable flavor. these roots are fit for use when first taken from the pitt, are Soft of a Sweetish taste and much the consistancy of a roasted onion; but if they are Suffered to remain in bulk 24 hours after being cooked they Spoil. if the design is to make bread or cakes of those roots they undergo a Second preperation of baking being previously pounded after the first baking between two Stones untill they are reduced to the consistancy of dough and then rolled in grass in cakes of 8 or 10 pounds, are returned to the Sweat intermixes with fresh roots in order that the steam may get freely to those loaves of bread. when taken out the Second time the Indn. woman make up this dough into cakes of various Shapes and Sizes, usually from ½ to ¾ of an inch thick and expose it on sticks to dry in the Sun, or place it over the smoke of their fires.— The bread thus prepared if kept free from moisture will Sound for a great length of time. this bread or the dryed roots are frequently eaten alone by the nativs without further preperation, and when they have them in abundance they form an ingrediant in almost every dish they prepare. this root is palateable but disagrees with us in every shape we have ever used it. the nativs are extreemly fond of this root and present it their visiters as a great treat. when we first arrived at the Chopunnish last fall at this place our men who were half Starved made So free a use of this root that it made them all Sick for Several days after.[6]

1. The cinnamon phase of the black bear, *Ursus americanus;* see May 31, 1806.

2. Camp Chopunnish on the Clearwater River.

3. Camas; see previous entry. Lewis's detailed description of the plant's morphology, floral development, and ecology—clearly the result of several hours of study—illustrates his strong command of botanical terminology and his impressive powers of observation. Despite the quality of this academic exercise, it was the specimen of camas he collected on June 23 that was needed for Pursh to describe it as a new species. The outstanding documentation of camas ethnobotany was Lewis's most valuable achievement of the day. Hitchcock et al., 1:780–82. It was apparently Biddle who drew a red vertical line through part of this passage.

4. It was probably Biddle who placed a red vertical line through the first few lines of the next paragraph.

5. Beginning about here another red vertical line cuts across several lines of text, perhaps Biddle's work again.

6. First noted on September 20, 1805.

[Lewis]   *Thursday June 12th 1806,*

All our hunters except Gibson returned about noon; none of them had killed anything except Sheilds who brought with him two deer. in the evening they resumed their hunt and remained out all night. an indian visited us this evening and spent the night at our camp. Whitehouse returned with his horse at 1 P. M. the days are now very warm and the Musquetoes[1] our old companions have become very troublesome. The Cutnose[2] informed us on the 10th before we left him that two young men would overtake us with a view to accompany me to the falls of the Missouri. nothing interesting occurred in the course of this day. our camp is agreeably situated in a point of timbered land on the eastern border of an extensive level and beautifull prarie which is intersected by several small branches near the bank of one of which our camp is placed. the quawmash is now in blume and from the colour of its bloom at a short distance it resembles lakes of fine clear water, so complete is this deseption that on first sight I could have swoarn it was water.

[Clark]   *Thursday June 12th 1806.*

All our hunters except Gibson returned about noon; none of them had killed any thing except Shields who brought with him two deer. in the evening they resumed their hunt and remained out all night. an Indian visited us this evening and Spent the night at our Camp. Whitehouse returned with his horse at 1 P. M. the days are very worm and the Musquetors our old Companions have become very troublesom.

The Cutnose informed us on the 10th before we left him that two young Chiefs would overtake us with a view to accompany us to the Falls of the Missouri and probably to the Seat of our Governmt. nothing interesting occured in the course of this day. our camp is agreeably Situated in a point of timbered land on the eastern borders of an extensive leavel and butifull prarie which is intersected by Several Small branches near the bank of one of which our Camp is placed. the quawmash is now in blume at a Short distance it resemhles a lake of fine clear water, So complete is this deseption that on first Sight I could have Sworn it was water.

1. *Aedes vexans* is the most common mosquito throughout the remainder of the party's route but other possibilities include *A. spenserii* and *A. hendersoni;* the latter is found especially among cottonwood trees.

2. Otherwise Neeshneparkkeook; see May 5, 1806.

[Lewis]   *Friday June 13th 1806.*

Reubin Feilds and Willard were ordered to proceed on our road to a small prarie 8 miles distant on this side of Collins's Creek and there hunt until our arrival;[1] they departed at 10 A. M. about noon seven of our hunters returned with 8 deer; they had wounded several others and a bear but did not get them. in the evening Labuish and Cruzatte returned and reported that the buzzards[2] had eaten up a deer which they had killed butchered and hung up this morning. The indian who visited us yesterday exchanged his horse for one of ours which had not perfectly recovered from the operation of castration and received a small ax and a knife to boot, he seemed much pleased with his exchange and set out immediately to his village, as if fearfull that we would cansel the bargain which is customary among themselves and deemed only fair. we directed the meat to be cut thin and exposed to dry in the sun. we made a digest of the Indian Nations West of the Rocky Mountains which we have seen and of whom we have been repeated informed by those with whom we were conversent. they amount by our estimate to 69,000 [*NB?: about 80,000*] Souls.—[3]

[Clark]   *Friday June 13th 1806.*

Ordered Rubin Fields and Willard to proceed on to a Small prarie in the Mountains about 8 miles and there hunt untill we arrive the Set out at 10 A. M. Soon after they Set out all of our hunters returned each with a deer except Shields who brought two in all 8 deer. Labeech and P. Crusatt went out this morning killed a deer & reported that the buzzds. had eate up the deer in their absence after haveing butchered and hung it up. The indian who visited us yesterday exchanged his horse with one of our party for a very indiferant one in which exchange he rcived a Small ax a Knife &c. Soon after he had exchanged he returned to his village well Satisfied. we caused the meat to be cut thin and dried in the sun. I make a list of the Indian Nations their place of residence, and probable number of Soles of each nation from estimation and indian information &c.

1. Perhaps Crane Meadow; see June 15, 1806.
2. Perhaps the turkey vulture, *Cathartes aura* [AOU, 325]. Burroughs, 203–4.
3. See Estimate of the Western Indians in Chapter 30. It is not clear to which of the several copies Lewis refers.

[Lewis]   *Saturday June 14th 1806.*

Sent our hunters out early this morning. Colter killed a deer and brought it in by 10 A. M. the other hunters except Drewyer returned early without having killed anything. Drewyer returned. we had all our articles packed up and made ready for an early departure in the morning. our horses were caught and most of them hubbled and otherwise confined in order that we might not be detained. from hence to traveller's rest[1] we shall make a forsed march; at that place we shal probably remain one or two days to rest ourselves and horses and procure some meat. we have now been detained near five weeks in consequence of the snows; a serious loss of time at this delightfull season for traveling. I am still apprehensive that the snow and the want of food for our horses will prove a serious imbarrassment to us as at least four days journey of our rout in these mountains lies over hights and along a ledge of mountains never intirely destitute of snow. every body seems anxious to be in motion, convinced that we have not now any time to delay if the calculation is to reach the United States this season; this I am detirmined to accomplish if within the compass of human power.

[Clark]   *Saturday June 14th 1806*

Sent out Hunters this morning   Colter killed a deer and brought it in by 10 A M   Drewyer did not return untill night   he wounded deer but could get none &c   [*blank*] neither of the other hunters killed ⟨any⟩ nothing. we had our articles packed up ready for a Start in the morning, our horses Collected and hobble that they may not detain us in the morning. we expect to Set out early, and Shall proceed with as much expedition as possible over those Snowey tremendious mountains which has detained us near five weeks in this neighbourhood waiting for the Snows to melt Suffcent for us to pass over them. and even now I Shudder with the expectation with great dificuelties in passing those Mountains, from the debth of Snow and the want of grass Sufficient to Subsist our horses as about 4 days we Shall be on the top of the Mountain which we have every reason to beleive is Covered with Snow the greater part of the year.

1. The party's camp of September 9–11, 1805, and again June 30–July 3, 1806; see June 30, 1806.

[Lewis] *Sunday June 15th 1806.*

We had some little difficulty in collecting our horses this morning they had straggled off to a greater distance than usual. it rained very hard in the morning and after collecting our horses we waited ⟨an hour⟩ for it to abait, but as it had every appearance of a settled rain we set out at 10 A. M. we passed a little prarie at the distance of 8½ me.[1] to which we had previously sent R. Feilds and Willard. we found two deer which they had killed and hung up. at the distance of 2½ miles further we arrived at Collins's Creek where we found our hunters; they had killed another deer, and had seen two large bear together the one black and the other white.[2] we halted at the creek, dined and graized our horses. the rains have rendered the road very slippery insomuch that it is with much difficulty our horses can get on several of them fell but sustained no injury. after dinner we proceeded up the creek about ½ a mile, passing it three times, thence through a high broken country to an Easterly fork of the same creek about 10½ miles and incamped near a small prarie in the bottom land.[3] the fallen timber in addition to the slippry roads made our march slow and extreemly laborious on our horses. the country is exceedingly thickly timbered with long leafed pine, some pitch pine, larch, white pine, white cedar or arborvita of large size,[4] and a variety of firs. the undergrowth principally reed root[5] from 6 to 10 feet high with all the other speceis enumerated the other day. the soil is good; in some plaices it is of a red cast like our lands in Virginia about the S. W. mountains.[6] Saw the speckled woodpecker,[7] bee martin[8] and log cock or large woodpecker.[9] found the nest of a humming bird,[10] it had just began to lay its eggs.— Came 22 Miles today.

[Clark] *Sunday June 15th 1806*

Collected our horses early with the intention of makeing an early Start. Some hard Showers of rain detained us untill [*blank*] A M at which time we took our final departure from the quawmash fields and proceeded with much dificuelty owing to the Situation of the road which was very Sliprey, and it was with great dificulty that the loaded horses Could assend the hills and Mountains they frequently Sliped down both assending and decending those Steep hills. at 9 miles we passed through a Small prarie in which was quawmash in this Prarie Reubin Fields & Willard had killed and hung up two deer at 2 miles further we arrived at the Camp of R. Fields & Willard on Collin's Creek, they arrived at this Creek last evening and had killed another Deer near the Creek. here we let our horses graze in a Small glade and took dinner. the rain Seased and Sun Shown out. after ⟨dinner⟩ detaining about 2 hours we proceeded on passing the Creek three times and passing over Some ruged hills or Spurs of the rocky Mountain, passing the Creek on which I encamped on the 17th Septr. last[11] to a Small glade of about 10 acres thickly Covered with grass and quawmash, near a large Creek and encamped. we passed through bad fallen timber and a high Mountain this evening. from the top of this Mountain I had an extensive view of the rocky Mountains to the South[12] and the Columbian plains for great extent[13] also the S W. Mountains[14] and a range of high Mountains which divides the waters of Lewis's & Clarks rivers and seems to termonate nearly a West Cours.[15] Several high pts. to the N & N. E. Covered with Snow. a remarkable high rugd mountain in the forks of Lewis's river nearly South and covered with Snow.[16] The vally up the Chopunnish river[17] appears extensive tolerably leavel and Covered with timber. The S W. Mountain is very high in a S S W. derection.

1. Crane Meadows, north of Lolo Creek in Clearwater County, Idaho. Space, 30; *Atlas* map 71.

2. The white bear is the grizzly bear, *Ursus horribilis*.

3. They camped on Eldorado Creek, in Idaho County, Idaho, not named on *Atlas* maps 70 or 71, near the mouth of Lunch Creek. Space, 31.

4. As the party ascends into the mountains, they leave dry forest types behind and enter a zone with higher precipitation and moist forests similar to those they saw on the Pacific Coast. Two characteristic species of the moist forest are noted here: western white pine, *Pinus monticola* Dougl., and western redcedar, *Thuja plicata* Donn. (white cedar or arborvitae refer to the similar eastern species *T. occidentalis* L.). Western redcedars reach sizes up to sixteen feet in diameter, much larger on average than white cedar. Little (CIH), 62-W, 90-W.

5. Reed root is the redroot (redstem ceanothus) of June 10.

6. The Columbia Basalt underlies this entire area. It contains abundant iron-bearing minerals such as augite and olivine. In dry climates the basalt weathers brown to dark brown, but in wet climates the basalt weathers more easily to a reddish-brown or brick-red

hematite. The soil here contains hematite disseminated among several other soil-forming materials.

7. Identified by Coues (HLC), 3 : 1044, as Cabanis's woodpecker, *Dryobates villosus hyloscopus*. Burroughs, 240, says that Cabanis's woodpecker is not found north of California, and declares this to be the Rocky Mountain hairy woodpecker, *Dendrocopos villosus monticola*. Cutright (LCPN), 433, agrees with Coues. Both are now subsumed under the hairy woodpecker, *Picoides villosus* [AOU, 393]. See also Holmgren, 34.

8. Western kingbird, *Tyrannus verticalis* [AOU, 447]; see June 10, 1805. Burroughs, 244.

9. Pileated woodpecker, *Dryocopus pileatus* [AOU, 405]; see March 4, 1806. Holmgren, 32; Burroughs, 242.

10. Identified by Coues (HLC), 3 : 1044 and n. 8, as the broad-tailed hummingbird, *Selasphorus platycercus* [AOU, 432], a new species. See also Cutright (LCPN), 301, 306, 437. Holmgren, 31, thinks it could be one of four species, including the broad-tailed.

11. Cedar Creek, in Idaho County; the actual date was September 19, 1805. Space, 14; Peebles (RLC), 22; *Atlas* map 70.

12. Perhaps the Clearwater Mountains in Idaho County.

13. Nez Perce and Camas prairies, according to Peebles (RLC), 22.

14. Perhaps the Wallowa Mountains in Wallowa County, Oregon. Ibid.

15. Assuming Clark's River to be, as usual, the Bitterroot and Clark Fork rivers in Montana, and Lewis's River to be the Salmon and the Snake, the separating range would be the Bitterroot Mountains. From where Clark could see them, the mountains would appear to run northwesterly.

16. Presumably the Seven Devils Mountains, in Idaho and Adams counties, Idaho, between the Snake and the Salmon.

17. The North Fork of the Clearwater, in Clearwater County. *Atlas* map 71.

[Lewis]   *Monday June 16th 1806.*

We collected our horses very readily this morning, took breakfast and set out at 6 A. M.; proceeded up the creek about 2 miles through some handsom meadows of fine grass abounding with quawmash, here we passed the creek[1] & ascended a ridge which led us to the N. E. about seven miles when we arrived at a small branch of hungry creek.[2] the difficulty we met with from the fallen timber detained us untill 11 oC before we reached this place. here is a handsome little glade in which we found some grass for our horses we therefore halted to let them graize and took dinner knowing that there was no other convenient situation for that purpose short of the glaids on hungry creek where we intended to encamp, as the last probable place, at which we shall find a sufficient quantity of grass for many days. this morning Windsor busted his rifle near the muzzle. before we reached this little branch on which we dined we saw in the hollows and N. hillsides large quatities of snow yet undisolved; in some places it was from two to three feet deep. vegetation is proportionably backward; the dogtooth violet[3] is just in blume, the honeysuckle,[4] huckburry[5] and a small speceis of white maple[6] are begining to put fourth their leaves; these appearances in this comparatively low region augers but unfavourably with rispect to the practibility of passing the mountains, however we determined to proceed, accordingly after taking a haisty meal we set out and continued our rout though a thick wood much obstructed with fallen timber, and intersepted by many steep ravines and high hills. the snow has increased in quantity so much that the greater part of our rout this evening was over the snow which has become sufficiently firm to bear our horshes, otherwise it would have been impossible for us to proceed as it lay in immence masses in some places 8 or ten feet deep. we found much difficulty in pursuing the road as it was so frequently covered with snow. we arrived early in the evening at the place that Capt. C. had killed and left the flesh of a horse for us last September.[7] [*EC?: 19th they got there*] here is a small glade in which there was some grass, not a sufficiency for our horses but we thought it most advisable to remain here all night as we apprehended if we proceeded further we should find less grass. the air is pleasent in the course of the day but becomes very cold before morning notwithstanding the shortness of the nights. Hungry creek is but small at this place but is deep and runs a perfect torrent; the water is perfectly transparent and as cold as ice. the pitch pine, white pine some larch and firs constite the timber; the long leafed pine extends a little distance on this side of the main branch of Collins's creek, and the white cedar not further than the branch of hungry creek on which we dined. I killed a small brown pheasant today,[8] it feeds on the tender leaves and buds of the fir and pitch pine. in the fore part of the day I observed the Cullumbine[9] the blue bells[10] and the yelow flowering pea[11] in blume. there is an abundance of a speceis of anjelico[12] in these mountains, much stonger to the taist and more highly scented than that speceis common to the U' States. know of no particular virtue or property it possesses; the natives dry it cut it in small peices which they string on a small cord and place about their necks; it smells very pleasantly. we came 15 miles today.

[Clark] *Monday June 16th 1806*

Collected our horses early and Set out 7 A M proceeded on up the Creek through a gladey Swompy bottom with grass and quawmash Crossed the Creek to the East and proceeded on through most intolerable bad fallen timber over a high Mountain on which great quantity of Snow is yet lying premisquissly through the thick wood, and in maney places the banks of snow is 4 feet deep. we noned it or dined on a Small Creek in a small open Vally where we found Some grass for our horses to eate, altho Serounded by Snow no other Convenient Situation Short of the glades on Hungery Creek where we intended to encamp, as the last probable place, at which we Shall find a Sufficent quantity of grass for maney days. This morning Windsor bursted his rifle near the Muzzle. Vigitation is propotionable backward; the dog tooth Violet is just in blume, the honeysuckle, huckleberry and a Small Species of white maple are beginning to put foth their leaves, where they are clear of the Snow, those appearances in this comparratively low region augers but unfavourably with respect to the practibility of passing the Mountains, however we deturmine to proceed, accordingly after takeing a hasty meal we Set out and Continued our rout through a thick wood much obstructed with fallen timber, and interupted by maney Steep reveins and hills which wer very high. the Snow has increased in quantity So much that the great part of our rout this evening was over the Snow which has become Sufficently firm to bear our horses, otherwise it would have been impossible for us to proceed as it lay in emince masses in Some places 8 or ten feet deep. We found much dificulty in finding the road, as it was So frequently covered with Snow. we arived early in the evening at the place I had killed and left the flesh of a horse for the party in my rear last Septr. here is a Small glade in which there is Some grass, not a Sufficency of our horses, but we thought it adviseable to remain here all night as we apprehended if we proceeded further we should find less grass. The air is pleasant in the Course of the day, but becomes very cold before morning not withstanding the Shortness of the night. Hungary Creek is but Small at this place but is deep and runs a perfect torrent; the water is perfectly transparent and as Cold as ice.   the titch pine, white pine Some Larch and firs consists the timber, the long leafed pine extends but a Short distance on the Mts. Capt. L. killed a Small brown pheasant today, it feeds on the tender leaves and buds of the fir and pitch pine.   in the forepart of the day I observed the Cullumbine the blue bells and the Yellow flowering pea in blume.   there is an abundance of a Species of Anjelico in the mountains much Stronger to the taiste, and more highly Scented than that Species common to the U' States. I know of no particular virtue or property it possesses   the nativs dry it Cut it in Small pieces which they string on a Small Cord and place about the necks; it Smells pleasently.   we Come 15 Ms. today.

1. Eldorado Creek, in Idaho County, Idaho. Space, 31; Peebles (RLC), 22.

2. Actually a branch of Fish Creek, in Idaho County, not named on *Atlas* map 70. Space, 31.

3. Dogtooth violet, also called fawn, or glacier, lily, *Erythronium grandiflorum* Pursh. It was an undescribed western species that Lewis had collected at lower elevations twice earlier (May 8 and June 5, 1806). Hitchcock et al., 1 : 787–88; Cutright (LCPN), 301, 308, 408.

4. Orange honeysuckle, *Lonicera ciliosa* (Pursh) DC.; he preserved a specimen of this undescribed species on this day and two weeks earlier at Camp Chopunnish. Hitchcock et al., 4 : 458; Cutright (LCPN), 308, 410.

5. Mountain huckleberry, *Vaccinium membranaceum* Dougl. ex Hook. Hitchcock et al., 4 : 32; Cutright (LCPN), 212, 422.

6. Rocky Mountain maple, *Acer glabrum* Torr., the only species of maple in this part of the Rocky Mountains. Hitchcock et al., 3 : 412.

7. At what is now called Horsesteak Meadow, on Hungery Creek, just below Windy Saddle in Idaho County. The location is marked "Small prarie, Killed a horse," on *Atlas* map 70. Clark's party killed the horse on September 19, 1805 (as Elliott Coues correctly noted it), and Lewis found it the following day. Space, 32.

8. Perhaps the Oregon ruffed grouse, *Bonasa umbellus sabini,* but see March 3, 1806. The red vertical line from here through the remainder of the entry was apparently drawn by Biddle.

9. The columbine in this area is the red, or Northwest crimson, columbine, *Aquilegia formosa* Fisch. Hitchcock et al., 2 : 333; Cutright (LCPN), 306, 402.

10. Tall bluebells, *Mertensia paniculata* (Ait.) G. Don, is common in this region. Hitchcock et al., 4 : 225.

11. Mountain thermopsis, *Thermopsis montana* Nutt., is common in this habitat and has bright yellow "pea" flowers. Ibid., 3 : 352.

12. The angelica-like plant abundant here is licorice-root, *Ligusticum verticillatum* (Geyer) Coult. & Rose. Ibid., 3:540. It is highly scented as noted. Lewis would have difficulty distinguishing between *Angelica* and *Ligusticum* without fruits, which would not have been present on this date.

[Lewis]   *Tuesday June 17th 1806.*

we collected our horses and set out early; we proceeded down hungry creek about seven miles passing it twice; we found it difficult and dangerous to pass the creek in consequence of its debth and rapidity; we avoided two other passes of the creek by ascending a very steep rocky and difficult hill.   beyond this creek the road ascends the mountain to the hight of the main leading ridges which divides the Waters of the Chopunnish and Kooskooske rivers.[1]   this hill or reather mountain we ascended about 3 miles when we found ourselves invelloped in snow from 12 to 15 feet deep even on the south sides of the hills with the fairest exposure to the sun; here was winter with all it's rigors; the air was cold, my hands and feet were benumbed.   we knew that it would require five days to reach the fish wears at the entrance of Colt Creek,[2] provided we were so fortunate as to be enabled to follow the proper ridges of the mountains to lead us to that place; ⟨of this Drewyer our principal dependance as a woodsman and guide was entirely doubtfull;⟩ short of that point we could not hope for any food for our horses not even underwood itself as the whole was covered many feet deep in snow.   if we proceeded and should get bewildered in these mountains the certainty was that we should loose all our horses and consequently our baggage instruments perhaps our papers and thus eminently wrisk the loss of the discoveries which we had already made if we should be so fortunate as to escape with life.   the snow boar our horses very well and the travelling was therefore infinitely better that the obstruction of rocks and fallen timber which we met with in our passage over last fall when the snow lay on this part of the ridge in detached spots only.   under these circumstances we conceived it madnes in this stage of the expedition to proceed without a guide who could certainly conduct us to the fish wears on the Kooskooske [*NB: Travellers (Creek) Rest*], as our [*NB: See note*][3] horses could not possibly sustain a journey of more than five days without food.   we therefore came to the resolution to return with our horses while they were yet strong and in good order and indevour to keep them so untill we could procure an indian to conduct us over the snowey mountains, and again to proceed as soon as we could procure such a guide, knowing from the appearance of the snows that if we remained untill it had desolved sufficiently for us to follow the road that we should not be enabled to return to the United States within this season. having come to this resolution, we ordered the party to make a deposit for all the baggage which we had not immediate use for,[4] and also all the roots and bread of cows which they had except an allowance for a few days to enable them to return to some place at which we could subsist by hunting untill we procured a guide. ⟨I⟩ [*word crossed out, illegible*] we left ⟨my⟩ our instruments papers &c beleiving them safer here than to wrisk them on horseback over the roads and creeks which we had passed. our baggage being laid on scaffoalds and well covered we began our retrograde march at 1 P. M. having remained about 3 hours on this snowey mountain. we returned by the rout we had come to hungry creek, which we ascended about 2 miles and encamped.[5] we had here more grass for our horses than the preceeding evening yet it was but scant. the party were a good deel dejected tho' not so as I had apprehended they would have been. this is the first time since we have been on this long tour that we have ever been compelled to retreat or make a retrograde march. it rained on us most of this evening.—

[Clark]   *Tuesday June 17th 1806*

We Collected our horses and Set out early; we proceeded down hungary Creek about 7 miles passing it twice; we found it dificuelt and dangerous to pass the creek in consequence of it's debth and rapidity; we avoided two other passes of the creek, by assending a Steep rockey and difficuelt hill. beyond this Creek the road assends the mountain to the hight of the main leading ridges, which divides the waters of the Kooskooske and Chopunnish Riv's. This mountain we ascended about 3 miles when we found ourselves invelloped in snow from 8 to 12 feet deep even on the South Side of the mountain. I was in front and Could only prosue the derection of the road by the trees which had been peeled by the nativs for the iner bark of which they Scraped and eate, as those pealed trees were only to be found Scattered promisquisley, I with great difficulty

32

prosued the direction of the road one mile further to the top of the mountain where I found the Snow from 12 to 15 feet deep, but fiew trees with the fairest exposure to the Sun; here was Winter with all it's rigors; the air was Cold my hands and feet were benumed.   we knew that it would require four days to reach the fish weare at the enterance of Colt Creek, provided we were So fortunate as to be enabled to follow the poper ridge of the mountains to lead us to that place; of this all of our most expert woodsmen and principal guides were extreemly doubtfull; Short of that point we could not hope for any food for our horses not even under wood itself as the whole was covered many feet deep in Snow.   if we proceeded and Should git bewildered in those Mountains the Certainty was that we Should lose all of our horses and consequencely our baggage enstrements perhaps our papers and thus eventially resque the loss of our discoveries which we had already made if we Should be So fortunate as to escape with life.   the Snow bore our horses very well and the traveling was therefore infinately better than the obstruction of rocks and fallen timber which we met with in our passage over last fall when the Snow lay on this part of the ridge in detached spops only.   under these Circumstances we Conceived it madness in this stage of the expedition to proceed without a guide who Could Certainly Conduct us to the fish-wears on the Kooskooske, as our horses could not possibly Sustain a journey of more than 4 or 5 days without food.   we therefore Come to the resolution to return with our horses while they were yet strong and in good order, and indeaver to keep them So untill we could precure an indian to conduct us over the Snowey Mountains, and again to proceed as soon as we could precure Such a guide, knowing from the appearance of the snows that if we remained untill it had disolved Sufficiently for us to follow the road that we Should not be enabled to return to the United States within this Season.   having come to this resolution, we ordered the party to make a deposit of all the baggage which we had not imediate use for, and also all the roots and bread of Cows which they had except an allowance for a fiew days to enable them to return to Some place at which we could Subsist by hunting untill we precured a guide.   we left our instrements, and I even left the most of my papers believing them Safer here than to Wrisk them on horseback over the road, rocks and water which we had passed.   our baggage being laid on Scaffolds and well covered, we began our retragrade march at 1 P. M. haveing remain'd about three hours on this Snowey mountain.   we returned by the rout we had advanced to hungary Creek, which we assended about 2 miles and encamped.   we had here more grass for our horses than the proceeding evening, yet it was but scant.   the party were a good deel dejected, tho' not as much So as I had apprehended they would have been. this is the first time Since we have been on this long tour that we have ever been compelled to retreat or make a retragrade march.   it rained on us the most of this evening.   on the top of the Mountain the Weather was very fluctiating and uncertain snowed cloudy & fair in a few minets.

1. At this point the Kooskooske is the Lochsa River, in Idaho County, Idaho. Space, 32; *Atlas* maps 70, 71.

2. Colt Killed Creek, "Killed Colt Creek" on *Atlas* map 70; present White Sand Creek in Idaho County. See September 14, 1805.

3. From conversations with Clark after the expedition, Biddle expanded on the matters of guides and leaving supplies unattended in the wilderness. Biddle Notes [ca. April 1810], Jackson (LLC), 2:544.

4. The baggage was cached on what is now called Willow Ridge, just west of Sherman Saddle in Idaho County. It was a mile or more northeast of Clark's "Encamped 18th Septr 1805" on *Atlas* map 70. Space, 32; Peebles (RLC), 22; Peebles (LT), map.

5. On the south side of Hungery Creek, in Idaho County. On *Atlas* map 70 the site lies between Clark's "Encamped 18th Septr 1805" and the main party's "Campd 19th."   Space, 32; Peebles (LT), map.

[Lewis]   *Wednesday June 18th 1806.*

This morning we had considerable difficulty in collecting our horses they having straggled off to a considerable distance in surch of food on the sides of the mountains among the thick timber; at 9 OCk. we collected them all except one of Drewyers and one of Sheildes; we set out leaving Sheilds and LaPage to collect the two lost horses and follow us. We dispatched Drewyer and Shannon to the Chopunnish Indians in the plains beyond the Kooskooske in order to hasten the arrival of the indians who had promised to accompany us or to procure a gude at all events and rejoin us as soon as possible.   we sent by them a rifle which we offered as a reward to any of them who would engage to conduct us to traveller's rest; we also dirrected them if they found difficulty in induciny any of them to accompany us to offer the reward of two other guns to be given them immediately and ten horses at the falls of Missouri. we had not proceeded far this morning before Potts cut his leg very badly with one of the large knives; he cut one of the large veigns on the inner side of the leg; I found much difficulty in stoping the blood which I could not effect untill I applyed a tight bandage with a little cushon of wood and tow on the veign below the wound. Colter's horse fel with him in passing hungry creek and himself and horse were driven down the creek a considerable distance rolling over each other among the rocks. he fortunately escaped without injury or the loss of his gun. by 1 P. M. we returned to the glade on the branch of hungry Creek where we had dined on the 16th inst.[1] here we again halted and dined. as there was much appearance of deer about this place we left R. and J. Feilds with directions to hunt this evening and tomorrow morning at this place and to join us in the evening at the meadows of Collin's creek where we intend remaining tomorrow in order to rest our horses and hunt. after dinner we proceeded on to Collin's Creek and encamped in a pleasant situation at the upper part of the meadows about 2 ms. above our encampment of the 15th inst.[2] we sent out several hunters but they returned without having killed anything. they saw a number of salmon [*NB: trout*][3] in the creek and shot at them several times without success. we directed Colter and Gibson to fix each of them a gigg in the morning and indevour to take some of the salmon. the hunters saw much fresh appearance of bear but very little of deer. we hope by means of the fish together with what deer and bear we can kill to be enabled to subsist untill our guide arrives without the necessity of returning to the quawmash flats. there is a great abundance of good food here to sustain our horses.—

[Clark]   *Wednesday June 18th 1806*

This morning we had considerable dificuelty in collecting our horses they haveing Strageled of to a considerable distance in Serch of food on the Sides of the mountains among the thick timber, at 9 oClock we Collected them all except 2 one of Shields & one of Drewyer's. we Set out leaving Shields and LePage to collect the two lost horses and follow us.

We dispatched Drewyer and Shannon to the Chopunnish Indians in the plains beyond the Kooskooske in order to hasten the arrival of the Indians who promised to accompany us, or to precure a guide at all events and rejoin us as Soon as possible. We Sent by them a riffle which we offered as a reward to any of them who would engage to conduct us to Clarks river at the entrance of Travellers rest Creek; we also directed them if they found difficuelty in induceing any of them to accompany us to offer the reward of two other guns to be given them immediately and ten horses at the falls of Missouri. we had not proceeded far this morning before J. Potts cut his leg very badly with one of the large knives; he cut one of the large veins on the iner side of the leg; Colters horse fell with him in passing hungary creek and himself and horse were driven down the Creek a considerable distance roleing over each other among the rocks. he fortunately escaped with[out] much injurey or the loss of his gun. he lost his blanket. at 1 P. M we returned to the glade on a branch of hungary Creek where we had dined on the 16th instant. here we again halted and dined. as there was some appearance of deer about this place we left J. & R Field with directions to hunt this evening and tomorrow morning at this place and join us in the evening in the Meadows on Collin's Creek where we intended to remain tomorrow in order to restour horses and hunt. after dinner we proceeded on to the near fork of Collins Creek and encamped in a pleasant Situation at the upper part of the Meadows about 2 miles above our encampment of the 15th inst. we Sent out Several hunters but they returned without having killed any thing—. they saw a number of large fish in the Creek and Shot at them Several times without Suckcess. we Gibson and Colter to fix each of themselves a gigg in the morning and indeaver to take Some of those fish. the hunters Saw much fresh appearance of Bear, but very little deer Sign. we hope by the means of the fish together with what deer and bear we can kill to been abled to Subsist untill our guide arives without the necessaty of returning to the quawmash flats. there is great abundance of good food here to Sustain our horses. we are in flattering expectations of the arrival of two young chiefs who informed us that they intended to accompany us to the U. States, and Should Set out from their village in 9 nights after we left them on the 19th inst. if they Set out at that time Drewyer & Shannon will meet them, and probably join us on the 20th or 21st—. Musquetors Troublesome.

1. A branch of Fish Creek, in Idaho County, Idaho; see June 16, 1806.

2. On Eldorado Creek, at the mouth of Dollar Creek in Idaho County. As Lewis notes, it was above the camp of June 15. It was somewhat south of Lewis's "Campd 20th" (September 20, 1805) on *Atlas* map 70. Space, 33; Peebles (RLC), 22; Peebles (LT), map.

3. Steelhead trout, *Oncorhynchus mykiss* (formerly *Salmo gairdneri*). See the next entry, June 19, and March 12 and 13, 1806.

[Lewis]   *Thursday June 19th 1806.*

Our hunters were out very early this morning, they returned before noon with one deer only.   the Fishermen had been more unsuccessfull, they returned without a single fish and reported they could find but few and those they had tryed to take in vain.   they had broke both their giggs which were of indian fabrication made of bone. I happened to have a pointed peice of iron in my pouch which answered by cuting in two peices to renew boath giggs.   they took one fish this evening which proved to be a salmon trout much to our mortification, for we had hoped that they were the salmon of this spring arrival and of course fat and fine.   these trout are of the red kind they remain all winter in the upper parts of the rivers and creeks and are generally poor at this season. At 2 P. M. J & R Feilds arived with two deer; John Sheilds and LaPage came with them, they had not succeeded in finding their horses.   late in the evening Frazier reported that my riding horse that of Capt Clark and his mule had gone on towards the Quawmash flatts and that he had pursued their tracks on the road about 2½ miles.   we determined to send out all the hunters in the morning in order to make a fair experiment of the pactability of our being able to subsist at this place and if not we shall move the day after to the Quawmash flatts.   the musquetoes have been excessively troublesome to us since our arrival at this place particularly in the evening. Cruzatte brought me several large morells[1] which I roasted and eat without salt pepper or grease   in this way I had for the first time the true taist of the morell which is truly an insippid taistless food.   our stock of salt is now exhausted except two quarts which I have reserved for my tour up Maria's River and that I left the other day on the mountain.—

[Clark]   *Thursday June 19th 1806*

This morning early Collins Labeesh & Crusat turned out to hunt, and Gibson & Colter fixed two Indian giggs and went in Serch of fish in the Creek. I took my gun and walked up the Creek about 4 Miles Saw some bear Sign and one fish only. Gibson killed only one fish which we found to be the Salmon Trout of the dark Species.   this fish was of the common Size pore, and indifferently flavoured. Labeesh killed one Deer neither of the others killed any thing.   about 1 P. M. Jo. & R Fields Shields & LaPage came up. Reubin & Joseph Fields brought two Deer which R. had killed in the Small glade on a branch of Hungary Creek where we had left them yesterday. Shields & LaPage did not find the two horses which we lost yesterday morning.   they report that they hunted with great diligence in the vicinity of our camp of the 17th without suckcess.   in my walk of this day up the Creek I observed a great abundance of fine grass[2] sufficient to Sustain our horses any length of time we chose to Stay at this place. Several glades of quawmash.   the S W. Sides of the hills is fallen timber and burnt woods, the N. E. Sides of the hills is thickly timbered with lofty pine, and thick under growth   This evening Several Salmon trout were Seen in the Creek, they hid themselves under the banks of the Creek which jutted over in Such a manner as to secure them from the Stroke of our giggs nets and spears which were made for the purpose of taking those Salmon trout.   we concluded to delay at this place another day with a view to give time to the two young Chiefs to arrive in case they set out on the 19th inst. as they informed us they Should   they will have Sufficient time to join us tomorrow or early the next day. Should we get a guide from this place it will Save us two days march through some of the worst road through those Mountains, crouded with fallin timber mud holes and steep hills &c.   we directed all the hunters to turn out early and kill something for us to live on &c. Musquetors troublesom

1. Most likely the black morel, *Morchella angusticeps* Pk., a spring mushroom highly prized by people who have access to salt and "grease." Miller (MNA), 214. The word is underlined in red, apparently by Biddle.

2. The dominant grasses of the area are Idaho fescue, *Festuca idahoensis* Elmer, and bluebunch wheatgrass, *Agropyron spicatum* (Pursh) Scribn. & Smith; see September 21, 1805.

[Lewis]   *Friday June 20th 1806.*

Our hunters set out early this morning; most of them returned before noon. R. Feilds killed a brown bear the tallons of which were remarkably short broad at their base and sharply pointed this was of the speceis which the Chopunnish call *Yah-kar*.[1]   it was in very low order and the flesh of the bear in this situation is much inferior to lean venison or the flesh of poor Elk. Labush and Cruzatte returned late in the evening with one deer which the former had killed.   we also caught seven salmon trout in the course of the day.   the hunters assured us that their greatest exertions would not enable them to support us here more than one or two days longer from the great scarcity of game and the difficult access of the country, the under brush being very thick and great quantities of fallen timber.   as we shall necessarily be compelled to remain more than two days for the return of Drewyer and Shannon we determined to return in the morning as far as the quawmash flatts and indeavour to lay in another stock of meat for the mountains, our former stock being now nearly exhausted as well as what we have killed on our return.   by returning to the quawmash flatts we shall sooner be informed whether or not we can procure a guide to conduct us through the mountains; should we fail in procuring one, we have determined to wrisk a passage on the following plan immediately, because should we wait much longer or untill the snow desolves in such manner as to enable us to follow the road we cannot hope to reach the United States this winter; this is that Capt. C. or myself shall take four of our most expert woodsmen with three or four of our best horses and proceed two days in advance taking a plentifull supply of provision.   for this party to follow the road by the marks which the baggage of the indians has made in many places on the sides of the trees by rubing against them, and to blaize the trees with a tomahawk as they proceeded.   that after proceeding two days in advance of hungary creek two of those men would be sent back to the main party who by the time of their return to Hungary Creek would have reached that place.   the men so returning would be enabled to inform the main party of the probable success of the preceeding party in finding the road and of their probable progress, in order that should it be necessary, the main party by the delay of a day or two at hungary creek, should give the advance time to mark the road through before the main party could overtake them, and thus prevent delay on the part of the rout where no food is to be obtained for our horses. should it so happen that the advance could not find the road by the marks on the trees after attempting it for two days, the whole of then would return to the main party. in which case we wold bring back our baggage and attempt a passage over these mountains through the country of the Shoshones further to the South by way of the main S. Westerly fork of Lewis's river and Madison or Gallatin's rivers, where from the information of the Chopunnish there is a passage which at this season of the year is not obstructed by snow, though the round is very distant and would require at least a month in it's performance.[2] The Shoshones informed us when we first met with them that there was a passage across the mountains in that quarter but represented the difficulties arrising from steep high and rugged mountains and also an extensive and barren plain which was to be passed without game, as infinitely more difficult than the rout by which we came. from the circumstance of the Chopunnish being at war with that part of the Shoshones who inhabit the country on this side of the Mountains through which the road passes I think it is highly probable that they cannot be well informed with rispect to the road, and further, had there been a better road in that quarter the Shoshones[3] on the East fork of Lewis's river who knew them both would not have recommended that by which we came to this country. the travelling in the mountains on the snow at present is very good, the snow bears the horses perfictly; it is a firm coase snow without a crust, and the horses have good foot hold without sliping much; the only dificulty is finding the road, and I think the plan we have devised will succeed even should we not be enabled to obtain a guide. Although the snow may be stated on an average at 10 feet deep yet arround the bodies of the trees it has desolved ⟨generally⟩ much more than in other parts not being generally more than one or two feet deep immediately at the roots of the trees, and; of course the marks left by the rubing of the indian baggage against them is not concealed. the reason why the snow is comparitively so shallow about the roots of the trees I presume proceeds as well from the snow in falling being thrown off from their bodies by their thick and spreading branches as from the reflection of the sun against the trees and the warmth which they in some measure acquire from the earth which is never frozen underneath these masses of snow. Bratton's horse was also discovered to be absent this evening. I presume he has also returned to the flatts.

[Clark]   *Friday June 20th 1806*

The hunters turned out early in different directions, our guiggers also turned out with 2 guigs a Bayonet fixed on a pole, a Scooping nett and a Snar made of horse.[4]   near the ford of the Creek in a deep hole we killed Six Salmon trout & 2 others were killed in the Creek above in the evening. Reubin Field killed a redish brown bear which was very meagure.   the tallons of this bear was remarkably Short broad at their base and Sharply pointed, this was of the Species the Chopunnish call *Yahkar*.   as it was in very low order the flesh was indifferent. Labiesh & Crusat returned late in the evening with one deer which the former had killed.   the hunters assured us that, their greatest exertions would not enable them to support us here more than one or two days longer, from the great scercity of game and the dificuelt access of the Country, the under brush being very thick and great quantities of fallen timber.   as we shall necessarily be compelled to remain more than two days for the return of Drewyer & Shannon we determine to return in the morning as far as the quawmash flatts, and endeaver to lay in another Stock of meat for the mountains, our former Stock now being nearly exhosted as well as what we have killed on our rout.   by returning to the quawmash flatts we Shall Sooner be informed wheather or not we can precure a guide to conduct us through the Mountains; Should we fail in precureing one, we are deturmined to wrisk a passage on the following plan immediatcly, be cause Should we wait much longer, or untill the Snow disolves in Such manner as to enable us to follow the road we cannot expect to reach the U States this Winter; this is that Capt. L. or myself shall take four of our most expert woods men with 3 or four of our best horses and proceed two days in advance takeing a plentiful Supply of provisions.   for this party to follow the road by the mark the indins have made in many places with their baggage on the Sides of the trees by rubbing against them, and to blaize the trees with a tomahawk as they proceed.   that after proceeding two days in advance of Hungary Creek, two of those men would be sent back to the party who by the time of their return to hungary Creek would have reached that place. the men So returning would be enabled to inform the main party of the probable Suckcess of the proceeding party in finding the road and of their probable progress, in order that Should it be necessary, the main party by a delay of a day or two a hungary Creek, should give the advance time to make the road through before the main party could overtake them, and thus prevent delay on that part of the rout where no food is to be obtained for our horses. Should it So happen that the advance Should not find the road by the marks of the trees after attempting it for two days, the whole of them would return to the main party. in which Case we would bring back our baggage and attempt a passage over the Mountains through the Country of the Shoshones further to the South, by way of the main S Westerly fork of Lewis's river and Madisons or Gallitins river's, where from the information of the Chopunnish, there is a passage where at this season of the year is not obstructed by snow, though the round is very distant and would require at least a month in it's preformance. The Shoshones informed us when we first met with them that there was a passage across the Mountains in that quarter but represented the difficuelties arriseing from Steep ruggid high mountains, and also an extensive and barren plain which was to be passed without game, as infinitely more difficuelt than the rout by which we Came. from the Circumstance of the Chopunnish being at war with that part of the Shoshones who inhabit the Country on this side of the Mountains through which the road passes, I think it is highly probable they cannot be well informed with respect to the road, and further, had there been a better road in that quarter the Shoshones on the East fork of Lewis's river who knew them boath would not have recommend'd that by which we came to this country. The travelling in the Mountains on the Snow, at present is very good, the Snow bears the horses perfectly; it is a firm coase Snow without a crust, and the horses have good foot hold without slipping much; the only dificuelty is finding the road, and I think the plan we have ⟨deci⟩ devised will Suckceed even Should we not be enabled to obtain a guide. altho the Snow may be Stated on an average at 10 feet deep, yet arround the body of the trees it has disolved much more than in other parts, not being generally more than one or two feet deep imediately at the roots of the trees, and of course the marks made by the rubbing of the Indian baggage against them is not Concealed. The reason why the Snow is ⟨not⟩ comparitively So Shallow about the roots of the trees, I prosume proceeds as well from the ⟨roots⟩ Snow in falling being thrown off from their bodies by the thick and Spreading branches, as from the reflection of the Sun against the trees and the warmth which they in Some measure acquire from the earth which is never frozen underneath those masses of Snow.   4 of our horses are absent.

1. The cinnamon phase of the black bear; see June 11, 1806. *Yá·ka,* "brown bear," is the Nez Perce term for the black bear; see May 31, 1806.
2. This route would be up the Snake River in its long curve through southern Idaho, including the arid Snake River Plain. They would then cross the Continental Divide through one of several passes west of present Yellowstone Park into southwestern Montana near the headwaters of the Missouri forks. The Nez Perces may also have been thinking of the route from the upper Snake River through the Yellowstone plateau (the present park), to the Yellowstone River; this was used by various mountain tribes, and was later called the Bannock Trail. Either way would have been a long and circuitous route. Allen (PG), 347, 379 and n. 61; Ehrenberg, 77; Sprague (GG), 213, 436.
3. The Lemhi Shoshones (Sacagawea's people), whom they met on the Lemhi River in eastern Idaho in August 1805.
4. Horsehair, presumably.

[Lewis]   *Saturday June 21st 1806.*

We collected our horses early set out on our return to the flatts.   we all felt some mortification in being thus compelled to retrace our steps through this tedious and difficult part of our rout, obstructed with brush and innumerable logs of fallen timber which renders the traveling distressing and even dangerous to our horses.   one of Thompson's horses is either choked this morning or has the distemper very badly I fear he is to be of no further service to us.   an excellent horse of Cruzatte's snagged himself so badly in the groin in jumping over a parsel of fallen timber that he will evidently be of no further service to us.   at the pass of Collin's Creek we met two indians who were on their way over the mountain; they had brought with them the three horses and the mule that had left us and returned to the quawmash grounds.   these indians returned with us about ½ a mile down the creek where we halted to dine and graize our horses at the same place I had halted and remained all night with the party on the [*blank*] of Septembr last.[1]   as well as we could understand the indians they informed us that they had seen Drewyer and Shannon and that they would not return untill the expiration of two days; the cause why Drewyer and Shannon had not returned with these men we are at a loss to account for.   we pressed these indians to remain with us and to conduct us over the mountain on the return of Drewyer and Shannon.   they consented to remain two nights for us and accordingly deposited their store of roots and bread in the bushes at no great distance and after dinner returned with us, as far as the little prarie[2] about 2 miles distant from the creek, here they halted with their horses and informed us they would remain untill we overtook them or at least two nights. they had four supenumery horses with them.   we sent on four hunters a head to the quawmash flatts to take an evenings hunt; they so far succeeded as to kill one deer.   we left Reubin and J. Feilds at the Creek where we dined together with Sergt Gass in order to hunt about that place untill our return.   at seven in the evening we found ourselves once more at our old encampment[3] where we shall anxiously await the return of Drewyer and Shannon.—

[Clark]   *Saturday June 21st 1806*

   We collected our horses early and Set out on our return to the flatts. we all felt Some mortification in being thus compelled to retrace our Steps through this tedious and difficuelt part of our rout, obstructed with brush and innumerable logs and fallen timber which renders the traveling distressing and even dangerous to our horses.   one of Thompsons horses is either choked this morning or has the distemper badly. I fear he is to be of no further Survice to us.   an excellent horse of Cruzatt's snagged himself So badly in the groin in jumping over a parcel of fallen timber that he will eventually be of no further Survice to us.   at the pass of Collin's Creek we met two indians who were on their way over the mountains, they had brought with them the three horses and the Mule which had left us and returned to the quawmash ground.   those indians returned with us about ½ a mile down the Creek where we ⟨expected⟩

halted to dine and graze our horses. as well as we Could understand the indians they informed us they had Seen Geo Drewyer & Shannon, and that they would not return untill the expiration of two days. the cause why Drewyer & Shannon did not return with these men we are at a loss to account for. we pressed those indians to remain with us and conduct us over the Mountains on the return of Drewyer & Shannon. they consented to remain two nights for us and accordingly deposited their Stores of roots & Bread in the bushes at no great distance and after Dinner returned with us, as far as the little prarie about 2 Miles distance from the Creek, here they halted with their horses and informed us they would remain untill we overtook them or at least 2 nights. they had four Supernoumery horses with them. We Sent on four hunters a head to the quawmash flatts to make an evening hunt; they So far Suckceeded as to kill one deer. We left R. and Jo. Fields at the Creek where we dined, and Sergt. Gass in order to hunt about that place untill our return. at 7 in the evening we found ourselves once more at our old encampment where we Shall anxiously await the return of Drewyer & Shannon.

1. The camp of September 21, 1805, on Lolo Creek in Clearwater County, Idaho. *Atlas* map 71.

2. Crane Meadows; see June 15, 1806. Peebles (RLC), 23.

3. The camp of June 10–15, 1806, on Weippe Prairie ("quawmash flatts"). Peebles (LT), map; *Atlas* map 71.

[Lewis]   *Sunday June 22nd 1806.*

this morning by light all hands who could hunt were sent out; the result of this days perfomance was greater than we had even hoped for. we killed eight deer and three bear. we dispatched Whitehouse to the Kooskooske near our old encampment above Collins's Creek[1] in order to procure some Salmon which we have understood the natives are now taking in considerable quantities near that place. we gave Whitehouse a few beads which Capt. C. had unexpectedly found in one of his waistcoat pockets to purchase the fish. nothing further worthy of notice occurred in the course of this day. the last evening was cool but the day was remarkably pleasent with a fine breize from the N. W. neither Drewyer Shannon nor Whitehouse returned this evening.— Potts's legg is inflamed and very painfull to him.   we apply a poltice of the roots of Cows.—[2]

[Clark]   *Sunday June 22nd 1806*

This morning by light all hands who Could hunt were Sent out, the result of the days performance was greater than we had even hopes for.   we killed eight Deer and three Bear.   we despatched whitehouse to the Kooskooke near our old encampment above Collins Creek in order to precure Some Salmon which we understood the nativs are now takeing in considerable quantities near that place.   we gave whitehouse a fiew beeds which I unexpectedly found in one of my waistcoat pockets to purchase the fish.   nothing further occured in the Course of this day.   the last evening was Cool but the day was remarkably pleasant with a fine breeze from the N. W.   neither Shannon Drewyer nor whitehouse returned this evening.— Potts legg is inflamed and very painfull to him. we apply a poltice of the root of Cowes.—.

    1. Camp Chopunnish.
    2. Here Lewis found another use for cous. Cutright (LCPN), 284.

[Lewis]   *Monday June 23rd 1806.*

Apprehensive from Drewyer's delay that he had met with some difficulty in procuring a guide, and also that the two indians who had promised to wait two nights for us would set out today, we thought it most advisable to dispatch Frazier and Wiser to them this morning with a vew if possible to detain them a day or two longer; and directed that in the event of their not being able to detain the indians, that Sergt. Gass, R & J. Feilds and Wiser should accompany the indians by whatever rout they might take to travellers rest and blaize the trees well as they proceeded and wait at that place untill our arrivall with the party.   the hunters as usual wer dispatched early this morning.   the does now having their fawns the hunters can bleat them up[1] and in that manner kill them with more facility and ease.   the indians pursue the game so much on horseback in this neighbourhood that it is very shye.   our hunters killed 4 deer and a bear today.   at [4?] P. M. Drewyer Shannon and Whitehouse returned. Drewyer brought with him three indians who had consented to accompany us to the falls of the Missouri for the compensation of two guns. one of those men is the brother of the cutnose and the other two[2] are the same who presented Capt. Clark and myself each with a horse on a former occasion at the Lodge of the broken arm. these are all young men of good character and much respected by their nation. we directed the horses to be brought near camp this evening and secured in such manner that they may he readily obtained in the morning being determined to make an early start if possible.— Colter one of our hunters did not return this evening.

[Clark]   *Monday June 23rd 1806*

Apprehensive from Drewyer & Shannons delay that they had met with Some difficuelty in precureing a guide, and also that the two indians who had promised to wait two nights for us would Set out today, we thought it most adviseable to dispatch Wizer & Frazier to them this morning with a view if possible to detain them a day or two longer; and directed that in the event of their not being able to detain the indians, that Sergt. Gass, Jo. & R. Field & Wiser Should accompany the Indians by whatever rout they might take to travellers rest and blaize the trees well as they proceeded, and wait at that place untill our arival with the party. the hunters as usial were dispatched early this morning. The does now haveing their young the hunters can blait them up, and in that manner kill them with more facillity and ease. the indians pursue the game So much on horse back in this neighbourhood that it is very Shye. our hunters killed [*blank*] deer today. at 4 P. M. Shannon Drewyer & Whitehouse returned. Shannon & Drewyer brought with them three indians who had consented to accompany us to the falls of the Missouri for the Compensation of 2 guns. one of those men is the brother of the *Cutnose* and the other two are the Same who presented Capt L. and myself with a horse on a former occasion at the Lodge of the broken arm, and the two who promised to pursue us in nine nights after we left the river, or on the 19th inst. Those are all young men of good Charrector and much respected by their nation. those men infor us that thir nation as well as the Wallar-wallars have made peace with the Shoshones agreeable to our late advice to them. they also inform us that they have heard by means of the Skeetsomis Nation & Clarks river that the Big bellies of Fort de Prarie[3] Killed great numbers of the Shoshons and *Otte lee Shoots*[4] which we met with last fall on the East fork of Lewis's river and high up the West fork of Clarks river &c.

We directed the horses to be brought near Camp and secured in Such a manner that they may be readily obtained in the morning being deturmined to make an early Start if possible—.— Colter one of our hunters did not return this evening—.

1. Bleating like a fawn to attract the does. Criswell, 15.
2. Some Nez Perce accounts say that one was a son of Twisted Hair and one a son of Hohots Ilppilp. Space, 34. The presentation of horses was made on May 12, 1806.
3. Atsina Indians; see May 28, 1805.
4. The Flatheads (Salish); see September 4, 1805. The name may represent a Flathead term, *uɫ-išú-t,* "those down below" (see September 5, 1805).

[Lewis]   *Tuesday June 24th 1806.*

We collected our horses early this morning and set out accompanyed by our three guides. Colter joined us this morning having killed a bear, which from his discription of it's poverty and distance we did not think proper to send after.   we nooned it as usual at Collins's Creek where we found Frazier, solus;[1] the other four men having gone in pursuit of the two indian men who had set out from Collins's Creek two hours before Frazier and Wizer arrived.   after dinner we continued our rout to Fish Creek a branch of Collins's Creek where we had lain on the 19th & 20th inst.[2]   here we found Sergt. Gass Wiser and the two indians whom they had prevailed on to remain at that place untill our arrival; R. & J. Feilds had only killed one small deer only while they lay at Collins's Creek and of this they had been liberal to the indians insomuch that they had no provision; they had gone on to the branch of hungary Creek at which we shall noon it tomorrow in order to hunt.   we had fine grass for our horses this evening.

[Clark]   *Tuesday June 24th 1806*

We collected our horses early this morning and Set out accompanied by our 3 guides. Colter joined us this morning haveing killed a Bear,

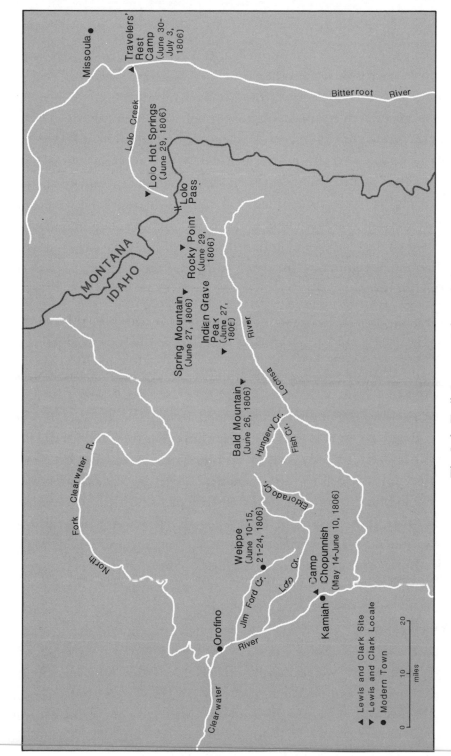

Missoula ●

Travelers'
Rest
Camp
(June 30–
July 3,
1806) ◄

Bitterroot River

Lolo Creek

Loo Hot Springs
(June 29, 1806) ▼

Lolo Pass ◄

MONTANA
IDAHO

Rocky Point
(June 29,
1806) ▼

Spring Mountain
(June 27, 1806) ▼

Indian Grave
Peak
(June 27,
1806) ▼

River

Bald Mountain
(June 26, 1806) ▼

Lochsa

Hungery Cr.

Fish Cr.

North Fork Clearwater R.

Eldorado Cr.

Weippe
(June 10–15,
21–24, 1806) ●

Jim Ford Cr.

Lolo Cr.

Camp
Chopunnish
(May 14–June 10, 1806) ◄

Orofino ●

River

Kamiah ●

Clearwater

◄ Lewis and Clark Site
▼ Lewis and Clark Locale
● Modern Town

0   10   20
    miles

1. The Lolo Trail, June 10–July 3, 1806

which from his discription of it's poverty and distance we did not think proper to send after. We nooned it as usial at Collins's Creek where we found Frazier, solus; the other four men haveing gorn in pursute of the two indians who had Set out from Collin's Creek two hours before Fraziers arrival Wiser arrived there. after dinner we Continued our rout to fish Creek a branch of Collin's creek where we had lain the 15th[3] 18th 19th & 20th inst. here we found Sargt. Gass, Wiser and the two indian men whome they had prevaild on to remain at that place untill our arival; Jos. & R. Field had killed one Small deer only while they lay at Collins creek, and of this they had been liberal to the indians insomuch that they had no provisions; they had gone on to the branch of hungary Creek at which we shall noon it tomorrow in order to hunt. we had fine grass for our horses this evening.—

1. Alone.
2. The camp of June 18–21, 1806, on Eldorado Creek in Idaho County, Idaho.
3. They did not camp there on June 15, 1806; see that date and June 18.

[Lewis]   *Wednesday June 25th 1806.*

last evening the indians entertained us with seting the fir trees on fire. they have a great number of dry lims near their bodies which when set on fire creates a very suddon and immence blaze from bottom to top of those tall trees. they are a beatifull object in this situation at night. this exhibition reminded me of a display of fireworks. the natives told us that their object in seting those trees on fire was to bring fair weather for our journey.— We collected our horses readily and set out at an early hour this morning. one of our guides complained of being unwell, a symptom which I did not much like as such complaints with an indian is generally the prelude to his abandoning any enterprize with which he is not well pleased. we left them at our encampment and they promised to pursue us in a few hours. at 11 A. M. we arrived at the branch of hungary creek where we found R. & J. Feilds. they had not killed anything. here we halted and dined and our guides overtook us. at this place I met with a plant[1] the root of which the shoshones eat. it is a small knob root a good deel in flavor an consistency like the Jerusalem Artichoke. it has two small oval smooth leaves placed opposite on either

50

side of the peduncle just above the root.   the scape is only about 4 inches long is round and smooth.   the roots of this plant formed one of those collections of roots which Drewyer took from the Shoshones last summer on the head of Jefferson's river.   after dinner we continued our rout to hungary Creek and encamped about one and a half miles below our encampment of the 16th inst.—[2]   the indians continued with us and I beleive are disposed to be faithfull to their engagement. I gave the sik indian a buffaloe robe he having no other covering except his mockersons and a dressed Elkskin without the hair. Drewyer and Sheilds were sent on this morning to hungry Creek in surch of their horses which they fortunately recovered.—

[Clark]   *Wednesday June 25th 1806*

   last evening the indians entertained us with Setting the fir trees on fire.   they have a great number of dry limbs near their bodies which when Set on fire create a very Sudden and emmence blaize from bottom to top of those tail trees.   they are a boutifull object in this Situation at night.   this exhibition remide me of a display of firewoks.   the nativs told us that their object in Setting those trees on fire was to bring fair weather for our journey—. We Collected our horses and Set out at an early hour this morning.   one of our guides Complained of being unwell, a Symptom which I did not much like as such complaints with an indian is generally the prelude to his abandoning any enterprize with which he is not well pleased.   we left 4 of those indians at our encampment they promised to pursue us in a fiew hours.   at 11 A. M. we arrived at the branch of hungary Creek where we found Jo. & R. Fields.   they had not killed anything.   here we halted and dined and our guides overtook us.   at this place the squaw Collected a parcel of roots of which the Shoshones Eat.   it is a Small knob root a good deel in flavour and Consistency like the Jerusolem artichoke.   it has two Small Smooth oval leaves placed opposit on either Side of the peduncle just above the root.   the scope is only about 4 inches long is round and Smooth.   the roots of this plant forms one of the Colection of roots which D—. took from the Shoshones last fall on the head of Jefferson river.   after dinner we continued our rout to hungary creek and encamped about one and a half

miles below our Encampment of the 16th inst:— The indians all continue with us and I beleive are disposed to be faithfull to their engage-
ments. Capt. L. gave the Sick indian a Small buffalow robe which he
brought from the Missouri, this indian having no other Covering except
his mockersons and a dressed Elk Skin without the hair—. Drewyer &
Shields were sent on this morning to hungary Creek in serch of their
horses which they fortunately recovered.—.   came [*blank*] miles to daye.

1. A good description of western spring beauty, *Claytonia lanceolata* Pursh. It is one of
the first species to bloom in spring, and its white flowers would have been evident where
snow had recently melted along the trail. The roots are small but very good-tasting.
Clark's entry for the day credits Sacagawea, "the squaw," with collecting the roots. This is
one of the few documented instances where Sacagawea is clearly credited with bringing a
botanical item to the attention of the captains. The species was unknown to science at the
time, and Lewis collected the type specimen two days later. Hitchcock et al., 2:229; Cutright (LCPN), 306, 308, 406. The Jerusalem artichoke used for comparison is *Helianthus
tuberosus* L. Drouillard brought a specimen of western spring beauty to Lewis on August
22, 1805, but the captain was unable to describe it sufficiently at that time. It was tenta-
tively identified in the editorial note as Nuttall sunflower, *H. nuttallii* T. & G. It is now
clear that the species he saw then and the one he describes here is western spring beauty.
2. Probably at or near the main party camp of September 19, 1805, on an unnamed
creek running into Hungery Creek in Idaho County, Idaho; it is marked "Campd 19th"
on *Atlas* map 71. Space, 14, 35; Peebles (RLC), 24; Peebles (LT), map.

[Lewis]   *Thursday June 26th 1806.*

This morning we collected our horses and set out after an early breakfast or at 6 A. M.   we passed by the same rout we had travelled on the
17th inst. to our deposit on the top of the snowey mountain to the N. E.
of hungary Creek.[1]   here we necessarily halted about 2 hours to arrange
our baggage and prepare our loads.   we cooked and made a haisty meal
of boiled venison and mush of cows.   the snow has subsided near four
feet since the 17th inst.   we now measured it accurately and found from
a mark which we had made on a tree when we were last here on the 17th
that it was then 10 feet 10 inches which appeared to be about the common debth though it is deeper still in some places.   it is now generally
about 7 feet.[2]   on our way up this mountain about the border of the
snowey region we killed 2 of the small black pheasant[3] and a female of
the large dommanicker or speckled pheasant,[4] the former have 16 fath-

ers in their tail and the latter 20 while the common pheasant[5] have only 18. the indians informed us that neither of these speceis drumed; they appear to be very silent birds for I never heared either of them make a noise in any situation.[6] the indians haistened to be off and informed us that it was a considerable distance to the place which they wished to reach this evening where there was grass for our horses. accordingly we set out with our guides who lead us over and along the steep sides of tremendious mountains entirely covered with snow except about the roots of the trees where the snow had sometimes melted and exposed a few square feet of the earth. we ascended and decended severall lofty and steep hights but keeping on the dividing ridge between the Chopunnish and Kooskooske rivers we passed no stream of water.[7] late in the evening much to the satisfaction of ourselves and the comfort of our horses we arrived at the desired spot and encamped on the steep side of a mountain convenient to a good spring. [*NB: having passed a few miles our camp of 18 Sepr 1805*][8] here we found an abundance of fine grass for our horses. this situation was the side of an untimbered mountain with a fair southern aspect where the snows from appearance had been desolved about 10 days. the grass was young and tender of course and had much the appearance of the greenswoard.[9] there is a great abundance of a speceis of bear-grass[10] which grows on every part of these mountains it's growth is luxouriant and continues green all winter but the horses will not eat it. soon after we had encamped we were overtaken by a Chopunnish man who had pursued us with a view to accompany me to the falls of the Missouri. we were now informed that the two young men whom we met on the 21st and detained several days are going on a party of pleasure mearly to the Oote-lash-shoots or as they call them Sha-lees[11] a band of the Tush-she-pah nation who reside on Clark's river in the neighbourhood of traveller's rest. one of our guides lost 2 of his horses, which he returned in surch of; he found them and rejoined us a little before dark.—

[Clark]   *Thursday June 26th 1806*

We collected our horses and Set out early and proceeded on Down hungary Creek a fiew miles and assended to the Summit of the mountain where we deposited our baggage on the 17th inst. found every thing

Safe and as we had left them.   the Snow which was 10 feet 10 inches deep on the top of the mountain, had sunk to 7 feet tho' perfectly hard and firm.   we made Some fire Cooked dinner and dined, while our horses Stood on snow 7 feet deep at least.   after dinner we packed up and proceeded on.   about the borders of the Snowey region we killed 2 Small black pheasents and a female of the large dommanicker or Speckled pheasent, the former have 16 feathers in the tail and the latter 20 while the common Pheasent have 18.   the indians informed us that neither of these Speces drumed; they appear to be very Silent birds for I never heard any of them make any noise.   the Indians hastened ⟨to the⟩ us off and informed us that it was a considerable distance to the place they wished to reach this evening where there was grass for our horses. accordingly we Set out with our guides who led us over and along the Steep Sides of tremendious Mountains entirely covered with Snow except about the roots of the trees where the Snow was partially melted and exposed a Small Spot of earth.   we assended and deceded Several Steep lofty hights but keeping on the dividing ridge of the Chopunnish & Kooskooske river we passed no Stream of water.   late in the evening much to the Satisfaction of ourselves and the Comfort of the horses we arived at the desired Spot and Encamped on the Steep Side of a Mountain Convenient to a good Spring.   here we found an abundance of fine grass for our horses.   this Situation was the Side of an untimbered mountain with a fair Southern aspect where the Snow from appearance had been disolved about 10 days, the grass was young and tender of course and had much the appearance of the Green Swoard.   there is a great abundance of Species of bear grass which grows on every part of those Mountains, its growth is luxurient and continues green all winter but the horses will not eate it. Soon after we had encamped we were over taken by a Chopunnish man who had pursued us with a view to accompany Capt Lewis to the falls of Missouri.   we were now informed that the two young men we met on the 21st and detained Several days were going on a party of pleasure mearly to the *Oat-lash-shoots* or as they call them *Sha-lees* a band of the *Tush-she-pâh* Nation who reside on Clarks river in the neighbourhood of the Mouth of Travelers rest.   one of our Guides lost 2 of his horses, he returned in Serch of them he found them & rejoined us at

Dark. all of the Indians with us have two & 3 horses each. I was taken yesterday with a violent pain in my head which has tormented me ever Since, most violently

1. The cache on Willow Ridge, in Idaho County, Idaho; see June 17, 1806.

2. Space, 36, judges the spring of 1806 to have been unusually late, since the snow is usually gone in the area by late June, except in isolated drifts and shaded spots.

3. Probably the blue grouse, *Dendragapus obscurus* [AOU, 297]; see August 1, 1805, and March 3, 1806.

4. Spruce grouse, *Dendragapus canadensis* [AOU, 298]; see March 3, 1806.

5. Presumably the ruffed grouse, *Bonasa umbellus* [AOU, 300], "common" because Lewis was familiar with it in the East. A red vertical line runs through this passage about the birds, perhaps Biddle's doing.

6. Space, 36, confirms that these birds do not drum, though they make other noises during the mating season or in calling their young.

7. The Lolo Trail runs along the ridge or divide between the North Fork of the Clearwater (Chopunnish) and the Lochsa (Kooskooske), primarily in Idaho County. *Atlas* maps 69, 70.

8. This camp was on Bald Mountain, in Idaho County. As Biddle notes, it was northeast of the camp of September 18, 1805, marked "Party Camped 18th" on *Atlas* map 70. Space, 36; Peebles (LT), map; Peebles (RLC), 26.

9. Greensward usually refers to a lush, green meadow rather than to a specific species. The grasses would be those noted at June 19, 1806. A red vertical line runs through most of the remainder of the entry, again probably Biddle's work.

10. Beargrass, *Xerophyllum tenax* (Pursh) Nutt., is indeed abundant here. When he says he sees "a speceis of bear-grass" he implies that he knows the eastern species, *X. asphodeloides* (L.) Nutt., and that this plant is different. He is correct. However, the eastern species is called turkey-beard, so Lewis's use of the name beargrass is curious. The wiry leaves are not edible, as he surmised, but as he noted on the type specimen label, they were used "by the natives to make baskets and other ornaments" (see also January 17, 1806). Hitchcock et al., 1:812; Cutright (LCPN), 422.

11. Salish (Flatheads). The name "Tush-she-pah" apparently represents the Shoshone term *tatasiba*, "the people with shaved heads," meaning the Flatheads (see September 4, 1805).

[Lewis]   *Friday June 27th 1806.*

We collected our horses early and set out. the road still continued on the heights of the same dividing ridge on which we had traveled yesterday for nine miles or to our encampment of the ⟨18th⟩ [NB: *17th*][1] of September last. about one mile short of this encampment on an elivated point we halted by the request of the Indians a few minutes and smoked the pipe. on this eminence the natives have raised a conic mound of stones of 6 or eight feet high and on it's summit erected a pine pole of 15 feet long.[2] from hence they informed us that when passing over with their familes some of the men were usually sent on foot by the fishery at the entrance of Colt Creek in order to take fish and again met the main party at the Quawmash glade on the head of the Kooskooske river.[3] from this place we had an extensive view of these stupendous mountains principally covered with snow like that on which we stood; we were entirely surrounded by those mountains from which to one unacquainted with them it would have seemed impossible ever to have escaped; in short without the assistance of our guides I doubt much whether we who had once passed them could find our way to Travellers rest in their present situation for the marked trees on which we had placed considerable reliance are much fewer and more difficult to find than we had apprehended. these fellows are most admireable pilots; we find the road wherever the snow has disappeared though it be only for a few hundred paces. after smoking the pipe and contemplating this seene sufficient to have damp the sperits of any except such hardy travellers as we have become, we continued our march and at the distance of 3 ms. decended a steep mountain and passed two small branches of the Chopunnish river just above their forks[4] and again ascended the ridge on which we passed several miles and at a distance of 7 ms. arrived at our encampment [*NB: 16th*] of September near which we passed 3 small branches[5] of the Chopunnish river and again ascended to the dividing ridge on which we continued nine miles when the ridge became lower and we arrived at a situation very similar to our encampment of the last evening tho' the ridge was somewhat higher and the snow had not been so long desolved of course there was but little grass.[6] here we encamped for the night having traveled 28 miles over these mountains without releiving the horses from their packs or their having any food. the indians inform us that there is [*NB: in the mountains a little to our left*] an abundance of the mountain sheep or what they call white buffaloe.[7] we saw three black-tailed or mule deer[8] this evening but were unable to get a shoot at them. we also saw several tracks of those animals in the snow. the indians inform that there is great abundance of Elk in the vally about the Fishery on the

Kooskooske River.[9] our meat being exhausted we issued a pint of bears oil to a mess which with their boiled roots made an agreeable dish. Potts's legg which has been much swolen and inflamed for several days is much better this evening and gives him but little pain. we applyed the pounded roots and leaves of the wild ginger[10] & from which he found great relief.— neare our encampment we saw a great number of the yellow lilly with reflected petals in blume;[11] this plant was just as forward here at this time as it was in the plains on the 10th of may.

[Clark]   *Friday June 27th 1806*

We collected our horses early and Set out. the road Still Continue on the hights of the Dividing ridge on which we had traveled yesterday for 9 Ms. or to our encampment of the 16th Septr. last.[12] about 1 m. Short of the encampment we halted by the request of the Guides a fiew minits on an ellevated point and Smoked a pipe on this eminance the nativs have raised a conic mound of Stons of 6 or 8 feet high and erected a pine pole of 15 feet long. from hence they informed us that when passing over with their families some of the men were usually Sent on foot by the fishery at the enterance of Colt Creek in order to take fish and again meet the party at the quawmash glade on the head of Kooskoske river. from this place we had an extencive view of these Stupendeous Mountains principally Covered with Snow like that on which we Stood; we were entirely Serounded by those mountains from which to one unacquainted with them it would have Seemed impossible ever to have escaped, in short without the assistance of our guides, I doubt much whether we who had once passed them could find our way to Travellers rest in their present Situation for the marked trees on which we had placed Considerable reliance are much fewer and more difficuelt to find than we had apprehended. those indians are most admireable pilots; we find the road wherever the Snow has disappeared tho' it be only fora fiew paces. after haveing Smoked the pipe and Contemplating this Scene Sufficient to have dampened the Spirits of any except Such hardy travellers as we have become, we continued our march and at the dist. of 3 m. decended a Steep mountain and passed two Small branches of the Chopunnish river just above their fok, and again assend the ridge on which we passed. at the distance of 7 m. arived at our Encampment of 16th Septr. last passed 3 Small branches passed on a dividing ridge rugid and we arived at a Situation very Similar to our Situation of last night tho' the ridge was Somewhat higher and the Snow had not been So long disolved of course there was but little grass. here we Encamped for the night haveing traveled 28 Ms. over these mountains without releiveing the horses from their packs or their haveing any food. the Indians inform us that there is an abundance of the Mountain Sheep, or what they Call white Buffalow on those Mountains. we Saw 3 black tail or mule deer this eveining but were unable to get a Shoot at them. we also Saw Several tracks of those animals in the snow. our Meat being exhosted we ⟨send 2⟩ issued a point of *Bears Oil* to a mess which with their boiled roots made an agreeable dish. Jo. Potts leg which had been much Swelled and inflaimed for several days is much better this evening and givs him but little pain. we applied the poundd root & leaves of wild ginger from which he found great relief. Near our encampment we saw great numbers of the Yellow lilly with reflected petals in blume; this plant was just as foward here at this time as it was in the plains on the 10th of May. My head has not pained me so much to day as yesterday and last night.

1. It appears that this was initially a blank space into which Biddle put "18th," then crossed it out and substituted "17th," all in red ink. He also added "16th" later in the entry in an apparent blank space.

2. In Idaho County, Idaho, on the first high point west of Indian Grave Peak. Lewis describes it as a mile short of the party's camp of September 17, 1805, marked on *Atlas* map 70. A rock mound stands there today, much smaller than the one described by Lewis. Space, 37.

3. A reference to Packer Meadows, in Idaho County, in the vicinity of the party's camp of September 13, 1805. Space, 37; *Atlas* map 69.

4. Gravey and Serpent creeks, according to Space, 37. Horseshoe and Serpent creeks, according to Peebles (RLC), 27; Peebles (LT), map.

5. Including Howard and Moon creeks. Space, 37; Peebles (LT), map.

6. On Spring Hill, or Spring Mountain, a little south of the Clearwater-Idaho county line, roughly midway between the camps of September 15 and 16 on *Atlas* map 70. Space, 37; Peebles (LT), map; Peebles (RLC), 27.

7. The mountain goat, *Oreamnos americanus,* of which they never obtained a complete specimen; see Lewis's description at February 22, 1806. Alexander Mackenzie heard of the "small white buffalo" from Canadian Indians on his journey to the Arctic Ocean in 1789, but he never saw one. Lamb, 209, 214; Cutright (LCPN), 444.

8. *Odocoileus hemionus,* mule deer.

9. In the valley of the Lochsa River, near the mouth of White Sand Creek ("Killed Colt Creek" on *Atlas* map 70), in Idaho County. Elk are more properly wapiti, *Cervus elaphus.*

10. Lewis, or perhaps actually Clark, now adds long-tailed wild ginger, *Asarum caudatum* Lindl., to John Potts's poultice of cous ("pounded roots") from June 22. Wild ginger is not known to occur at this elevation, and would not have had expanded leaves on this early date if it did occur here. The party must have carried a supply of leaves from lower elevations where the species is common, perhaps for cooking. Hitchcock et al., 2:102; Cutright (LCPN), 306, 403.

11. The dogtooth violet of June 16. He collected it on May 8, but made no mention of it on May 10. A red vertical line crosses through this passage, perhaps Biddle's mark, and a dark vertical line runs through preceding lines.

12. Actually September 17; see Lewis's entry. It appears that someone has overwritten the number 15 to make it 16.

[Lewis]   *Saturday June 28th 1806.*

This morning we collected our horses and set out as usual after an early breakfast. several of our horses had straggled to a considersble distance in surch of food but we were fortunate enough to find them in good time they look extreemly gant this morning, however the indians informed us that at noon we would arrive at a place where there was good food for them. we continued our rout along the dividing ridge passing one very deep hollow and at the distance of six miles passed our encampment of the ⟨16⟩ [*NB: 15th*][1] of September last, one and a half miles further we passed the road which leads by the fishery falling in on the wright immediately on the dividing ridge.[2] about eleven O'clock we arrived at an untimbered side of a mountain with a Southern aspect just above the fishery here we found an abundance of grass for our horses as the Indians had informed us. as our horses were very hungary and much fatiegued and from information no other place where we could obtain grass for them within the reach of this evening's travel we determined to remain at this place all night having come 13 miles only.[3] the water was distant from our encampment we therefore melted snow and used the water principally. the whole of the rout of this day was over deep snows. we find the traveling on the snow not worse than without it, as the easy passage it gives us over rocks and fallen timber fully compensate for the inconvenience of sliping, certain it is that we travel considerably faster on the snow than without it. the snow sinks from 2 to 3 inches with a hors, is coarse and firm and seems to be formed of the larger and more dense particles of the snow; the surface of the snow is reather harder in the morning than after the sun shines on it a few hours, but it is not in that situation so dense as to prevent the horse from obtaining good foothold.   we killed a small black pheasant; this bird is generally found in the snowey region of the mountains and feeds on the leaves of the pine and fir.[4]   there is a speceis of small whortleburry[5] common to the hights of the mountains, and a speceis of grass with a broad succulent leaf which looks not unlike a flag;[6] of the latter the horses are very fond, but as yet it is generally under the snow or mearly making it's appearance as it confined to the upper parts of the highest mountains.—

[Clark]   *Saturday June 28th 1806*

This morning we Colected our horses and Set out as usial after an early brackfast.   we continued our rout along the dividig ridge over knobs & through deep hollows   passed our encampmt of the 14 Sept. last near the forks of the road leaving the one on which we had Came one leading to the fishery to our right imediately on the dividing ridge.   at 12 oClock we arived at an untimberd side of a mountain with a southern aspect just above the fishery   here we found an abundance of grass for our horses as the guids had informed us.   as our horses were hungary and much fatiegued and from information no other place where we could obtain grass for them within the reach of this evening's travel we deturmined to remain at this place all night haveing come 13 m. only.   the water was distant from our Encampment we therefore melted Snow and used the water.   the whole of the rout of this day was over deep Snow.   we find the travelling on the Snow not worse than without it, as easy passage it givs us over rocks and fallen timber fully compensates for the inconvenience of sliping, certain it is that we travel considerably faster on the snow than without it.   the Snow Sinks from 2 to 3 inches with a horse, is course and firm and seems to be formed of the larger particles   the surface of the snow sees to be rather harder in the morning than after the Sun Shines on it a fiew hours, but it is not in that situation so dense as to prevent the horses from obtaining good foothold. I killed a Small black pheasant; this bird is generally found in the Snowey region of the mountains and feeds on the leaves of the pine & fir.   there is a Species of Small huckleberry common to the hights of the mountains, and a Species of grass with a broad succulent leaf which looks not unlike a flag; of the latter the horses are very fond, but as yet it is generally under the Snow, or mearly makeing it's appearance as it confined to the upper part of the highest mountains.

1. Again, a substitution and a revision in an apparent blank space. Clark gives the date of the previous camp as September 14. Biddle has it right; they were passing the camp of September 15.

2. They deviated here from their westbound route, which went down into the valley of the Lochsa River in Idaho County, Idaho. Now they continued eastward on the Lolo Trail, as it is known today, along the ridge. This portion of the eastbound route does not appear on *Atlas* map 70. Space, 38; Peebles (LT), map.

3. The camp was near Powell Junction on the present Forest Road 500 in Idaho County, also near Papoose Saddle and a few miles north of Powell Ranger Station and the camp of September 14, 1805, on *Atlas* map 70. Space, 38; Peebles (LT), map.

4. The middle portion of this sentence is crossed through with a red vertical line, perhaps done by Biddle.

5. Grouseberry, whortleberry, *Vaccinium scoparium* Leiberg, is a common subalpine, low shrub that produces very small, but delicious, red berries. Hitchcock et al., 4:35.

6. Smooth woodrush, *Luzula hitchcockii* Hamet-Ahti, is not a grass but a member of the woodrush family. It occurs only at high elevations and is particularly abundant where snow accumulations regularly provide moister conditions.

[Lewis]   *Sunday June 29th 1806.*

We collected our horses early this morning and set out, having previously dispatched Drewyer and R. Fields to the warm springs to hunt.   we pursued the hights of the ridge on which we have been passing for several days, it terminated at the distance of 5 ms. from our encampment and we decended to, and passed the main branch of the Kooskooske[1] 1 ½ ms. above the entrance of Quawmash creek[2] wid falls in on the N. E. side.   when we decended from this ridge we bid adieu to the snow.   near the river we fund a deer which the hunters had killed and left us.   this was a fortunate supply as all our oil was now exhausted and we were reduced to our roots alone without salt.   the Kooskooske at this place is about 30 yds. wide and runs with great volocity.   the bed as all the mountain streams is composed of smooth stones.[3]   beyond the river we as-

cended a very steep acclivity of a mountain about 2 Miles and arrived at
it's summit where we found the old road which we had pased as we went
out, coming in on our wright.   the road was now much plainer and more
beaten, which we were informed happened from the circumstance of the
Ootslashshoots visiting the fishery frequently from the vally of Clark's
river; tho' there was no appearance of there having been here this spring.
at noon we arrived at the quawmas flatts on the Creek of the same name[4]
and halted to graize our horses and dine having traveled 12 miles.   we
passed our encampment of the [*NB: 13th*][5] of September at 10 ms. where
we halted   there is a pretty little plain of about 50 acres plentifully
stocked with quawmash and from apperances this fromes one of the
principal stages or encampments of the indians who pass the mountains
on this road.   we found after we had halted that one of our packhorses
with his load and one of my riding horses were left behind.   we dispatched J. Feilds and Colter in surch of the lost horses.   after dinner we
continued our march seven miles further to the warm springs[6] where we
arrived early in the evening and sent out several hunters, who as well as
R Fields and Drewyer returned unsuccessful; late in the evening Colter
and J. Fields joined us with the lost horses and brought with them a deer
which they had killed, this furnished us with supper.   these warm springs
are situated at the base of a hill of no considerable hight on the N side
and near the bank of travellers rest creek[7] which at that place is about 10
yards wide.   these springs issue from the bottoms and through the interstices of a grey freestone rock,[8] the rock rises in iregular masy clifts in a
circular range arround the springs on their lower side.   immediately
above the springs on the creek there is a handsome little quamas plain of
about 10 acres.   the prinsipal spring is about the temperature of the
warmest baths used at the hot springs in Virginia. In this bath which had
been prepared by the Indians by stoping the run with stone and gravel, I
bathed and remained in 19 minutes, it was with dificulty I could remain
thus long and it caused a profuse sweat   two other bold springs adjacent
to this are much warmer, their heat being so great as to make the hand of
a person smart extreemly when immerced. I think the temperature of
these springs about the same as the hotest of the hot springs in Vir-

ginia. both the men and indians amused themselves with the use of a bath this evening. I observed that the indians after remaining in the hot bath as long as they could bear it ran and plunged themselves into the creek the water of which is now as cold as ice can make it; after remaining here a few minutes they returned again to the warm bath, repeating this transision several times but always ending with the warm bath. I killed a small black pheasant near the quamash grounds this evening which is the first I have seen below the snowy region. I also saw some young pheasants which were about the size of Chickens of 3 days old. saw the track of two bearfoot indians who were supposed to be distressed rufugees who had fled from the Minnetares.[9]

[Clark]   *Sunday June 29th 1806*

We colected our horses and Set out haveing previously dispatched Drewyer & R. Field to the Warm Springs to hunt. we prosued the hights of the ridge on which we have been passing for several days; it termonated at the distance of 5 M. from our encampment, and we decended to & passed the main branch of Kooskooke 1 ½ Ms. above the enterance of Glade Creek which falls in on the N. E. Side. we bid adew to the Snow. near the River we found a Deer which the hunters had killed and left us. this was a fortunate Supply as all our bears oil was now exhosted, and we were reduced to our roots alone without Salt. the river is 30 yds wide and runs with great velossity. the bead as all the Mountain streams is composed of Smooth Stone. beyond this river we assended a Steep Mountain about 2 Miles to it's Sumit where we found the old road which we had passed on as we went out. comeing in on our right, the road was now much plainer and much beaten. at noon we arived at the quaw-mash flatts on Vally Creek and halted to graize our horses and dined haveing traveled 12 Miles here is a pretty little plain of about 50 acres plentifully Stocked with quawmash and from appearance this forms one of the principal Stages of the indians who pass the mountains on this road. we found that one of our pack horss with his load and one of Capt. L.s. horses were missing we dispatched Jo. Field & Colter in serch of the lost horse's. after dinner we continued our march 7 ms further to the worm Springs where we arrived early in the evening, and Sent out Several hunters, who as well as R. Field & Drewyer returned unsuksessfull; late in the evening Jo. Field & Colter joined us with the lost horses and brought with them a Deer which J. F. had killed, this furnished us with a Supper.

Those Worm or Hot Springs are Situated at the base of a a hill of no considerable hight, on the N. Side and near the bank of travellers rest Creek which is at that place about 10 yds wide. these Springs issue from the bottom and through the interstices of a grey freestone rock, the rock rises in irregular masy clifts in a circular range, arround the Springs on their lower Side. imediately above the Springs on the Creek there is a handsom little quawmash plain of about 10 acres. the principal Spring is about the temperature of the Warmest baths used at the Hot Springs in Virginia. in this bath which had been prepared by the Indians by stopping the river with Stone and mud, I bathed and remained in 10 minits it was with dificuelty I could remain this long and it causd a profuse swet. two other bold Springs adjacent to this are much warmer, their heat being so great as to make the hand of a person Smart extreemly when immerced. we think the temperature of those Springs about the Same as that of the hotest of the hot Springs of Virginia. both the Men and the indians amused themselves with the use of the bath this evening. I observe after the indians remaining in the hot bath as long as they could bear it run and plunge themselves into the Creek the water of which is now as Cold as ice Can make it; after remaining here a fiew minits they return again to the worm bath repeeting this transision Several times but always ending with the worm bath. Saw the tracks of 2 bearfooted indians—.

1. Present Crooked Fork, in Idaho County, Idaho, "North Fork" on *Atlas* map 69. Space, 38; Peebles (LT), map; Peebles (RLC), 27.

2. Brushy Creek in northeast Idaho County; it is not named on *Atlas* maps 69 or 70. Space, 38; Peebles (RLC), 27; Peebles (LT), map.

3. The stones result principally from mass wasting of the formations through which the river cuts. The stones in the streambed become rounded and polished as the current moves them downstream, especially during spring runoff.

4. Packer Meadows on Pack Creek, in Idaho County, in the vicinity of their camp of September 13, 1805, on *Atlas* map 69. Space, 39; Peebles (RLC), 27; Peebles (LT), map.

5. Another addition to an apparent blank space in Biddle's customary red ink.

6. They crossed into Missoula County, Montana, and camped at the Lolo Hot Springs; see September 13, 1805. Space, 39; Peebles (RLC), 27; Peebles (LT), map; *Atlas* map 69.

7. Present Lolo Creek, in Missoula County. *Atlas* map 69.

8. The term freestone was applied to any layered stone that could be split easily to produce slabs or blocks; it generally was used in reference to sedimentary rocks such as sandstone or limestone. The rocks near Lolo Hot Springs, however, are igneous rocks of granitic composition and were derived from the Jurassic-Cretaceous Idaho batholith intrusion. Lewis probably called these rocks freestone either because they are fractured and appear layered or because these rocks have the tendency to spall off in slabs (ex-foliate). The temperature of the water at Lolo Hot Springs was measured at 111°F in 1974, and the discharge was measured at 180 gallons per minute.

9. From the cramped nature of the writing, it appears that this last sentence was probably inserted later. The "Minnetares" here might be either Atsinas or Hidatsas. A red vertical line runs through the last sentences of the entry, probably to strike out the material about the "pheasants" and perhaps done by Biddle.

[Lewis]   *Monday June 30th 1806.*

We dispatched Drewyer and J. Fields early this morning to hunt on the road and indeavour to obtain some meat for us.   just as we had prepared to set out at an early hour a deer came in to lick at these springs and one of our hunters killed it; this secured us our dinners, and we proceeded down the creek sometimes in the bottoms and at other times on the top or along the steep sides of the ridge to the N. of the Creek.   at one mile from the springs we passed a stout branch of the creek on the north side and at noon having travelled 13 ms. we arrived at the entrance of a second Northen branch of the creek[1] where we had nooned it on the 12th of Septr. last.   here we halted, dined and graized our horses.   while here Sheilds took a small tern[2] and killed a deer.   at this place a road turns off to the wright which the indians informed us leads to Clarks river[3] some distance below where there is a fine extensive vally in which the Shalees or Ootslashshoots sometimes reside.   in descending the creek this morning on the steep side of a high hill my horse sliped with both his hinder feet out of the road and fell, I also fell off backwards and slid near 40 feet down the hill before I could stop myself such was the steepness of the declivity; the horse was near falling on me in the first instance but fortunately recovers and we both escaped unhirt. I saw a small grey squirrel[4] today much like those of the Pacific coast only that the belly of this was white. I also met with the plant in blume which is sometimes called the lady's slipper or mockerson flower.[5] it is in shape and appearance like ours only that the corolla is white, marked with small veigns of pale red longitudinally on the inner side. after dinner we resumed our march. soon after seting out Sheilds killed another deer and in the course of the evening we picked up three others which Drewyer had killed along the road making a total of 6 today. Deer are very abundant in the neighbourhood of travellers rest of both speceis,[6] also some bighorns[7] and Elk. a little before sunset we arrived at our old encampment on the south side of the creek a little above it's entrance into Clark's river.[8] here we encamped with a view to remain two days in order to rest ourselves and horses & make our final arrangements for seperation. we came 19 ms. after dinner the road being much better than it has been since we entered the mountains we found no appearance of the Ootslashshoots having been here lately. the indians express much concern for them and apprehend that the Minnetares of fort de Prarie have distroyed them in the course of the last winter and spring, and mention the tracks of the bearfoot Indians which we saw yesterday as an evidence of their being much distressed.— our horses have stood the journey supprisingly well, most of them are yet in fine order, and only want a few days rest to restore them perfectly.—

Courses and estimated distances from the Quawmash Flats on the West side of Rocky Mountains to Travellers rest.—[9]

ms.

East— 11 To Collins's Creek 25 yds. wide, passing a small prarie at 9 ms. road hilly, thickly timbered.

N. 45° E. 13 to the crossing of Fish Creek 10 yds. wide passing a small creek at 6 ms.

N. 75° E. 9 to a small branch of hungry Creek. the road passing along a ridge with much fallen timber. some snow at the extremity of this course.

N. 22½ E.	5	to the heads of the main branch of hungry Creek. road hilly, some snow.
N. 75 E.	3	down hungry Creek on it's Noth side, passing 2 small branches on it's N. side, the lst at ½ m and the 2nd at 1½ ms. further.
N. 75 E.	6	still continuing on the N. side of the creek to the foot of the mountain, passing 3 north branches and 1 South branch of the Crek.
N. 45 E.	3	to the summit of the mountain where we deposited our baggage on the 17th inst.
N. 45 E.	15	to an open prarie on the side of a mountain having kept the dividing ridge between the Waters of the Kooskooske and Chopunnish rivers.
N. 45° E.	28	to an open prarie on the South Side of a mountain, having still kept the same dividing ridge mentioned in the last Course, though you ascend many steep mountains and decend into many deep hollows.
East—	3	to an extemity of a ridge where we decend to a deep hollow. much fallen timber caused in the first instance by fire and more recently by a storm from S. W.
N. 45° E.	10	Along a high snowey ridge to an open hillside of considerable Extent passing the road at 4½ ms. which turns off to the right and leads by the fishery at the entrance of Colt Creek.
N. 45° E.	12	To the quawmash flatts at the head of a branch of the Kooskooske, passing the Kooskoske 35 yd. wide at 5 miles. from hungry Creek to this river the road may be said to be over snow as so small a proportion of it is distitute of it. after passing this river the road dose not agin ascend to the snowy hights. at 7 ms. on this course again fell into the road which leads by the fishery about 4 ms. ⟨from⟩ above the mouth of Quawmash Creek.
North—	4	to the Hotspring Creek on the main branch of travellers rest.
N. 20° E.	3	to the warm or hot Springs down the N. side of the creek.
N. 20° E.	3	down the creek passing a Northern branch 3 yds. wide at 1 M. also the Creek itself twice a short distance below the Northern bran
N. 45° E.	10	along the North side of the creek to the entrance of a N. branch of the same 8 yds. wide. a road leads up this branch.

N. 60° E.	9	down the N. side of travellers rest creek to the prarie of the Creek and the Vally of Clark's R.
East—	9	to our encampment on the S side of travelers rest, passing the creek 1 M. above and 2 from it's mouth
Total	156	

[Clark]   Monday June 30th 1806

We dispatched Drewyer & Jo. Field early this morning ahead to hunt. just as we had prepard. to set out at an early hour, a deer Came in to lick at the Springs and one of our hunters killed it; this Secired to us our dinner.   and we proceeded down the Creek, Sometimes in the bottoms and at other times on the tops or along the Steep Sides of the ridge to the N of the Creek.   at 1 ½ m. we passd our encampment of the 12th of Septr. last.   we noon'd it at the place we had on the 12 of Septr. last   whiles here Shields killed a deer on the N. fork near the road.   here a rode leads up the N. fork and passed over to an extensive vally on Clarks river at Some distance down that river as our guids inform us.   after dinner we resumed our march. Soon after Setting out Shields killed another deer, and we picked up 3 others which G Drewyer had killed along the road. Deer are very abundant in the neighbourhood of travellers rest of boath Specis, also Some big horn and Elk.   a little before Sunset we arrived at our old encampment on the S. Side of the Creek a little above its enterance into Clarks river.   here we Encamped with a view to remain 2 days in order to rest ourselves and horses and make our final arrangements for Seperation.   we found no signs of the Oatlashshots haveing been here lately.   the Indians express much Concern for them and apprehend that the Menetarries of Fort d Prar have destroyed them in the course of the last Winter and Spring, and mention the tracts of the bearfooted indians which we Saw yesterday as an evidence of their being much distressed—.   our horses have stood the journey Supirisinly well and only want a fiew days rest to restore them.

[Clark][10]

Descended the mountain to Travellers rest leaveing those tremendious mountanes behind us—in passing of which we have experiensed Cold and hunger of which I shall ever remember.   ⟨as we⟩ in passing over this part of the Rocky mountains from Clarks river, to the quawmash flats from the 14th to the 19th of Septr. 1805 we marched through Snow, which fell on us on the night of the 14th and nearly all the day of the 15 in addition to the [c]old rendered the air cool and the way difficuelt.   our food was horses of which we eate three.— On our return we Set out from the quawmash flats on the 15th of June and commenes the assent of the rocky mountains; the air became cool and vigitation backward—   on the 16th we met with banks of Snow and in the hollars and maney of the hill Sides the Snow was from 3 to 4 feet deep and Scercely any grass vegitation just commencing where the Snow had melted—   on the 17th at meridian, the Snow became So deep in every derection from 6 to 8 feet deep we could not prosue the road ⟨or direction,⟩   there being no grass for our horses we were obliged to return to the quawmash flatts to precure meat to live on as well as grass for our horses—   leaveing our baggage on the mountains We precured 5 Indians as pilots and on the 24th of June 1806 we again under took those Snowey regn.   on the 26th we with our baggage arived at an open plain serounded with Snow where there was grass for horses   on the 27th & 28th also passing over Snow 6 or 8 feet deep all the way   on 29th passed over but little Snow—   but saw great masses of it lying in different directions

1. Grave Creek, in Missoula County, Montana, not named on *Atlas* map 69. Space, 39.

2. Probably "turn"; at least, no one has attempted to identify any tern on this date.

3. Clark Fork, near Alberton in Missoula County. Space, 39.

4. Probably Richardson's red squirrel, *Tamiasciurus hudsonicus richardsoni*. See February 24 and 25, 1806; and Burroughs, 98–99. It was probably Biddle who drew a red vertical line through this passage and the next about the lady's slipper.

5. Mountain lady's slipper, *Cypripedium montanum* Dougl. ex Lindl., an extraordinarily beautiful but rare species that was unknown to science at this time. Hitchcock et al., 1:833–35; Cutright (LCPN), 306, 407.

6. Meaning both the mule deer and the white-tailed deer, *Odocoileus virginianus*.

7. Bighorn sheep, *Ovis canadensis*.

8. Their old Travelers' Rest camp of September 9–11, 1805; it lies on the south side of Lolo Creek, just south of the present village of Lolo, about two miles up the creek from the Bitterroot River, in Missoula County. Space, 4; Appleman (LC), 332; *Atlas* map 69.

9. This table of courses and distances appears in Lewis's Codex L, pp. 70–71, in the midst of his entry for July 1, 1806. It covers the journey from Weippe Prairie to Travelers' Rest, June 24–30, and so is placed on the last date of that trip.

10. This material comes from Clark's separate remarks in his weather observations for June 1806. He added this passage to the end of his weather entry of June 30, filling out some blank space in Codex M, p. 150. Since it is more appropriate to daily-entry material, it is placed here by date.

[Lewis and Clark]   [*Weather, June 1806*][1]

Day of the Month	State of the weather at ☉ rise	Wind at ☉ rise	State of the weather at 4 P. M.	Wind at 4 P. M.	State of the Koskooske[2] at ☉ rise		
					raised or fallen	Feet	Inches and parts
1st	f a r T & L.	S E	f a c	N W	r	1	6
2ed	c a c	N W	f a c	S E	r		8
3rd	c a f & c	S E	c a f	S E	r		6
4th	c a r	S. E.	f a c	N W	r		1½
5th	f	S E.	f	N W	r		4
6th	f	S. E.	f	N W	f	1	
7th	c a r	N W	c a f r & h	N W	f		3
8th	c	S E	c a f	N W	f		7
9th	c	S E	f a c	N W	f		3½
10th	f	S E	f	N W	f		1
11th	f	S E	f	N W			
12th	f a r T L	S E	f	N W			
13th	c	S E	c a f	N W			
14th	f	S E	f	N W			
15th	c	N W	r a f & r	N W			
16th	f a c	S E	c a f	S E			
17th	c a r	E	c a f & r	S E			
18th	c a r	E	c a r & h	S W			
19th	f a c	S E	f	N W			
20th	f	S E	f	N W			
21st	f	S E	f	N W			
22cd	f	N W	f	N W			
23rd	f	N W	f	N W			
24th	f	N W	f a c[3]	N W			
25th	c a r	S E	c a r	N W			
26th	c a r	S E	f	S E			
27th	f a r & T.[4]	S E	f	S E			
28th	f.	S E	f	S E			
29th	f	S E	f a r h & T.	S E			
30th	f	S E	f	N W			

[*Remarks*]⁵

1st   about dark last evening had a slight rain from a heavy thunder cloud which passed to the E & N. E. of us.

2nd   have slept comfortably for several nights under one blankett ony. The river from sunrise untill 10 A. M. yesterday raised 1½ inches; from that [t]ime untill dark fell 4½, and in the course of the last night raised again 8 Inches as stated in the diary. the Indians inform us that the present rise of the river is the greatest which it annually takes, and that when the water now subsides to about the hight it was when we arrived here the mountains will be passable. I have no doubt but that the melting of the mountain snows in the begining of June is what causes the annual inundation of the lower portion of the Missouri from the 1st to the Middle of July.—

3d   The weather has been much warmer for five days past than previously, particularly the mornings and nights—

4th   rained greater part of last night but fell in no great quantity— yesterday the water was at it's greatest hight at noon, between which and dark it fell 15 inches and in the course of the night raised 1½ inches⁶ as stated in the diary. from the indian information the river will now subisde and may therefore be said to have been at it's greatest annual hight on the 3rd inst. at noon.—

5th   last night was colder than usual but no frost.— the river fell 3½ inches in the course of the day⁷ and raised 4 I. last night as [s]tated in the diary. this fluctuating state of the river no doubt is caused by the influence of the sun in the course of the day on the snows of the mountains; the accession of water thus caused in the day dose not reach us untill night when it produces a rise in the river.— The wild rose is in blume. the river fell 10 Ins. in the course of this day.

6th   in the course of the last night the river raised a little but fell by morning 1 inch lower than what it stood at last evening. the seven bark and the yellow vining honeysuckle are just in blume. a few of the does have produced their young. strawberries⁸ ripe near the river—⁹

7th   rain but slight both last evening and today. but little hail tho' large. The river fell three inches last night and 7 yesterday. The goose berries¹⁰ fully grown also the servis berry.

8th   river fell 8 In. in the course of yesterday 7 last night

9th   river fell 9 In. yesterday.[11]

10th   do   fell 5½ in. couse of yesterday[12]   having left the river today I could not longer keep it's state; it appears to be falling fast and will probably in the course of a few days be as low as when we first arrived there.   it is now about 6 feet lower than it has been.[13]

11th   at *the quawmash Flats*[14]

12th   slight sprinkle of rain in the forepart of the night.—

13th   The days for several past have been warm, the Musquetoes trouble-some

15th   it began to rain at 7 A. M. and contined by showers untill 5 P. M.[15]

16th[16]   on the tops of the hills the dog tooth violet is just in bloom   grass about 2 inches high   small Huckkleberry just puting fourth it's leaves &c.

17th   rained slightly a little after sunset   air cool.   rained from 1 to 3 P. M.[17]

18th   obliged to return.[18]

19th   returned to quawmash flats.[19]

22ed   hard frost this morning tho' no ice. Strawberries ripe at the Quaw-mash flats, they are but small and not abundant.—

23rd   hard frost this morning   ice one eighth of an inch thick on standing water

24th   Set out a 2d time from quawmash flats[20]

25th   rained a little last night, some showers in the evening.—

26th   Slight rain in the fore part of the last evening—[21]

27th   Thunder shower last ⟨the⟩ evening   some rain a little before dark last evening.[22]

28th   nights are cool in these mountains but no frost.

29th   night cold   hard frost this morning.   the quawmash and Straw-berries are just begining to blume at the flatts on the head of the Kooskooske.[23]   The Sun flower[24] also just beginning to blume, which is 2 months later than those on the Sides of the Western Mountains near the falls of Columbia.[25]

30th   We are here Situated on Clarks river in a Vally between two high mountains of Snow.[26]

1. Lewis's weather table for June 1806 appears in Codex L, pp. 147, 149 (reading backwards); Clark's is in Codex M, pp. 151–52 (reading backwards). The present version follows Lewis, noting any significant variations in Clark.

2. Clark does not have any information on the state of the Clearwater (Kooskooske) River; Lewis ceased recording it after they left the river on June 10.

3. Clark has only "f."

4. Clark has only "f. a. r."

5. Both captains have remarks in the margins of their weather tables and separately. Lewis's version appears here, but there are some significant variations in Clark's remarks that are noted.

6. The rest of this sentence is missing in Clark's version; he resumes with "from the indian."

7. The rest of this sentence is missing in Clark's journal; he resumes with "this fluctuating state."

8. Either wild strawberry, *Fragaria virginiana* Duchesne, or woodland strawberry, *F. vesca* L. Hitchcock et al., 3 : 108–9.

9. In his marginal remarks Clark writes, "hot Sultery day." In his separate remarks there is no sentence about strawberries.

10. See gooseberry possibilities at June 10, 1806.

11. Clark adds "& 3½ last night."

12. In his marginal remarks Clark has "R. fell 5½ ins: do. & ⟨2?⟩ 1 ins: last night." "Do." (ditto) refers to corresponding word "yesterday" in the remarks for June 9. In his separate remarks Clark says, "The river fell 1 inch last night and I 5½ yesterday." He has no sentence about the data on the river ceasing and resumes with "it appears."

13. Here Clark adds, "left the river and proceeded the quawmash flatts."

14. This marginal remark appears only in Clark's Codex M.

15. Clark adds, "we Set out on the rocky mountains."

16. Clark has no remarks for this day.

17. An obviously impressed Clark adds, "assend a mtn. *Snow 15 feet deep on top.*"

18. This marginal remark appears only in Clark's Codex M.

19. This marginal remark also appears only in Clark's version.

20. Another marginal remark which only Clark has.

21. Clark adds, "in the snowey region."

22. The last two words are not in Clark's version.

23. The remainder of this remark appears only in Clark's separate comments in Codex M.

24. Any one of several species of *Helianthus,* otherwise not identifiable.

25. The Western Mountains would be the Cascade Range in Oregon and Washington; the falls are the Celilo Falls.

26. Lewis's marginal remark for this date consists of four repetitions of "do" (ditto), indicating a repetition of the June 29 remark "night cold hard frost this morning." He has no other remarks for the day. The sentence is Clark's marginal remark. Clark continues

with a lengthy passage in his separate remarks summarizing their experiences crossing the mountains on both the westbound and eastbound trips, "in passing of which we have experienced Cold and hunger of which I Shall ever remember." The passage serves to fill out page 150 in Codex M, which would otherwise have been largely blank. It has been placed with the daily journal entry of June 30, 1806.

[Lewis]   *Tuesday July 1st 1806.*

    This morning early we sent out all our hunters.   set Sheilds at work to repair some of our guns which were out of order   Capt. Clark & my self consurted the following plan viz.   from this place I determined to go with a small party by the most direct rout to the falls of the Missouri, there to leave Thompson McNeal and goodrich to prepare carriages and geer for the purpose of transporting the canoes and baggage over the portage, and myself and six volunteers to ascend Maria's river with a view to explore the country and ascertain whether any branch of that river lies as far north as Latd. 50 and again return and join the party who are to decend the Missouri, at the entrance of Maria's river. I now called for the volunteers to accompany me on this rout, many turned out, from whom I scelected[1] Drewyer the two Feildses, Werner, Frazier and Sergt Gass accompanied me   the other part of the men are to proceed with Capt Clark to the head of Jefferson's river where we deposited sundry articles and left our canoes.[2]   from hence Sergt Ordway with a party of 9 men are to decend the river with the canoes; Capt C. with the remaining ten including Charbono and York will proceed to the Yellowstone river at it's nearest approach to the three forks of the missouri, here he will build a canoe and decend the Yellowstone river with Charbono the indian woman, his servant York and five others to the missouri where should he arrive first he will wait my arrival. Sergt Pryor with two other men are to proceed with the horses by land to the Mandans and thence to the British posts on the Assinniboin with a letter to Mr. Heney [*NB: Haney*][3] whom we wish to engage to ⟨procure⟩ prevail on the Sioux Chefs to join us on the Missouri, and accompany them with us to the seat of the general government.   these arrangements being made the party were informed of our design and prepared themselves accordingly.   our hunters killed 13 deer in the course of this day of which 7 were fine bucks, deer are large and in fine order.   the indians inform us that there are a great number of white buffaloe or mountain sheep of the snowey hights of the mountains West of this [*NB: Clarks*] river; they state that they inhabit the most rocky and inaccessible parts, and run but badly, that they kill them with great ease with their arrows when they can find them.[4] the indian warrior who overtook us on the 26th Ult. made me a present of an excellent horse which he said he gave for the good council we had given himself and nation and also to assure us of his attattchment to the white men and his desire to be at peace with the Minnetares of Fort de Prarie. we had our venison fleeced and exposed in the sun on pole to dry. the dove[5] the black woodpecker,[6] the lark woodpecker,[7] the logcock, the prarie lark,[8] sandhill crain, prarie hen with the short and pointed tail,[9] the robin,[10] a speceis of brown plover,[11] a few curloos, small black birds,[12] ravens[13] hawks and a variety of sparrows as well as the bee martin[14] and the several speceis of Corvus genus are found in this vally.—

Windsor birst his gun near the muzzle a few days since; this Sheilds cut off and I then exchanged it with the Cheif for the one we had given him for conducting us over the mountains. he was much pleased with the exchange and shot his gun several times; he shoots very well for an inexperienced person.[15]

The little animal found in the plains of the Missouri which I have called the *barking squirrel*[16] weighs from 3 to 3½ pounds. it's form is that of the squirrel. it's colour is an uniform light brick red grey, the red reather predominating. the under side of the neck and bely are lighter coloured than the other parts of the body. the legs are short, and it is wide across the breast and sholders in propotion to it's size, appears strongly formed in that part; the head is also bony muscular and stout, reather more blontly terminated wider and flatter than the common squirrel. the upper lip is split or divided to the nose. the ears are short and lie close to the head, having the appearance of being cut off, in this particular they resemble the guinea pig. the teeth are like those of the squrrel rat &c. they have a false jaw or pocket between the skin and the mustle of the jaw like that of the common ground squrrel but not so large in proportion to their size. they have large and full whiskers on each side of the nose, a few long hairs of the same kind on each jaw and over the eyes. the eye is small and black. they have five toes on each foot of which the two outer toes on each foot are much shoter than those in the center particularly the two inner toes of the fore feet, the toes of the fore feet are remarkably long and sharp and seem well adapted to cratching or burrowing those of the hind feet are neither as long or sharp as the former; the nails are black.   the hair of this animal is about as long and equally as course as that of the common grey squrrel of our country, and the hair of the tail is not longer than that of the body except immediately at the extremity where it is somewhat longer and frequently of a dark brown colour.   the part of generation in the female is placed on the lower region of the belly between the hinder legs so far forward that she must lie on her back to copolate.   the whole length of this animal is one foot five inches from the extremity of the nose to that of the tail of which the tail occupyes 4 inches.   it is nearly double the size of the whistleing squirrel of the Columbia.   it is much more quick active and fleet than it's form would indicate.   these squirrels burrow in the ground in the open plains usually at a considerable distance from the water yet are never seen at any distance from their burrows.   six or eight usually reside in one burrow to which there is never more than one entrance.   these burrows are of great debth. I once dug and pursued a burrow to the debth of ten feet and did not reach it's greatest debth.   they generally associate in large societies placing their burrows near each other and frequently oc-cupy in this manner several hundred acres of land.   when at rest above ground their position is generally erect on their hinder feet and rump; thus they will generally set and bark at you as you approach them, their note being much that of the little toy dogs, their yelps are in quick succes-sion and at each they a motion to their tails upwards.   they feed on the grass and weeds within the limits of their village which they never appear to exceed on any occasion.   as they are usually numerous they keep the grass and weeds within their district very closely graized and as clean as if it had been swept.   the earth which they throw out of their burrows is usually formed into a conic mound around the entrance.   this little ani-mal is frequently very fat and it's flesh is not unpleasant.   as soon as the hard frosts commence it shuts up it's burrow and continues within untill spring.   it will eat grain or meat.[17]

[Clark]   *Tuesday July 1st 1806* on Clark's river

We Sent out all the hunters very early this morning   by 12 OClock they all returned haveing killd. 12 Deer Six of them large fat Bucks, this is like once more returning to the land of liveing a plenty of meat and that very good.   as Capt. Lewis and Myself part at this place we make a division of our party and such baggage and provisions as is Souteable.   the party who will accompany Capt L. is G. Drewyer, Sergt. Gass, Jo. & R. Fields, Frazier & Werner, and Thompson Goodrich & McNear as far as the Falls of Missouri at which place the 3 latter will remain untill I Send down the Canoes from the head of Jeffersons river.   they will then join that party and after passing the portage around the falls, proceed on down to the enterance of Maria where Capt. Lewis will join them after haveing as-sended that river as high up as Latd. 50° North.   from the head of Jeffer-sons river I shall proceed on to the head of the Rockejhone [18] with a party of 9 or 10 men and desend that river.   from the R Rockejhone I Shall dispatch Sergt. Pryor with the horses to the Mandans and from thence to the Tradeing Establishments of the N. W. Co on the Assinniboin River with a letter which we have written for the purpose to engage Mr. H. Haney to endeaver to get Some of the principal Chiefs of the Scioux to accompany us to the Seat of our government &.   we divide the Loading and apportion the horses. Capt L. only takes 17 horses with him, 8 only of which he intends to take up the Maria &c. One of the Indians who ac-companed us Swam Clarks river and examined the Country around, on his return he informed us that he had discovered where a Band of the *Tushepaws* had encamped this Spring   passed of 64 Lodges, & that they had passed Down Clarks river and that it was probable that they were near the quawmash Hatts on a Easterly branch of that river.   those guides expressed a desire to return to their nation and not accompany us fur-ther, we informed them that if they was deturmined to return we would kill some meat for them, but wished that they would accompy Capt. Lewis on the rout to the falls of Missouri only 2 nights and show him the right road to cross the Mountains.   this they agreed to do.   we gave a medal [19] of the Small Size to the young man Son to the late Great Chief of the Chopunnish Nation who had been remarkably kind to us in every instance, to all the others we tied a bunch of blue ribon about the hair, which pleased them very much. the Indian man who overtook us in the Mountain, presented Capt. Lewis with a horse and said that he opened his ears to what we had said, and hoped that Cap Lewis would see the Crovanters of Fort De Prarie[20] and make a good peace that it was their desire to be at peace. Shew them the horse as a token of their wishes &c.

1. It appears that Lewis has crossed out this sentence to here then added the words "accompanied me" to make a new sentence.

2. Camp Fortunate at the forks of the Beaverhead River, in Beaverhead County, Montana; see August 17, 1805. *Atlas* map 66.

3. Hugh Heney, whom they met at the Mandan-Hidatsa villages; see December 16, 1804.

4. A red vertical line crosses through this sentence, apparently done by Biddle.

5. Mourning dove, *Zenaida macroura* [AOU, 316]. Holmgren, 34. The remainder of this paragraph has Biddle's red line through it.

6. Lewis's woodpecker, *Melanerpes lewis* [AOU, 408]; see May 27, 1806. Holmgren, 34; Burroughs, 239–40.

7. Common, or northern, flicker, *Colaptes auratus* [AOU, 412]. Burroughs, 241–42; Holmgren, 34.

8. Probably the horned lark, *Eremophola alpestris* [AOU, 474]. Holmgren, 31.

9. Sharp-tailed grouse, *Tympanuchus phasianellus* [AOU, 308]; see March 1, 1806. Holmgren, 29; Burroughs, 213.

10. American robin, *Turdus migratorius* [AOU, 761].

11. Probably the upland sandpiper, *Bartramia longicauda* [AOU, 261]; see July 22, 1805. Holmgren, 33; Burroughs, 227.

12. Either the rusty blackbird, *Euphagus carolinus* [AOU, 509], or Brewer's blackbird, *E. cyanocephalus* [AOU, 510]. Holmgren, 28.

13. Common raven, *Corvus corax* [AOU, 486].

14. Either the eastern kingbird, *Tyrannus tyrannus* [AOU, 444], or the western kingbird, more likely the latter.

15. Here on pp. 70–71 of Lewis's Codex L appears his table of courses and distances for June 24–30, 1806. It has been placed under the last of those dates.

16. Prairie dog; see Clark's description at September 7, 1804. The first few lines of this passage are crossed out with a red vertical line, probably Biddle's doing.

17. These last two sentences are crowded in at the bottom of p. 73, Codex L. Thwaites (LC), 5:178, transcribed the passages as, "and continues untill spring. it will eat neither grain or meat." Accepting the present reading, it is assumed that Lewis left out the negative but did mean that the prairie dog ate neither grain nor meat.

18. More correctly, the French term *Roche Jaune,* for the Yellowstone River.

19. Probably the 55 mm Jefferson medal; see August 3, 1804.

20. Gros ventres or big bellies, again the Atsinas.

[Lewis]   *Wednesday July 2ed 1806.*

We sent out the hunters early this morning, they returned not so suc-
cesfull as yesterday having killed 2 deer only. Sheilds continued repairing
the gunns which he compleated by evening. all arrangements being
now compleat we determined to set out in the morning.   in the course of
the day we had much conversation with the indians by signs, our only
mode of communicating our ideas.   they informed us that they wished
to go in surch of the Ootslashshoots their friends and intended leaving us
tomorrow morning, I prevailed on them to go with me as far as the East
branch of Clark's River[1] and put me on the road to the Missouri. I gave
the Cheif a medal of the small size; he insisted on exchanging names with
me according to their custom which was accordingly done and I was
called Yo-me-kol-lick which interpreted is *the white bearskin foalded.* in
the evening the indians run their horses, and we had several foot races
betwen the natives and our party with various success.   these are a race
of hardy strong athletic active men.   nothin worthy of notice transpired
in the course of the day. Goodrich and McNeal are both very unwell with
the pox which they contracted last winter with the Chinnook women
this forms my inducement principally for taking them to the falls of the
Missouri where during an intervail of rest they can use the murcury
freely. I found two speceis of native clover here, the one with a very narrow small leaf and a pale red flower, the other nearly as luxouriant as our
red clover with a white flower the leaf and blume of the latter are proportionably large.[2] I found several other uncommon plants specemines of
which I preserved.[3] The leaf of the cottonwood[4] on this river is like that
common to the Columbia narrower than that common to the lower part
of the Missouri and Mississippi and wider than that on the upper part of
the Missouri.   the wild rose, servise berry, white berryed honeysuckle,
seven bark, elder,[5] alder aspin,[6] choke cherry and the broad and narrow
leafed willow[7] are natives of this valley.   the long leafed pine forms the
principal timber of the neighbourhood, and grows as well in the river
bottoms as on the hills.   the firs and larch are confined to the higher
parts of the hills and mountains.[8]   the tops of the high mountains on either side of this river are covered with snow.   the musquetoes have been
excessively troublesome to us since our arrival at this place.

[Clark]   *Wednesday July 2nd 1806*

Sent out 2 hunters this morning and they killed 2 Deer. the Musquetors has been So troublesom day and night Since our arrival in this Vally that we are tormented very much by them and Cant' write except under our Bears. We gave the Second gun to our guides agreeable to our promis, and to each we gave Powder & ball   I had the greater part of the meat dried for to Subsist my party in the Mountains between the head of Jeffersons & Clarks rivers where I do not expect to find any game to kill.   had all of our arms put in the most prime order   two of the rifles have unfortunately bursted near the muscle, Shields Cut them off and they Shute tolerable well   one which is very Short we exchanged with the Indian whoe we had given a longer gun to induc them to pilot us across the Mountains.   we caused every man to fill his horn with powder & have a sufficincy of Balls &c.   the last day in passing down Travellers rest Creek Capt Lewis fell down the Side of a Steep Mountain near 40 feet but fortunately receved no dammage.   his hors was near falling on him but fortunately recovered and they both escaped unhurt. I killed a Small grey squurel and a Common pheasant. Capt L. Showed me a plant in blume which is Sometimes called the ladies Slipper or Mockerson flower.   it is in shape and appearance like ours only that the corolla is white marked with Small veigns of pale red longitudinally on the inner Side, and much Smaller. The Indians and Some of our men amused themselves in running races on foot as well as with their horses.

1. The Clark Fork, or Hellgate, River, meeting the Bitterroot west of present Missoula, in Missoula County, Montana.

2. The smaller species is small-head, or woolly, clover, *Trifolium microcephalum* Pursh. Lewis had on the previous day collected a specimen that was used by Pursh to describe the new species. The larger clover is likely longstalk clover, *T. longipes* Nutt. Hitchcock et al., 3:366, 364; Cutright (LCPN), 307–8, 421. It was probably Biddle who marked the red vertical line through these botanical passages.

3. Lewis preserved specimens of at least four undescribed species at Travelers' Rest. The most notable was a small herb with a very large flower, recognized by Pursh as a representative of a new genus, and fittingly named *Lewisia*. Lewis's genus now consists of about twenty western North American species. The species discovered here is bitterroot, *L. rediviva* Pursh. The common name refers to its bitter-tasting roots, which were an important source of food and a major trade item for the native people. Lewis's initial de-

scription is at August 22, 1805. The other new species collected here were: thinleaf owl-clover, *Orthocarpus tenuifolius* (Pursh) Benth.; wormleaf stonecrop, *Sedum stenopetalum* Pursh; and the small-head clover mentioned in the previous note. Hitchcock et al., 2:235, 573, 4:354; Cutright (LCPN), 307–8, 410, 412, 419.

4. Black cottonwood, *Populus trichocarpa* T. & G. It has narrower leaves than plains cottonwood, *P. deltoides* Marsh., and broader leaves than narrowleaf cottonwood, *P. angustifolia* James, both encountered earlier. Hitchcock et al., 34–37; Little (CIH), 153-W, 149-W; Little (MWH), 114.

5. Common elderberry, *Sambucus canadensis* L.

6. Quaking aspen, *Populus tremuloides* Michx., is observed among other common Rocky Mountain shrubs noted earlier. Hitchcock et al., 2:35.

7. Many species of willow occur in the valley. The narrow-leaved species is sandbar, or coyote, willow, *Salix exigua* Nutt.; broad-leaved species include Bebb willow, *S. bebbiana* Sarg., Scouler willow, *S. scouleriana* Barratt, and yellow willow, *S. lutea* Nutt. Ibid., 2:51–52, 45–46, 66–67; Dorn, 227–28.

8. Lewis notes a vegetation pattern similar to that observed on the western side of the Bitterroot Range. The ponderosa pine predominates in the hot and dry climate of the low-elevation valley bottom, while the other conifers gain dominance on cooler and moister mountain slopes.

Chapter Thirty-Seven

Lewis's Exploration of the Marias

July 3–August 12, 1806

[Lewis] July 3rd[1]

Courses and distances from travellers rest.

North   7   m. to the crossing of Clarke's river,[2] valley wide tops of the hills covered with Long leaf pine. bottoms pine and Cottonwood. passed a small branch at 3 M on W. side and at 1 M. further the entrance of a small creek on E. side.[3] at 5 miles Co-kâh-lâr coosh or buffaloe river falls in on the East side.[4] Clark river 120 yds. wide buffaloe river [*blank*] yard wide— set out at 8 A. M. halted at 11 A. M. to make a raft. dined here.

N. 75 E   7   m. through a handsome level plain to the point where the Cokahlar ishkit River enters the mountains, or where the hills close it in on both sides. we halted ⟨one⟩ five mile short of this place on a little stream ⟨which runs down from the 2nd largest of the rivers⟩ [*X: nothern*] we encamped.[5] Sent out the hunters they killed three deer gave the indians half. the musqutoes troublesome built fires for our horses.[6] we did not get over the river until 6 P. M. I fell in the water and wet the chronometer. we made three rafts. indians express great apprehension with rispect to the Minetares. saw the fresh track of a horse in the main road which leads up this river which the indians supposed to be the Shalees. Took leave of Capt. C. and party to-day. gave one of my shirts and a handkercheif to the two Indians whom we met on Collin's Creek and detained some [days?]

[Lewis]   *Thursday July 3rd 1806.*

All arrangements being now compleated for carrying into effect the several scheemes we had planed for execution on our return, we saddled our horses and set out I took leave of my worthy friend and companion Capt. Clark and the party that accompanyed him. I could not avoid feeling much concern on this occasion although I hoped this seperation was only momentary. I proceeded down Clark's river seven miles with my party of nine men and five indians.[7] here the Indians recommended our passing the river which was rapid and 150 yds. wide. 2 miles above this place I passed the entrance of the East branch of Clark's River which discharges itself by two channels; the water of this river is more terbid than the main stream and is from 90 to 120 yds. wide. as we had no other means of passing the river we busied ourselves collecting dry timber for the purpose of constructing rafts; timber being scarce we found considerable difficulty in procuring as much as made three small rafts. we arrived at 11 A. M. and had our rafts completed by 3 P. M. when we dined and began to take over our baggage which we effected in the course of 3 hours the rafts being obliged to return several times. the Indians swam over their horses and drew over their baggage in little basons of deer skins which they constructed in a very few minutes for that purpose.[8] we drove our horses in after them and they followed to the opposite shore. I remained myself with two men who could scarcely swim untill the last; by this time the raft by passing so frequently had fallen a considerable distance down the river to a rapid and difficult part of it crouded with several small Islands and willow bars which were now overflown; with these men I set out on the raft and was soon hurried down with the current a mile and a half before we made shore, on our approach to the shore the raft sunk and I was drawn off the raft by a bush

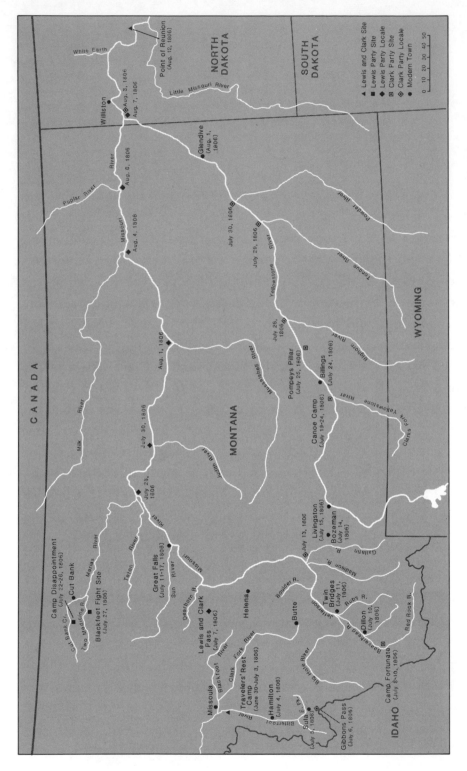

2. On the Marias and Yellowstone Rivers, July 3–August 12, 1806

84

and swam on shore the two men remained on the raft and fortunately effected a landing at some little distance below. I wet the chronometer by this accedent which I had placed in my fob as I conceived for greater security. I now joined the party and we proceeded with the indians about 3 Ms. to a small Creek and encamped at sunset. I sent out the hunters who soon returned with three very fine deer of which I gave the indians half   These people now informed me that the road which they shewed me at no great distance from our Camp would lead us up the East branch of Clark's river and a river they called Cokahlarishkit or the *river of the road to buffaloe*[9] and thence to medicine river[10] and the falls of the Missouri where we wished to go.   they alledged that as the road was a well beaten track we could not now miss our way and as they were affraid of meeting with their enimies the Minnetares they could not think of continuing with us any longer, that they wished now to proceed down Clark's river in surch of their friends the Shalees.   they informed us that not far from the dividing ridge between the waters of this and the Missouri rivers[11] the roads forked   they recommended the left hand as the best rout but said they would both lead us to the falls of the Missouri. I directed the hunters to turn out early in the morning and indeavour to kill some more meat for these people whom I was unwilling to leave without giving them a good supply of provision after their having been so obliging as to conduct us through those tremendious mountains.   the musquetoes were so excessively troublesome this evening that we were obliged to kindle large fires for our horses   these insects tortured them in such manner untill they placed themselves in the smoke of the fires that I realy thought they would become frantic.   about an hour after dark the air become so coald that the musquetoes disappeared.

Courses and distances July 3rd 1806.

North—   7   M. down the West side of Clark's river to the place at which we passed it.   forded travelers rest C. ½ a mile below our camp, passed a branch on west side at 2½ m. further   also at 1 m. further passed the entrance of a small creek on the E side of Clark's river, and two miles short of the extremity of the course passed the entrance of the East branch of Clark's river which discharges itself in two channels. Clark's river 150 yds.

wide the East branch from 90 to 120. the vally of Clarks river is extensive beatifull level plains and praries. the tops of the hills and mountains on either hand are covered with long leafed pine larch and fir; near the river the bottoms are timbered with long leafed pine and cottonwood.

N. 75 E.   7   M. through a handsom leve plain to the point at which the
ms.   14   East branch enters the mountains or where the hills set in near it on either side. we halted and encamped on a small creek 5 miles short of the extremity of this course. a Creek 15 yds. wide falls into the E. branch on it's N. side one mile short of the mountain.[12]

We saw the fresh track of a horse this evening in the road near our camp which the indians supposed to be a Shale spye.[13] we killed a prarie hen with the short and pointed tail she had a number of young which could just fly.

1. Here begins Lewis's fragmentary Codex La, which runs through July 15. Lewis may have intended it as preliminary field notes for the period when he was traveling through the mountains to the Great Falls of the Missouri, to be copied into Codex L, but in fact there are no entries in Codex L after July 4 until July 15, when he apparently resumed keeping the notebook journal. He left a set of blank pages in Codex L to fill in with the missing dates (see July 4, 1806), which he never did. The bottoms and edges of the pages in Codex La are quite tattered, making some transcriptions questionable. These are shown in brackets with question marks, as appropriate. The captains split the party into two groups on this day to pursue separate explorations, Lewis on the Marias River and the Missouri and Clark on the Yellowstone, until they reunited on August 12, 1806. This chapter covers Lewis's trip and the next chapter follows Clark.

2. Lewis went down the west side of the Bitterroot and the Clark Fork and crossed the latter, as he notes, some two miles below the junction of the Bitterroot and the Clark Fork, in Missoula County, Montana, northwest of present Missoula.

3. Miller Creek, in Missoula County.

4. The Clark Fork. The word is a Nez Perce name, qoq̇á·lx̣ 'ískit, "bison trail."

5. On Grant Creek near its junction with the Clark Fork River, northwest of Missoula.

6. The smoke from the fires would keep the mosquitoes from bothering the horses.

7. The white men in Lewis's party were Gass, Drouillard, Joseph and Reubin Field, Werner, Frazer, Thompson, McNeal, and Goodrich.

8. Lewis is evidently describing a method of crossing streams used by Indians of some northwestern tribes in which goods were placed on inflated rafts of deerskin and towed across. Gustavus Sohon's depiction of Flatheads using this method in the 1850s appears in Fahey, following p. 46.

9. The route would go up the Clark Fork and the Blackfoot rivers in Missoula County.

10. Sun River, which meets the Missouri just above the Great Falls at Great Falls, Cascade County, Montana. *Atlas* maps 54 and 61.

11. The Continental Divide.

12. Rattlesnake Creek, Missoula County.

13. A Salish (Flathead) scout.

[Lewis]   *July 4th 1806.*

An Indian arrived alone from the West side of the mountains.[1] ⟨it⟩ he had pursued and overtook us here. sent out the hunters early to kill some meat to give the indians as they would not go with us further and I was unwilling after they service they had rendered to send them away without a good store of provision. they are going down Clark's River in surch of the Shalees their ⟨relations⟩ friends, and from thence intend returning by this rout home again, they fleescd their meat informed us that they should dry it and leave it for their homeward journey.— Set out at 12. had killed no deer.

N. 75 E	5	M. passed a large creek 15 yds wide at four miles[2] and entered the mountain passed this creek at one mile on which we were encamped. open plain ⟨narrow⟩ wide bottom to the river
S. 75 E.	3	M. along the north side of the river bottom widens a prairie ⟨passed a small rapids⟩
N 45 E	1	m. passing a small branch at the extremity of this cors[3]
S. 45 E	1	M. to the forks of the east branch of Clark's River[4] a handsom wide plain below on the S. side
S East	8	M. up the buffaloe road river or Co-kâh-lah-,'ishkit river[5]
	Ms.18	through a timbered country, mountains high rocky and but little bottoms. land poor— encamped[6] in a handsom high timbered bottom near the river where there was fine grass killed grown squirrel of speceis different from any I had seen

[Lewis]   *Friday July 4th 1806.*

I arrose early this morning and sent out Drewyer and the Fieldses to hunt. at 6. A. M. a man of the Pallote pellows [*NB?: Pelloat pallahs*][7] arrived from the West side of the Rocky mountains; he had pursued us a few days after our departure and overtook us at this place; he proved to be the same young man who had first attempted to pass the rocky mountains early in June last when we lay on the Kooskooske and was obliged to relinquish the enterprize in consequence of the debth and softness of the snow. I gave a shirt a handkercheif and a small quantity of ammunition to the indians. at half after eleven the hunters returned from the chase unsuccessfull. I now ordered the horses saddled smoked a pipe with these friendly people and at noon bid them adieu. they had cut the meat which I gave them last evening thin and exposed it in the sun to dry informing me that they should leave it in this neighbourhood untill they returned as a store for their homeward journey. it is worthy of remark that these people were about to return by the same pass by which they had conducted us through the difficult part of the Rocky Mountains, al-tho they were about to decend Clark's river several days journey in surch of the Shale's their relations,[8] a circumstance which to my mind furnishes sufficient evidence that there is not so near or so good a rout to the plains of Columbia by land along that river as that which we came. the several war routs of the Minetarees which fall into this vally of Clark's river con-center at traveller's rest beyond which point they have never yet dared to venture in pursuit of the nations beyond the mountains. all the nations also on the west side of the mountain with whom we are acquainted in-habiting the waters of Lewis's river & who visit the plains of the Missouri pass by this rout. these affectionate people our guides betrayed every emmotion of unfeigned regret at seperating from us; they said that they were confidint that the Pahkees,[9] (the appellation they give the Minne-tares) would cut us off. the first 5 miles of our rout was through a part of the extensive plain in which we were encamped, we then entered the mountains with the East fork of Clark's river through a narrow confined pass on it's N. side continuing up that river five ms. further to the en-trance of the Cokahlahishkit R which falls in on the N. E. side, is 60 yds. wide deep and rapid. the banks bold not very high but never over-flow. the East fork below its junction with this stream is 100 yds. wide and above it about 90. the water of boath are terbid but the East branch much the most so; their beds are composed of sand and gravel; the East fork possesses a large portion of the former. neither of those streams are navigable in consequence of the rapids and shoals which obstruct their currents. thus far a plain or untimbered country bordered the river which near the junction of these streams spread into a handsome level plain of no great extent; the hills were covered with long leafed pine and fir. I now continued my rout up the N. side of the Cokahlahishkit river through a timbered country for 8 miles and encamped in a handsom bottom on the river where there was an abundance of excelence grass for our horses. the evening was fine, air pleasent and no musquetoes. a few miles before we encamped I killed a squirrel of the speceis common to the Rocky Mountains and a ground squirrel of a speceis which I had never before seen,[10] I preserved the skins of both of these animals.

Courses and distances July 4th 1806.

S. 75° E. 3 M. a long the N. side of the river, at 2 Ms. the bottom widens into a handsome prarie. river 110 yds. wide.

N. 45 E. 1 M. through a high plain, passed a small branch at the extremity of this course.

S. 45 E. 1 M. through a low leavel prarie to the entrance of the Cokahlahishkit river falling in on the N. side 60 yds. wide deep and rapid not navigable in consequence of the obstruction of rocks rapids &c.

East 8
ms. 13 M. up the north side of the Cokahlah-ishkit R. through a timbered country, mountains high and rocky. river bottoms narrow and land poor. encamped at the extremity of this course on the bank of the river in a handsom timbered bottom.[11]

1. A "Pallote pellow," according to the Codex L entry, next. They may be Palouse Indians, or more likely Nez Perces. The complicated linguistic matter is discussed at June 8, 1806.

2. Rattlesnake Creek, Missoula County, Montana; shown as "15 yds. wide" on fig. 4.

3. Marshall Creek, in Missoula County. They were passing through the northern part of present Missoula, on the north side of the Clark Fork. The last part of the route was along what later became Mullan Road and eventually Broadway Street through Missoula.

4. The junction of Blackfoot River and the Clark Fork, in Missoula County, east of Missoula.

5. Lewis went northeasterly up Blackfoot River.

6. In Missoula County, by Lewis's estimate some eight miles up the Blackfoot River from its junction with the Clark Fork, on the north side (see fig. 4).

7. This appears to be Biddle's writing, but in dark rather than his customary red ink.

8. The Salish ("Shale's"), or Flatheads, were not linguistically or culturally related to the Nez Perce. However, they were close allies, camped together for extended periods, and undoubtedly intermarried.

9. The Shoshone term probably refers to the tribe's enemies, including Blackfeet, Arapahoes, Atsinas, and Assiniboines. Linguistic determinations are discussed at August 13, 1805.

10. Probably Richardson's red squirrel; see February 24 and 25, 1806. The other squirrel can not be identified.

11. At this point in Codex L (p. 81) is the phrase "a Suplement to Come in here enclosed," apparently in Clark's hand. Following are several blank pages (82–98, with two pages unnumbered), into which Lewis apparently intended to fill the events of July 5–14, 1806, perhaps from the notes in Codex La.

[Lewis] *July 5th 1806.*

Set out at 6 A. M.— steered

N. 75 E.	6½	M. passed a stout C. N Side at 2½ M. anoth[er] just above[1] saw an old indian encampment of 11 lodges of bark and [leather?] on S. side at 3½ M. killed a deer.
N. 25 E.	12 ⟨10⟩	m. passing a ⟨large⟩ small creek at ⟨½⟩ one m. on S sid[2] on which there is a handsom and extensive Valley and plain for 10 or 12 ms. also another creek 12 yd. wide at ½ a mile further on N. side[3] and another 8 yds. wide on ⟨S.⟩ N. [L?] side at 5 ms further[4] one & ½ m. short of the extremity of this course arrive at a high prarie on ⟨S.⟩ N. [L?] side from one to three miles in width extending up the river.[5] halted and dined in the mouth of a little drane on the left of the plain where there was a considerable quantity of quawmash. saw a gang of antelopes[6] here of which we killed one the does at this season herd with each other and have their young. the bucks are alone there are many wild horses on Clarkes river about the place we passed it we saw some of them at a distance. there are said to be many of them about the head of the yellowstone river.—
East	6	m. to the entrance of Werner's Creek[7] 35 yds. wide through a high extensive prairie on N. side. hills low and timbered

the entrance of a Creek 4 yards wide which discharges
itself into Werners Creek

S. 75° E. 2½ M. to the river passing through an extensive
and handsom plain on Werners Creek croping
that creek at 1 M. and leaving a high prarie
hills to the right, seperating the plain from
the river. saw two swan in this beautifull
Creek.

East 3 M. to the entrance of a large Creek 20 yds.
wide ~called Seamans Creek~ passing a creek at 1 M. 8 yds. wide. this
course with the river, the road passing through
an extensive high prarie rendered very uneven
by a vast number of little hillucks and sink
~holes~ -holes. at the head of these two creeks
high broken mountains stand at the distance
of 10 M. forming a kind of cove generally
of open untimbered country. we encamped
on the lower side of the east creek just
above it's entrance. here a war party had
encamped about 2 months since and concealed
their fires.——

31 M.

July 6th 1806

Set out a little after sunrise passed the creek a
little above our encampment.

East 14 M. to the point at which the river leaves
the extensive plains and enters the mountains.
these plains I called the knob plains. the prarie of
the knobs from the number of knobs being irregularly scattered through it. passed the
N. fork of the Cokahlarishkit River at 7 Ms.
it is 45 yds wide deep and rapid. had some difficulty in passing it. passed a

culty in
passing it.
passed a
large
crooked
pond

3. Monture (Seaman's) Creek, Powell County, Montana,
July 5, 1806, Codex La, p. 4

91

with the long leafed pine, larch, and some fir. the road passes at some distance to the left of the river and ⟨their⟩ this couses ⟨are⟩ is with the river.

N. 22 W.　4　miles to a high insulated knob just above the entrance of a Creek 8 yards wide which discharges itself into Werners ⟨run⟩ Creek.[8]

N. 75 E.　2½　M. to the river passing through an extensive and handsom plain on Werner's Creek, crossing that creek at 1 m. and leaving a high prarie hill to the right seperating the plain from the river. saw two swan in this beautiful Creek.—

East　3
31 m.　m. to the entrance of a large creek 20 yds. wide Called Seamans' Creek[9] passing a creek at 1 m. 8 yds. wide.[10] this course with the river, the road passing through an extensive high prarie rendered very uneven by a vast number of little hillucks and sinkholes ⟨holds⟩. at the heads of these two creeks high broken mountains stand at the distance of 10 m. forming a kind of Cove generally of open untimbered country.— we encamped on the lower side of the last creek just above it's entrance.[11] here a war party had encamped about 2 months since and conceald their fires.—[12]

1. The two are West Twin and East Twin creeks, flowing into the Blackfoot River at Twin Creeks, Missoula County, Montana.

2. Union Creek, in Missoula County.

3. Gold Creek, in Missoula County; shown as "12 yds wide" on fig. 4.

4. Belmont Creek, in Missoula County; "8 yds. wide" on fig. 4.

5. Present Ninemile Prairie, running along the Blackfoot River in Missoula County.

6. Pronghorn, *Antilocapra americana*.

7. Present Clearwater River, reaching the Blackfoot in Missoula County.

8. This portion of the course appears to be in Clark's hand, substituting for the same material which is mostly lost in tatters at the bottom of the page. The stream flowing into the Clearwater is apparently Blanchard Creek (see fig. 4).

9. Present Monture Creek in Powell County, Montana. Lewis's spelling here suggests the presently favored name for his dog; see September 11, 1803. Jackson (DS).

10. Present Cottonwood Creek, in Powell County.

11. On the west side of Monture Creek, just upstream from its entrance into Blackfoot River, in Powell County (see fig. 4).

12. Under this entry and extending into the next in Codex La, p. 4, is a sketch map by

Lewis depicting part of his route (fig. 3). It may represent the area around the mouth of Monture (Seaman's) Creek, but the actual route (shown by a dotted line) is hard to reconcile with that shown on Clark's map in Codex N (fig. 4).

[Lewis]   July 6th 1806.

Set out a little after sunrise   passed the creek a little above our encampment.[1]

East   14   M. to the point at which the river leaves the extensive plains and enters the mountains   these plains I called ⟨the *knob plains*⟩ the prarie of the knobs[2] from ⟨the⟩ a number of knobs being irregularly scattered through it.   passed the N. fork 1 of the Cokahlarishkit River[3] at 7 M.   it is 45 yds. wide deep and rapid.   had some difficulty in passing it.   passed a large crooked pond[4] at 4 ms. further.   great Number of the burrowing squirrls in this prarie of the speccis common to the plains of Columbia.[5]   saw some goats and deer.   the hunters killed one of the latter.   the trail which we take to be a returning war-party of the Minnetares of Fort de prarie becomes much fresher.   they have a large pasel of horses.   saw some Curloos,[6] bee martains woodpeckers plover robins, doves, ravens, hawks and a variety of sparrows common to the plains also some ducks.   the North fork is terbid as is also the main branch which is about 50 yds. wide   the other streams are clear.   these plains continue their course S 75 E. and are wide where the river leaves them.   up this valley and creek a road passes to Dearbourn's river and thence to the Missouri.—

N. 60 E   1½   up the river.   here we halted and dine and our hunters overtook us with a deer which they had killed.   river bottoms narrow and country thickly timbered. Cottonwood and pine grow intermixed in the river bottoms musquitoes extreemely troublesome.   we expect to meet with the Minnetares and are therefore much on our guard both day and night.   the bois rague[7] in blume.—   saw the common small blue flag[8] and peppergrass.[9]   the southern wood and two other speceis of shrub are common in the prarie of knobs.   preserved specemines of them.[10]   passed several old indian encampments of ⟨stick⟩ brush lodges.—

S 80 E   2   m. to two nearly equal forks of the river[11]   here the road forks   also one leading up each branch   these are the forks of which I presume the indians made mention.   passed a creek on N. side 12 yds. wide shallow and clear.[12]

N 75 E.   8   m. to our encampment of this evening over a steep high
Ms. 25   balld toped hill for 2 m. thence through and to the left of a large low bottom 2 M.   thence three miles through a thick wood along the hill side bottoms narrow.   thence 1 m. to our encampment[13] on a large creek some little distance above it's mouth through a beatifull plain on the border of which we passed the remains of 32 old lodges.   they appear to be those of the Minnetares as are all those we have seen today.   killed ⟨another⟩ five deer and a beaver today.[14]   encamped on the creek   *much sign* of beaver in this extensive bottom.

1. Apparently Monture Creek, in Powell County, Montana, Lewis's Seaman's Creek.

2. Nevada Valley, in Powell County.

3. North Fork Blackfoot River, which meets the Blackfoot River south of Ovando in Powell County.

4. There are various lakes in this part of Powell County, east of the North Fork of the Blackfoot River. The largest are Kleinschmidt Lake and Browns Lake. One of these, most likely the former, is probably represented by a crescent shape marked "Pond" in the appropriate location on fig. 4. It appears that Biddle has substituted some of the words in this sentence, which were lost in tears at the bottom of the page. The words are in dark rather than his usual red ink.

5. Probably the Columbian ground squirrel.

6. Longed-billed curlew, *Numenius americanus* [AOU, 264].

7. Meaning the French *bois rouge*, "red wood," referring to the red, woody stems of red osier dogwood, *Cornus sericea* L. (or *C. stolonifera* Michx.). Hitchcock et al., 3:588–90.

8. Western blue flag, *Iris missouriensis* Nutt., a new species. Ibid., 1:817–18; Cutright (LCPN), 311, 326, 410.

9. Peppergrasses are small, generally weedy, herbs of the mustard genus *Lepidium*. Lewis may have seen one of several native species such as tall peppergrass, *L. virginicum* L. It is equally likely, however, that he was using this common name for one of the many other mustards of the region, many of which are very similar in appearance. Hitchcock et al., 2:519–21.

10. Big, or common, sagebrush, *Artemisia tridentata* Nutt. The other two species of shrubs collected on this day are Antelope bush, bitter brush, *Purshia tridentata* (Pursh) DC., and silverberry, *Elaeagnus commutata* Bernh., both new to science. Ibid., 5:70, 3:162, 460; Cutright (LCPN), 326, 408, 416.

11. Perhaps the junction of Poorman Creek from the south and Blackfoot River, in

Lewis and Clark County, Montana. At this fork, on fig. 4, Clark has made a dotted line representing the Indian trail going southeasterly, while Lewis's trail goes northeast. It is also possible that Lewis has misplaced this course and that it should go as the second course of July 7, since Lewis's camp was more than one mile below the entrance of Poorman Creek. The two forks would then be Landers Fork and Blackfoot River. These two streams more nearly fit the captain's description here.

12. Probably Arrastra Creek in Powell County, flowing into Blackfoot River.

13. On Beaver Creek, in Lewis and Clark County, some two miles west of present Lincoln (see fig. 4).

14. Beaver, *Castor canadensis.*

[Lewis]   July 7 1806.

Set out at 7 A. M.—

N. 75 E.	6	M. with the road through a level beatifull plain on the North side of the river much timber in the bottoms hills also timbered with pitch pine. no longleafed pine since we left the praries of the knobs. crossed a branch of the creek 8 yds. wid. on which we encamped at ¼ m.[1] also passed a creek 15 yd. wide at ¼ further.[2] ⟨crossed the main creek⟩
North	6	ms.— passed the main creek[3] at a mile ½ and kept up it on the wright hand side through handsom plain bottoms to the foot of a ridge which we ascended the main stream boar N W & W. as far as I could see it a wright hand fork falls into this creek at 1 M. above the commencement of this course.[4]
N. 15 E.	8	m. over ⟨a⟩ two ridges and again striking the wrighthand fork[5] at 4 ms. then continued up it on the left hand side much appearance of beaver many dams. bottoms not wide and covered with low willow and grass. halted to dine at a large beaver dam the hunters killed 3 deer and a fawn. deer are remarkably plenty and in good order. Reubin Fields wounded a moos deer[6] this morning near our camp. my dog much worried.
N. 10 E.	3	m. up the same creek on the east side through a handsome narrow plain.
N 45 E.	2	m. passing the dividing ridge betwen the waters of the Columbia and Missouri rivers at ¼ of a mile.[7] from this gap which is low and an easy ascent on the W. side the fort mountain[8] bears North Eaast, and appears to be distant about 20

Miles. the road for one and ¾ miles desends the hill and continues down a branch.

N. 20 W.   7   ms. over several hills and hollows along the foot of the moun-
           32   tain hights passing five small rivulets running to the wright. saw some sighn of buffaloe early this morning in the valley where we encamped last evening from which it appears that the buffaloe do sometimes penetrate these mountains a few miles. we saw no buffaloe this evening. but much old appearance of dung, tracks &c. encamped on a small run under the foot of the mountain.[9] after we encamped Drewyer killed two beaver and shot third which bit his knee very badly and escaped

1. Probably Keep Cool Creek, in Lewis and Clark County, Montana (nameless on fig. 4).

2. Probably Spring Creek, in Lewis and Clark County, not shown on any expedition map.

3. Landers Fork Blackfoot River, in Lewis and Clark County. Coues wrote "Lander's Fork," a name bestowed in the 1850s, on the stream in fig. 4.

4. By "wrighthand fork" Lewis may mean Blackfoot River, the main stream.

5. The right hand fork is now Alice Creek, Lewis and Clark County. It is shown on fig. 4 as joining Landers Fork to become the Blackfoot River.

6. Moose, *Alces alces,* not a new species.

7. Lewis crossed Hard Scrabble Creek near its mouth with Alice Creek and then went up Alice Creek, which he also crossed. He and his party then went over the Continental Divide through Lewis and Clark Pass, somewhat misnamed since Clark never saw it. The pass is about seventeen miles northeast of present Lincoln; it is shown as "Gap" on fig. 4. In crossing it the party returned to the territory of the United States. This was the route that the Hidatsas had told them of at Fort Mandan, which they had missed on the westward journey. However, had they not followed the Missouri and its forks to their headwaters, they would have missed the Shoshones and would have been deprived of the services of Old Toby and the use of the Indian horses, which would have greatly decreased their chances of making it across the Rockies. Appleman (LC), 317–18.

8. Square Butte, in Cascade County, Montana; see fig. 4 and July 15, 1805.

9. About three miles east of Table Mountain, in Lewis and Clark County (see fig. 4).

[Lewis]   July 8th 1806.

Set out at 6 A. M.

N 25 W.   3½   m. to the top of a hill from whence we saw the Shishequaw mountain[1] about 8 M. distant, immediately before us. passed

⟨torrant⟩ *Dearborne's river*[2] at 3 m.   this stream comes form the S. W. out of the mountains which are about 5 Ms. to our left.   the bed of the river is about 100 yds. wide tho' the water occupys only about 30 yds.   it appears to spread over it's bottoms at certain seasons of the year and runs a mear torrant tearing up the trees by the roots which stand in it's bottom ⟨hense the name we have given it.⟩[3]   the Shishiquaw mountain is a high insulated conic mountain standing several miles in advance of the Eastern range of the rocky mountains. Country broken and mountanous to our wright.

No ·rh   14½   ms. ⟨leaving the⟩ through an open plain to Shishequaw Creek[4] 20 yds. wide bottoms and considerable qantity of timber it leaves the mountain to the S E and enters the ⟨mountains⟩ [*EC?: plains*].   we struck it about 10 miles below the mountain which boar S. 32 W. from us.   the road continued along the foot of the mountain to the West of north which not being anything like our course and the country becoming tolerably level at the commencement of this course we steered through the plains leaving the road with a view to strike Medicine river and hunt down it to it's mouth in order to procure the necessary skins to make geer, and meat for the three men whom we mean to leave at the falls as none of them are hunters.   we halted and dined on Shishequaw Creek   R. Fields killed a fine buck and a goat; Josh. Fields saw two buffaloe below us some distance which are the first that have been seen.   we saw a great number of deer goats and wolves as we passed through the plains this morning but no Elk or buffaloe.   saw some barking squirrils   much rejoiced at finding ourselves in the plains of the Missouri which abound with game.—

N. 50 E   2   m. to the discharge of Shishequaw Creek into the Medicine River[5] through an extensive beautifull and level bottom.

N. 85° E.   8
28

m. to our encampment of this evening on a large island.[6]   the bottoms continue level low and extensive plains level and not very elivated partcularly on the N. E. side of the river.   the land of neither the plains nor bottoms is fertile.   it is of a light colour intermixed with a considerable proportion of gravel[7]   the grass generally about 9 inghes high.   the hunters were unsuccessful this evening. I killed a very large and the whitest woolf I have seen—[8]

1. Present Haystack Butte, in Lewis and Clark County, Montana, shown clearly on fig. 4.

2. Dearborn River, in Lewis and Clark County, which they named on July 18, 1805. Reaching it so far above its junction with the Missouri, where they had first seen it, Lewis apparently did not recognize it at first and called it Torrant River. It was apparently Biddle who wrote in the substitution in dark ink.

3. Perhaps Biddle's deletion.

4. Elk Creek (faintly noted on fig. 4), a branch of Sun River, Lewis and Clark's Medicine River, in Lewis and Clark County.

5. The meeting of Elk Creek and Sun River in Lewis and Clark County.

6. On an island in Sun River, between Lewis and Clark and Cascade counties, just north of Montana Highway 21 (see fig. 4).

7. The rock underlying this area is the Two Medicine Formation; it is composed primarily of alternating layers of sandstone and shale. The gravel occupies river terraces and is mostly outwash that was deposited during the later part of the Pleistocene glaciations. The sandy soil of these plains allows water to percolate downward rapidly so that only hardy, deep-rooted, drought-resistant plants can survive.

8. The gray wolf, *Canis lupus*.

[Lewis]   *July 9th 1806.*

Set out early and had not proceeded far before it began to rain.   the air extreemly cold.   halted a few minutes in some old lodges untill it cased to rain in some measure.   we then proceeded and it rained without intermission   wet us to the skin.

| N. 80° E. | 4 | ms. through a handsome level wide bottom[1] in which there is a considerable quanty of narrow leafed cottonwood timber.[2] the river is generally about 80 yds. wide rapid yet I think it migt be navigated.   it's bed is loose gravel and pebbles.   the banks low but seldom overflow.   water clear. |
| S 85 E | 4 | ms Still on the S W. side of the river through wide and level bottoms some timber. Joseph feilds killed a very fat buffaloe bull and we halted to dine.   we took the best of the meat as much as we could possibly carry on our horses.   the day continuing rainy and cold I concluded to remain all day.[3]   we feasted on the buffaloe.   saw a number of deer wolves and Antelopes.   killed two deer. |

1. Lewis proceeded down Sun River, passing from Lewis and Clark County, Montana, to Cascade County.

2. Narrowleaf cottonwood.

3. On the south side of Sun River, near the mouth of Simms Creek, in Cascade County, a little over one mile northwest of present Simms (see fig. 4).

[Lewis]   *July 10th 1806.*

Set out early and continued down the S W bank of the river—

N 75 E   24   m. to our encampment in a grove of cottonwood timber.[1] the latter part of this course for 7 miles there is no timber in the river bottom, the other parts of the river possesses bottoms of the wide leafed cottonwood.[2] much the greater part of the bottom is untimbered. the bottoms are wide and level the high praries or plains are also beautiful level and smooth. great quantities of prickly pear of two kinds on the plains.[3] the ground is renderd so miry by the rain which fell yesterday that it is excessively fatiegueing to the horses to travel. we came 10 miles and halted for dinner the wind blowing down the river in the fore part of the day was unfavourable to the hunters they saw several gangs of Elk but they having the wind of them ran off. in the evening the wind set from the West and we fell in with a few elk of which R. Fields and myself killed 3 one of which swam the river and fell on the opposite so we therefore lost it's skin I sent the packhorses on with Sergt. Gass directing them to halt and encamp at the first timber which proved to be about 7 ms. I retained frazier to assist in skining the Elk. we wer about this time joined by drewer. a large brown bear swam the river near where we were and drewyer shot and killed it. by the time we butchered thes 2 elk and bar it was nearly dark we loaded our horses with the best of the meat and pursud the party and found them encamped as they had been directed in the first timber. we did not reach them until 9 P. M. they informed us that they had seen a very large bear in the plains which had pursued Sergt. Gass and Thomson some distance but their horses enabled them to keep out of it's reach. they were afraid to fire on the bear least their horses should throw them as they were unaccustomed to the gun. we killed five deer 3 Elk and a bear today saw vast herds of buffaloe in the evening below us on the river. ⟨he⟩ we hered them bellowing about us all night. vast assemblages of wolves. saw a large herd of Elk making down the river. passed a considerable

rapid in medicine river after dark. the river about a hundred yards wide is deep and in many parts rappid and today
has been much crouded with islands. from our encampment down we know the river and there is no rapids and
scarcely any courant. goosberries[4] are very abundant of the
common red kind and are begining to ripen. no currants on
this river. both species of the prickly pears just in blume.—

1. The camp was on the south side of Sun River, in Cascade County, Montana, some
four to five miles northwest of the city of Great Falls (see fig. 4).

2. Plains cottonwood.

3. Two species of prickly pear occur in the area: brittle prickly pear, *Opuntia fragilis*
(Nutt.) Haw., and plains prickly pear, *O. polyacantha* Haw. Dorn, 97; Hitchcock et al.,
3:458–59.

4. Bristly, or redshoot, gooseberry, *Ribes setosum* Lindl., is the most likely, but white-
stem gooseberry, *R. inerme* Rydb., is also a possibility. Dorn, 148–49; Hitchcock et al.,
3:83, 74–75.

[Clark]   [*undated*][1]

Courses and Computed Destances from the Enterance of
Travellers rest Creek into Clarks River to the Falls of Missouri

North	7	Miles to the crossing of Clarks river, vally wide the top of the hills covered with long leafed pine bottoms pine & Cotton wood passed a Small branch at 3 miles on W. Side and at 1 m. further a Small Creek on the E. Side. at 5 miles Clarks river is joined by an Easterly fork 120 yards wide.
N 75° E.	7	miles through a handsom leavel plain to the point where the East fork enters the mountains, or where the hills close it in on both Sides. passed a large Creek 15 yd. wide at ⟨5?⟩ 6 miles also one at 3 miles.

(July 4)

S 75° E.	3	miles allong the North Side of the river, the bottoms widen. a prarie.
N. 45° E.	1	M. passing a small branch at the extremity of this course—.
S. 45° E	1	M. to the forks of the East fork of Clarks river a handsom wide plain below on the South Side.
⟨East	8	Miles to the enterance of warners Creek 35 yards wide through a high extensive plain⟩

East	8	Miles on a Buffalow road up Co-kah-lah-ishkit river through a timbered Country mountains high rocky and but little bottom land pore.

July 5th

N. 75° E	3½	Miles passed a Stout Creek on N. Side at 2½ miles another just above.
N. 25° E	12	Miles passed a Small creek at 1 mile on the S. Side on which there is a handsome and extencive vally and plain for 10 or 12 miles also another Creek 12 yds wide at ½ a mile on the N. Side, and another 8 yds wide on the N. Side at 5 miles. and one ½ mile Short of the extremity of the course arrived at a high prarie on the S. Side from one to 3 miles in width, extending up the river. great number of wild horses on Clarks river about the place Capt. L. crossed it. we saw several
East	6	Miles to the enterance of Warners Creek 35 yards wide through a high extencive prarie on the N. Side. hills low and timbered with the long leafed pine, larch and Some fir. the road passes at some distance to the left of the river and these courses is with the river.
N. 22° W.	4	Miles to a high insulated Knob just above the enterance of a Creek 8 yards wide which discharges itself into Werners Creek.
N. 75° E	2½	Miles to the river passing through a handsom plain on Werners Creek crossing that Creek at one mile and leaveing a high prarie hill to the right seperateing the plain from the river. Saw 2 swan in this butifull Creek.
East	3	Miles to the enterance of a large Creek 20 yards wide called Seamons Creak, passed a creek at 1 mile 8 yds wide, (this course is with the river) the road passing through a high extencive prarie, a vast number of little hillocks and Sink holes. at the head of those 2 Creeks is high broken mountains Standing at the distance of 10 m. forming a kind of cove Generaly of open untimbered Country.

July 6th

East	14	Miles to this point at which the river leaves the extencive plains and enters the mountains these plains is called the prarie of the Knobs, passed the North fork of Cokahlar,ishket

river at 7 miles, it is 45 yards wide deep & rapid. passed a large crooked pond at 4 miles further. Great number of burrowing Squirels of the Species common to the Columbian plains. the main branch is 50 yards wide and turbid the other Streams are clear, these plains continue their course S. 75° E and are wide where the river leaves them. up this vally and Creek a road passes to the Missouri.

N. 60° E. 1½ miles up the river. bottoms narrow and and country thickly timered. Cotton wood and pine grow intermxed in the river bottoms passed Several old indian encampments.

N. 80° E. 2 miles to two nearly equal forks of the river here the road forks also one leading up each river. passed a Creek on N. side 12 yd. wide.

N. 75° E. 8 Miles over a Steep high bald toped hill for 2 miles thence 3 m. through a thick woods along the hill Side. bottoms narrow. crossed a large Creek in a butifull plain much beaver Sign.

July 7th

N. 75° E. 6 M. through a leavel butifull plain on the N. side of the river much timber in the bottoms, hills also timbered with pitch pine crossed a branch of the Creek 8 yds. wide at ¼ M. also passed a creek 15 yds. wide at ¼ further.

North 6 ms. passed the main Creek at 1 Ms. and kept up it on the right hand Side through a handsom plain. the main Stream [*EC: Lander's fork*] bore N W. & W as far as I could See it, a right hand fork falls into this creek at 1 me. above the Commcmt. of this course.

N. 15° E 8 Ms. over two ridges one again Strikeing the right hand fork at 4 ms. then Continuing up it on the left hand Side. much apperance of beaver maney dams. bottoms not wide and covered with willow and grass.

N. 10° E 3 ms. up the Same Creek on the E. Side through a handsom narrow plain.

N. 45° E. 2 Ms. passing the dividing ridge between the waters of the Co-
(106¾) lumbia from those of the Missouri at ¼ of a mile. from this gap which is low and an easy asent, the road decends and continues down a creek.

N. 20° W. 7   Ms. over Several hills and hollows along the foot of the mountain, passed 5 small riverlets [*EC: tributaries of Dearborn R*] running to the right.

July 8th 1806.

N. 25° W. 3   ms. to the top of a hill from whince we saw the Shishequaw Mountain about 8 ms. distant imediately before us, passed torrent river at 3 ms. this Stream comes from the S. W. out of the mountains which are about 5 miles to our left the bead of the river is 100 yds. wide tho' the water only occupies about 30 yds. it runs a mear torrent taring the trees up by the roots which Stand in it's bottoms, we discover this to be Dearborns River.[2] "The Shishequaw Mountain is a high insulated conic mountain Standing Several miles in advance of the Eastern range of the rocky Mountains" near trhe Meadecine River.

North   14½   Miles through an open plain to Sishequaw Creek 20 yards wide about 10 ms. below the mtn. which bears S. 32° W. from us, haveing left the road to our left which keeps near the mts.

N. 50° E   2   Ms. to the ⟨mouth⟩ discharge of Shishequaw Creek into
(28¼)   Medecine River through an extencive leavel and butifull bottom.

N. 85° E   8   Ms. down the Medecine river to a large Island. the bottoms are extensive low and leavel. the lands of neither the Plain or bottom are fertile it is of a light colour intermixed with a considerable portion of gravel. the grass Generaly about 9 inches high.

July 9th

N. 80° E. 4   Ms. through a handsom leavel wide bottom in which there is a considerable quantity of the narrow leafed Cotton wood timber. The river is generally about 80 yds wide rapid it's bed is loose Gravel and pebbles its banks low but sildom overflow. water clear.

S. 85° E. 4   ms. down on the S W. Side of Medecine river through wide and leavel bottoms Some timber—.

July 10th

N. 75° E. 24   Miles down the river. 7 ms. of the latter part of the course no timber. passed a rapid bottom wide and extensive a great number of small islands in the river.

S. 75° E   <u>8</u>   miles to the Missouri at the White Bear Islands at the head of
      <u>183</u>   the portage above the falls, passed through the plains. at
                 which place Capt. Lewis continued untill the 15th July 1806
                 and left 6 men and proceeded towards the head of Marias
                 river with the other 3 men as before mentioned—

The most derect and best Course from the dividing ridge which divides the waters of the Columbia from those of the Missouri at the Gap where Capt Lewis crossed it is to leave a Short range of mountains which pass the missouri at the Pine Island rapid to the right passing at it's base and through the plains pass fort mountain to the White bear Isds or medecine river, a fine road and about 45 miles, reducing the distance from Clarks river to 145 miles— one other road passes from the enterance of Dearborns River over to a South branch of the Cohahlarishkit river [*EC: via Cadotte's Pass? or Still further South?*] and down that river to the main fork and down on the N. Side of the main fork to Clarks river &c.—

    1. This is Clark's summary in Codex N, pp. 144–48 (reading backwards) of Lewis's route from Travelers' Rest to Sun River, July 3–10, 1806. It is placed here by date. Clark must have received this information after the men reunited in August 1806.
    2. The final words, beginning with "we discover," appear to have been substituted for some erased material. The material within quotes comes from Lewis's entry of July 8.

[Lewis]   *July 11th 1806.*

the morning was fair and the plains looked beatifull the grass much improved by the late rain. the air was pleasant and a vast assemblage of little birds which croud to the groves on the river sung most enchantingly. we set out early. I sent the hunters down Medicine river to hunt Elk and proceeded with the party across the plain to the white bear Islands which I found to be 8 ms. distant my course S. 75 E.— through a level beautifull and extensive high plain covered with immence hirds of buffaloe.— it is now the season at which the buffaloe begin to coppelate and the bulls keep a tremendious roaring we could hear them for many miles and there are such numbers of them that there is one continual roar. our horses had not been acquainted with the buffaloe they appeared much allarmed at their appearance and bellowing. when I ar-

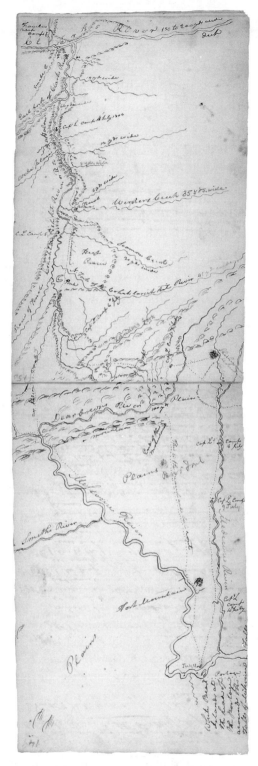

4. Lewis's Route from Travelers' Rest to the Missouri River,
ca. July 3–11, 1806, Codex N, pp. 149–50

rived in sight of the whitebear Islands[1] the missouri bottoms on both sides of the river were crouded with buffaloe   I sincerely belief that there were not less than 10 thousand buffaloe within a circle of 2 miles arround that place. I met with the hunters at a little grove of timber opposite to the island where they had killed a cow[2] and were waiting our arrival.   they had met with no elk. I directed the hunters to kill some buffaloe as well for the benifit of their skins to enable us to pass the river as for their meat for the men I meant to leave at this place.   we unloaded our horses and encamped opposite to the Islands.   had the cow skined and some willows sticks collected to make canoes of the hides   by 12 OCk. they killed eleven buffaloe most of them in fine order.   the bulls are now generally much fatter than the cows and are fine beef. I sent out all hands with the horses to assist in buthering and bringing in the meat by 3 in the evening we had brought in a large quantity of fine beef and as many hides as we wanted for canoes ⟨covering⟩ shelters and geer. I then set all hands to prepare ⟨the⟩ two canoes ⟨in order to pass the river⟩   the one we made after the mandan fassion with a single skin in the form of a bason[3] and the other we constructed of two skins on a plan of our own. we were unable to compleat our canoes this evening.   the wind blew very hard.   we continued our operations untill dark and then retired to rest. I intend giving my horses a couple of[4] days rest at this place and deposit all my baggage which is not necessary to my voyage up medicine [EC?: maria's] river.

1. Lewis's party camped here on the west bank of the Missouri, in Cascade County, Montana, opposite the White Bear Islands (see June 18, 1805) and a little below the mouth of Sand Coulee Creek on the opposite bank (see fig. 4). Atlas maps 42, 54, 61.

2. The first buffalo, Bison bison, they had killed since July 16, 1805.

3. The hemispherical "bullboat" of the Mandans and Hidatsas; see October 6, 1804.

4. At this point Lewis has the crossed-out date "July 12th 1806." The last sentence in this entry was probably an afterthought, added when the next day's date had already been written in.

[Lewis]   *July 12th 1806.*

we arrose early and resumed our operations in compleating our canoes which we completed by 10 A. M.   about this time two of the men whom I had dispatched this morning in quest of the horses returned with seven of them only.   the ⟨othe⟩ remaining ten of our best horses were absent and not to be found. I fear that they ⟨have⟩ are stolen. I dispatch two men on horseback in surch of them.   the wind blew so violently that I did not think it prudent to attempt passing the river.—   at ⟨3 PM⟩ Noon Werner returned having found three others of the horses near Fort Mountain. Sergt. Gass did not return untill 3 P. M. not having found the horses.   he had been about 8 ms. up medecine river. I now dispatched Joseph Fields and Drewyer in quest of them.   the former returned at dark unsuccessfull and the latter continued absent all night.   at 5 P. M. the wind abated and we transported our baggage and meat to the opposite shore in our canoes which we found answered even beyond our expectations.   we swam our horses over also and encamped at sunset.[1]   quetoes extreemly troublesome. I think the river is somewhat higher than when we were here last ⟨spring⟩ summer.   the present season has been much more moist than the preceeding one.   the grass and weeds are much more luxouriant than they were when I left this place on the 13th of July 1805.— saw the brown thrush,[2] pigeons,[3] doves &c.—

the yellow Currants begining to ripen.[4]

1. This camp was on the east bank of the Missouri, in Cascade County, Montana, somewhat below the old White Bear Islands camp and south of the city of Great Falls. The area, but not the camp, appears on *Atlas* maps 42, 54, 61.
2. Brown thrasher, *Toxostoma rufum* [AOU, 705].
3. Perhaps passenger pigeons, *Ectopistes migratorius* [AOU, 315].
4. Probably golden currant, *Ribes aureum* Pursh. Booth & Wright, 107.

[Lewis]   13th July.

removed above to my old station opposite the upper point of the white bear island.[1]   ⟨had⟩ formed our camp and set Thompson &c at work to complete the geer for the horses.   had the cash opened[2]   found my bearskins entirely destroyed by the water, the river having risen so high that the water had penitrated.   all my specimens of plants also lost.   the Chart of the Missouri fortunately escaped.[3]   opened my trunks and boxes and exposed the articles to dry.   found my papers damp and several articles damp.   the stoper had come out of a phial of laudinum and the contents had run into the drawer and distroyed a gret part of my medicine in such manner that it was past recovery.   waited very impatiently for the return of Drewyer   he did not arrive. Musquetoes excessively troublesome insomuch that without the protection of my musquetoe bier I should have found it impossible to wright a moment.   the buffaloe are leaving us fast and passing on to the S. East.   killed a buffaloe picker[4] [*EC?: pecker*]   a beatifull bird.

1. The White Bear Islands camp of June 18, 1805, on the east bank of the Missouri in Cascade County, Montana. *Atlas* maps 42, 54, 61.

2. For the cache at the upper portage camp, see June 26, July 9 and 10, 1805. See Cutright (LCPN), 312–13, on the loss of specimens.

3. This map is apparently lost. See June 27, 1805, and Introduction to the *Atlas*.

4. The brown-headed cowbird, *Molothrus ater* [AOU, 495], so called because it picks ticks and other pests from the backs of the buffalo and cattle; not a new species. Burroughs, 256.

[Lewis]   *14th July*

Had the carriage wheels dug up   found them in good order.   the iron frame of the boat had not suffered materially.   had the meat cut thiner and exposed to dry in the sun.   and some roots of cows of which I have yet a small stock pounded into meal for my journey. I find the fat buffaloe meat a great improvement to the mush of these roots.   the old cash being too damp to venture to deposit my trunks &c in I sent them over to the Large island and had them put on a high scaffold among some thick brush and covered with skins. I take this precaution lest some indians may visit the men I leave here before the arrival of the main party and rob them.   the hunters killed a couple of wolves, the buffaloe have almost entirely disappeared.   saw the bee martin.   the wolves are in great numbers howling arround us and loling about in the plains in view at the distance of two or three hundred yards. I counted 27 about the carcase of a buffaloe which lies in the water at the upper point of the large island.   these are generally of the large kind.[1] Drewyer did not return this evening.—

1. Again, the gray wolf.

[Lewis]   *15 July 1806.*[1]

Sent McNeal down this morning to the lower part of the portage to see whether the large perogue and cash were safe.—[2] Drewyer returned without the horses and reported that he had tracked them to beyond our camp of the

[Lewis]   *Tuesday July 15th 1806.*[3]

Dispatched McNeal early this morning to the lower part of portage in order to learn whether the Cash and white perogue remained untouched or in what state they were.   the men employed in drying the meat, dressing deerskins and preparing for the reception of the canoes.   at 1 P. M. Drewyer returned without the horses and reported that after a diligent surch of 2 days he had discovered where the horses had passed Dearborn's river at which place there were 15 lodges that had been abandoned about the time our horses were taken; he pursued the tracks of a number of horses from these lodges to the road which we had traveled over the mountains which they struck about 3 ms. South of our encampment of the 7th inst. and had pursued this road Westwardly; I have no doubt but they are a party of the Tushapahs who have been on a buffaloe hunt. Drewyer informed that there camp was in a small bottom on the river of about 5 acres inclosed by the steep and rocky and lofty clifts of the river and that so closely had they kept themselves and horses within this little spot that there was not a track to be seen of them within a quarter of a mile of that place.   every spire of grass was eaten up by their horses near their camp which had the appearance of their having remained here some time.   his horse being much fatiegued with the ride he had given him and finding that the indians had at least 2 days the start of him thought it best to return.   his safe return has releived me from great anxiety. I had already settled it in my mind that a whitebear had killed him and should have set out tomorrow in surch of him, and if I could not find him to continue my rout to Maria's river. I knew that if he met with a bear in the plains even he would attack him.   and that if any accedent should happen to seperate him from his horse in that situation the chances in favour of his being killed would be as 9 to 10. I felt so perfectly satisfyed that he had returned in safety that I thought but little of the horses although they were seven of the best I had. this loss great as it is, is not intirely irreparable, or at least dose not defeat my design of exploring Maria's river. I have yet 10 horses remaining, two of the best and two of the worst of which I leave to assist the party in taking the canoes and baggage over the portage and take the remaining 6 with me; these are but indifferent horses most of them but I hope they may answer our purposes. I shall leave three of my intended party, (viz) Gass, Frazier and Werner, and take the two Feildses and Drewyer. by having two spare horses we can releive those we ride. having made this arrangement I gave orders for an early departure in the morning, indeed I should have set out instantly but McNeal road one of the horses which I intend to take and has not yet returned. a little before dark McNeal returned with his musquet broken off at the breech,[4] and informed me that on his arrival at willow run [*NB?: on the portage*] he had approached a white bear within ten feet without discover him the bear being in the thick brush, the horse took the allarm and turning short threw him immediately under the bear; this animal raised himself on his hinder feet for battle, and gave him time to recover from his fall which he did in an instant and with his clubbed musquet he struck the bear over the head and cut him with the guard of the gun[5] and broke off the breech, the bear stunned with the stroke fell to the ground and began to scratch his head with his feet; this gave McNeal time to climb a willow tree which was near at hand and thus fortunately made his escape. the bear waited at the foot of the tree untill late in the evening before he left him, when McNeal ventured down and caught his horse which had by this time strayed off to the distance of 2 ms. and returned to camp. these bear are a most tremenduous animal; it seems that the hand of providence has been most wonderfully in our favor with rispect to them, or some of us would long since have fallen a sacrifice to their farosity. there seems to be a sertain fatality attatched to the neighbourhood of these falls, for there is always a chapter of accedents prepared for us during our residence at them. the musquetoes continue to infest us in such manner that we can scarcely exist; for my own part I am confined by them to my bier at least ¾ths of my time. my dog even howls with the torture he experiences from them, they are almost insupportable, they are so numerous that we frequently get them in our thrats as we breath.—

1. The last entry in Codex La. After Lewis's writing, and at right angles to it, Clark has added, "a part of M. L. notes to Come into the book No. 12—after the 4' July." The word "after" may be Coues's insertion. "No. 12" would be Codex L in Biddle's numbering system, and the meaning is that Codex La fits into the gap in Codex L. Coues has continued Clark's sentence with these words: "where ten blank leaves were left by M. L. for the insertion of this matter. Dec. 20, 1892. Coues." See Appendix C, vol. 2.

2. The "lower portage camp" on the Missouri, in Chouteau County, Montana, below the mouth of Belt Creek; see June 16, 1805. It appears as the camp of June 16–29, 1805, on *Atlas* maps 42, 54, and 61.

3. Codex L resumes on this date; see July 4, 1806.

4. Presumably the U.S. Model 1795 musket, caliber .69; obviously it was not designed for the use to which McNeal put it. Russell (GEF), 150–57; Russell (FTT), 36–37.

5. Probably the trigger guard.

[Lewis]   *Wednesday July 16th 1806.*

I dispatched a man early this morning to drive up the horses as usual, he returned at 8 A. M. with one of them only.   allarmed at this occurrence I dispatched one of my best hands on horseback in surch of them he returned at 10 A. M. with them and I immediately set out.   sent Drewyer and R. Fields with the horses to the lower side of Medecine river, and proceeded myself with all our baggage and J. Fields down the missouri to the mouth of Medecine river in our canoe of buffaloe skins. we were compelled to swim the horses above the whitebear island and again across medicine river as the Missouri is of great width below the mouth of that river.   having arrived safely below Medicine river we immediatly sadled our horses and proceeded down the river to the handsom fall[1] of 47 feet where I halted about 2 hours and took a haisty sketch of these falls; in the mean time we had some meat cooked and took dinner after which we proceeded to the grand falls[2] where we arrived at sunset.   on our way we saw two very large bear on the opposite side of the river.   as we arrived in sight of the little wood below the falls we saw two other bear enter it; this being the only wood in the neighbourhood we were compelled of course to contend with the bear for possession, and therefore left our horses in a place of security and entered the wood which we surched in vain for the bear, they had fled.   here we encamped and the evening having the appearance of rain made our beds and slept under a shelving rock.   these falls have abated much of their grandure since I first arrived at them in June 1805, the water being much lower at preset than it was at that moment, however they are still a sublimely grand object. I determined to take a second drawing of it in the morning.   we saw a few buffaloe as we passed today, the immence hirds which were about this place on our arrival have principally passed the river and directed their course downwards.   we see a number of goats or antilopes always in passing through the plains of the Missouri above the Mandans.   at this season they are thinly scattered over the plains but seem universally distributed in every part; they appear very inquisitive usually to learn what we are as we pass, and frequently accompany us at no great distance for miles, frequently halting and giving a loud whistle through their nostrils, they are a very pretty animal and astonishingly fleet and active.   we spent this evening free from the torture of the Musquetoes.   there are a great number of geese which usually raise their young above these falls about the entrance of Medicine river   we saw them in large flocks of several hundred as we passed today. I saw both yesterday and today the Cookkoo[3] or as it is sometimes called the *rain craw*.   this bird is not met with west of the Rocky Mountains nor within them.—

1. Present Rainbow Falls, in Cascade County, Montana; see June 14, 1805.

2. Lewis camped here, on the north side of the Missouri River at the Great Falls, in Cascade County, Montana. *Atlas* maps 42, 54, 61.

3. Either the yellow-billed cuckoo, *Coccyzus americanus* [AOU, 387], or the black-billed cuckoo, *C. erythropthalmus* [AOU, 388]. Holmgren, 29. The range of the former does extend well beyond the Rockies to the west.

[Lewis]   *Thursday July 17th 1806.*

I arrose early this morning and made a drawing of the falls.[1]   after which we took breakfast and departed.   it being my design to strike Maria's river about the place at which I left it on my return to it's mouth in the begining of June 1805. I steered my course through the wide and level plains which have somewhat the appearance of an ocean,[2] not a tree nor a shrub to be seen.   the land is not fertile, at least far less so, than the plains of the Columbia or those lower down this river, it is a light coloured soil intermixed with a considerable proportion of coarse gravel without sand, when dry it cracks and appears thursty and is very hard, in it's wet state, it is as soft and slipry as so much soft soap.[3] the grass is naturally but short and at present has been rendered much more so by the graizing of the buffaloe, the whole face of the country as far as the eye can reach looks like a well shaved bowlinggreen, in which immence and numerous herds of buffaloe were seen feeding attended by their scarcely less numerous sheepherds the wolves. we saw a number of goats as usual today, also the party coloured plover with the brick red head and neck;[4] this bird remains about the little ponds which are distributed over the face of these plains[5] and here raise their young. we killed a buffaloe cow as we passed throug the plains and took the hump and tonge which furnish ample rations for four men one day.   at 5 P. M. we arrived at *rose* [*NB?: Tansy*] river[6] where I purposed remaining all night as I could not reach maria's river this evening and unless I did there would be but little probability of our finding any wood and very probably no water either. on our arrival at the river we saw where a wounded and bleading buffaloe had just passed and concluded it was probable that the indians had been runing them and were near at hand.   the Minnetares of Fort de prarie and the blackfoot indians rove through this quarter of the country and as they are a vicious lawless and reather an abandoned set of wretches I wish to avoid an interview with them if possible.[7] I have no doubt but they would steel our horses if they have it in their power and finding us weak should they happen to be numerous wil most probably attempt to rob us of our arms and baggage; at all events I am determined to take every possible precaution to avoid them if possible. I hurried over the river to a thick wood and turned out the horses to graize; sent Drewyer to pursue and kill the wounded buffaloe in order to determine whether it had been wounded by the indians or not, and proceeded myself to reconnoitre the adjacent country having sent R. Fields for the same purpose a different rout. I ascended the river hills and by the help of my glass examined the plains but could make no discovery, in about an hour I returned to camp, where I met with the others who had been as unsuccessfull as myself. Drewyer could not find the wounded buffaloe. J. Fields whom I had left at camp had already roasted some of the buffaloe meat and we took dinner after which I sent Drewyer and R. Fields to resume their resurches for the indians; and set myself down to record the transactions of the day.   [*NB?: Tansy*] *rose* [*EC: Teton*] river is at this place fifty yards wide, the water which is only about 3 feet deep occupys about 35 yds. and is very terbid of a white colour.   the general course of this river is from East to west so far as I can discover it's track through the plains, it's bottoms are wide and well timbered with cottonwood both the broad and narrow leafed speceis.   the bed of this stream is small gravel and mud; it's banks are low but never overflow, the hills are about 100 or 150 feet high; it possesses bluffs of earth like the lower part of the Missouri; except the debth and valocity of it's stream and it is the Missouri in miniture.   from the size of rose river at this place and it's direction I have no doubt but it takes it's source within the first range of the Rocky mountains.   the bush which bears the red berry[8] is here in great plenty in the river bottoms

Courses and distances July 17th 1806.

N. 10° W.   20   m. from the great falls of the Missouri to rose river where we
           ms. 20   encamped on it's northern bank in a grove of cottonwood.—

The spies returned having killed 2 beaver and a deer.   they reported that they saw no appearance of Indians.—

1. Lewis again shows his strong desire to have an accurate representation of the Great Falls; no drawing of the falls by Lewis has been found. See June 13, 1805.

2. An early instance of this comparison, which would become common in describing the Great Plains.

3. The Blackleaf Formation and Marias River Shale underlie the area traversed by Lewis. Except along steep-sided coulees, however, these formations are covered by glacial till consisting mainly of silt and clay; the more clay-rich portions are known as gumbo-till. The gravel is both glacial outwash and pebbles or cobbles left behind after the more easily eroded part of the till is removed. Because of the abundant clay- and silt-sized material in the soil, it cracks open when it dries. The clay or gumbo-till which forms the soil becomes extremely plastic when wet.

4. The avocet, *Recurvirostra americana* [AOU, 225], already described before the expedition. Lewis's detailed description is at May 1, 1805.

5. These ponds are in Chouteau County, Montana, northwest of present Floweree, in the vicinity of the area called Antelope Flat; one of them is present Antelope Lake. The

ponds are glacial kettles, outwash-channel depressions, and wind blowouts that fill during heavy rains; they usually dry up by mid or late summer. Lewis is traveling nearly north from the Great Falls of the Missouri. The route does not appear on any *Atlas* maps.

6. Teton River in Chouteau County; for the naming of it, see June 4 and 6, 1805. Lewis camped here, some ten miles northwest of present Carter.

7. Lewis's information on these people came primarily from their enemies, like the Shoshones and the Nez Perces, but his experience of July 27, 1806, no doubt confirmed his unfavorable opinion.

8. Buffaloberry, *Shepherdia argentea* (Pursh) Nutt.

[Lewis]   *Friday July 18th 1806.*

We set out this morning a little before sunrise   ascended the river hills and continued our rout as yesterday through the open plains   at about 6 miles we reached the top of an elivated plain which divides the waters of the rose river from those of Maria's river.   from hence the North mountains, the South mountains, the falls mountains and the Tower Mountain[1] and those arround and to the East of the latter were visible.   our course led us nearly parrallel with a creek of Maria's river which takes it's rise in these high plains at the place we passed them; at noon we struck this creek about 6 ms. from its junction with Maria's river[2] where we found some cottonwood timber; here we halted to dine and graize our horses.   the bed of this creek is about 25 yds. wide at this place but is nearly dry at present, the water being confined to little pools in the deeper parts of it's bed.   from hence downwards there is a considerable quantity of timber in it's bottom.   we passed immence herds of buffaloe on our way in short for about 12 miles it appeared as one herd only the whole plains and vally of this creek being covered with them; saw a number of wolves of both speceis,[3] also Antelopes and some horses.   after dinner we proceeded about 5 miles across the plain to Maria's river where we arrived at 6 P. M.   we killed a couple of buffaloe in the bottom of this river and encamped on it's west side in a grove of cottonwood some miles above the entrance of the creek.[4]   being now convinced that we were above the point to which I had formerly ascended this river and faring that a fork of this stream might fall in on the Northside between this place and the point to which I had ascended it, I directed Drewyer who was with me on my former excurtion, and Joseph Fields to decend the river early in the morning to the place from whence I had returned, and examine whether any stream fell inn or not. I keep a strict lookout every night, I take my tour of watch with the men.

Courses and distances of July 18th 1806.

N. 25 W.	7	ms. to the source of Buffloe Creek passing the dividing ridge between the waters of Maria's and rose [*EC?: Tansy or Teton*] river at 6 ms. praries more hilly than yesterday. many prickly pears now in blume.
N. 15 W	12	ms. down buffaloe Creek to the place at which we dined. here timber commences on this stream. 25 yds. wide no running water.
North	5	ms. to Maria's River 130 yds. wide 3 feet deep encamped on
Ms. 24		South side.—

1. These are all names which the captains had bestowed in 1805. The North Mountains are the Bears Paw Mountains. The South Mountains would be either the Highwood or the Judith mountains, although the latter could not be seen from this point. The Falls Mountains may be either the Little or Big Belt mountains. The Tower Mountains are the Sweetgrass Hills. See May 24 and 25, 1805, and June 5, 1805.

2. Lewis's Buffalo Creek, now Dugout Coulee, flowing north toward the Marias in Chouteau and Liberty counties, Montana.

3. The coyote, *Canis latrans*, and the gray wolf.

4. Lewis camped on Marias River, in Liberty County, a few miles above the mouth of Dugout Coulee.

[Lewis]   *Saturday July 19th 1806.*

Drewyer and J. Fields set out early this morning in conformity to my instructions last evening.   they returned at ½ after 12 OCk. and informed me that they had proceeded down the river to the place from which I had returned on the [*blank*] of June last[1] and that it was 6 miles distant.   they passed the entrance of buffaloe Creek at 2 ms.   the course of the river from hence downwards as far as they were is N. 80 E.   they killed 8 deer and two Antelopes on their way; most of the deer were large fat mule bucks.   having completed my observation of the sun's meridian Altitude we set out, ascended the river hills having passed the river and proceeded through the open plains up the N. side of the river 20 miles and encamped.[2]   at 15 miles we passed ⟨the⟩[*illegible*] a large creek[3] on

N. side a little above it's entrance; there is but little running water in this creek at present, it's bed is about 30 yds. wide and appears to come from the broken *Mountains*[4] so called from their raggid and irregular shape there are three of them extending from east to West almost unconnected, the center mountain terminates in a conic spire and is that which I have called the tower mountain   they are destitute of timber.   from the entrance of this creek they bore N. 10° W.   the river bottoms are usually about ½ a mile wide and possess a considerable quantity of timber entirely cottonwood; the underbrush is honeysuckle[5] rose bushes[6] the narrow leated willow and the bush which bears the acid red berry called by the french engages *grease de buff*. [*NB: buffaloe grease*][7] just as we halted to encamp R. Fields killed a mule doe.   the plains are beautifull and level but the soil is but thin.[8]   in many parts of the plains there are great quantities of prickly pears.   saw some herds of buffaloe today but not in such quantities as yesterday, also antelopes, wolves, gees, pigeons, doves, hawks, ravens crows larks sparrows &c.   the Curlooe has disappeared.

On the South side of Maria's river ⟨8⟩ 2[9] ms. above the entrance of Buffaloe Creek

Observed Meridian Altd. of ☉'s L. L.
with Octant by the back observatn.   } 59° 35′

Latitude deduced from this observation.   [*blank*]

Courses and distances July 19th 1806.

S. 80 W.	20	Ms. up Maria's river to the place of our encampment on it's N.
	Ms. 20	side. passed a large creek on South Side[10] with some timber in it's vally at 8 ms. also another large creek [*EC: Sweetgrass Creek*][11] on N. side at 15 ms. this last is 30 yds. wide but little water at present. the bluffs of the river and creeks are steep and principally formed of earth, though there are sometimes thin stratas of freestone intermixed near the top of the bluffs.—[12]

1. On June 5, 1805, Lewis reached a point on the Marias River above the mouth of Horse Coulee, in Liberty County, Montana.

2. The camp was on the Marias, in Toole County, Montana, a mile or so west of the Liberty County line.

3. Willow Creek, in Liberty County.

4. The Sweetgrass Hills, in Toole and Liberty counties; the three mountains are West Butte, Gold Butte (Tower Mountain), and East Butte.

5. Either common snowberry, or Western snowberry, *Symphoricarpos occidentalis* Hook. Booth & Wright, 234.

6. Probably western wild rose, or possibly prickly rose, *Rosa acicularis* Lindl. Ibid., 119.

7. Buffaloberry again; the French term is *graisse de boeuf*.

8. The semiarid climate, the steep slopes, and the wind combine to retard soil formation.

9. The penciled-in "2" may be an addition by Coues; the "8" is not clear and could be another number.

10. Pondera Creek, reaching the Marias in Liberty County. Someone, perhaps Coues, has penciled in a question mark in parentheses after the word "South."

11. Present Willow Creek.

12. Near its mouth, Pondera Creek cuts through glacial till, the base of the Telegraph Creek Formation and into the top of the Marias River Shale. The freestone is the lower sandstone of the Telegraph Creek Formation.

[Lewis]   *Sunday July 20th 1806*

We set at sunrise and proceed through the open plain as yesterday up the North side of the river.   the plains are more broken than they were yesterday and have become more inferior in point of soil; a great quanty of small gravel is every where distributed over the surface of the earth which renders travling extreemly painfull to our bearfoot horses.   the soil is generally a white or whiteish blue clay, this where it has been trodden by the buffaloe when wet has now become as firm as a brickbat and stands in an inumerable little points quite as formidable to our horses feet as the gravel.   the mineral salts common to the plains of the missouri has been more abundant today than usual.   the bluffs of the river are about 200 feet high, steep irregular and formed of earth which readily desolves with water, slips and precipitates itself into the river as before mentioned frequentlly of the bluffs of the Missouri below which they resemble in every particular, differing essentially from those of the Missouri above the entrance of this river, they being composed of firm red or yellow clay which dose not yeald readily to the rains and a large quantity of rock.[1] the soil of the river bottom is fertile and well timbered, I saw some trees today which would make small canoes.   the timber is generally low.   the underbrush the same as before mentioned.   we have seen fewer buffaloe today than usual, though more Elk and not less wolves and Antelopes also some mule deer; this speceis of deer seems most prevalent in this quarter. saw some gees ducks and other birds common to the country. there is much appearance of beaver on this river, but not any of otter.[2] from the apparent decent of the country to the North and above the broken mountains I am induced to beleive that the South branch of the Suskashawan receives a part of it's waters from the plain even to the borders of this river[3] and from the brakes visible in the plains in a nothern direction think that a branch of that river decending from the rocky mountains passes at no great distance from Maria's river and to the N. E. of the broken mountains. the day has proved excessively warm and we lay by four hours during the heat of it; we traveled 28 miles and encamped as usual in the river bottom on it's N. side.[4] there is scarcely any water at present in the plains and what there is, lies in small pools and is so strongly impregnated with the mineral salts that it is unfit for any purpose except the uce of the buffaloe. these animals appear to prefer this water to that of the river. the wild liquorice[5] and sunflower[6] are very abundant in the plains and river bottoms, the latter is now in full blume; the silkgrass and sand rush[7] are also common to the bottom lands. the musquetoes have not been ⟨very little⟩ troublesome to us since we left the whitebear islands.—

Courses and distances July 20th 1806.

S. 80° W.   28   ms. with the river in it's course upwards to our encampment of this evening on it's N. side.   river 120 yds. wide and deep, water appears to be but little diminsed, somewhat more transparent.   passed a creek on S. side at 6 ms. also another 22 ms. on the N. side[8] this last has no water some little timber.   bed 15 yds. wide.—   the general course of this river is very streight, and it meanders through a vally of about ½ a mile in width from side to side.

1. Late Pleistocene glacial ice in this area displaced the Marias River southward from its preglacial course. The displaced Marias River then cut a new valley in older glacial till and into shale of the Colorado Group. This downcutting produced a more rugged topography here than it did farther to the east. The gravel is both glacial outwash and cobbles that were left behind when the finer-grained portion of the till eroded. The glacial till that overlies the Colorado Group was derived from this same formation farther

to the north. In this area the till is composed of silt- and clay-sized particles and is highly impregnated with salts such as calcium-magnesium sulfate/bicarbonate. When the clay dries out it becomes exceedingly firm, resembling adobe. The bluffs near the river are composed mainly of glacial till. The till does not dissolve but erodes easily in contact with running water. The running water undercuts the banks and they slide or fall down into the river. The firm red or yellow clay and rock along the Missouri above the mouth of the Marias is part of the Kootenai Formation.

2. *Lutra canadensis.*

3. Lewis was still hoping that the Marias would provide Americans with access to the Saskatchewan River country and its fur trade. In fact, the entire basin of the Milk River lies between the South Saskatchewan and any part of the Missouri system.

4. Lewis camped on the north side of the Marias River in southern Toole County, Montana, some five miles southwest of the present town of Shelby, and perhaps a mile west of Interstate Highway 15.

5. Wild liquorice, *Glycyrrhiza lepidota* (Nutt.) Pursh. Booth & Wright, 130.

6. Probably the early flowering perennial, Nuttall's Sunflower, *Helianthus nuttallii* T. & G. ssp. *rydbergii* (Britt.) Long, typically found in riverbottoms. It flowers earlier than the annual sunflowers, *H. annuus* L., and *H. petiolaris* Nutt. Another possibility for such an early flowering, perennial, upland sunflower is stiff sunflower, *H. rigidus* (Cass.) Desf. ssp. *subrhomboideus* (Rybd.) Heiser (also known as *H. laetiflorus*). Booth & Wright, 274; Barkley, 377–79.

7. Based on the bottomland habitat and association with the scouring ("sand") rush (*Equiseum* sp.), the silkgrass is almost certainly hemp dogbane, *Apocynum cannabinum* L., long known as a textile fiber plant commonly used by natives. See August 20, 1805.

8. Coues (HLC), 3 : 1090–91 n. 43, argues that the actual order and direction of these two streams has been reversed in Lewis's wording. According to Coues, the first stream, from the south some eighteen miles above the previous night's camp, is the Dry Fork of Marias River, in Toole County. Coues identifies the second stream, six miles above the first on the north side of the Marias, as Medicine Rock Coulee, a name perhaps present in his time but not found on current maps; it would probably be an unnamed creek occupying a glacial channel that passes through Shelby. On the other hand, if Lewis's first creek did enter from the south at six miles as he has it, it could be Dead Indian Coulee. The second stream in Lewis's record almost has to be coming from the south and therefore would be Dry Fork since there is no stream of any consequence coming from the north in this day's route and Dry Fork most nearly fits his mileage estimates.

[Lewis]   *Monday July 21st 1806.*

We set out at sunrise and proceeded a short distance up the North side of the river; we found the ravines which made in on this side were so steep and numerous that we passed [*EC?: crossed*] the river in doing which the pack horse which carried my instruments missed the ford and wet the instruments. this accident detained us about half an hor. I took the Instruments out wiped them and dryed their cases, they sustained no naterial injury. we continued on the S. side of the river about 3 [*EC?: 3*] miles when we again passed over to the N. side and took our course through the plains at some distance from the river. we saw a large herd of Elk this morning. the buffaloe still become more scarce. at 2 P. M. we struck a northern branch of Marias river[1] about 30 yds. wide at the distance of about 8 miles from it's entrance. this stream is closely con- fined between clifts of freestone rocks[2] the bottom narrow below us and above the rocks confine it on each side; some little timber below but not any above; the water of this stream is nearly clear. from the appearance of this rock and the apparent hight of the bed of the streem I am induced to beleive that there are falls in these rivers somewhere about their junc- tion. being convinced that this stream came from the mountains I de- termined to pursue it as it will lead me to the most nothern point to which the waters of Maria's river extend which I now fear will not be as far north as I wished and expected. after dinner we set out up the North branch keeping on it's S. side; we pursued it untill dark and not finding any timber halted and made a fire of the dung of the buffaloe. we lay on the south side in a narrow bottom under a Clift.[3] our provision is nearly out, we wounded a buffaloe this evening but could not get him.

Courses and distances July 21st 1806.

S. 80° W.	15	ms. with the river upward. it forks at the extremity of this course and the main or Southern branch bears S. 75 W. about 30 ms. to the mountains
N. 40° W.	6	m. up the North branch. 30 yd. wide confined closly be- tween clifts of rocks, shallow rapid and not navigable
N. 25° W.	7	m. still with the N. fork upwards. we struck the river at 2
Miles	28	miles from the eommencement of this course, passed it and continued on it's South side. hills broken. land poor.

1. Cut Bank Creek, the northern fork of Marias River, Two Medicine River being the south fork; the two meet on the Pondera-Glacier county line in Montana.

2. The glacial relocation of the Marias River and its tributaries caused each to downcut a new valley. Near the junction of the Marias River and Cut Bank Creek, the formations

are the Telegraph Creek Formation and the Virgelle Sandstone; from about six miles south of their evening camp, the Two Medicine Formation borders Cut Bank Creek. These formations contain abundant, erosion-resistant sandstone layers. The streams, thus, cut narrow, trench-like valleys.

3. Lewis camped on the west side of Cut Bank Creek, in Glacier County, a mile or so southwest of the present town of Cut Bank.

[Lewis]   *Tuesday July 22ed 1806.*

We set out very early this morning as usual and proceeded up the river. for the first seven miles of our travel this morning the country was broken the land poor and intermixed with a greater quantity of gravel than usual; the ravines were steep and numerous and our horses feet have become extreemly soar in traveling over the gravel[1] we therefore traveled but slow.[2] we met with a doe Elk which we wounded but did not get her. the river is confined closely between clifts of perpendicular rocks in most parts. after the distance of seven miles the country became more level les gravly and some bottoms to the river but not a particle of timber nor underbush of any discription is to be seen. we continued up the river on it's South side for 17 miles when we halted to glaize our horses and eat; there being no wood we were compelled to make our fire with the buffaloe dung which I found answered the purpose very well. we cooked and eat all the meat we had except a small peice of buffaloe meat which was a little tainted. after dinner we passed the river and took our course through a level and beautifull plain on the N. side. the country has now become level, the river bottoms wide and the adjoining plains but little elivated above them; the banks of the river are not usually more than from 3 to four feet yet it dose not appear ever to overflow them. we found no timber untill we had traveled 12 miles further when we arrived at a clump of large cottonwood trees in a beautifull and extensive bottom of the river about 10 miles below the foot of the rocky mountains where this river enters them; as I could see from hence very distinctly where the river entered the mountains and the bearing of this point being S of West I thought it unnecessary to proceed further and therefore encamped resolving to rest ourselves and horses a couple of days at this place and take the necessary observations.[3] this plain on which we are is very high; the rocky mountains to the S. W. of us appear but low from their base up yet are partially covered with snow nearly to their bases. there is no timber on those mountains within our view; they are very irregular and broken in their form and seem to be composed principally of clay with but little rock or stone. the river appears to possess at least double the vollume of water which it had where we first arrived on it below; this no doubt proceeds from the avapparation ⟨of⟩ caused by the sun and air and the absorbing of the earth in it's passage through these open plains.[4] The course of the mountains still continues from S. E. to N. W. the front rang appears to terminate abrubtly about 35 ms. to the N. W. of us.[5] I believe that the waters of the Suskashawan apporoach the borders of this river very nearly. I now have lost all hope of the waters of this river ever extending to N Latitude 50° though I still hope and think it more than probable that both *white earth* river and milk river extend as far north as latd. 50°—[6] we have seen but few buffaloe today no deer and very few Antelopes; gam of every discription is extreemly wild which induces me to beleive that the indians are now, or have been lately in this neighbourhood. we wounded a buffaloe this evening but our horses were so much fatiegued that we were unable to pursue it with success.—

Courses and distances July 22ed 1806.

N. 30° W.   7   ms. with the course of the river upwards. river closely confined between low but steep and rocky Clifts. water transpent.

S. 80° W.   10   ms. through the plains, the river making a considerable bend to the wright or N W

S. 75° W.   11   ms. through the plains on the N side of the river which here
Ms. 28   made a considerable bend to the left or South. we passed the river to it's N. side at one mile from the commencement of this course and again recrossed it at the extremity of the course and encamped on it's S. side.—

1. In preglacial times, Cut Bank Creek flowed northeast from the mountains, passed about seven miles north of Cut Bank, and either joined the Milk River in Canada or it joined the Marias River near Tiber Dam. Glacial ice, however, diverted the stream to the south, causing it to cut a new valley west of Cut Bank in sandstone rocks. From about seven miles north of Cut Bank to the mountains, the creek occupies its preglacial channel, and the topography is much more subdued near the creek. The gravel is both glacial out-

wash and pebbles or cobbles left behind after the finer-grained portion of the till has been removed.

2. Lewis continued up the west side of Cut Bank Creek in Glacier County, Montana. After a few miles his course turned west, still following the creek.

3. This was the camp Lewis would name Camp Disappointment, where they would remain until July 26. It was in Glacier County, on the Blackfeet Indian Reservation, along the south side of Cut Bank Creek just above the mouth of Cut Bank John Coulee (sometimes given under its previous name, Trail Coulee), about twelve miles northeast of present Browning and some six miles north of U.S. Highway 2.

4. Although much glacial material blankets the lower portion of the mountains, and Cretaceous shale forms their base, the mountains are composed of extremely resistant Precambrian quartzite, argillite, and limestone. Part of the volume of the Cut Bank Creek–Marias River system is lost to evaporation, but at least an equal amount is lost to recharge to the permeable sand, gravel, and sandstone through which the stream passes. The late snowmelt of 1806, combined with a winter 1805–6 snowpack that greatly exceeded present average snowpacks, would have created a much greater volume of water than normal, especially in the upper portion of the drainage. Nevertheless, it is not likely that Cut Bank Creek could have been carrying twice the volume of water that the lower Marias River did. Stream-gauging records show that Cut Bank Creek at Cut Bank has an average monthly maximum flow of about 600 cubic feet per second (cfs) and at the mouth of the Marias River the average flow for the Marias River for the following month is about 950 cfs (prorated to adjust for releases from the Tiber Reservoir). Therefore, at the place where Lewis reached the Marias, the equivalent average flow would be between 900 and 1,100 cfs. On the other hand, if Lewis had been comparing the flow in the area immediately downstream from the junction of Cut Bank Creek and Two Medicine River (about 2,000 cfs) with that at the place where he reached the Marias River, his estimate would be close to the mark.

5. Lewis was looking toward the main ridge of the Continental Divide in Glacier National Park, Montana.

6. White Earth River is Little Muddy River, or Creek, in Williams County, North Dakota; see April 21, 1805. In later years Clark explained to Biddle that the hope was to find rivers extending to 50° North so as to gain more territory for the United States. Biddle Notes [ca. April 1810], Jackson (LLC), 2:544.

[Lewis]   *Wednesdy July 23rd 1806.*

I dispatched Drewyer an Joseph fields this morning to hunt. I directed Drewyer who went up the river to observe it's bearings and the point at which it entered the mountains, this he did and on his return I observed the point at which the river entered to bear S 50° W. distant about ten miles the river making a considerable bend to the West just above us.

both these hunters returned unsuccessful and reported that there was no game nor the appearance of any in this quarter.   we now rendered the grease from our tainted meat and made some mush of cows with a part of it, reserving as much meal of cows and grease as would afford us one more meal tomorrow. Drewyer informed us that there was an indian camp of eleven leather lodges which appeared to have been abandoned about 10 days, the poles only of the lodges remained.   we are confident that these are the Minnetares of fort de prarie and suspect that they are probably at this time somewhere on the main branch of Maria's river on the borders of the buffaloe, under this impression I shall not strike that river on my return untill about the mouth of the North branch.[1]   near this place I observe a number of the whistleing squirrel of the speceis common to the plains and country watered by the Columbia river, this is the first instance in which I have found this squirrel in the plains of the Missouri.[2]   the Cottonwood of this place is also of the speceis common to the Columbia.[3]   we have a delightfull pasture for our horses where we are.

Observed Meridian Altd. of ☉'s L. L. with Octant by the back observation— $62°\ 00'\ 00''$

Latitude deduced from this observation [*blank*]
observed equal altitudes of the Sun with the Sextant.

	h	m	s			h	m	s	
A. M.	7	40	57	P. M.		4	32	40	Altd. of ☉
"		42	30	"			33	13	$56°\ 8'\ 45''$
"		43	5	"			34	43	

The clouds obscured the moon and put an end to further observa tion.   the rok which makes its appearance on this part of the river is of a white colour fine grit and makes excellet whetstones; it lies in horizontal stratas and makes it's appearance in the bluffs of the river near their base.[4]   we indeavoured to take some fish but took only one small trout.[5] Musquetoes uncommonly large and reather troublesome.

1. The junction of Cut Bank Creek and Two Medicine River.
2. Columbian ground squirrel. Burroughs, 99–101, 322 n. 8.

3. Lewis recognizes that black cottonwood, the only cottonwood west of the Continental Divide, continues east along the eastern Rocky Mountain foothills of north-central Montana. See also July 26, 1806. Barkley, 562; Little (CIH), 153-W.

4. Lewis camped near the contact between two Upper Cretaceous formations, the Horsethief Sandstone and the St. Marys River Formation; both of these formations show distinct layering. The rock that Lewis thought would make excellent whetstones is likely one of the fine-grained sandstones in the Horsethief Sandstone.

5. Perhaps cutthroat trout, *Oncorhynchus clarki* (formerly *Salmo clarkii*).

[Lewis]   *Thursday July 24th 1806.*

At 8 A. M. the sun made it's appearance for a few minutes and I took it's altitude but it shortly after clouded up again and continued to rain the ballance of the day   I was therefore unable to complete the observations I wished to take at this place. I determined to remain another day in the hope of it's being fair.   we have still a little bread of cows remaining of which we made a kettle of mush which together with a few pigeons that we were fortunate enough to kill served us with food for this day. I sent the hunters out but they shortly returned without having killed anything and declared that it was useless to hunt within 6 or 8 miles of this place that there was no appearance of game within that distance.   the air has become extreemly cold which in addition to the wind and rain renders our situation extreemly unpleasant.   several wolves visited our camp to-day, I fired on and wounded one of them very badly.   the small speceis of wolf[1] barks like a dog, they frequently salute us with this note as we pass through the plains.

1. Coyote.

[Lewis]   *Friday July 25th 1806.*

The weather still continues cold cloudy and rainy, the wind also has blown all day with more than usual violence from the N. W.   this morning we eat the last of our birds and cows, I therefore directed Drewyer and J. Fields to take a couple of the horses and proceed to the S. E. as far as the main branch of Maria's river[1] which I expected was at no great distance and indeavour to kill some meat; they set out immediately and I remained in camp with R. Fields to avail myself of every opportunity to make my observations should any offer, but it continued to rain and I did not see the sun through the whole course of the day   R. Fields and my-self killed nine pige[ons] which lit in the trees near our camp   on these we dined.   late in the evening Drewyer and J. Fields returned the former had killed a fine buck on which we now fared sumptuously.   they informed me that it was about 10 miles to the main branch of Maria's River, that the vally formed by the river in that quarter was wide extensive and level with a considerable quantity timber; here they found some wintering camps of the natives and a great number of others of a more recent date or that had from appearance been evacuated about 6 weeks; we consider ourselves extreemly fortunate in not having met with these people. I determined that if tomorrow continued cloudy to set out as I now begin to be apprehensive that I shall not reach the United States within this season unless I make every exertion in my power which I shall certainly not omit when once I leave this place which I shall do with much reluctance without having obtained the necessary data to establish it's longitude—as if the fates were against me my chronometer from some unknown cause stoped today, when I set her to going she went as usual.

1. Two Medicine River.

[Lewis]   *Saturday July 26th 1806.*

The moring was cloudy and continued to rain as usual, tho' the cloud seemed somewhat thiner. I therefore posponed seting out untill 9 A. M. in the hope that it would clear off but finding the contrary result I had the horses caught and we set out biding a lasting adieu to this place which I now call camp disappointment. I took my rout through the open plains S. E. 5 ms. passing a small creek[1] at 2 ms. from the mountains wher I changed my direction to S. 75 E. for 7 ms. further and struck a principal branch[2] of Maria's river 65 yds. wide, not very deep, I passed this stream to it's south side and continued down it 2 ms. on the last mentioned course when another branch[3] of nearly the same dignity formed a junction with it, coming from the S. W.   this last is shallow and rappid; has the appearance of overflowing it's banks frequently and discharging vast torrants of water at certain seasons of the year.   the beds of both these

streams are pebbly particularly the S. branch.   the water of the N. branch
is very terbid while that of the S. branch is nearly clear not withstanding
the late rains. I passed the S. branch just above it's junction and continued down the river which runs a little to the N of E 1 ms. and halted to
dine and graize our horses.[4]   here I found some indian lodges which appeared to have been inhabited last winter in a large and fertile bottom
well stocked with cottonwood timber.   the rose honeysuckle and red-
berry bushes constitute the undergrowth there being but little willow in
this quarter both these rivers abov their junction appeared to be well
stocked with timber or comparitively so with other parts of this country.   here it is that we find the three species of cottonwood which I have
remarked in my voyage assembled together   that speceis common to the
Columbia I have never before seen on the waters of the Missouri, also the
narrow and broad leafed speceis.[5]   during our stay at this place R. Fields
killed a buck a part of the flesh of which we took with us.   we saw a few
Antelopes some wolves and 2 of the smallest speceis of fox[6] of a redish
brown colour with the extremity of the tail black.   it is about the size of
the common domestic cat and burrows in the plains.   after dinner I continued my rout down the river to the North of Eat about 3 ms. when the
hills putting in close on the S side I determined to ascend them to the
high plain which I did accordingly, keeping the Fields with me; Drewyer
passed the river and kept down the vally of the river. I had intended to
decend this river with it's course to it's junction with the fork which I had
ascended and from thence have taken across the country obliquely to
rose river and decend that stream to it's confluence with Maria's river.[7]
the country through which this portion of Maria's river passes to the fork
which I ascended appears much more broken than that above and between this and the mountains. I had scarcely ascended the hills before I
discovered to my left at the distance of a mile an assembleage of about
30 horses, I halted and used my spye glass by the help of which I discovered several indians on the top of an eminence just above them who appeared to be looking down towards the river I presumed at Drewyer.
about half the horses were saddled.   this was a very unpleasant sight,
however I resolved to make the best of our situation and to approach
them in a friendly manner. I directed J. Fields to display the flag which I

had brought for that purpose and advanced slowly toward them, about this time they discovered us and appeared to run about in a very confused manner as if much allarmed, their attention had been previously so fixed on Drewyer that they did not discover us untill we had began to advance upon them, some of them decended the hill on which they were and drove their horses within shot of it's summit and again returned to the hight as if to wate our arrival or to defend themselves. I calculated on their number being nearly or quite equal to that of their horses, that our runing would invite pursuit as it would convince them that we were their enimies and our horses were so indifferent that we could not hope to make our escape by flight; added to this Drewyer was seperated from us and I feared that his not being apprized of the indians in the event of our attempting to escapc hc would most probably fall a sacrefice.   under these considerations I still advanced towards them; when we had arrived ⟨at the distance of⟩ within a quarter of a mile of them, one of them mounted his horse and rode full speed towards us, which when I discovered I halted and alighted from my horse; he came within a hundred paces halted looked at us and turned his horse about and returned as briskly to his party as he had advanced; while he halted near us I held out my hand and becconed to him to approach but he paid no attention to my overtures.   on his return to his party they all decended the hill and mounted their horses and advanced towards us leaving their horses behind them, we also advanced to meet them. I counted eight of them but still supposed that there were others concealed as there were several other horses saddled. I told the two men with me that I apprehended that these were the Minnetares of Fort de Prarie and from their known character I expected that we were to have some difficulty with them; that if they thought themselves sufficiently strong I was convinced they would attempt to rob us in which case be their numbers what they would I should resist to the last extremity prefering death to that of being deprived of my papers instruments and gun and desired that they would form the same resolution and be allert and on their guard.   when we arrived within a hundred yards of each other the indians except one halted I directed the two men with me to do the same and advanced singly to meet the indian with whom I shook hands and passed on to those in his rear, as he did also to the two men in my rear; we now all assembled and alighted from our horses; the Indians soon asked to smoke with us, but I told them that the man whom they had seen pass down the river had my pipe and we could not smoke untill he joined us. I requested as they had seen which way he went that they would one of them go with one of my men in surch of him, this they readily concented to and a young man set out with R. Fields in surch of Drewyer. I now asked them by sighns if they were the Minnetares of the North which they answered in the affermative;[8] I asked if there was any cheif among them and they pointed out 3   I did not believe them however I thought it best to please them and gave to one a medal to a second a flag and to the third a handkercheif, with which they appeared well satisfyed.   they appeared much agitated with our first interview from which they had scarcely yet recovered, in fact I beleive they were more allarmed at this accedental interview than we were.   from no more of them appearing I now concluded they were only eight in number and became much better satisfyed with our situation as I was convinced that we could mannage that number should they attempt any hostile measures.   as it was growing late in the evening I proposed that we should remove to the nearest part of the river and encamp together, I told them that I was glad to see them and had a great deel to say to them.   we mounted our horses and rode towards the river which was at but a short distance, on our way we were joined by Drewyer Fields and the indian.   we decended a very steep bluff about 250 feet high to the river where there was a small bottom of nearly ½ a mile in length and about 250 yards wide in the widest part,[9] the river washed the bluffs both above and below us and through it's course in this part is very deep; the bluffs are so steep that there are but few places where they could be ascended, and are broken in several places by deep nitches which extend back from the river several hundred yards, their bluffs being so steep that it is impossible to ascend them; in this bottom there stand tree solitary trees[10] near one of which the indians formed a large simicircular camp[11] of dressed buffaloe skins and invited us to partake of their shelter which Drewyer and myself accepted and the Fieldses lay near the fire in front of the sheter.   with the assistance of Drewyer I had much conversation with these people in the course of the evening. I

learned from them that they were a part of a large band which lay encamped at present near the foot of the rocky mountains on the main
branch of Maria's river one ½ days march from our present encampment;
that there was a whiteman with their band; that there was another large
band of their nation hunting buffaloe near the broken mountains and
were on there way to the mouth of Maria's river where they would probably be in the course of a few days.   they also informed us that from
hence to the establishment where they trade on the Suskasawan river is
only 6 days easy march or such as they usually travel with their women
and childred which may be estimated at about 150 ms.[12] that from these
traders they obtain arm amunition sperituous liquor blankets &c in exchange for wolves and some beaver skins. I told these people that I had
come a great way from the East up the large river which runs towards the
rising sun, that I had been to the great waters where the sun sets and had
seen a great many nations all of whom I had invited to come and trade
with me on the rivers on this side of the mountains, that I had found most
of them at war with their neighbours and had succeeded in restoring
peace among them, that I was now on my way home and had left my
party at the falls of the missouri with orders to decend that river to the
entrance of Maria's river and there wait my arrival and that I had come in
surch of them in order to prevail on them to be at peace with their neighbours particularly those on the West side of the mountains and to engage
them to come and trade with me when the establishment is made at the
entrance of this river to all which they readily gave their assent and declared it to be their wish to be at peace with the Tushepahs whom they
said had killed a number of their relations lately and pointed to several of
those present who had cut their hair as an evidince of the truth of what
they had asserted. I found them extreemly fond of smoking and plyed
them with the pipe untill late at night. I told them that if they intended to
do as I wished them they would send some of their young men to their
band with an invitation to their chiefs and warriors to bring the whiteman
with them and come down and council with me at the entrance of Maria's
river and that the ballance of them would accompany me to that place,
where I was anxious now to meet my men as I had been absent from
them some time and knew that they would be uneasy untill they saw

me. that if they would go with me I would give them 10 horses and some tobacco. to this proposition they made no reply, I took the first watch tonight and set up untill half after eleven; the indians by this time were all asleep, I roused up R. Fields and laid down myself; I directed Fields to watch the movements of the indians and if any of them left the camp to awake us all as I apprehended they would attampt to seal [steal] our horses. this being done I fell into a profound sleep and did not wake untill the noise of the men and indians awoke me a little after light in the morning.—

1. Willow Creek, a tributary of Cut Bank Creek, in Glacier County, Montana.

2. Two Medicine River, in Glacier County.

3. Badger Creek, meeting Two Medicine River in Glacier County. Just below its mouth the party passed into Pondera County, Montana.

4. That is, about one mile below the mouth of Badger Creek, on Two Medicine River in Pondera County. Actually, the general course of the river is a little south of east in this area.

5. Lewis makes an astute ecological observation; the three major cottonwood species typical of the plains, the Rocky Mountains, and the Pacific Coast all occur together here in the eastern foothills of the Rocky Mountains. The species of the Columbia is black cottonwood, the "narrow [leafed]" is narrowleaf cottonwood, and the "broad leafed" is plains cottonwood. Cf. Cutright (LCPN), 316, 316 n. 7.

6. Swift fox, *Vulpes velox*. See July 6 and 8, 1805.

7. Lewis intended to follow Two Medicine River to its junction with Cut Bank Creek, then head southeasterly to Teton River and follow that stream down to the junction with the Marias.

8. This conversation almost certainly was in sign language. Actually these Indians were Piegans, members of one of the three main divisions of the Blackfeet confederation, the other two being the Bloods and the Blackfeet proper. They were an Algonquian-language people who had evidently moved west onto the high plains centuries before. In the eighteenth century they acquired the horse and became a classic example of the bison-hunting nomads of the Great Plains. In 1754 Anthony Hendry, or Henday, a Hudson's Bay Company trader, was the first white man to make direct contact with these people, in Canada. Equipped with horses and traders' guns, by Lewis and Clark's time they had become "the dominant military power on the northwestern plains, feared by all neighboring tribes." Their range straddled the present U.S.-Canadian boundary in southern Alberta and northwest Montana. Relatively friendly toward Canadian traders, they became notorious for their enmity toward the American mountain men. Some writers have traced the origin of this hostility to these Piegans' violent encounter with Lewis's party, but it is just as likely to have arisen because the Blackfeet resented the Americans trading firearms to their enemies, like the Shoshones, Crows, Flatheads, and Nez Perces. Today some of the Blackfeet live on the Blackfeet Reservation in northwest Montana, and others on reserves

in Canada. Many years after the encounter with Lewis, Wolf Calf, supposedly a member of this Piegan party, gave an account of the episode which was printed in Wheeler, 2:311–12. Ewers (BRNP); Ronda (LCAI), 243–44; Bradley (MS), 135.

9. This campsite was in Pondera County, on the Blackfeet Reservation, along the south side of Two Medicine River about four miles below the mouth of Badger Creek and downstream from Kipps Coulee, about one and one-half miles south of the Glacier-Pondera county line and some fourteen miles southwest of the town of Cut Bank. A spot identified as the actual site has been marked in recent years based largely on the work of Helen West, along with Robert Anderson, and Ed Mathison in 1964 (see West). A more recent study by Bergantino casts doubts on the marked site being the actual spot of the camp of July 26–27, 1806. The limitations of Lewis's journal comments, course and distance references, and compass sightings, along with the similarity of terrain in the area opens the possibility that other nearby spots may be likely competitors for the designation. Due to the difficulties involved, an incontestible locating of the site may never be made. The same can be said for pinpointing most Lewis and Clark camps.

10. Three very old cottonwoods were standing in the location West identified as the campsite. Their proximity to the marked site seemed to validate the designation. Nevertheless, the results of borings have been inconclusive and the trees cannot be positively identified as the ones Lewis mentions. The trees presently suffer from heart rot and were partially burned some years ago.

11. Lewis probably means "hemispherical"; skins thrown over a rough dome formed of branches made a type of temporary shelter common to many Western tribes.

12. Lewis's estimated distance would take one to the Bow River in Alberta, where there was a North West Company post reportedly abandoned in 1804. However, the company's principal post for the Blackfeet trade was Rocky Mountain House, founded in 1799 on the North Saskatchewan River, near the site of the present Alberta community of the same name. That would be a distance of some 240 miles from Lewis's current location, a considerable journey to make in six days even for these mobile people. Innis, 234; Coues (NLEH), 2:705; Ewers (BRNP), 31; Glover, 79 n. 1.

[Lewis]   *July 27th 1806 Sunday.*

This morning at day light the indians got up and crouded around the fire, J. Fields who was on post had carelessly laid his gun down behid him near where his brother was sleeping, one of the indians the fellow to whom I had given the medal last evening sliped behind him and took his gun and that of his brothers unperceived by him, at the same instant two others advanced and seized the guns of Drewyer and myself, J. Fields seing this turned about to look for his gun and saw the fellow just runing off with her and his brothers he called to his brother who instantly jumped up and pursued the indian with him whom they overtook at the distance of 50 or 60 paces from the camp sized their guns and rested them from him and R Fields as he seized his gun stabed the indian to the heart with his knife   the fellow ran about 15 steps and fell dead;[1] of this I did not know untill afterwards, having recovered their guns they ran back instantly to the camp; Drewyer who was awake saw the indian take hold of his gun and instantly jumped up and sized her and rested her from him but the indian still retained his pouch, his jumping up and crying damn you let go my gun awakened me   I jumped up and asked what was the matter which I quickly learned when I saw drewyer in a scuffle with the indian for his gun. I reached to seize my gun but found her gone, I then drew a pistol from my holster and terning myself about saw the indian making off with my gun   I ran at him with my pistol and bid him lay down my gun ⟨at the instant⟩ which he was in the act of doing when the Fieldses returned and drew up their guns to shoot him which I forbid as he did not appear to be about to make any resistance or commit any offensive act, he droped the gun and walked slowly off, I picked her up instantly, Drewyer having about this time recovered his gun and pouch asked me if he might not kill the fellow which I also forbid as the indian did not appear to wish to kill us, as soon as they found us all in possession of our arms they ran and indeavored to drive off all the horses   I now hollowed to the men and told them to fire on them if they attempted to drive off our horses, they accordingly pursued the main party who were drving the horses up the river and I pursued the man who had taken my gun who with another was driving off a part of the horses which were to the left of the camp, I pursued them so closely that they could not take twelve of their own horses but continued to drive one of mine with some others; at the distance of three hundred paces they entered one of those steep nitches in the bluff with the horses before them   being nearly out of breath I could pursue no further, I called to them as I had done several times before that I would shoot them if they did not give me my horse and raised my gun, one of them jumped behind a rock and spoke to the other who turned arround and stoped at the distance of 30 steps from me and I shot him through the belly,[2] he fell to his knees and on his wright elbow from which position he partly raised himself up and fired at me, and turning himself about crawled in behind a rock which was a few

feet from him.   he overshot me, being bearheaded I felt the wind of his
bullet very distinctly.[3]   not having my shotpouch I could not reload my
peice and as there were two of them behind good shelters from me I did
not think it prudent to rush on them with my pistol which had I discharged I had not the means of reloading untill I reached camp; I therefore returned leasurely towards camp, on my way I met with Drewyer
who having heared the report of the guns had returned in surch of me
and left the Fieldes to pursue the indians, I desired him to haisten to the
camp with me and assist in catching as many of the indian horses as were
necessary and to call to the Fieldes if he could make them hear to come
back that we still had a sufficient number of horses, this he did but they
were too far to hear him.   we reached the camp and began to catch the
horses and saddle them and put on the packs.   the reason I had not my
pouch with me was that I had not time to return about 50 yards to camp
after geting my gun before I was obliged to pursue the indians or suffer
them to collect and drive off all the horses.   we had caught and saddled
the horses and began to arrange the packs when the Fieldses returned
with four of our horses; we left one of our horses and took four of the
best of those of the indian's; while the men were preparing the horses I
put four sheilds and two bows and quivers of arrows which had been left
on the fire, with sundry other articles; they left all their baggage at our
mercy.   they had but 2 guns and one of them they left   the others were
armed with bows and arrows and eyedaggs.[4]   the gun we took with us.
I also retook the flagg but left the medal about the neck of the dead man
that they might be informed who we were.   we took some of their buffaloe meat and set out ascending the bluffs by the same rout we had decended last evening leaving the ballance of nine of their horses which we
did not want.   the   Feildses told me that three of the indians whom they
pursued swam the river one of them on my horse.   and that two others
ascended the hill and escaped from them with a part of their horses, two I
had pursued into the nitch one lay dead near the camp and the eighth we
could not account for but suppose that he ran off early in the contest.
having ascended the hill we took our course through a beatiful level plain
a little to the S of East.   my design was to hasten to the entrance of Maria's river as quick as possible in the hope of meeting with the canoes and

party at that place having no doubt but that they would pursue us with a large party and as there was a band near the broken mountains or probably between them and the mouth of that river we might expect them to receive inteligence from us and arrive at that place nearly as soon as we could, no time was therefore to be lost and we pushed our horses as hard as they would bear.   at 8 miles we passed a large branch 40 yds. wide which I called battle river.[5]   at 3 P. M. we arrived at rose river about 5 miles above where we had passed it as we went out, having traveled by my estimate compared with our former distances and couses about 63 ms.[6] here we halted an hour and a half took some refreshment and suffered our horses to graize; the day proved warm but the late rains had supplyed the little reservors in the plains with water and had put them in fine order for traveling, our whole rout so far was as level as a bowling green with but little stone and few prickly pears.   after dinner we pursued the bottoms of rose river but finding inconvenient to pass the river so often we again ascended the hills on the S. W. side and took the open plains; by dark we had traveled about 17 miles further, we now halted to rest ourselves and horses about 2 hours, we killed a buffaloe cow and took a small quantity of the meat.   after refreshing ourselves we again set out by moon light and traveled leasurely, heavy thunderclouds lowered arround us on every quarter but that from which the moon gave us light.   we continued to pass immence herds of buffaloe all night as we had done in the latter part of the day.   we traveled untill 2 OCk in the morning having come by my estimate after dark about 20 ms.   we now turned out our horses and laid ourselves down to rest in the plain very much fatiegued as may be readily conceived.[7]   my indian horse carried me very well   in short much better than my own would have done and leaves me with but little reason to complain of the robery.

1. This man's name is variously given as He-that-looks-at-the-calf and Sidehill Calf. Ewers (BRNP), 48; Ronda (LCAI), 242; Wheeler, 2:311–12.

2. There is some doubt as to whether this man died of his wound or not, since the fragmentary evidence conflicts on whether one or two Piegans lost their lives. Apparently there is no doubt that the man stabbed by Reubin Field died. Bradley (MS), 135; Wheeler, 2:311–12; Glover, 273.

3. The Piegan almost certainly carried a North West trade musket, much less accurate

than Lewis's rifle; indeed, "30 steps" would be about the limit of accuracy for such a weapon. In any case, a man shot in the abdomen was unlikely to shoot very well. Ewers (ILUM), 34–44; Russell (GEF), 104–30, 162–64; Hanson.

4. A type of dagger or stabbing knife with a hole or eye in the handle for inserting a loop; see April 15, 1806.

5. Present Birch Creek in Pondera County, Montana, a tributary of Two Medicine River.

6. Heading southeasterly from the site of the fight, Lewis's party passed near present Conrad in Pondera County and reached the Teton (Rose) River in either northeast Teton County or western Chouteau County, Montana.

7. This camp was some miles west of Fort Benton in Chouteau County.

[Lewis] *July 28th 1806 Monday.*

The morning proved fair, I slept sound but fortunately awoke as day appeared, I awaked the men and directed the horses to be saddled, I was so soar from my ride yesterday that I could scarcely stand, and the men complained of being in a similar situation however I encourged them by telling them that our own lives as well as those of our friends and fellow travellers depended on our exertions at this moment; they were allert soon prepared the horses and we again resumed our march; the men proposed to pass the missouri at the grog spring[1] where rose river approaches it so nearly and pass down on the S. W. side, to this I objected as it would delay us almost all day to reach the point [*EC: mouth of Marias*] by this circuetous rout and would give the enemy time to surprise and cut off the party at the point if they had arrived there,[2] I told them that we owed much to the safety of our friends and that we must wrisk our lives on this occasion, that I should proceed immediately to the point and if the party had not arrived that I would raft the missouri a small distance above, hide our baggage and march on foot up the river through the timber untill I met the canoes or joined them at the falls; I now told them that it was my determination that if we were attacked in the plains on our way to the point that the bridles of the horses should be tied together and we would stand and defend them, or sell our lives as dear as we could. we had proceeded about 12[3] miles on an East course when we found ourselves near the missouri; we heared a report which we took to be that of a gun but were not certain; still continuing down the N. E. bank of the missouri about 8 miles further, being then within five miles of the grog spring we heared the report of several rifles very distinctly on the river to our right, we quickly repared to this joyfull sound and on arriving at the bank of the river had the unspeakable satisfaction to see our canoes coming down.[4] we hurried down from the bluff on which we were and joined them striped our horses and gave them a final discharge imbrarking without loss of time with our baggage. I now learned that they had brought all things safe having sustaned no loss nor met with any accident of importance. Wiser had cut his leg badly with a knife and was unable in consequence to work.[5] we decended the river opposite to our principal cash[6] which we proceeded to open after reconnoitering the adjacent country. we found that the cash had caved in and most of the articles burried therin were injured; I sustained the loss of two very large bear skins which I much regret; most of the fur and baggage belonging to the men were injured. the gunpowder corn flour poark and salt had sustained but little injury the parched meal was spoiled or nearly so. having no time to air these things which they much wanted we droped down to the point to take in the several articles which had been buried at that place in several small cashes;[7] these we found in good order, and recovered every article except 3 traps belonging to Drewyer which could not be found. here as good fortune would have it Sergt. Gass and Willard who brought the horses from the falls joined us at 1 P. M. I had ordered them to bring down the horses to this place in order to assist them in collecting meat which I had directed them to kill and dry here for our voyage, presuming that they would have arrived with the perogue and canoes at this place several days before my return. having now nothing to detain us we passed over immediately to the island in the entrance of Maria's river to launch the red perogue, but found her so much decayed that it was impossible with the means we had to repare her and therefore mearly took the nails and other ironwork's about her which might be of service to us and left her. we now reimbarked on board the white peroge and five small canoes and decended the river about 15 ms. and encamped on the S. W. side near a few cottonwood trees,[8] one of them being of the narrow leafed speceis and was the first of that kind which we had remarked on our passage up the river. we encamped late but having little meat I sent out a couple of hunters who soon returned with a sufficient quantity of the flesh of a fat cow.   there are immence quantities of buffaloe and Elk about the junction of the Missouri and Maria's rivers.—   during the time we halted at the entrance of Maria's river we experienced a very heavy shower of rain and hail attended with violent thunder and lightning.

1. The Grog Spring does not appear on any expedition maps, but it was located in Chouteau County, Montana, a few miles northeast of Fort Benton in the vicinity of the very close approach of the Teton and Missouri rivers to each other; see June 12, 1805. Grog is a mixture of rum and water.

2. Lewis's fear was that Blackfeet pursuing his party might instead encounter the group coming down the Missouri from the Great Falls and that this group, unaware of the danger, would be taken by surprise. He had to reach the mouth of the Marias, the designated rendezvous with this river party, in time to warn them.

3. This number is not entirely clear, since it appears possible that "2" was written over "9" or vice versa; Thwaites (LC), 5:227, has "12."

4. Lewis had left Sergeant Gass, Werner, Frazer, Thompson, McNeal, and Goodrich at the Great Falls on July 16, 1806, to recover materials from the caches and to portage around the falls. On July 19 Sergeant Ordway joined them at the White Bear Islands camp, having come down with canoes from the Three Forks where he had separated from Clark on July 13. Ordway's party consisted of Collins, Colter, Cruzatte, Howard, Lepage, Potts, Weiser, Whitehouse, and Willard. The two joined and came down the Missouri to meet Lewis. There is some question as to whether Lewis's dog Seaman was with this party or with Lewis's party on the Marias. Osgood (ODS), 15–17.

5. This occurred on July 23 while they were portaging around the falls, according to Ordway.

6. This cache in Chouteau County, between the Marias and the Missouri, was about a mile upriver from the camp of June 3–12, 1805. See Clark's entry of June 10, 1805. *Atlas* maps 42, 53, 61.

7. Located at the camp of June 3–12, 1805, at the mouth of the Marias in Chouteau County. *Atlas* maps 42, 53, 61.

8. Lewis's camp was on the south bank of the Missouri in Chouteau County, a little below the mouth of Crow Coulee. It is marked on *Atlas* map 42, which suggests that Lewis had this and the other original draft maps of the route from the Mandan villages to the Great Falls (*Atlas* maps 33–42) with him at this time. See Introduction to the *Atlas*, p. 9. MRC map 75.

[Lewis]   *Tuesday July 29th 1806.*

Shortly after dark last evening a violent storm came on from N. W. attended with rain hail Thunder and lightning which continued the greater part of the night.   no having the means of making a shelter I lay in the water all night.   the rain continued with but little intermission all day. I intend halting as soon as the weather proves fair in order to dry our baggage which much wants it.   I placed the two Fieldses and Colter and Collins in the two smallest canoes ⟨on⟩with orderes to hunt, and kill meat for the party and obtain as many Elkskins as are necessary to cover our canoes and furnish us with shelters from the rain.   we set out early and the currant being strong we proceeded with great rapidity.   at 11 A. M. we passed that very interesting part of the Missouri where the natural walls appear, particularly discribed in my outward bound journey.[1] we continued our rout untill late in the evening and encamped on the N. E. side of the river at the same place we had encamped on the 29th of May 1805.[2]   on our way today we killed 9 bighorns of which I preserved the skins and skeletons of 2 females and one male; the flesh of this anin-mal is extreemly delicate tender and well flavored, they are now in fine order.   their flesh both in colour and flavor much resembles mutton though it is not so strong as our mutton.   the eye is large and prominant, the puple of a pale sea green and iris of a light yellowish brown colour. these animals abound in this quarter keeping themselves principally con-fined to the steep clifts and bluffs of the river.   we saw immence hirds of buffaloe in the high plains today on either hand of the river.   saw but few Elk.   the brown Curloo has left the plains I presume it has raised it's young and retired to some other climate and country.   as I have been very particular in my discription of the country as I ascended this river I presume it is unnecesssesary here to add any-thing further on that sub-ject.   the river is now nearly as high as it has been this season and is so thick with mud and sand that it is with difficulty I can drink it.   every little rivulet now discharges a torrant of water bringing down immece boddies of mud sand and filth from the plains and broken bluffs.—

1. The Stone Walls and White Cliffs of the Missouri, in Chouteau County, Montana; see May 31, 1805. *Atlas* maps 41, 53, 60; MRC map 74.

2. Lewis's camp was in Chouteau County, on the north side of the Missouri about a mile above the mouth of Arrow Creek (Lewis and Clark's Slaughter River); as Lewis indi-cates, it is marked on *Atlas* map 41 at the site of the camp of May 29, 1805. MRC map 73.

[Lewis]   *Wednesday July 30th 1806.*

The rain still continued this morning it was therefore unnecessary to remain as we could not dry our baggage   I Consequently set out early as usual and pursued my rout downwards.   the currant being strong and the men anxious to get on they plyed their oars faithfully and we went at the rate of about seven miles an hour.   we halted several times in the course of the day to kill some bighorns being anxious to procure a few more skins and skeletons of this animal; I was fortunate enough to procure one other malle and female for this purpose which I had prepared accordingly.   seven others were killed by the party also 2 buffaloe one Elk 2 beaver with & a female brown bear with tallons 6¼ inches in length. I preserved the skin of this bear also with the tallons; it was not large and in but low order.   we arrived this evening at an island about 2 ms. above Goodriches Island and encamped on it's N. E. side.[1]   the rain continued with but little intermission all day; the air is cold and extreemly disagreeable.   nothing extraordinary happened today

1. *Atlas* map 40 seems to place Lewis's campsite on Goodrich's Island, just below the campsite of May 25, 1805. Ordway and Gass say the camp was on the island. However, Lewis's journal entry places the camp on the upriver side of the sharp bend above Goodrich's Island. His wording leaves it unclear whether he actually camped on the nameless island or on the bank northeast of it in Blaine County, Montana. This area is a few miles below Cow Creek and Cow Island Crossing. MRC map 71.

[Lewis]   *Thursday July 31st 1806.*

The rain still continuing I set out early and proceeded on as fast as possible.   at 9 A. M. we fell in with a large herd of Elk of which we killed 15 and took their skins.   the bottoms in the latter part of the day became wider better timbered and abound in game.   the party killed 14 deer in the course of the day without attempting to hunt but little for them.   we also killed 2 bighorns and 1 beaver; saw but few buffaloe.   the river is still rising and excessively muddy more so I think than I ever saw it.   we experienced some very heavy showers of rain today.   we have been passing high pine hills all day.   late in the evening we came too on the N. E. side of the river and took sheter in some indian lodges built of sticks, about 8 ms. below the entrance of North mountain creek.[1]   these lodges appeared to have been built in the course of the last winter.   these lodges with the addition of some Elk skins afforded us a good shelter from the rain which continued to fall powerfully all night. I think it probable that the minnetares of Fort de Prarie visit this part of the river; we meet with their old lodges in every bottom.—

1. Rock Creek, in Phillips County, Montana; see May 24, 1805. The course of the Missouri has changed considerably in this vicinity, so the mileage below the creek mouth may not now apply. The camp was in either Fergus or Phillips County. *Atlas* map 39; MRC map 70.

[Lewis]   [*Weather, July 1806*][1]

Day of the Month	State of the weather at ☉ rise	Wind at ☉ rise	State of the weather at 4 P. M.	Wind at 4 P. M.
1st	c a f	N W	f	N W
2cd	f	S E	f	S E
3rd	f	S E	f	N W
4th	f	S E	f	N W
5th	f	N E	f	S W
6th	f	N E	f	S W
7	c a r T & L.	S W	c a f & r	W
8th	f	S W	f	W.
9th	c a r	N. E.	r.	N. E.
10th	f a r	N W.	f	W.
11th	f	N W	f	N. W.
12th	f	N W	f	N W
13th	f	N E	f	N E
14th	f	S W	f	S W
15th	f	S W	f	E
16th	f	S W	f	S W
17th	f a T L	S W	f	S W
18th	f	S W	f	N E
19th	f	S E	f	N E
20th	f	E	f	N.
21st	f	N.	f	N. E.
22cd	f	S E	f	N. E.

23rd	f a T & L		S E		f		S W
24th	c a r T & L		N W		c a r t L		N W.
25th	c a r		N W		c a r		N W
26th	c a r		N		f		N W
27th	f		N W		f		S W
28th	f a r T & L.		N E		c a f h r T & L		N E
29th	r a r T & L—		S W		c a r		N E
30th	r a r		N E		r		N E
31st	c a r		N E		r		N W

[Remarks][2]

1st   a speceis of wild clover with a small leaf just in blume.

3rd   the turtle dove[3] lays it's eggs on the ground in these plains and is now seting, it has two eggs only and they are white.

5th   a great number of pigeons breeding in this part of the mountains musquetoes not so troblesome as near Clark's river. some ear flies[4] of the common kind and a few large horse flies.[5]

6th   the last night cold with a very heavy dew.

7   a cloud came on about sunset and continued to rain moderately all night. rained at 3 P. M.

8th   heavy white frost last night. very cold.

9th   rained slightly last night. air cold. rained constantly all day air extreemly cold it began to rain about 8 A. M. and continued with but little intermission all day in the evening late it abated and we obtained a view of the mountains we had just passed they were covered with snow apparrently several feet deep which had fallen during this day.—

10th   rain ceased a little after dark.

11th   wind very hard in the latter part of the day

12th   wind violent all last night and today untill 5 P. M. when it ceased in some measure

16th   Saw the Cookkoo or rain crow and the redheaded woodpecker.[6] the golden rye[7] now heading. both species of the prickly pare[8] in blume.— the sunflower in blume.

17th   wind violent all day. distant thunder last evening to the West.

23rd   a distant thundercloud last evening to the west.   mountains covered with snow.

24th   a violent gust of thunder Lightning last evening at 6 P. M.   rain and wind all night untill this evening with some intervales.

25th   rained and wind violent all day and night.

26th   wind violent   rain continues.

28th   a thundershower last night from N. W. but little rain where we were. heavy hail storm at 3 P. M.   the prickly pear has now cast it's blume

29th   heavy rain last night, continued with small intervales all night

30th   rained almost without intermission

31st   do   do   do   do

1. Since Lewis and Clark separated on July 3 and were apart for the rest of the month, their weather observations for most of the month are unrelated; therefore they appear separately, without notice of discrepancies. Lewis's table is in Codex L, pp. 146, 148 (reading backwards). Coues's penciled page number for 148 is mislabeled as "page 147."

2. Lewis's remarks in Codex L appear both in the margin of his weather table and separately.

3. The mourning dove.

4. Probably deer fly, *Chrysops* sp.

5. Horse fly, *Tabanus* sp.

6. Red-headed woodpecker, *Melanerpes erythrocephalus* [AOU, 406].

7. Some unknown species of *Elymus*.

8. See Lewis's entry of July 10, 1806.

[Lewis]   *Friday August 1st 1806.*

The rain still continuing I set out early as usual and proceeded on at a good rate.   at 9 A. M. we saw a large brown bear swiming from an island to the main shore we pursued him and as he landed Drewyer and myself shot and killed him; we took him on board the perogue and continued our rout.   at 11 A. M. we passed the entrance of Mussel shell river.[1]   at 1 in the evening we arrived at a bottom on S. W. side where there were several spacious Indian lodges built of sticks and an excellent landing. as the rain still continued with but little intermission and appearances seemed unfavorable to it's becomeing fair shortly, I determined to halt at this place at least for this evening and indeavour to dry my skins of the bighorn which had every appearance of spoiling, an event which I would not should happen on any consideration as we have now passed the country in which they are found and I therefore could not supply the deficiency were I to loose these I have. I halted at this place being about 15 ms. below Missel shell river,[2] had fires built in the lodges and my skins exposed to dry. shortly after we landed the rain ceased tho' it still continued cloudy all this evening. a white bear came within 50 paces of our camp before we perceived it; it stood erect on it's hinder feet and looked at us with much apparent unconsern, we seized our guns which are always by us and several of us fired at it and killed it. it was a female in fine order, we fleesed it and extracted several gallons of oil. this speceis of bar are rearly as poor at this season of the year as the common black bear nor are they ever as fat as the black bear is found in winter; as they feed principally on flesh, like the wolf, they are most fatt when they can procure a sufficiency of food without rispect to the season of the year. the oil of this bear is much harder than that of the black bear being nearly as much so as the lard of a hog. the flesh is by no means as agreeable as that of the black bear, or Yahkah or partycoloured bear[3] of the West side of the rocky mountains. on our way today we killed a buck Elk in fine order the skins and a part of the flesh of which we preserved. after encamping this evening the hunters killed 4 deer and a beaver. The Elk are now in fine order particularly the males. their horns have obtained their full growth but have not yet shed the velvet or skin which covers them. the does are found in large herds with their young and a few young bucks with them. the old bucks yet herd together in parties of two to 7 or 8.—

1. Musselshell River, on the Petroleum-Garfield County line, Montana; see May 20, 1805. *Atlas* map 39; MRC map 69.

2. This camp was in Petroleum or Phillips County, some two to three miles below the camp of May 19, 1805, just above what was later called Horseshoe Point. The area is now inundated by Fort Peck Reservoir. They remained here until August 3. *Atlas* map 38; MRC map 68.

3. The Yahkah is the cinnamon phase of the black bear; see May 31 and June 20, 1806. Here Lewis seems to use "partycolored" for the same bear, but perhaps he means the grizzly, which he calls the "variagated" bear on May 14, 1806.

[Lewis]   *Saturday August 2cd 1806.*

The morning proved fair and I determined to remain all day and dry the baggage and give the men an opportunity to dry and air their skins and furr.   had the powder parched meal and every article which wanted drying exposed to the sun.   the day proved warm fair and favourable for our purpose. I permitted the Fieldses to go on a few miles to hunt. by evening we had dryed our baggage and repacked it in readiness to load and set out early in the morning.   the river fell 18 inches since yesterday evening.   the hunters killed   several deer in the course of the day.   nothing remarkable took place today.   we are all extreemly anxious to reach the entrance of the Yellowstone river where we expect to join Capt. Clark and party.

[Lewis]   *Saturday August 3rd 1806.*

I arrose early this morning and had the perogue and canoes loaded and set out at half after 6 A. M.   we soon passed the canoe of Colter and Collins who were on shore hunting, the men hailed them but received no answer we proceeded, and shortly after overtook J. and R. Fields who had killed 25 deer since they left us yesterday; deer are very abundant in the timbered bottoms of the river and extreemly gentle.   we did not halt today to cook and dine as usual having directed that in future the party should cook as much meat in the evening after encamping as would be sufficient to serve them the next day; by this means we forward our journey at least 12 or 15 miles Pr. day.   we saw but few buffaloe in the course of this day, tho' a great number of Elk, deer, wolves, some bear, beaver, geese a few ducks, the party coloured covus,[1] one Callamet Eagle,[2] a number of bald Eagles,[3] red headed woodpeckers &c.   we encamped this evening on N. E. side of the river 2 ms. above our encampment of the 12th of May 1805.[4]   soon after we encamp Drewyer killed a fat doe.   the Fieldses arrived at dark with the flesh of two fine bucks, besides which they had killed two does since we passed them making in all 29 deer since yesterday morning. Collins and Colter did not overtake us this evening.

1. The black-billed magpie, *Pica pica* [AOU, 475].
2. Golden eagle, *Aquila chrysaetos* [AOU, 349].

3. Bald eagle, *Haliaeetus leucocephalus* [AOU, 352].

4. On the north side of the Missouri in Valley County, Montana, below the mouth of Cattle Creek, as Lewis notes about two miles above the camp of May 12, 1805. The site is now inundated by Fort Peck Reservoir. *Atlas* map 38; MRC map 66.

[Lewis]   *Monday August 4th 1806.*

Set out at 4 A. M. this morning.   permited Willard and Sergt. Ordway to exchange with the Feildses and take their small canoe to hunt today.   at ½ after eleven O'Ck. passed the entrance of big dry river;[1] found the water in this river about 60 yds. wide tho' shallow.   it runs with a boald even currant.   at 3 P. M. we arrived at the entrance of Milk river[2] where we halted a few minutes.   this stream is full at present and it's water is much the colour of that of the Missouri; it affords as much water at present as Maria's river and I have no doubt extends itself to a considerable distance North.   during our halt we killed a very large rattlesnake of the speceis common to our country.[3]   it had 176 scuta on the abdomen and 25 on the tail, it's length 5 feet.   the scutae on the tail fully formed.   after passing this river we saw several large herds of buffaloe and Elk   we killed one of each of these animals and took as much of the flesh as we wished.   we encamped this evening two miles below the gulph on the N. E. side of the river.[4] Tonight for the first time this season I heard the small whippoorwill or goatsucker of the Missouri cry.[5] Colter and Collins have not yet overtaken us. Ordway and Willard delayed so much time in hunting today that they did not overtake us untill about midnight.   they killed one bear and 2 deer.   in passing a bend just below the gulph it being dark they were drawn by the currant in among a parsel of sawyers,[6] under one of which the canoe was driven and throwed Willard who was steering overboard; he caught the sawyer and held by it; Ordway with the canoe drifted down about half a mile among the sawyers under a falling bank, the canoe struck frequently but did not overset; he at length gained the shore and returned by land to learn the fate of Willard whom he found was yet on the sawyer; it was impossible for him to take the canoe to his relief   Willard at length tied a couple of sticks together which had lodged against the sawyer on which he was and set himself a drift among the sawyers which he fortunately escaped and was taken up about a mile below by Ordway with the canoe; they sustained no loss on this occasion. it was fortunate for Willard that he could swim tolerably well.—

1. Present Big Dry Creek, in Garfield County, Montana. *Atlas* map 37; MRC map 65.

2. On Milk River, meeting the Missouri in Valley County, Montana, see May 8, 1805. *Atlas* map 37; MRC map 65.

3. Perhaps the prairie rattlesnake, *Crotalus viridus viridus*. Benson (HLCE), 90.

4. The camp was in Valley or McCone County, Montana, some two miles above the camp of May 7, 1805. *Atlas* map 37; MRC map 64.

5. Common poorwill, *Phalaenoptilus nuttallii* [AOU, 418]. Holmgren, 34; Burroughs, 236.

6. A submerged tree with a portion sticking out of the water and cutting the river in a sawing fashion, thus a navigational hazard.

[Lewis]   *Tuesday August 5th 1806.*

Colter and Collins not having arrived induced me to remain this morning for them. the hunters killed four deer this morning near our encampment. I remained untill noon when I again reimbarked and set out concluding that as Colter and Collins had not arrived by that time that they had passed us after dark the night of the 3rd inst. as Sergt Ordway informed me he should have done last evening had not the centinel hailed him. we continued our rout untill late in the evening when I came too and encamped on the South side about 10 miles below little dry river.[1] on our way we killed a fat cow and took as much of the flesh as was necessary for us. The Feildses killed 2 large bear this evening one of them measured nine feet from the extremity of the nose to that of his tail, this is the largest bear except one that I have seen. we saw several bear today as we passed but did not kill any of them. we also saw on our way immence herds of buffaloe & Elk, many deer Antelopes, wolves, geese Eagles &c. but few ducks or prarie hens.[2] the geese cannot fly at present; I saw a solitary Pillacon[3] the other day in the same situation. this happens from their sheding or casting the fathers of the wings at this season.

1. Prairie Elk Creek in McCone County, Montana; see May 6, 1805. The camp was in McCone County, some four miles southwest of the present town of Wolf Point. *Atlas* map 36; MRC maps 63, 64.

2. Perhaps the greater prairie-chicken, *Tympanuchus cupido pinnatus* [AOU, 305]. Burroughs, 211; Holmgren, 29.

3. American white pelican, *Pelecanus erythrorhynchos* [AOU, 125]. Burroughs, 179; Holmgren, 32.

[Lewis]   *Wednesday August 6th 1806.*

A little after dark last evening a violent storm arrose to the N. E. and shortly after came on attended with violent Thunder lightning and some hail; the rain fell in a mere torrant and the wind blew so violently that it was with difficulty I could have the small canoes unloaded before they filled with water; they sustained no injury.   our situation was open and exposed to the storm.   in attending to the canoes I got wet to the skin and having no shelter on land I betook myself to the orning of the perogue which I had, formed of Elkskin, here I obtained a few hours of broken rest; the wind and rain continued almost all night and the air became very cold.   we set out early this morning and decended the river about 10 miles below Porcupine river[1] when the wind became so violent that I laid by untill 4 P. M.   the wind then abaiting in some measure we again resumed our voyage, and decended the river about 5 miles below our encampment of the 1st of May 1805 where we halted for the night on the S. W. side of the river.[2]   after halting we killed three fat cows and a buck.   we had previously killed today 4 deer a buck Elk and a fat cow. in short game is so abundant and gentle that we kill it when we please. the Feildses went on ahead this evening and we did not overtake them. we saw several bear in the course of the day.—

1. Poplar River, in Roosevelt County, Montana; see May 3, 1805. *Atlas* map 36; MRC map 62.

2. Lewis camped in Richland County, Montana, some ten miles east of the present town of Poplar. *Atlas* map 36; MRC map 62.

[Lewis]   *Thursday August 7th 1806.*

It began to rain about midnight and continued with but little intermission until 10 A. M. today.   the air was cold and extreemly unpleasant. we set out early resolving if possible to reach the Yelowstone river today which was at the distance of 83 ms. from our encampment of the last evening; the currant favoured our progress being more rapid than yesterday, the men plied their oars faithfully and we went at a good rate. at 8 A. M. we passed the entrance of Marthy's river[1] which has changed it's entrance since we passed it last year, falling in at preasent about a quarter of a mile lower down. at or just below the entrance of this river we meet with the first appearance of Coal birnt hills and pumicestone,[2] these appearances seem to be coextensive. here it is also that we find the first Elm[3] and dwarf cedar[4] on the bluffs, the ash[5] first appears in the instance of one solletary tree at the Ash rapid, about the Elk rapid[6] and from thence down we occasionly meet with it scattered through the bottoms but it is generally small. from Marthy's river to Milk river on the N. E. side there is a most beautifull level plain country; the soil is much more fertile here than above.[7] we overtook the Feildses at noon. they had killed 2 bear and seen 6 others, we saw and fired on two from our perogue but killed neither of them. these bear resort the river where they lie in wate at the crossing places of the game for the Elk and weak cattle; when they procure a subject of either they lie by the carcase and keep the wolves off untill they devour it. the bear appear to be very abundant on this part of the river. we saw a number of buffaloe Elk &c as we passed but did not detain to kill any of them. we also saw an unusual flight of white gulls about the size of a pigeon with the top of their heads black.[8] at 4 P. M. we arrived at the entrance of the Yellowstone river.[9] I landed at the point and found that Capt. Clark had been encamped at this place and ⟨was gone⟩ from appearances had left it about 7 or 8 days. I found a paper on a pole at the point which mearly contained my name in the hand wrighting of Capt. C. we also found the remnant of a note which had been attatched to a peace of Elk's horns in the camp; from this fragment I learned that game was scarce at the point and musquetoes troublesome which were the reasons given for his going on; I also learnt that he intended halting a few miles below where he intended waiting my arrival. I now wrote a note directed to Colter and Collins provided they were behind, ordering them to come on without loss of time; this note I wraped in leather and attatced onto the same pole which Capt. C. had planted at the point; this being done I instantly reimbarked and decended the river in the hope of reaching Capt. C's camp before night. about 7 miles below the point on the S. W. shore I saw some meat that had been lately fleased and hung on a pole; I directed Sergt. Ordway to go on shore examine the place; on his return he reported that he saw the tracks of two men which appeared so resent that he beleived they had been there today, the fire he found at the plce was blaizing and appeared to have been mended up afresh or within the course of an hour past.   he found at this place a part of a Chinnook hat which my men recognized as the hat of Gibson;[10] from these circumstances we included that Capt. C's camp could not be distant and pursued our rout untill dark with the hope of reaching his camp in this however we were disappointed and night coming on compelled us to encamp on the N. E. shore in the next bottom above our encampment of the 23rd and 24th of April 1805.[11]   as we came too a herd of buffaloe assembled on the shore of which we killed a fat cow.—

1. Big Muddy Creek, in Roosevelt County, Montana; see April 29, 1805. It is labeled "50 yds wide Handson vallie" on *Atlas* map 35; see *Atlas* map 48. MRC map 61.

2. The coal-bearing Fort Union Formation borders the Missouri River for about fifteen miles upstream from the mouth of Big Muddy Creek, but the Missouri River valley is wider upstream from that creek than it is below, so the coal easily could have been missed. The burnt hills and "pumicestone" (clinker) are produced by the burning of the coal beds. It was probably Biddle who drew a red vertical line through this geological material and the passages about trees.

3. American elm, *Ulmus americana* L. Little (CIH), 196-W.

4. Creeping juniper, *Juniperus horizontalis* Moench. It was collected in 1804 with two other juniper species. Cutright (LCPN), 105, 127, 373.

5. Green ash, *Fraxinus pennsylvanica* Marsh., extends up the Missouri River into Fergus and Chouteau counties, Montana. Little (CIH), 130-W.

6. For Ash and Elk Fawn Rapids, see *Atlas* maps 52, 60; the first lies in Chouteau and Fergus counties, the second in Fergus and Blaine counties.

7. The terrace that borders the northern edge of the Missouri River between the Milk and Poplar rivers was formed in preglacial times when the Missouri River occupied a position more to the north than it does at present. The terrace north of the river from the Poplar River to fifteen miles upstream from Big Muddy Creek is poorly developed and was formed during the late Pleistocene.

8. Identified by Coues (HLC), 3:1112–13 n. 20, as Forster's tern, *Sterna forsteri* [AOU, 69]. Holmgren, 30, adds Bonaparte's gull, *Larus philadelphia* [AOU, 60], as a possibility. See also March 6, 1806.

9. Lewis's party has returned to North Dakota, where the Yellowstone enters the Missouri in McKenzie County. *Atlas* maps 35, 48, 56; MRC map 60. Clark left his note to Lewis on August 4, 1806; see his entry for that date.

10. The captains purchased an unknown number of hats made of cedar bark from some Clatsop women on February 22, 1806, and distributed them among the party. Evidently at least one was still being worn over five months later.

11. This camp was in Williams County, North Dakota, a few miles south of present Trenton. *Atlas* map 35; MRC map 59.

[Lewis]   *Friday August 8th 1806.*[1]

Beleiving from the recent appearances about the fire which we past last evening that Capt Clark could be at no great distance below I set out early; the wind ⟨by⟩ heard from the N. E. but by the force of the oars and currant we traveled at a good rate untill 10 A. M. by which time we reached the center of the beaver bends about 8 ms. by water and 3 by land above the entrance of White earth river.[2]   not finding Capt. Clark I knew not what calculation to make with rispect to his halting and therefore determined to proceed as tho' he was not before me and leave the rest to the chapter of accedents.   at this place I found a good beach for the purpose of drawing out the perogue and one of the canoes which wanted corking and reparing.   the men with me have not had leasure since we left the West side of the Rocky mountains to dress any skins or make themselves cloaths and most of them are therefore extreemly bare. I therefore determined to halt at this place untill the perogue and canoe could be repared and the men dress skins and make themselves the necessary cloathing.   we encamped on the N. E. side of the river;[3] we found the Musquetoes extreemly troublesome but in this rispect there is but little choise of camps from hence down to St. Louis.   from this place to the little Missouri there is an abundance of game   I shall therefore when I leave this place travel at my leasure and avail myself of every opportunity to collect and dry meat untill I provide a sufficient quantity for our voyage not knowing what provision Capt C. has made in this rispect. I formed a camp unloaded the canoes and perogue, had the latter and one of the canoes drawn out to dry, fleased what meat we had collected and hung it on poles in the sun, after which the men busied themselves in dressing skins and making themselves cloaths. Drewyer killed 2 Elk and a deer this evening.   the air is cold yet the Musquetoes continue to be troublesome.—

1. Here end the daily entries in Codex L; the remainder consists of weather diaries for June, July, and August (through the twelfth), 1806. Immediately following this entry is a notation by Clark: "a Suplt. to Come in here." The reference is to Codex Lb, which contains Lewis's last few daily entries; see Appendix C, vol. 2. On the end flyleaf is the following notation in Lewis's hand (see August 12, 1806, for information about these men):

Joseph Dickson } from the Illinois the former
Forrest Hancock } the latter from Boon's settlement

2. In Williams and McKenzie counties, North Dakota, above present Williston. "White earth river" is present Little Muddy River, in Williams County; see April 21, 1805. *Atlas* map 35; MRC map 59.

3. In Williams County, several miles southwest of Williston. *Atlas* map 35; MRC map 59.

[Lewis]   *Saturday August 9th 1806.*[1]

The day proved fair and favourable for our purposes. the men were all engaged dressing skins and making themselves cloathes except R & J. Fields whom I sent this morning over the river with orders to proceed to the entrance of the White earth river in surch of Capt. C. and to hunt and kill Elk or buffaloe should they find any convenient to the river. in the evening these men returned and informed me that they saw no appearance of Capt. Clark or party. they found no game nor was there a buffaloe to be seen in the plains as far as the eye could reach. nothing remarkable took place in the course of the day. Colter and Collins have not yet overtaken us I fear some missfortune has happened them for their previous fidelity and orderly deportment induces me to beleive that they would not thus intentionally delay.[2] the Perogue is not yet sufficiently dry for reparing. we have no pitch and will therefore be compelled to use coal and tallow.

1. Here begins Lewis's journal Codex Lb, consisting of pages torn from one of the red notebooks. It runs only to August 12, after which Lewis ceased writing because of the discomfort of the wound he received on August 11. See Appendix C, vol. 2.

2. Evidently Collins's "deportment" had improved greatly since the early days of the expedition; see vol. 2.

[Lewis]   *Sunday August 10th 1806.*

The morning was somewhat cloudy I therefore apprehended rain however it shortly after became fair. I hastened the repairs which were necessary to the perogue and canoe which were compleated by 2 P. M. those not engaged about this business employed themselves as yesterday. at 4 in the evening it clouded up and began to rain which puting a stop to the opperation of skindressing we had nothing further to detain us, I therefore directed the vessels to be loaded and at 5 P. M. got under way the wind has blown very hard all day but did not prove so much so this evening as absolutely to detain us. we decended this evening as low nearly as the entrance of white Earth river and encamped on the S. W. side.[1] the musquetoes more than usually troublesome this evening.

1. Lewis's camp was in McKenzie County, North Dakota, nearly opposite present Williston and a little above Little Muddy River. The site is probably inundated by Garrison Reservoir (Lake Sakakawea); it would be just above the camp of April 21, 1805. *Atlas* map 34; MRC map 59.

[Lewis]   *Monday August 11th 1806.*

We set out very early this morning. it being my wish to arrive at the birnt hills[1] by noon in order to take the latitude of that place as it is the most northern point of the Missouri, enformed the party of my design and requested that they would exert themselves to reach the place in time as it would save us the delay of nearly one day; being as anxious to get forward as I was they plyed their oars faithfully and we proceeded rapidly. I had instructed the small [c]anoes that if they saw any game on the river to halt and kill it and follow on; however we saw but little game untill about 9 A. M. when we came up with a buffaloe swiming the river which I shot and killed; leaving the small canoes to dress it and bring on the meat I proceeded. we had gone but little way before I saw a very large grizzly bear and put too in order to kill it, but it took wind of us and ran off. the small canoes overtook us and informed that the flesh of the buffaloe was unfit for uce and that they had therefore left it half after 11 A. M. we saw a large herd of Elk on the N. E. shore and I directed the men in the small canoes to halt and kill some of them and continued on in the perogue to the birnt hills; when I arrived here it was about 20 minutes after noon and of course the observation for the ☉'s meridian Altitude was lost; jus opposite to the birnt hills there happened to be a herd of Elk on a thick willow bar and finding that my observation was lost for the present I determined to land and kill some of them   accordingly we put too and I went out with Cruzatte only.[2]   we fired on the Elk I killed one and he wounded another, we reloaded our guns and took different routs through the thick willows in pursuit of the Elk; I was in the act of firing on the Elk a second time when a ball struck my left thye about an inch below my hip joint, missing the bone it passed through the left thye and cut the thickness of the bullet across the hinder part of the right thye; the stroke was very severe; I instantly supposed that Cruzatte had shot me in mistake for an Elk as I was dressed in brown leather and he cannot see very well; under this impression I called out to him damn you, you have shot me, and looked towards the place from whence the ball had come, seeing nothing I called Cruzatte several times as loud as I could but received no answer; I was now preswaded that it was an indian that had shot me as the report of the gun did not appear to be more than 40 paces from me and Cruzatte appeared to be out of hearing of me; in this situation not knowing how many indians there might be concealed in the bushes I thought best to make good my retreat to the perogue, calling out as I ran for the first hundred paces as loud as I could to Cruzatte to retreat that there were indians hoping to allarm him in time to make his escape also; I still retained the charge in my gun which I was about to discharge at the moment the ball struck me.   when I arrived in sight of the perogue I called the men to their arms to which they flew in an instant, I told them that I was wounded but I hoped not mortally, by an indian I beleived and directed them to follow me that I would return & give them battle and releive Cruzatte if possible who I feared had fallen into their hands; the men followed me as they were bid and I returned about a hundred paces when my wounds became so painfull and my thye so stiff that I could scarcely get on; in short I was compelled to halt and ordered the men to proceed and if they found themselves overpowered by numbers to retreat in order keeping up a fire. I now got back to the perogue as well as I could and prepared my self with a pistol my rifle and air-gun being determined as a retreat was impracticable to sell my life as deerly as possible.   in this state of anxiety and suspense remained about 20 minutes when the party returned with Cruzatte and reported that there were no indians nor the appearance of any; Cruzatte seemed much allarmed and declared if he had shot me it was not his intention, that he had shot an Elk in the willows after he left or seperated from me. I asked him whether he did not hear me when I called to him so frequently which he absolutely denied. I do not beleive that the fellow did it intentionally but after finding that he had shot me was anxious to conceal his knowl-edge of having done so.[3] the ball had lodged in my breeches which I knew to be the ball of the short rifles such as that he had,[4] and there being no person out with me but him and no indians that we could discover I have no doubt in my own mind of his having shot me. with the assis-tance of Sergt. Gass I took off my cloaths and dressed my wounds myself as well as I could, introducing tents of patent lint into the ball holes,[5] the wounds blead considerably but I was hapy to find that it had touched nei-ther bone nor artery. I sent the men to dress the two Elk which Cruzatte and myself had killed which they did in a few minutes and brought the meat to the river. the small canoes came up shortly after with the flesh of one Elk. my wounds being so situated that I could not without in-finite pain make an observation I determined to relinquish it and pro-ceeded on. we came within eight miles of our encampment of the 15th of April 1805 and encamped on N. E. side.[6] as it was painfull to me to be removed I slept on board the perogue; the pain I experienced excited a high fever and I had a very uncomfortable night. at 4 P. M. we passed an encampment which had been evacuated this morning by Capt. Clark, here I found a note from Capt. C. informing me that he had left a letter for me at the entrance of the Yelow stone river, but that Sergt. Pryor who had passed that place since he left it had taken the letter; that Sergt. Pryor having been robed of all his horses had decended the Yelowstone river in skin canoes and had over taken him at this encampment. this I fear puts an end to our prospects of obtaining the Sioux Cheifs to accom-pany us as we have not now leasure to send and enjage Mr. Heney on this service, or at least he would not have time to engage them to go as early as it is absolutely necessary we should decend the river.

1. The present Crow Hills in southeastern Williams County, North Dakota, which they had passed on April 17, 1805. *Atlas* map 34; MRC map 58.

2. This area in McKenzie County, North Dakota, opposite the Crow Hills, would now be inundated by Garrison Reservoir. *Atlas* map 34; MRC map 58.

3. Both Ordway and Gass seem to believe that Cruzatte was entirely ignorant of having shot Lewis; see their entries for this day.

4. The .54 caliber Model 1803 rifle.

5. As noted in another instance on May 5, 1806, the tents were rolls of lint used to keep the wound open to allow new tissue to grow from the inside out and promote drainage. Lewis was fortunate to escape serious infection. Cutright (LCPN), 285, 324; Chuinard (OOMD), 392–94.

6. Lewis camped in southwestern Mountrail County, North Dakota, a little above the mouth of present White Earth River. The site would now be inundated by Garrison Reservoir. *Atlas* map 34; MRC map 57.

[Lewis]   *Thursday August 12th 1806.*[1]

Being anxious to overtake Capt. Clark who from the appearance of his camps could be at no great distance before me, we set out early and proceeded with all possible expedition   at 8 A. M. the bowsman informed me that there was a canoe and a camp he beleived of whitemen on the N. E. shore. I directed the perogue and canoes to come too at this place and found it to be the camp of two hunters from the Illinois by name Joseph Dickson and Forest Hancock.[2] these men informed me that Capt. C. had passed them about noon the day before. they also informed me that they had left the Illinois in the summer 1804 since which time they had been ascended the Missouri, hunting and traping beaver; that they had been robed by the indians and the former wounded last winter by the Tetons of the birnt woods;[3] that they had hitherto been unsuccessfull in their voyage having as yet caught but little beaver, but were still determined to proceed. I gave them a short discription of the Missouri, a list of distances to the most conspicuous streams and remarkable places on the river above and pointed out to them the places where the beaver most abounded. I also gave them a file and a couple of pounds of powder with some lead.   these were articles which they assured me they were in great want of. I remained with these men an hour and a half when I took leave of them and proceeded.   ⟨at one OCK in the⟩ while I halted with these men Colter and Collins who seperated from us on the 3rd ist. rejoined us.   they were well no accedent having happened.   they informed me that after proceeding the first day and not overtaking us that they had concluded that we were behind and had delayed several days in waiting for us and had thus been unable to join us untill the present momet. my wounds felt very stiff and soar this morning but gave me no considerable pain. there was much less inflamation than I had reason to apprehend there would be. I had last evening applyed a poltice of peruvian barks.[4] at 1 P. M. I overtook Capt. Clark and party and had the pleasure of finding them all well.[5] as wrighting in my present situation is extreemly painfull to me I shall desist untill I recover and leave to my frind Capt. C. the continuation of our journal.[6] however I must notice a singular Cherry[7] which is found on the Missouri in the bottom lands about the beaverbends and some little distance below the white earth river. this production is not very abundant even in the small tract of country to which it seems to be confined. the stem is compound erect and subdivided or branching without any regular order it rises to the hight of eight or ten feet seldom puting up more than one stem from the same root not growing in cops as the Choke Cherry dose. the bark is smooth and of a dark brown colour. the leaf is peteolate, oval accutely pointed at it's apex, from one and a ¼ to 1 ½ inches in length and from ½ to ¾ of an inch in width, finely or minutely serrate, pale green and free from bubessence. the fruit is a globular berry about the size of a buck-shot of a fine scarlet red; like the cherries cultivated in the U' States each is supported by a seperate celindric flexable branch peduncle which issue from the extremities of the boughs the peduncle of this cherry swells as it approahes the fruit being largest at the point of insertion. the pulp of this fruit is of an agreeable ascid flavour and is now ripe. the style and stigma[8] are permanent. I have never seen it in blume.

1. Lewis's journalizing in Codex Lb, and for the expedition, ends at this entry. There follows a note by Clark: "To be anexed to Book No. 12 at the last." Book No. 12 is Biddle's designation for Codex L. Coues has added the dates of Codex Lb, "Aug. 9–12 1806."

2. Joseph Dickson, or Dixon, having lived in Pennsylvania and Tennessee, settled in Cahokia, Illinois, with his wife and children in 1802; he spent much of his time hunting and trapping in Missouri, where he met Forrest Hancock, who had come to Boone's Settlement in 1799. The two started up the Missouri in August 1804; they may have spent the following winter in the vicinity of Sioux City, Iowa. The next year they worked with the trader Charles Courtin, wintering in Teton Sioux country. Their meeting with Clark on this day (see Clark's entry), was the expedition party's first direct contact with the European world since April 1805. John Colter, who may have known Dickson before, persuaded the captains to let him join the two in a trapping venture to the Yellowstone, in

what has become known as the "Fourth Expedition" to the region, those of Charles LeRaye (which is highly questionable), François Antoine Larocque, and Clark being the first three. How far up the Yellowstone they traveled is not known, but the party broke up over some dispute and Colter and Hancock returned to the Mandan villages. Dickson spent the winter of 1806–7 alone on the Yellowstone, enduring great hardship. On his journey downriver in the spring, he barely escaped the hostility of the Arikaras. Thereafter he remained in Illinois and became a highly respectable citizen, having "got religion" as a result of his suffering in the Rockies. Dickson (HH); Dickson (JD); Harris, 33–58 (which varies considerably from other accounts).

3. The Brulé, or Bois Brulé, Sioux; see September 24, 1804, and Fort Mandan Miscellany, in vol. 3.

4. Peruvian bark, or *cinchona*, was a general remedy for fevers. Chuinard (OOMD), 65, 156–57 n. 8.

5. The two parties reunited at the place Clark had halted for lunch, in Mountrail County, North Dakota, some six miles south of present Sanish. The site does not appear on any *Atlas* map, but it was below Little Knife River (the captains' Goat Pen Creek). The site is now inundated by Garrison Reservoir. Mattison (GR), 49–50; *Atlas* map 34; MRC map 56.

6. In fact, Lewis never resumed writing his journals after this date.

7. Lewis's last botanical description in the journals is of the pin, or bird, cherry, *Prunus pensylvanica* L. f. It is a biogeographically interesting species of the northern Midwest that is more common in the East, with relic populations in the Black Hills of South Dakota and in the Colorado front range of the Rockies. The specimen he described here may be the one in the Lewis and Clark herbarium, Academy of Natural Sciences, Philadelphia. The cherry "cultivated in the U' States" he used for comparison is probably black cherry, *P. serotina* Ehrh. Barkley, 148; Cutright (LCPN), 325–26.

8. Coues patched the damaged page at this point with a two-cent postage stamp (Scott #220) bearing the words "Dec. 20 1892 Coues." He also used a portion of the stamp to patch another tear a few pages earlier.

[Lewis]   [*Weather, August 1806*][1]

day of the month	State of the weather at ⊙ rise	Wind at ⊙ rise	State of the weather at 4 P. M.	Wind at 4 P. M.
1st	r a r	N E	r a r	N W
2cd	f a r	N W	f.	N W
3rd	f	S E	f.	S E
4th	f	S E	f.	S E
5th	c a f	N W	f.	S. E.
6th	f a r T & L	N. E.	f.	N. E.
7th	r a r	N E	c a r	N E

8th	f	N. E	f	N E
9th	f	N E	f.	S. E.
10th	f	N. E	c a r	N E
11th	f	N. E	f.	N W
12th	f	N W		

[*Remarks*]²

2cd   it became fair soon after dark last evening and continued so.—

6th   a violent gust of Thunder Lightning wind and hail last night.

7th   rained from 12 last night untill 10 A M today—.

8th   wind hard but not so much so as to detain us.—

9th   heavy dew last night.   air cold.

10th   a slight shower about 3 P. M.   wind hard.

11th   air cool this evening   wind hard.

12th   wind violent last night.

1. Lewis's weather table for August 1806 is in Codex L, p. 145. He apparently ceased keeping it after his reunion with Clark on August 12, as with his other journal-keeping, due to the wound he received on the eleventh. Clark's weather table appears separately at the end of the month in Chapter 39.

2. These remarks are found only in the margin of Lewis's weather table.

Chapter Thirty-Eight

Clark's Exploration of the Yellowstone

July 3–August 12, 1806

[Clark]   *Thursday July 3rd 1806*

we colected our horses and after brackfast. I took My leave of Capt
Lewis and the indians and at 8 A M Set out with [*blank*] men[1] interpreter Shabono & his wife & child (as an interpreter & interpretess for
the Crow Inds[2] and the latter for the Shoshoni) with 50[3] horses. we
proceeded on through the Vally of Clarks river[4] on the West Side of the
[river] nearly South 18 [13?] Miles and halted on the upper Side of a
large Creek, haveing Crossed 8 Streams 4 of which were Small. this
vally is from 10 to 15 Ms. in width tolerably leavel and partially timberd
with long leaf & pitch pine,[5] Some cotton wood, Birch,[6] and Sweet willow[7]
on the borders of the Streams. I observed 2 Species of Clover[8] in this
vally one the white Clover Common in the Western parts of the U.
States, the other Species which is much Smaller than either the red or
white both it's leaf & blossom the horses are excessively fond of this
Species. after letting our horses graze a Sufficient length of time to fill
themselves, and taking dinner of Venison we again resumed our journey
up the Vally which we found more boutifully versified with Small open
plains covered with a great variety of Sweet cented plants, flowers & grass.
this evening we Crossed 10 Streams 8 of which were large Creeks[9] which
comes roleing their Currents with Velocity into the river. those Creeks
take their rise in the mountains to the West[10] which mountains is at this

161

time Covered with Snow for about ⅓ of the way from their tops downwards. Some Snow is also to be Seen on the high points and hollows of the
Mountains to the East of us.[11] our Course this evening was nearly South
18 Ms. makeing a total of 36 miles today. we encamped on the N. Side
of a large Creek[12] where we found tolerable food for our horses. Labeish
killed a Deer this evening. We Saw great numbers of deer and 1 bear today. I also observed the burring Squirel of the Species Common about
the quawmarsh flatts West of the Rocky Mountains.[13] Musquetors very
troublesom.— one man Jo: Potts very unwell this evening owing to
rideing a hard trotting horse; I give him a pill of Opiom which Soon releve him.

1. With Clark were Sergeants Ordway and Pryor, Bratton, Collins, Colter, Cruzatte,
Gibson, Hall, Howard, Labiche, Lepage, Potts, Shannon, Shields, Weiser, Whitehouse,
Willard, Windsor, York, Toussaint and Jean Baptiste Charbonneau, and Sacagawea.

2. The Crow language is quite similar to that of the Hidatsas, with which Charbonneau and Sacagawea were familiar.

3. Biddle has added a pointing hand symbol and the numerals "50" to Clark's apparent blank space, both in red ink.

4. Clark's party headed south up the Bitterroot River, going from Missoula County to
Ravalli County, Montana. The route appears as a dotted line labeled "Capt Clarks rout
returning" on *Atlas* map 68; the starting point at Travelers' Rest is on *Atlas* map 69. The
stream where they halted at noon may have been Kootenai Creek in Ravalli County; if so,
they had crossed Mormon and Carlton creeks in Missoula County, and One Horse,
Sweeney, and Bass creeks in Ravalli County.

5. Ponderosa pine and lodgepole pine, respectively.

6. Water, or river, birch, *Betula occidentalis* Hook. Hitchcock et al., 2:77–81.

7. Sweet willow is the name used earlier for large, tree-sized willow species, which on
the Missouri River was primarily the peach-leaved willow, *Salix amygdaloides* Anderss. In
this area, however, Pacific willow, *S. lasiandra* Benth., is the more probable tree. Little
(CIH), 189-W; Little (MWH), 173-W.

8. Clark notices the same species that Lewis mentioned on July 2.

9. Including Big, Sweathouse, Bear, and Fred Burr creeks in Ravalli County. *Atlas*
map 68 shows numerous streams in this area on the west side of the Bitterroot River without naming any of them.

10. The Bitterroot Range along the Montana-Idaho boundary. *Atlas* map 68.

11. The Sapphire Mountains in Missoula and Ravalli counties. *Atlas* map 68.

12. On Blodgett Creek in Ravalli County, near U.S. Highway 93 and some three miles
north of present Hamilton. The site does not appear on *Atlas* map 68, but was some eight
miles north of the party's campsite of September 7, 1805.

13. The Columbian ground squirrel of Weippe Prairie, Clearwater County, Idaho.

[Clark]   *Friday July 4th 1806*

I order three hunters to Set out early this morning to hunt & kill Some meat and by 7 A. M. we Collected our horses took braekfast and Set out   proceeded on up the Vally on the West Side of Clarks river crossing three large deep and rapid Creeks, and two of a Smaller Size to a Small branch in the Spurs of the mountain and dined.[1]   the last Creek or river which we pass'd was So deep and the water So rapid that Several of the horses were Sweped down Some distance and the Water run over Several others which wet Several articles.   after Crossing this little river, I observed in the road the tracks of two men whome I prosume is of the Shoshone nation.   our hunters joined us with 2 deer in tolerable order. on the Side of the Hill near the place we dined Saw a gange of Ibex or big horn Animals I Shot at them running and missed. This being the day of the decleration of Independence of the United States and a Day commonly Scelebrated by my Country I had every disposition to Selebrate this day and therefore halted early and partook of a Sumptious Dinner of a fat Saddle of Venison and Mush of Cows (roots)   after Dinner we proceeded on about one mile to a very large Creek[2] which we assended Some distance to find a foard to cross   in crossing this creek Several articles got wet, the water was So Strong, alto' the debth was not much above the horses belly, the water passed over the backs and loads of the horses.   those Creeks are emensely rapid has great decnt [*NB: descent*]   the bottoms of the Creek as well as the low lands on each Side is thickly covered with large Stone.[3] after passing this Creek I inclined to the left and fell into the road on which we had passed down last fall near the place we had dined on the 7th of Sept. and continued on the road passing up on the W. Side of Clarks river 13 miles to the West fork of Sd. river and Encamped on an arm of the same[4]   I Sent out 2 men to hunt, and 3 in Serch of a foard to pass the river.   at dark they all returned and reported that they had found a place that the river might be passed but with Some risque of the loads getting wet   I order them to get up their horses and accompany me to those places &c.   our hunters killed 4 deer to day.   we made 30 ms. to day on a course nearly South   Vally from 8 to 10 mes. wide.   contains a good portion of Pitch pine.   we passed three large deep rapid Creeks this after noon[5]

1. Clark is still moving south on the west side of the Bitterroot River in Ravalli County, Montana. Among the streams crossed would be Blodgett, Canyon, Sawtooth, Roaring Lion, and Lost Horse creeks, none of them named on *Atlas* map 68. See also *Atlas* map 103.

2. Perhaps Rock Creek, in Ravalli County.

3. During the Pleistocene, numerous small glaciers advanced eastward into the Bitterroot Valley from the Bitterroot Mountains and left behind extensive deposits of boulder till in the stream valleys they occupied. Subsequent erosion removed much of the finer-grained material, leaving the boulders. The streams also carried large boulders downstream beyond the glaciers during flood flows.

4. Clark camped on the north side of the West Fork Bitterroot River, near its junction with the Bitterroot in Ravalli County. The site is not marked on *Atlas* map 68, but is on *Atlas* map 103; it is some five miles northwest of the camp of September 6, 1805.

5. Probably including Rock, Tin Cup, and Chaffin creeks, in Ravalli County, none of them named on *Atlas* maps 68 or 103.

[Clark]   *Saturday July 5th 1806*

I rose at day light this morning   despatched Labeash after a Buck which he killed late last evening; and I with the three men who I had Sent in Serch of a ford across the West fork of Clarks river, and examined each ford neither of them I thought would answer to pass the fork without wetting all the loads.   near one of those places pointed out by Colter I found a practiable foard and returned to Camp, ordered everything packed up and after Brackfast we Set out   passed 5 Chanels of the river which is divided by Small Islands   in passing the 6th & last Chanel Colter horse Swam and with Some dificuelty he made the Opposite Shore, Shannon took a different derection from Colter rained his horse up the Stream and passed over very well   I derected all to follow Shannon and pass quartering up the river which they done and passed over tolerably well the water running over the back of the 2 Smaller horses only.   unfortunately my trunk & portmantue Containing Sea otter Skins flags Some curiosites & necessary articles in them got wet, also an esortment of Medicine, and my roots.   about 1 mile we struck the East fork which had fallen and was not higher than when we passed it last fall   we had not proceeded up this fork more than 1 mile eer we struck the road by which we passed down last fall and kept it   at one mile we crossed the river at a very good foard and continued up on the East Side to the foot of the Mountain nearly opposite flour Crek[1] & halted to let our horses graze and dry our wet articles. I saw fresh Sign of 2 horses and a fire burning on the side of the road. I prosume that those indians are spies from the Shoshones. Shannon & Crusat killed each a deer this morning and J. Shields killed a female Ibex or bighorn on the side of the Mountain, this Animal was very meager. Shannon left his tomahawk at the place he killed his deer. I derect him to return for it and join me in the Vally on the East Side of this mountain.   gave Shields permission to proceed on over to the 1st Vally and there hunt untill my arival this evening at that place, after drying every article which detained us untill ½ past 4 P. M. we packed up and Crossed the Mountain into the vally where we first met with the flatheads[2]   here I overtook Shields he had not killed any thing. I crossed the river which heads in a high peecked mountain Covered with Snow N. E. of the Vally at about 20 Miles.[3]   [*NB: see note*][4]   Shields informed me that the Flat head indians passed up the Small Creek which we came down last fall about 2 miles above our Encampment of the 4th & 5th of, Septr. I proceeded up this South branch 2 Miles and encamped on the E. side of the Creek,[5] and Sent out several men to examine the road. Shields returned at dark and informed me that the best road turned up the hill from the creek 3 Miles higher up, and appeared to be a plain beaten parth.[6]   as this rout of the Oat lash shoots can be followed it will evidently Shorten our rout at least 2 days and as the indians informed me last fall a much better rout than the one we came out.   at all events I am deturmined to make the attempt and follow their trail if possible   if I can prosue [*EC: prosue = pursue*] it my rout will be nearer and much better than the one we Came from the Shoshones, & if I should not be able to follow their road; our rout can't possibly be much wors. The hunters killed two deer this evening. The after part of the day we only come 8 miles makeing a total of 20 Miles—. Shannon Came up about Sunset haveing found his tomahawk.

1. Clark crossed from the north to the south side of the West Fork Bitterroot River, in Ravalli County, Montana, then crossed the East Fork to its east side and continued south-easterly along that stream. Flour Creek ("Flower creek" in Biddle) is shown on *Atlas* map 68 ("Flour Camp Creek") flowing into the East Fork on the west side below the camp of September 6, 1805; it is present Warm Springs Creek.

2. Ross, or Ross's, Hole, in Ravalli County near present Sula, where the party met the Flatheads (Salish) on September 4, 1805. Appleman (LC), 326–27; *Atlas* maps 68, 103.

3. East Fork Bitterroot River heads near West Pintlar Peak on the Ravalli-Beaverhead County line, Montana, which is also the Continental Divide.

4. Biddle's interlineation refers to notes he took in conversation with Clark after the expedition. In this case, he wrote, "Shields & others I had sent out to examine the route which the Oolashoots we had met last fall had taken across the mountain when we had seen them 4 & 5 Sept. 1805 said he had found a large trail which turned up the hill from the creek 3 miles higher, an easterly branch of the creek we had come down last fall. Shannon found a trail not so large, nor so good." Biddle Notes [ca. April 1810], Jackson (LLC), 2:521.

5. Clark's camp is not marked on *Atlas* map 68 but is on maps 103, 104; it was in Ravalli County on Camp Creek, near Camp Creek Ranger Station and U.S. Highway 93, some two miles southeast of the party's camp of September 4–5, 1805.

6. Apparently the road which Clark pursued to Camp Fortunate, diverging from the old westbound route; see entries for subsequent days.

[Clark]   *Sunday 6th July 1806*

Some frost this morning   the last night was so cold that I could not Sleep.   we Collected our horses which were much scattered which detained us untill 9 A. M. at which time we Set out and proceeded up the Creek on which we camped 3 Miles[1] and left the road which we came on last fall to our right and assended a ridge with a gentle Slope to the dividing mountain which Seperates the waters from [*NB: of*] the Middle fork of Clarks river from those [*NB: of Wisdom*][2] and Lewis's river and passed over prosueing the rout of the Oat lash shute band which we met last fall to the head of [*NB: Glade Cr:*] a branch of Wisdom R and down the Said branch crossing it frequently[3] on each Side of this handsom glades in which I observe great quantities of quawmash just beginning to blume on each side of those glades the timber is small and a great propotion of it Killed by the fires. I observe the appearance of old buffalow roads and some heads on this part of the mountain.   [*NB: proving that formerly Buffs.[4] roved there & also that this is the best route, for the Buffs.* ⟨*who*⟩ *and the* ⟨*Buffs.*⟩ *Indians always have the best route & here both were joined*]   The Snow appears to lying in considerable masses on the mountain from which we decended on the 4th of Septr. last.[5] I observe great numbers of the whistleing Squirel[6] which burrows their holes Scattered on each Side of the glades through which we passed. Shields killed a *hare* of the large mountain Species.[7]   the after part of the day we passed on the hill Side N of the Creek for 6 Ms. Creek [*NB: down glade Cr*] and entered an extensive open Leavel plain in which the Indian trail Scattered in Such a manner that we Could not pursue it.   the Indian woman wife to Shabono informed me that she had been in this plain frequently and knew it well that the Creek which we decended was a branch of Wisdom river[8] and when we assended the higher part of the plain we would discover a gap in the mountains in our direction to the Canoes,[9] and when we arived at that gap we would See a high point of a mountain covered with snow in our direction to the canoes.[10]   we proceeded on 1 mile and Crossd. a large Creek[11] from the right which heads in a Snow Mountain and Fish Creek over which there was a road thro' a gap.[12]   we assended a Small rise and beheld an open boutifull Leavel Vally or plain of about 20 [*NB: 15*] Miles wide and near 60 [*NB: 30*] long extending N & S. in every direction around which I could see high points of Mountains Covered with Snow.[13] I discovered one at a distance very high covered with Snow which bore S. 80° E.[14] The Squar pointed to the gap through which she said we must pass which was S. 56° E. She said we would pass the river before we reached the gap.   we had not proceeded more than 2 Miles in the last Creek, before a violent Storm of wind accompand. with hard rain from the S W. imediately from off the Snow Mountains this rain was Cold and lasted 1½ hours. I discovd. the rain wind as it approached and halted and formd. a solid column to protect our Selves from the Violency of the gust.   after it was over I proceeded on about 5 Miles to Some Small dry timber on a Small Creek and encampd.[15] made large fires and dryed our Selves.   here I observed Some fresh Indian Signs where they had been gathering quawmash.   [*NB: This is the great plain where Shoshonees gather quawmash & cows &c.   our woman had done so.   many beaver*]

Courses and distance &c.[16]

	Miles
on the course which we had decended the branch of Clark's river to the first Flat heads or Oat lashshoot band the 4th of Septr. 1805—	3½
Thence up a jintle Slope of the dividing mountain which seperates the waters of the [*blank*] from those of Lewis's & Clark's rivers leaveing the old rout on which we Came out to the right on a course nearly S. E.—	3—

167

Thence N. 80° E. through a leavel piney Country on the top of the mountain to a glade at the head of a branch which runs towards the Missouri ⎫ 2 ½

Thence S. 50° E. down the branch Crossing it frequently & through small glades on either Side of the branch the glades at Some places a mile wide with Several Small Streams falling in on either Side up which there is Small glades to the narrows N E. ⎫ 7—

Thence N. 68d E. keeping down the North Side of the Creek on the Side of the hill.   the bottoms of the Creek Small open and much fallen timber to an extensive bottom S. Side ⎫ 4—

Thence S. 56° E. through an open Leavle plain passing a large Creek from the right at one mile to a quawmash flatt through which a Small Creek runs scattered through the bottom, and Encamped— ⎫ 6—

miles   26—0

1. Camp Creek, in Ravalli County, Montana, roughly parallel to U.S. Highway 93, unnamed on *Atlas* map 68.

2. Biddle has made his addition to Clark's apparent blank space.

3. Clark's party evidently crossed the Continental Divide from Ravalli County to Beaverhead County, Montana, by way of Gibbons Pass, then went down Trail Creek (Clark's Glade Creek) toward the valley of the Big Hole River (his Wisdom River). His route appears as a dotted line on *Atlas* map 68. Some of his courses appear on the route on *Atlas* map 103.

4. These were probably mountain bison (*Bison bison athabascae*), rather than plains bison (*Bison bison bison*) who had wandered into the mountains. The mountain Indians, since acquiring the horse and thus increasing their hunting efficiency, had greatly reduced the numbers of this animal by Lewis and Clark's time. See also Clark's entry for July 14, 1806. Christman.

5. The general area of Saddle Mountain in Ravalli County, from which the party descended on the date Clark mentions toward Ross Hole. *Atlas* maps 68, 103.

6. Again, the Columbian ground squirrel.

7. Perhaps Nuttall's cottontail, *Sylvilagus nuttallii;* if so, a new species. Burroughs, 123.

8. The Big Hole River. *Atlas* maps 65, 66, 67. On *Atlas* map 103 it is also "E. fork of Clarks R," certainly an error.

9. Big Hole Pass, at the upper end of the Big Hole Valley in Beaverhead County, through which present Montana Highway 278 passes. It was on the way to Camp Fortunate, at which place the canoes had been cached in August 1805. *Atlas* maps 67, 103.

10. Perhaps the Tendoy Mountains in Beaverhead County, south of Camp Fortunate; they were probably not visible from this point but came into view in a few miles.

11. Ruby Creek in Beaverhead County, which runs northeasterly to join Trail Creek and form the North Fork Big Hole River. A few miles to the east is the Big Hole Battlefield National Monument, site of an engagement between the Nez Perces and the U.S. Army on August 9–10, 1877. Both the Indians and the soldiers who attacked them reached the site by Clark's route through Gibbons Pass, named for the army commander in the battle. Brown (FNP), 250.

12. Ruby Creek heads in the Beaverhead Mountains of the Bitterroot Range near the heads of some of the tributaries of the North Fork Salmon River (Lewis and Clark's Fish Creek). The gap is another Big Hole Pass, east of Gibbonsville, Lemhi County, Idaho, in Beaverhead County, Montana. *Atlas* maps 67, 103.

13. The valley of the Big Hole River, in Beaverhead County; in its east central part lies the present town of Wisdom, still bearing Lewis and Clark's name for the river. *Atlas* maps 67, 103.

14. There are a number of high peaks in the Pioneer Mountains east of Clark's position, some of them over 10,000 feet. He may be using the word "mountain" as he often did to mean a whole range, or he may be seeing Tweedy Mountain in Beaverhead National Forest.

15. Apparently on Moose Creek, in the western part of the Big Hole Valley in Beaverhead County, some seven miles southwest of Wisdom. The spot appears on *Atlas* map 103.

16. Being in new territory, Clark has resumed keeping tabled courses and distances.

[Clark]   *Monday 7th July 1806*

This morning our horses were very much Scattered; I Sent out men in every direction in Serch of them.   they brought all except 9 by 6 oClock and informed me that they could not find those 9: I then ordered 6 men to take horses and go different directions and at a greater distance   those men all returned by 10 A. M. and informed me that they had circles in every direction to 6 or 8 miles around Camp and could not See any Signs of them, that they had reasons to believe that the indians had Stolen them in the course of the night, and founded their reasons on the quallity of the horses, all being the most valuable horses we had, and Several of them so attached to horses of inferior quallity which we have they could not be Seperated from each other when driveing with their loads on in the course of the day. I thought it probable that they might be stolen by Some Skulking Shoshones, but as it was yet possible that they may have taken our back rout or rambled to a greater distance I deturmined to leave a Small party and hunt for them to day, and proceed on with the main party and all the baggage to the Canoes, raise them out of the water and expose them to the sun to dry by the time this party Should overtake me. I left Sergt. Ordway, Shannon, Gibson Collins & Labeech with directions to hunt this day for the horses without they Should discover that the Inds. had taken them into the Mountains, and prosue our trail &c.   at ½ past 10 A M I set out and proceeded on through an open rich vally crossing four large Creeks[1] with extensive low and mirey bottoms, and a Small river[2] keeping the Course I had set out on S. 56° E   after crossing the river I kept up on the N E. side, Sometimes following an old road which frequently disappeared, at the distance of 16 miles we arived at a Boiling Spring[3] Situated about 100 paces from a large Easterly fork of the Small river in a leavel open vally plain and nearly opposit & E. of the 3 forks of this little river which heads in the Snowey Mountains to the S E. & S W of the Springs.   this Spring [NB: *15 yds in circumc, boils up all over bottom which is Stoney*] contains a very considerable quantity of water, and actually blubbers with heat for 20 paces below where it rises.   it has every appearance of boiling, too hot for a man to endure his hand in it 3 seconds. I directt Sergt. Pryor and John Shields to put each a peice of meat in the water of different Sises.   the one about the Size of my 3 fingers Cooked dun in 25 minits the other much thicker was 32 minits before it became Sufficiently dun.   this water boils up through some loose hard gritty Stone.   a little sulferish[4]   after takeing dininer and letting our horses graize 1 hour and a half we proceeded on Crossed this easterly branch and up on the N. Side of this middle fork 9 miles crossed it near the head of an Easterly branch and passed through a gap of a mountain on the Easterly Side of which we encamped near some butifull [NB: *Springs*] which fall into Willards Creek.[5] I directed that the rambling horses should be hobbled, and the Sentinal to examine the horses after the moon rose.   ⟨much⟩ Emence beaver sign.

Course distance &c. July 7th

		miles	
S. 56° E	to the boiling hot Spring ½ mile Easterly of the three upper forks of wisdom river near a large Creek from the East passed 4 large Creek from the Snow mountains on my right and a small river at 12 miles bottoms extensive & wet	16	0

S 45° E	on the ⟨E⟩ S E. Side of the middle fork	5	0
N. 50° E	to the Gap of a mountain crossing a Small branch at 2 Miles from the left and Encamped	4	0
		miles 25—	

This extensive vally Surround with covered with snow is extreemly fertile covered esculent plants &c and the Creeks which pass through it contains emence numbers of beaver &c. I now take my leave of this butifull extensive vally which I call the hot spring Vally, and behold one less extensive and much more rugid on Willards Creek for near 12 miles in length. remarkable Cold night

1. Clark headed southeasterly across the Big Hole Valley, crossing Rock, Lake, Big Swamp, and Little Lake creeks, in Beaverhead County, Montana, all affluents from the west of the Big Hole River. Although prominent, none is named on *Atlas* maps 67, 103, or 104.

2. The Big Hole River in Beaverhead County, the captains' "Wisdom River." The dotted line labeled "Capt Clarks rout returning in 1806" marks his route on *Atlas* map 67. See also *Atlas* maps 103, 104.

3. Just east of present Jackson on Warm Spring Creek in Beaverhead County. It is labeled "boiling Hot Spring which Cooked meat in 25 minits" on *Atlas* map 67; see also *Atlas* maps 103, 104.

4. The water of Jackson Hot Spring is not especially mineralized, containing about 660 parts per million (ppm) dissolved solids. Of this total, only about 0.6 ppm are hydrogen sulfide. This gas, however, usually can be detected at concentrations as low as 0.3 ppm. The temperature of the water was reported to be 136° F in 1974, and the discharge at that time was 260 gallons per minute. The spring emerges from Tertiary sandstone and sandy limestone, but has a deep source.

5. Clark crossed Warm Spring Creek and went southeasterly up Governor Creek and Bull Creek, roughly parallel to Montana Highway 278 in Beaverhead County. Just after passing Bull Creek he went east through Big Hole Pass, still near the path of the modern highway, and once over the pass, camped near the head of Divide Creek, the upper portion of Lewis and Clark's "Willards Creek." The route, but not the campsite, is marked on *Atlas* map 67. On *Atlas* map 103 the camp appears to be incorrectly labeled "Campd. 8 July"; it is correct on *Atlas* map 104, the best map of the three.

[Clark]   *Tuesday July 8th 1806*

Our horses being Scattered we were detained unill 8 A. M before we Set out. we proceeded on down Willards Creek on the S.W. Side about 11 miles near which the Creek passes through the mountain[1] we then

Steared S. 20° E. to the West branch of Jeffersons river in Snake Indian cove about 7 miles and halded two hours to let the horses graize.[2] after dinner we proceeded on down the forke which is here but Small 9 Miles to our encampment of 17 Augt.[3] at which place we Sunk our Canoes & buried Some articles, as before mentioned the most of the Party with me being Chewers of Tobacco become So impatient to be chewing it that they Scercely gave themselves time to take their Saddles off their horses before they were off to the deposit. I found every article Safe, except a little damp.[4] I gave to each man who used tobacco about two feet off a part of a role   took one third of the ballance myself and put up ⅔ in a box to Send down with the most of the articles which had been left at this place, by the Canoes to Capt. Lewis.   as it was late nothing Could be done with the Canoes this evening. I examined them and found then all Safe except one of the largest which had a large hole in one Side & Split in bow. The Country through which we passed to day was diversified high dry and uneaven Stoney open plains and low bottoms very boggy[5] with high mountains on the tops and North sides of which there was Snow, great quantities of the Species of hysoop[6] & shrubs common to the Missouri plains are Scattered in those Vallys and hill Sides. The road which we have traveled from travellers rest Creek to this place an excellent road.[7] and with only a few trees being cut out of the way would be an excellent waggon road   one Mountain of about 4 miles over excepted which would require a little digging   The distance is *164* Miles—. Shields killed an antelope   [*NB: this place is the head of Jeffer river where we left our canoes*][8]

Course Distance &c. July 8th

		Miles
S. 40° E.	down the Creek keeping on the S W Side of the Creek passing Several Small branches from the mountains to our right	11—
S 20° E	passing through a gap at 3 miles and thro' an open plain on either Side of the Gap to thc West branch of Jeffersons river	7—
East	down the Said branch of Jeffiersons river to a high point of land and struck thc road from thc Canoes to the Snake indian vally on Lewisis river on which we passed last Summer[9]	4—

N 45° E down the fork to the forks of Sd river at which place
we made a Deposit & left our canoes & Encamped } 5—

Miles 27—

1. Clark headed southeasterly down Divide Creek in Beaverhead County, Montana, to a point west of present Bannack, where the creek turns east to join Grasshopper Creek (the lower part of Lewis and Clark's Willard's Creek), which goes on east to join the Beaverhead (Jefferson River to the captains). *Atlas* map 67 shows the route as a rather faint dotted line; it is much clearer on *Atlas* maps 103, 104.

2. Clark now headed southerly following roughly the present route of a local road south from Bannack through the gap that leads into the captains' Shoshone (or "Snake indian") Cove to Horse Prairie Creek (the "West branch of Jeffersons river"). Lewis had first entered the valley on August 10, 1805. Clark paused on Horse Prairie Creek a few miles east of present Grant in Beaverhead County. *Atlas* maps 67, 103, 104.

3. He went down Horse Prairie Creek to the forks of the Beaverhead River and camped at Camp Fortunate, where the party had first stopped on August 17, 1805, on the east bank of the Beaverhead just below the forks in Beaverhead County, a site now under Clark Canyon Reservoir just above the dam. Here Clark's party remained until July 10. *Atlas* map 104. "Fortunate Camp" appears on *Atlas* map 66.

4. For this cache, see Lewis's entries for August 20, 21, and 22, 1805. Although Clark says everything was safe, only one plant specimen (golden currant) remains of those which were cached here. That includes all those collected between the Great Falls and Camp Fortunate. The dampness may have caused the rest to mildew. Cutright (LCPN), 329.

5. After descending from the divide between Big Hole River and Grasshopper Creek, Clark's party traveled principally across Tertiary sedimentary deposits and passed by several areas of Tertiary volcanic rocks. The boggy bottoms were along Grasshopper Creek and Horse Prairie Creek.

6. The abundant hyssop is big sagebrush.

7. At this point Clark inserted his courses and distances for the day; after them he continued his text, repeating the word "road." For convenience of reading we have continued the text and placed the courses and distances at the end of the entry.

8. Biddle placed his interlineation in a large blank space at the bottom of p. 59 in Codex M.

9. A reference to the trail west through Shoshone (or Snake Indian) Cove over Lemhi Pass to the valley of the Lemhi River ("East Fork of Lewis R" on *Atlas* map 67). See entries for August 1805.

[Clark] *Wednesday 9th July 1806*

rose early had the horses brought up. after which I had the Canoes raised washed, brough down and drawn up on Shore to dry and repard. Set Several men to work digging for the Tobacco Capt. Lewis informed me he had buried in the place the lodge Stood when we lay here last Summer, they Serched diligently without finding anything. at 10 A M Sergt. Ordway and party arrived with the horses we had lost. he reported that he found those horses near the head of the Creek on which we encamped,[1] makeing off as fast as they could and much Scattered. nothing material took place with his party in their absence. I had the Canoes repared men & lodes appotioned ready to embark tomorrow morning. I also formd. ⟨my⟩ the party to accomp me to the river Rejhone[2] from applicants and apportioned what little baggage I intended to carry as also the Spear horses. this day was windy and Cold. The Squar brought me a Plant[3] the root of which the nativs eat. this root most resembles a Carrot in form and Size and Something of its colour, being of a pailer yellow than that of our Carrot, the Stem and leaf is much like the Common Carrot, and the taste not unlike. it is a native of moist land.— John Sheilds and Collins each killed a Deer this morning. the wind dried our Canoes very much they will be Sufficiently dry by tomorrow morning to Set out in them down the river.

1. On Moose Creek, in Beaverhead County, Montana, where they camped on July 6, 1806.
2. The *Roche jaune*, or Yellowstone, River.
3. Although the description of a carrot-like leaf is not consistent, this may be ternate, or nineleaf, lomatium, *Lomatium triternatum* (Pursh) Coult. & Rose, a plant with an edible root which Lewis collected on May 6, 1806, on the Clearwater River in Idaho. *L. dissectum* (Nutt.) Math. & Const., fits the leaf description more closely, but is not especially typical of "moist land" and is not known to be palatable. Booth & Wright, 173–74; Cutright (LCPN), 289, 413.

[Clark]   *Thursday July 10th 1806*

last night was very cold and this morning everything was white with frost and the grass Stiff frozend. I had Some water exposed in a bason in which the ice was ¾ of an inch thick this morning. I had all the Canoes put into the water and every article which was intended to be Sent down put on board, and the horses collected and packed with what fiew articles I intend takeing with me to the River Rochejhone, and after brackfast we all Set out at the Same time[1] & proceeded on Down Jeffersons river on

the East Side through Sarviss [*NB: Service*] Vally and rattle snake mountain[2] and into that butifull and extensive Vally open and fertile which we
Call the beaver head Vally which is the Indian name   in their language
Har na Hap pap Chah.[3]   from the No.[4] of those animals in it & a pt. of
land resembling the head of one   this Vally extends from the rattle
Snake Mountain down Jeffersons river as low as fraziers Creek[5] above the
big horn mountain and is from 12 [*NB: 10*] to 30 [*NB: 15*] miles in width
and [*blank*] [*NB: about 50*] miles on a direct line in length and Jeffersons
river in passing through this Vally reives McNeals Creek,[6] Track Creek,[7]
Phalanthrophy river, Wisdom river,[8] Fields river[9] and Fraziers Creek
each throw in a considerable quantity of water and have innoumerable
beaver and otter on them; the bushes in their low bottoms are the resort
for great numbers of Deer, and in the higher parts of the Vally we see
Antelopes scattered feeding. I saw also on the Sides of the rock in rattle
snake mountain 15 big horn animals, those animals feed on the grass
which grow on the Sides of the mountn. and in the narrow bottoms on
the Water courses near the Steep Sides of the mountains on which they
can make their escape from the pursute of wolves Bear &c.   at Meridian
I halted to let the horses Graze having Come 15 Miles   I ordered the
[*NB: canoes*] to land. Sergt. Ordway informed me that the party with him
had Come on very well, and he thought the Canoes could go as farst as
the horses &c. as the river now become wider and not So Sholl, I deturmined to put all the baggage &c. which I intend takeing with me to the
river Rochejhone in the canoes and proceed on down with them myself to
the 3 forks or Madisons & galletens rivers.   leaveing the horses to be
taken down by Sergt. Pryor and 6 of the men of the party to accompany
me to the river Rochejhone and directed Sergt. Pryor to proceed on moderately and if possible encamp with us every night.   after dinner had my
baggage put on board and Set out, and proceeded on tolerable well to the
head of the 3000 Mile Island on which we had encamped on the [*NB:
11th*] of Augt last.[10]   the Canoes passed Six of my encampments assending,[11] opposit this island I encamped on the East side.[12]   the Musquetors
were troublesom all day and untill one hour after Sunset when it became
Cool and they disappeared.   in passing down in the Course of this day
we saw great numbers of beaver lying on the Shores in the Sun.   wild

young Gees and ducks are common in this river.   we killed two young gees this evening. I saw several large rattle Snakes in passing the rattle Snake Mountain   they were fierce.[13]

1. Ordway indicates that he was in charge of the canoe party, while Clark led the group with the horses on land.

2. They were setting off northeast down the Beaverhead River, in Beaverhead County, Montana. For "Sarvice berry Vallie" and the Rattlesnake Cliffs, shown on *Atlas* map 66, see August 10, 1805.

3. The valley of the Beaverhead and upper Jefferson rivers in Beaverhead and Madison counties, Montana. For the Beaverhead Rock, which Clark passed the next day on this downriver trip, see entries for August 8, 9, and 10, 1805. *Atlas* map 66. Rees, 5, gives the name Clark was trying to spell as *Hane-pompy-hah*, "Beaverhead valley."

4. Biddle added an "o" in red to Clark's "N."

5. Present South Boulder River, reaching the Jefferson in Madison County; see August 1, 1805. *Atlas* map 65.

6. Present Blacktail Deer Creek, reaching the Beaverhead River in Beaverhead County, near Dillon; see August 10 and 13, 1805. *Atlas* map 66.

7. Present Rattlesnake Creek in Beaverhead County, reaching the Beaverhead a few miles above Dillon; see August 14, 1805. It is "Track run" on *Atlas* map 66.

8. Modern Ruby (Philanthropy) and Big Hole (Wisdom) rivers meet the Beaverhead River near Twin Bridges, Madison County, to form Jefferson River. See entries for August 5 and 6, 1805. *Atlas* maps 65, 66.

9. "R Fields Vally Creek" on *Atlas* map 65; present Boulder River, meeting Jefferson River in Jefferson County, Montana. See August 1, 1805.

10. Biddle has added "11th" to Clark's apparent blank space. He seems to be mistaken; the island on which the party camped on August 11, 1805, according to *Atlas* map 66, was that labeled "Otter Isd." "3000 mile Island" is some three to four miles farther down the Beaverhead River, in Beaverhead County some ten miles northeast of Dillon.

11. Clark's camps of August 11–16, 1805. *Atlas* map 66.

12. On the east bank of the Jefferson River, in Beaverhead County, opposite Three Thousand Mile Island; see a previous note in this entry. *Atlas* map 66.

13. Immediately after this, at the very bottom of p. 62 of Codex M, Clark has the word "Course." However, there are no courses and distances for this day, in which he covered familiar ground.

[Clark]   *Friday 11th July 1806*

Sent on 4 of the best hunters in 2 Canoes to proceed on a fiew miles a head and hunt untill I came up with them, after an early brackfast I proceeded on down a very crooked Chanel, at 8 a. m I overtook one Canoe with a Deer which Collins had killed, at meridian passed Sergt. Pryors

Camp near a high point of land on the left Side which the Shoshones call the beavers head.[1]   the wind rose and blew with great violence from the S W imediately off Some high mountains Covered with Snow.   the violence of this wind retarded our progress very much and the river being emencly Crooked we had it imediately in our face nearly every bend.   at 6 P M I passed Phalanthrophy river which I proceved was very low.   the wind Shifted about to the N. E. and bley very hard tho' much wormer than the forepart of the day.   at 7 P M I arrived at the Enterance of Wisdom River and Encampd. in the Spot we had encamped the [*NB: 6th*] of August last.[2]   here we found a Bayonct which had been left & the Canoe quite safe.[3]   I directed that all the nails be taken out of this Canoe and paddles to be made of her Sides & here I came up with Gibson & Colter whome I had Sent on a head for the purpose of hunting this morning, they had killed a fat Buck and 5 young gees nearly grown. Wisdom river is very high and falling. I have Seen great Nos. of Beaver on the banks and in the water as I passed down to day, also some Deer and great numbers young gees, Sand hill cranes &c. &c. Sgt. Pryor left a deer on the shore

1. In Madison County, Montana; see August 8, 1805.

2. On the east side of Jefferson River, opposite the mouth of the Big Hole River, in Beaverhead County, Montana, some two miles northeast of present Twin Bridges. *Atlas* map 65. Again, Biddle has added the date to Clark's blank space.

3. For the leaving of this canoe, see August 7, 1805. Probably some of the men who had been serving in regular infantry units before the expedition brought along their bayonets. Almost certainly it was a spike bayonet with a socket to fit over the muzzle of a musket. Peterson, 84–86.

[Clark]   *Saturday 12th July 1806*

Sergt. Pryor did not join me last night he has proceeded on down. the beaver was flacking[1] [*NB: flapping their tails*] in the river about us all the last night.   this Morning I was detained untill 7 A M makeing Paddles and drawing the nails of the Canoe to be left at this place and the one we had before left here.   after completing the paddles &c and takeing Some Brackfast I set out   the Current I find much Stronger below the forks than above and the river tolerably streight as low as panther Creek[2] when it became much more Crooked   the Wind rose and blew

hard off the Snowey mountains to the N. W.[3] and renderd it very difficuelt to keep the canoes from running against the Shore   at 2 P. M. the
Canoe in which I was in was driven by a Suden puff of wind under a log
which projected over the water from the bank, and the man in the Stern
Howard was Caught in between the Canoe and the log and a little hurt
after disingaging our selves from this log the canoe was driven imediately
under a drift which projected over and a little abov the Water, here the
Canoe was very near turning over   we with much exertion after takeing
out Some of the baggage hauled her out, and proceeded on without re-
ceving any damage.   the men in the other Canoes Seeing our Situation
landed and come with as much Speed as possible through the briers and
thick brush to our assistance.   but from the thickness of the brush did
not get up to our assistance untill we had got Clear.   at 3 P M we halted
at the enterance of Fields Creek and dined here Willard and Collins over
took us with two deer which they had killd. this morning and by takeing a
different Side of an Island from which we Came, we had passed them.
after dinner I proceeded on and Encamped a little below our encampmt.
of the 31st of July last.[4]   the Musquetoes very troublesome this evening   Some old buffalow Signs. I killed 4 young gees and Collins killed 2
bever this evening.

1. Apparently an obsolete dialect form of "flapping." Criswell, 39.
2. Present Big Pipestone Creek, reaching the Jefferson River near Whitehall, in Jefferson County, Montana. See August 3, 1805. *Atlas* map 65.
3. Highland Mountains, in Jefferson and Madison counties.
4. Clark does not indicate on which side of the Jefferson River this camp was. It would
be in either Jefferson or Madison County, some two miles below the mouth of Antelope
Creek and the camp of July 31, 1805, near where U.S. Highway 287 crosses the Jefferson.
Atlas map 65.

[Clark]   July 13th 1806[1]
    at 5 oClock Set out

from the 3 forks at the head of Missouri
Courses distance &c

S. 85° E   6   Miles to Galletins river, passed over Some ridges, the river
                    Some ⟨distance⟩ makeing a bend to the S W. Camped on the

N. W. Side   passed through an open Smooth plain   the hill Sides contains a hard white rock which lies in a Slopeing position and Shows only in places   Several roads leading to my left hand—

[Clark]   *Sunday 13th July 1806*

Set out early this morning and proceded on very well to the enterance of Madicines river at our old Encampment of the 27th July last[2]   at 12 where I found Sergt. Pryor and party with the horses, they had arived at this place one hour before us.   his party had killed 6 deer & a white bear   I had all the horses driven across Madicine & gallitines rivers and halted to dine and let the horses feed imediately below the enterance of Gallitine.[3]   had all the baggage of the land party taken out of the Canoes and after dinner the 6 Canoes and the party of 10 men under the direction of Sergt. Ordway Set out.[4]   previous to their departur I gave instructions how they were to proceed &c. I also wrote to Capt Lewis by Sergt. Ordway—.   my party now Consists of the following persons Viz: Serjeant N. Pryor, Jo. Shields, G. Shannon William Bratton, Labiech, Windsor, H. Hall, Gibson, Interpreter Shabono his wife & Child and my man york; with 49 horses and a colt.   the horses feet are very sore and Several of them can Scercely proceed on.   at 5. P. M I Set out from the head of Missouri at the 3 forks, and proceeded on nearly East 4 miles and Encamped on the bank of Gallitines River which is a butifull navigable Stream.[5]   Saw a large Gange of Elk in the plains and Deer in the river bottoms. I also observe beaver and Several otter in galletines river as I passed along. Gibson killed an otter the fur of which was much longer and whiter than any which I had Seen. Willard killed 2 deer this morning.   all the meat I had put into the Canoes except a Sufficiency for Supper. The Country in the forks between Gallitins & Madisens rivers is a butifull leavel plain Covered with low grass.—   on the lower or N E. Side of Gallitins river the Country rises gradually to the foot of a mountain which runs nearly parrelal.   those plains are indefferant or the Soil of which is not very rich they are Stoney & Contain Several Stratas of white rock.[6]   the Current of the river is rapid and near the mouth contains Several islands, it is navigable for Canoes. I saw Several Antelope Common Deer, wolves, beaver, Otter, Eagles, hawks, Crows, wild gees both old and young, does &c. &c. I observe Several leading roads which appear to pass to a gap of the mountain in a E. N E. direction about 18 or 20 miles distant.[7] The indian woman who has been of great Service to me as a pilot through this Country recommends a gap in the mountain more South which I shall cross.—.[8]

1. Here begins a first draft found in the Voorhis Collection, Missouri Historical Society, written on letter paper; it gives Clark's courses and distances for July 13–19 and July 24–August 3, 1806. Thwaites published only parts of it; see the Introduction and Appendix C, vol. 2. It appears here before the Codex M entries for the same dates, since it was probably written as a preliminary draft; editorial notes will mainly be to the codex entries, which are much more detailed and written in narrative fashion. The number "37" is written in the margin, apparently without reference to the text and in an unknown hand.

2. At the junction of the Jefferson and Madison rivers in Broadwater County, Montana, about two miles northeast of present Three Forks. *Atlas* map 65.

3. On the Missouri River in Broadwater County, immediately below the junction of the Missouri and Gallatin rivers. *Atlas* map 65.

4. Ordway proceeded down the Missouri with the canoes to the Great Falls; with him were Collins, Colter, Cruzatte, Howard, Lepage, Potts, Weiser, Whitehouse, and Willard.

5. On a modern map Clark's general course appears more nearly southeast; he camped on the north side of the Gallatin River in Gallatin County, Montana, about a mile east of present Logan. *Atlas* maps 106, 113.

6. Clark's observation refers to the western part of the Horseshoe Hills which he crossed late in the afternoon. Several light-colored, resistant limestone beds of the Mississippian Madison Group, Devonian Jefferson Limestone, Cambrian Pilgrim Limestone, and Meagher Limestone crop out there and dip steeply to the northwest in an anticline-syncline zone. The stones are either the exposures of these formations or are derived from them by weathering—they are not river gravels.

7. This gap and the trails leading to it appear quite plainly on *Atlas* maps 106 and 113; it is Flathead Pass in the Bridger Range, in Gallatin County, leading easterly to the valley of Shields River. The Flatheads and Bannocks commonly passed this way to hunt buffalo on the plains. Sprague (GG), 424.

8. Bozeman Pass; see July 15, 1806. In this area, familiar to her from childhood, Sacagawea did indeed act as a guide, as legend has her doing much more extensively.

[Clark]   [July 14, 1806]

S 78° E.   6   Miles to a part of the river haveing passed through an open leavel butifull plain covered with low grass river bind to the

N E. Passed Several buffalow roeds all leading to a gap in the mountain to the N. E. of me

S 70° E.   6   miles to a plain East of the river haveing crossed Several Streams ⟨of⟩ & the river ⟨the river⟩ ⟨the Streams⟩ (passed out of my direction in the first part of this Course [)] an intolerable rout caused by Beaver daming the Stream a muddy wet rout, and Come into the course abut one mile from thc commencement & then passed through a low leavel firm plain to the river and Crossd it into a low plain.

⟨East⟩ S 78° E   12   Miles to the most Sourtherly of the three forks of the East fork of Galletins river, all Small, the most Easterly branch Comeing out of the mountain, passing through an open Leavel plain   Passed 3 Small Streams from the Mountains to my right. Some Snow on the mountains to the S E. S. S W. West and at a distanc to the N. W.   none to be seen on those Easterly—   marked my name & day & year on a Cotton tree.

N 80° E.   3   miles to the Enterance of a banch into the middle fork from the N E at the foot of the mountain, haveing Crossed the E fork at 1½ above a thicket   a Spur on the mountain on the left   a Slopeing plain on the right Mountain forming a half Circle, and the middle fork entering the mountain a Short distance above.   much beaver Sign &c. Camped

[Clark]   *Monday 14th July 1806*

Sent Sheilds a head to kill a deer for our brackfast and at an early hour Set out with the party   Crossed Gallitines river which makes a Considerable bend to the N. E. and proceeded on nearly S. 78° E through an open Leavel plain   at 6 miles I Struck the river and crossed a part of it and attemptd to proceed on through the river bottoms which was Several Miles wide at this place, I crossed Several chanels of the river running through the bottom in defferent directions. I proceeded on about two miles crossing those defferent chanels all of which was damed with beaver in Such a manner as to render the passage impracticable and after Swamped as I may Say in this bottom of beaver   I was compelled to turn Short about to the right and after Some difficuelty made my way good to an open low but firm plain which was an Island and extended nearly the Course I wished to proceed.   here the Squar informed me that there was a large road passing through the upper part of this low plain from Madicins river through the gap which I was Stearing my Course to. I proceeded up this plain 4 miles and Crossed the main Chanel of the river, having passed through a Skirt of cotton timber to an open low plain on the N E. Side of the river and nooned it.[1]   the river is divided and on all the small Streams inoumerable quantities of beaver dams, tho' the river is yet navagable for Canoes. I overtook Shields Soon after I ⟨had⟩ set out; he had killed a large fat Buck. I saw Elk deer & Antelopes, and great deel of old Signs of buffalow.   their roads is in every direction. The Indian woman informs me that a fiew years ago Buffalow was very plenty in those plains & Vallies quit as high as the head of Jeffersons river, but fiew of them ever come into those Vallys of late years owing to the Shoshones who are fearfull of passing into the plains West of the mountains and Subsist on what game they Can Catch in the Mountains principally and the fish which they take in the E. fork of Lewis's river. Small parties of the Shoshones do pass over to the plains for a few days at a time and kill buffalow for their Skins and dried meat, and return imediately into the Mountains.   after Dinner we proceeded on a little to the South of East through an open leavel plain to the three forks of the E branch of Gallitines River[2] at about 12 miles, crossed the most Southerly of those forks[3] and Struck an old buffalow road [*NB: the one our Indn woman meant*] which I kept Continuing nearly the Same Course up the middle fork Crossed it and Camped on a small branch of the middle fork on the N E. Side at the commencement of the gap of the mountain—[4]   the road leading up this branch, Several other roads all old Come in from the right & left.   emence quantities of beaver on this Fork quit down, and their dams very much impeed the navigation of it from the 3 forks down, tho I beleive it practicable for Small Canoes by unloading at a fiew of the worst of those dams. Deer are plenty. Shannon Shields and Sergt. Pryor each killed one which were very fat much more So than they are Commonly at this Season of the year. The Main fork of Galletins River turn South and enter them mountains which are yet Covered with Snow. Madisens river makes a Great bend to the East and enters the Same mountain.   a leavel plain between the two rivers below the mountain.

    1. On *Atlas* map 106 the route appears as a dotted line marked "Capt. Clark's rout from the 3 forks of Missouri to R. Rochejone," and on *Atlas* map 113 as a double dotted line, "Captain William Clarks route from the 3 forks of the Missouri to the Rochejone or yellow Stone." He proceeded southeasterly, crossing and recrossing the Gallatin River as indicated, in Gallatin County, Montana.

    2. Clark reached the forks of East Gallatin River in the vicinity of present Bozeman, in Gallatin County. *Atlas* maps 106, 113.

    3. Present Bozeman Creek, in Gallatin County; on *Atlas* map 106 it is rather curiously marked "Co ni-ah Fork Clatsop Chief." For Coboway (Coni-ah), see December 12, 1805. *Atlas* map 113.

    4. Clark continued up the East Gallatin River and camped on Kelly Creek, some three to four miles east of Bozeman just north of Interstate Highway 90 near the site of Fort Ellis (established 1867). The site is noted on *Atlas* map 106 but not on map 113.

[Clark]   [July 15, 1806]

N. 45d E.	3	miles to the top of the gap of a mountain passing up on the N W. Side of the branch, Some thick under brush Such as young Cotton wood & W Thorn passing on a plain old buffalow road. the assent of the mtn. is very gradl.
East	3	miles to the top of a dividig ridge between the waters of the Missouri from those of the rochejhone passing down a branch and at 2½ miles Crossed a branch of the Middle fork of the East branch of Galitins river about ½ mile above the branch we Came down. runng to the right
S 45° E.	1	miles down a Small branch a road Coms in form the left leading over to the Easterly branch.
N. 75° E	8	Miles to the river Rochejhone passing down a branch on the North Side through a kind of vally Passed 3 Small Streams from the left & one at 6 ms. from the right and Struck the lower ⟨one⟩ ½ mile below the branch we Came down & 1½ miles below the plain the river Passes out of the rocky mountains high on each Side bottom in those mountains narrow. river about 120 yds wide bold and deep the water of a whiteish blue Colour a mountan which is ruged N. W has Snow on parts of it. Those above & on the East Side of the

river is rugid and covered with Snow   those on the West is also high but have no Snow.   much Dead timber on its N. Side.

From the gap of the Mtn. river

North	2	miles to a few Cotton under the bank and halted to let our horses graze & Dine. passed a very Small branch at ⟨½⟩ a mile below the one we Came down. I marked my ⟨the two first letters of⟩ my name and the day of the year &c. on one of the Cotton trees with red paint ⟨and Cut it in allso.⟩ The valley is open and extensive— watr. 3 ms.
North	1	mile Down river to a clump of trees in a gulley passed Som tall timber killed by fire, Saw a gang of Elk L.[1] Killed one psd. an Island (2½ ms.)
N. 15° E	4	miles to a bend of the at a deep bend to the West passed two Small runs and a large Isd. on which there was tall treess Several of them would make Small Canoes Saw a large Gang of Elk feeding on an Isld main Chanel on the E. Side Passed 11 Islands the 2 last of them large the others Small (6 ms)
N. 30° E	2	miles to the Enterans of [blank] river[2] 35 yds wide boald Current & Deep from the N W much timber on the Creek & beaver passed Several Islands Small road forks one Crossing this R about a Mile about its mouh the other passing over a high rocky hill below the Creek (2½)
N. 50° E.	3	miles river passing under a high hill rocky & Steep on the N W Side, an extensive low bottom opposit in which I Saw 3 gangues of Elk. passd Several Small Islands and Encamped on the bank of the river opposit to an Island (5)

[Clark]   *Tuesday 15th July 1806*

we collected our horses and after an early brackft at 8 A M Set out and proceeded up the branch to the head   thence over a low gap in the mountain   thence across the heads of the N E. branch of the [*NB: Easterly*][3] fork of Gallitins river which we Camped near last night passing over a low dividing ridge to the head of a water Course which runs into the Rochejhone, prosueing an old buffalow road which enlargenes by one which joins it from the most Easterly [*NB: Northerly*] branch of the East fork of Galetins R.[4] proceeding down the branch a little to the N. of East keeping on the North Side of the branch to the River *rochejhone* at which place I arrived at 2 P M.[5] The Distance from the three forks of the East-erly fork of Galletines river (from whence it may be navigated down with Small Canoes) to the river Rochejhone is 18 miles on an excellent high dry firm road with very incoiderable hills. from this river to the nearest part of the main fork of Gallitine is 29 miles mostly through a leavel plain. from the head of the Missouri at the 3 forks 48 miles through a leavel plain the most of the way as may be seen by the remarks

Course Distance & Remarks from the Three forks of Missouri to the River Rochejhone where it enters the Rocky Mounts.[6]

S 85° E   6   Miles through an open plain crossing a ridge to galletines river, it haveing made a bend to the S W. campd. the hill Sides over which we passed contain a hard white rock which lies in an inclined position and shows only in Stratus.[7] Several roads leading to a Gap in the mountain to my left.

S. 78° E.   6   Miles to a part of the river which is divided by numbers of beaver dams on one channel of the river. passed through an open leavel butifull plain covered with low grass. river makeing a bend to the N. E. from the place I crossed it this morning. passed numbers of buffalow roads which do not appear to be very old leading to the before mentioned gap.

S. 70° E.   6   Miles to the main principal Stream of the river which we crossed having crossed Several Streams near the Crossing. a leavel firm plain on the Island.

S. 78° E.   12   Miles to the most Southerly of the three easterly branches of the Easterly fork of Galletines river. passed through an open leavel plain in which there is three Small Streams of water from the Snow Mountains to the South.[8] Great quan-tities of Snow yet remains on the Mountains to the S. E South, S W. West, and at a distance to the N W. a very small quan-tity is also to be Seen on a nacked mountain to the East marked my W. C July 14th 1806 with powder on a Cotton tree at the river.

N. 80° E.   3   Miles to the enterance of a Small branch which falls into the Middle branch of the East fork of Galletine River having Crossed the middle branch at 2 miles, passed great numbers of beaver dams and ponds on the branch, and encamped.

here the mountain forms a kind of half circle in which the three branches enter them.   from which the mountains appear to run N W. from one extremity and W. from the othr

N. 45° E   3   Miles to the top of the mountain in a low gap passing up the branch on which we encamped last night, on a well beaten buffalow road, through Some thick under growth Such as young Cottonwood & thorn. Several beaver dams across this branch.   the assent gradual.

East   3   Miles to the top of the dividing ridge between the waters of the Missouri from those of the river Rochehone.   passing down a Small branch and at 2½ miles crossing a larger branch of the middle fork of the East fork of Galletins about ½ a Mile above the branch I came down, running to the right   a road coms in from the left, which passes through a low gap of the mtn. from the most easterly branch of the East fork.

S. 45° E.   1   Mile down a Small branch crossed two runs from the left[9] passing on the hill Side to the left of the branch.   the road firm and through an open country.   high mountains on each side partially Covered with pine.

N. 75° E   8
ms. 48   Miles to the River Rochejhone passing down on the Northerly side of the Same branch across which there is Several beaver dams. Crossed three Small Streams from the left with running water one of which is crouded with beaver dams.[10]   a Small stream coms in on the right at 6 ms.[11] Struck the Rochejhone ½ a mile below the branch we came down & 1½ ms. below where it passes out of the Rocky mountains.   river 120 yds wide bold, rapid and deep.

    in the evening after the usial delay of 3 hours to give the horses time to feed and rest and allowing our Selves time also to Cook and eate Dinner, I proceeded on down the river on an old buffalow road   at the distance of 9 miles below the mountains Shield River[12] discharges itself into the Rochejhone on it's N W. side above a high rocky Clift, this river is 35 yards wide deep and affords a great quantity of water   it heads in those Snowey Mountains to the N W with Howards Creek,[13] it contains some Timber Such as Cotton & willow in it's bottoms, and Great numbers of beaver   the river also abounds in those animals as far as I have Seen.

passed the creek and over a high rocky hill and encamped in the upper part of a large bottom.[14] The horses *feet* are very sore many of them Can Scercely proceed on over the Stone and gravel[15] in every other respect they are Sound and in good Sperits. I saw two black bear on the side of the mountains this morning. Several gangs of Elk from 100 to 200 in a gangue on the river, great numbers of Antelopes.   one Elk only killed to day.

The Roche passes out of a high rugid mountain covered with Snow.[16] the bottoms are narrow within the mountains but widen from ½ a m. to 2 ms. in the Vally below, those bottoms are Subject to over flow, they contain Some tall Cotton wood, and willow rose bushes & rushes Honey suckle &c.   a Second bottom on the N E. Side which rises to about 20 feet higher the first & is 1 m. wide   this bottom is coars gravel pebils & Sand with Some earth[17] on which the grass grow very Short and at this time is quit dry   this 2d bottom over flows in high floods[18]   on the opposit Side of the river the plain is much higher and extendes quite to the foot of the mountain. The mountains to the S. S. E on the East side of the river is rocky rugid and on them are great quantities of Snow.[19] a bold Snow mountain which bears East[20] & is imediately at & N W of the 3 forks of the East fork of Gallitins river may be Seen, there is also a high rugid Mtn. on which is Snow bearing North 15 or 20 miles.[21]   but fiew flowers to be Seen in those plains.   low grass in the high plains, and the Common corse grass, rushes and a species of rye[22] is the growth of the low bottoms.   the mountains have Some scattering pine on them, and on the Spurs and hill Sides there is some scrubby pine. I can See no timber Sufficient large for a Canoe which will Carry more than 3 men and Such a one would be too Small to answer my purpose

1. "L." is probably François Labiche.

2. Shields River, see below.

3. Biddle added brackets around Clark's words "N E. branch of the" and interlined his word above it, all in red ink.

4. Clark went easterly up Kelly Creek, then crossed Jackson Creek and went through Bozeman Pass in the Bridger Range, passing from Gallatin County to Park County, Montana. The route is clearly marked on *Atlas* maps 106 and 113.

5. He went east down the north side of Billman Creek, reaching the Yellowstone River at present Livingston in Park County. *Atlas* maps 106, 107, 113.

6. Here in Codex M Clark inserts his cumulative courses and distances from the Three Forks to the Yellowstone for July 13–15, 1806.

7. The strata of hard, white, rock lying in an inclined position was the limestone observed on July 13, 1806.

8. Hyalite, McDonald, and Baxter creeks, in Gallatin County west of Bozeman, coming from the Gallatin Mountains; nameless on *Atlas* maps 106, 113.

9. Quinn Creek and an unnamed stream in Park County. *Atlas* maps 106, 113.

10. Flynn Creek, Area Creek, and an unnamed stream, all in Park County. *Atlas* maps 106, 113.

11. Miner Creek in Park County. *Atlas* maps 106, 113.

12. After John Shields of the party; unlike so many streams the captains named for members of the Corps of Discovery, Shields River, which meets the Yellowstone in Park County a few miles northeast of Livingston and west of Sheep Mountain, retains the same name today. It is named on *Atlas* map 106 but not on map 113.

13. Shields River heads in the Crazy Mountains in northern Park County; near there is the head of Sixteenmile Creek, the captains' Howard's Creek, which flows west to meet the Missouri River in Gallatin County. *Atlas* map 64.

14. Clark camped on the north side of the Yellowstone River in Park County, just south of Sheep Mountain and some three miles below the mouth of Shields River. *Atlas* maps 106, 107, 113.

15. The gravel likely was both alluvium and slopewash deposits that cap the lower terrace on the northwest side of the Yellowstone River. The stone may be either the larger cobbles in those deposits or the blocky-weathering, Tertiary-Cretaceous Livingston Formation over which Clark's party passed just before making camp.

16. From where Clark viewed it the Yellowstone emerged from between the Gallatin Range on the west and the Absaroka Range on the east. *Atlas* maps 106, 113.

17. This terrace is actually on the northwest side of the river. Although the most conspicuous components of the Yellowstone terrace deposits are gravel and cobbles, sand- and silt-sized materials make up more than half the deposits.

18. It was probably Biddle who drew a red line through this sentence to strike it out.

19. The Absaroka Range and the Beartooth Mountains to the east of them.

20. This is impossible from Clark's position on the Yellowstone, but if he means "west," then Saddle Peak in the Bridger Range could be the mountain.

21. The Crazy Mountains.

22. Clark has returned to the shortgrass prairie of the high plains east of the Rocky Mountains, which is dominated by blue grama, *Bouteloua gracilis* (HBK.) Lag., buffalo-grass, *Buchloe dactyloides* (Nutt.) Engelm., and a variety of other species. The rye is probably basin wildrye, *Elymus cinereus* Scribn. & Merrill. Fernald, 182, 184; Mueggler & Stewart.

[Clark]   16th

N 80° E	9	miles to a bluff in a bend right the general course of the river very Straight passed a ⟨great number of⟩ Several Islands the most of them covered with Cottonwood and Willer The Trees too Small for Canoes. passed a large Creek from the right which I call [*blank*] Creek[1] (11 ms)
N. 10° W.	1	miles to a bend on the right side (1)
N. 50° E	1½	Miles to a ⟨bluff⟩ Clift of rocks in a bend on the right Side— (2 M)
N. 10° E	2½	Miles to a bend to the left opsd. a large Island main Channel on the right Dined on the Isld. killd a fat Buffalow & saw 2 w[hite] Bear. a gange of Elk 200 & a gang of Antelopes wild gees &c &c. (4 Ms)
N. 46° E[2]	4½	miles to a N W bend of the river at which place there is a very inconsiderable rapid under a low Clift of rocks on the N W Side, passed a branch at 2 miles and one on the S E. Side of the river at 3 miles. river making a genl. bend to the S. E.— W[ater] 7 ⟨6½⟩
N. 60° E	4	miles to Some high trees in a bend to the S E Side passed a drean N. W. Side high land on the S. E. Side a Short distance from the river. the first 2 ms of this cours a low Bluff on the N W. Side. by water 6 m
North	2½	Miles to the bend under a low bluff on N W. Side Buffalow Crossing just above passed 2 dreans on N W Side an extensive low bottom on the S E. Side 3 or 400 B or Elk in it (4)
N: 40° E	1	Mile to the enterance of a small Creak on the N W Side below which I incamped opposit to a Small Island by water 1 mile only Labiech killed an Elk. L. brought me a Small fish 8 ins long formed like a trout. the mouth placed like a Sturgion with a red Streak down each side from the gills to the tail

[Clark]   *Wednesday 16th July 1806*

I gave Labeech promission to proceed on early ⟨in⟩ this morning a head and kill a fat Elk or Buffalow.   our horses haveing rambled to a long distance down the river detained us much later than Common.   we did not Set out untill 9 A M.   we had not proceeded on far before I saw a buffalow & Sent Shannon to kill it   this buffalow provd. to be a very fat Bull   I had most of the flesh brought on an a part of the Skin to make mockersons [*NB: remarkable sort of bag round foot*] for Some of our lame horses.   proceeded on down the river without finding any trees Sufficently large for a Canoe about 10 miles and halted having passed over to an Island on which there was good food for our horses to let them graze & Dine. I have not Seen Labeech as yet. Saw a large gangue of about 200 Elk and nearly as many Antilope   also two white or Grey Bear in the plains, one of them I Chased on horse back about 2 miles to the rugid part of the plain where I was compelled to give up the Chase   two of the horses was So lame owing to their feet being worn quit Smooth and to the quick, the hind feet was much the worst   I had Mockersons made of green Buffalow Skin and put on their feet which Seams to releve them very much in passing over the Stoney plains.   after dinner I proceeded on   Soon after I had set Out Labeech joined us with part of a fat Elk which he had killed. I passed over a Stoney point at which place the river runs Close to the high land on the N W. side   crossed a small Creek and Encamped on the river a little below its' Enterance.[3] Saw emence heards of Elk feeding on the opposit side of the river. I saw a great number of young gees in the river.   one of the men brought me a fish of a species I am unacquainted; it was 8 inches long formed like a trout.   it's mouth was placed like that of the Sturgeon   a red streak passed down each Side from the gills to the tail.[4] The rocks which the high lands are faced with and which may also be seen in perpendicular Straters in the high plains, is a dark freestone.   the greater part of this rock is of an excellent grit for Grindstones hard and sharp.[5]   observe the Silkgrass[6] Sunflower[7] & Wild indigo[8] all in blume.   but fiew other flowers are to be Seen in those plains. The river and Creek bottoms abound in Cotton wood trees, tho' none of them Sufficiently large for Canoes.   and the current of the Rochejhone is too rapid [*NB: & not willing*] to depend on Skinn canoes. [*NB: which are not so easy managed & we did not know the river*] no other alternetive for me but to proceed on down untill I can find a tree Sufficently large &c. to make a Canoe.—

Courses Computed distance by Land and Water Down the River Rochejhone from the Rocky Mountain in Latd. 45° 22′ 30″ North and Longtd. [*blank*] W. July 15 & 16th 1806[9]

			Miles by watr.
North	2	miles on a direct Course from the gap of the mountain to a fiew Cotton trees under the bank and on the west or Larboard Side of the river & on a Small Chanel. I marked my name withe red paint and the day of the month & year also the distance & course of the portage on one of the Cotton trees. wide bottom on the Lard Side, the high Slopeing Prarie on the Stard Side	3½
North	1	Mile to a cluster of trees in a Gully. passed some tall timber laterly killed by fire in the low bottom. the high bottom appear to have been over flown	2½
N. 15° E.	4	Miles to a deep bend of the river to the West passed two Small runs and a large Island on which I Saw Some trees nearly large enough for Small canoes. main chanel on the East of the island. passed 11 Islands in this Course, the two lower of them large the others Small	7
N. 30° E.	2	Miles to the enterance of Shield— River of 35 yds. wide deep & a boald Current with a great perpotion of timber on its borders. this river is from the N W. much beaver sign. a high rugid rocky hill buts the river imediately below a very good buffalow road passing from the head of this river through a gap of the Mts. to the Missouri	3
N. 50° E 3 [EC: Camp July 15]		Miles passing a high rocky hill on the Lard. Side, to the enterance of a Small Creek on the Lard. Side passd. Several Small islands. an extensive low bottom on the Stard. Side in which there is great nos. of Elk feeding.	5

N. 80° E. 9 [*EC: July* *16th*]	Miles to a Bluff in a Stard. bend. the general course of the river very Streight passing Several islands, Most of them Covered with Cotton trees and willow. passed Stinking Cabin Creek 20 yards wide bold current from which falls in on the Stard Side. Timber up this Cree as far as I could see	11
N. 10° W. 1	Mile on the Course to a bend on the Stard. side	1
N. 50° E. 1½	Miles to a Clift of rocks in a bend to the Stard. side passing Some Small Islands	2
N 10° E. 2½	Miles on the Course to a Stard. Bend opsd. a large island. main Chanel on the Stard. Side	4
N. 46° E. 4½	Miles on the Course to a Lard Bend of the river at which place there is Some rocks in the middle of the river near a low Clift of rocks on the Lard. Side passing a branch at 2 miles, and one on the Stard. Side at 3 miles. river having a Genl. bend to the S. E.	7
N. 60° E. 4	Miles on the Course to Some high trees in a Std. bend. passing under a low bluff on the Lard. side for 2 ms. the high lands on the opposit Side Seperated from the river by a narrow low bottom passed several small islands.	6½
N. 2½	Miles on the Course to a low bluff in a Lard. bend below a great Crossing place of the buffalo. passed two Brooks on the Lard. side. an extensive low bottom on the Stard. side in which I saw great numbers of Elk feeding.	4
N. 40° E <u>1</u>	Mile on the Course to the enterane of a Small Creek on the Lard. Side below which I encamped below a Small Island in a Small bottom in which there was good grass	<u>1½</u>

       Miles <u><u>3</u>8</u> by land   *Miles by water* <u><u>5</u>8</u>

    1. "Stinking Cabin Creek" in the codex entry courses and distances; perhaps present Mission Creek, about a mile below Clark's campsite of July 15 on the opposite side of the Yellowstone River, or Locke Creek, some three miles below Mission Creek, both in Park

County, Montana. *Atlas* maps 107, 114. Clark is using a name supplied by the Mandans and Hidatsas (see Fort Mandan Miscellany, vol. 3). The "Stinking Cabin Creek" of the table therein would appear to be Boulder River in Sweet Grass County, Montana, one of the "Rivers Across" of July 18, 1806, below, or Shoshone River, Park and Greybull counties, Wyoming. Clark may well have misidentified the stream in the present instance, since the Indians at Fort Mandan obviously did not tell him of every affluent of the Yellowstone.

2. The number "60" appears above this course, but cannot be matched to any mileage total.

3. The camp was in Sweet Grass County, Montana, on the north side of the Yellowstone just below the mouth of Little Timber Creek; the stream is "Small Creek" on *Atlas* map 107, and "Grape Creek Small" on *Atlas* map 114.

4. Perhaps the mountain sucker, *Catostomus platyrhynchus;* if so, the first description. Burroughs, 264–65; Cutright (LCPN), 426.

5. The dark freestone is sandstone of the Livingston Formation and the Eagle Sandstone. Dips up to 70° occur along some of the anticlines and synclines, but no perpendicular strata have been mapped in this area. Many near-vertical igneous dikes, however, cut the surface several miles north of the river, but would not have been easily seen from Clark's route.

6. This is undoubtedly hemp dogbane, as noted under Lewis's entry of July 20, 1806. It is not a coincidence that Lewis also mentions silkgrass and sunflowers together in bottomland habitats.

7. See Lewis's entry of July 20, 1806.

8. This can be neither the false indigo, *Amorpha,* nor the wild false indigo, *Baptesia,* since neither are known from the area. The term wild indigo probably refers to a plant with pinnately compound leaves typical of true indigo, *Indigoifera.* It is probably a species of milkvetch, *Astragalus,* or of locoweed, *Oxytropis,* possibly purple locoweed, *O. lambertii* Pursh. Dorn, 134, 143.

9. Clark's courses and distances from the East Gallatin River down the Yellowstone; the "Rocky Mountain" here is more specifically the Bridger Range.

[Clark]   17 July

N. 30° E   1½   miles to a bend under a hill to the N. E Side.   river making a bend to the right in which there is 3 Island   by watr.   3 m

N. 65° E   5   miles to the enterance of 2 large Creeks on each Side of the river on those Creeks is much Cotton timer.   all the mountains to the S W is covered with Snow. Some Snow also on the mountains N. W.   the high Snow Mtn. is W. N. W.   river make 2 bends to right   9

N. 76° E   2½   miles to mouth of a brook   River make a bend to the right.   1½

N. 85 E	3	miles to a brook in a N E bend passd. a Small Island river makeing a Small bend to the right. 3½
S. 15° E.	3	miles to the enterance of a Creek on the right the road passing over a hill. under which the river passes from 1 to 2 ms.— 5
S. 60° E	3	miles to the enteranc a large Creek on the N W Side Crooked 30 yds wide one on the oposit Side nearly opposit. all these Creeks have a great quantity of Cotton Trees in this bottoms their water of a milkey colour. Dined. Saw a *Pelican* 5 ms.

after Dinner 17th July 1806 from the enterance of the R[1]

S 40° E	3	miles to high point on the N E Side opposit a high Clift in the opsd bend the river haveig made a bend to the right in which there is 2 islands. Saw a pilicin alone— by water 4 ms.
N. 80° E	3	miles by land to a bluff under a high pine hill on the N W Side passed 10 Islands a large Creek fallen in on the opposit side. 8
S. 60° E	3	miles to the enteranc of a Small ⟨Creek⟩ Brook on the right Side passing one large Island, river passing under the high land on N. E. Side. passed an Indian fort of logs & bark Lard.— 4 ms. ½
N. 80° E	3	miles to the enterance of a Small Creek on the Stard Side passed 2 large and 5 Small Islands the river Passing under high pine land on Lard Side for 2 miles.— 5 ⟨4⟩ ms. ½
N. 60° E	3	miles to point of wood in the Lard. bend passed 3 Islands narrow low bottom on each Side ½ mile wide Saw Several Buffalow opposit on the Stard side. encamped in the bottom opsd. a Small island. 5 ms

[Clark]   *Thursday 17th July 1806*

   The rain of last night wet us all.   [*NB: having no tent, & no covering but a buffaloe skin*]   I had the horses all Collected early and Set out, proceeded ove the point of a ridge and through an open low bottom   crossed a large Creek which heads in a high Snow toped Mountain to the N W. imediately opposit to the enterance of the Creek one Something larger falls in from the high Snow mountains to the S W. & South   those Creeks I call *Rivers across*[2]   they contain Some timber in their Vallys   at the distance of [*blank*] Miles by water we arive at the enterance of two Small rivers [*NB: otter creeks*][3] or large Creeks which fall in nearly opposit to each other   the one on the N E side is 30 yards wide. I call it Otter River the other Beaver R[4] below the enterance of this Creek I halted as usial to let the Horses graze &c. I saw a Single Pelican which is the first which I have Seen on this river.   after Dinner I proceeded on Down the Rochejhone passing over a low ridge through a Small bottom and on the Side of a Stoney hill for 2 miles and through a Small [*NB: bottom*] and again on the Side of a high hill for 1½ M. to a bottom in which we Incamped opposit a Small Island.[5] The high lands approach the river on either side much nearer than it does above and their Sides are partially covered with low pine & Cedar,[6] none of which are Sufficently large for Canoes, nor have I Seen a Cotton tree in the low bottoms Sufficently large for that purpose. Buffalow is getting much more plenty than they were above. not so many Elk & more deer Shannon killed one deer. I Saw in one of those Small bottoms which I passed this evening an Indian fort[7] which appears to have been built last Summer.   this fort was built of logs and bark.   the logs was put up very Closely   [*NB: ends supporting each other*] capping on each other about 5 feet [*NB: high*] and Closely chinked. around which bark was Set up on end so as to Cover the Logs.   the enterance was also guarded by a work on each Side of it and faceing the river.   this work is about 50 feet Diameter & nearly round.   the Squaw informs me that when the war parties [*NB: of Minnits Crows &, who fight Shoshonees*] find themselves pursued they make those forts to defend themselves in from the pursuers whose Superior numbers might other wise over power them and cut them off without receiveing much injurey on hors back &c.

Courses Distances Computed & Remarks 17th July

			Ms. by water
N. 30° E.	1½	Miles on the Course to a Larboard bend under a hill, river makeing a bend to the Stard. Side in which there is 3 islands Covered with timber	3

N. 65° E.	5	Miles on the Course to the Enterance of two large Creeks one on each Side imediately opposite each other which I call Rivers a Cross[8] a great proportion of timber on both of those Creeks. river making two bends to the Stard Side in the Course. High Snow Mts. W. N W, and those to the S. W is also covered with S.	9
N. 76° E.	1½	Miles to the enterance of a brook in the Lard. Bend	1½
N. 85° E	3	Miles on the Course to a Brook in a Lard Bend passed a small Island river bending a little to the Stard Side. Current rapid	3½
S. 15° E.	3	Miles on the Course to the enterance of *Thy snag'd* Creek[9] on the Stard. Side. river passing under a high rocky hill from 1 to 2 Miles	5
S. 60° E.	3	Miles on the Course to the enterance of a large creek on the Lard. Side, crooked and 30 yds wide which I call Otter River a large creek or Small river falls in nearly opposit Beaver R.[10] much timber on both of those streams. the water of a milky colour. passed islands. Saw a Single pelican & a pen to catch birds.	5½
S. 40° E.	3	Miles to a high point on the Lard. Side opposite a high Clift in the opposit bend, the river haveing made a bend to Std. in which there is 2 large Islands	5
N. 80° E.	4	Miles on the Course to a Clift under a high pine hill on the Lard. Side passing the enteranc of a large Creek on the Stard. Side which I call Brattens Ck.[11] and 10 islands in this Course	8
S. 60° E.	3	Miles to the enterance of a Small Brook[12] on the Stard. Side passing one large Island. an old indian fort of logs & bark river passed at the foot of a high hill on the Larboard Side	4½

N. 80° E.	3	Miles to the enterance of a Small Creek[13] on the Stard. Side, passing 2 large & 5 Small Islands, the river passing under a high pine hill for 2 miles. rocky	5
N. 60° E.	3	Miles to a point of wood in the Lard. Bend, passed 3 islands. the bottoms are narrow and low on each Side of the river, not exceeding ½ a mile in width. Encpd.	5

Ms.   <u>33</u> by Land   Ms. by water <u>55</u>

1. Opposite this page of his first draft Clark has a sketch map (fig. 5). On it are mileage figures apparently for July 15–19. While it bears the words "dined 18th" near one end and an apparent campsite symbol near the middle which might be the camp of July 17, it is difficult to reconcile this map with *Atlas* maps 107, 108, 114, and 115, showing the route of July 17–18—or to reconcile it with any other portion of the Yellowstone.

2. On the north is Big Timber Creek and on the south is Boulder River, in the vicinity of present Big Timber, Sweet Grass County, Montana. Big Timber Creek is likely to be that referred to by Thomas James, who passed by in 1810 when working for Manuel Lisa, as the "Twenty Five Yard" River; that width is the only notation given for that stream ("River 25 yds wide bold") on *Atlas* map 114, other than "rivers across." Similar designations, with varying widths, appear for Boulder River and for both streams on *Atlas* maps 107, 125, and 126. It is not unlikely that Lisa and his partners had a copy of Clark's map of the region, since Clark was a partner in the enterprise. "Twenty Five Yard" River has sometimes been identified with Shields River, but some confusion may have occurred over the years. James, 48; Oglesby, 69; Bradley (MMC), 29. The words "Rivers across" may have been added to a blank space and they may not be in Clark's hand, nor do they look to be a Biddle emendation.

3. Biddle crossed out Clark's words "Small rivers" and interlined "otter creeks," then crossed out those words, all in red ink.

4. Sweet Grass and Lower Deer creeks, respectively, in Sweet Grass County. *Atlas* maps 107, 114. The words from "Otter" to "R" were apparently substituted for some erased material.

5. The camp was on the north side of the Yellowstone a mile or two below the mouth of Hump Creek, in Sweet Grass County, just west of the Stillwater County line. It appears to be marked "Encamped 7th July 1806" on *Atlas* map 107, but Clark's numbers may have run together. See also *Atlas* map 115.

6. Limber pine, *Pinus flexilis* James, and Rocky Mountain juniper, red cedar, *Juniperus scopulorum* Sarg. Little (CIH), 56-W, 30-W; Mueggler & Stewart.

7. In Sweet Grass County, just above the mouth of Work Creek (which does not appear on *Atlas* maps 107 or 114) on the opposite side. As Sacagawea noted, a number of

tribes made use of such fortifications for emergency defense against superior numbers; sometimes they also used stones in construction. Thomas James describes one used by Crows on the Yellowstone in 1810, and Henry Brackenridge mentions an Arikara one in 1811. Ewers (ILUM), 117–30; James, 49; Brackenridge, 124. Just above this fort on *Atlas* map 114 is marked the site where a party of trappers led by Michael Immell and Robert Jones of the Missouri Fur Company were defeated by Blackfeet on May 31, 1823, with Immell and Jones being killed. The discovery of this map helped fur trade scholars locate this incident for the first time. Apparently the map was copied from some version of Clark's original on which Clark, as Indian superintendent for the region, had recorded the site. Morgan, 48–50; Wood & Moulton, 384.

8. Another addition to an apparent blank space in an unidentifiable hand.

9. Present Upper Deer Creek in Sweet Grass County, some two miles above Lower Deer Creek. The name obviously derives from the accident which happened to Gibson, recorded in Codex M as happening the following day, July 18. The name can be found on *Atlas* map 107 but not on map 114. It is not apparent why the incident should be commemorated by naming a creek passed the day before it happened. Clark may have misdated the episode in his codex journal, writing some time after it occurred, or mislocated the stream he intended to name after it in making final versions of his maps. Either would indicate uncharacteristic carelessness on his part.

10. Both "Otter River" and "Beaver R." appear to be later additions, the first to a blank space, the other as an interlineation.

11. Present Bridger Creek, in Sweet Grass County. *Atlas* maps 107, 114. "Brattens," after William Bratton of the party, replaces some erased material.

12. Present Work Creek in Sweet Grass County, not shown on *Atlas* maps 107, 114, or 115.

13. Clark's "Weasel Creek," today's Hump Creek. *Atlas* maps 107, 115.

[Clark]   18th July

East   3   miles to a Stard. Bend passing under a high pine hill on Lard
                            Side   Several Islands—   4½

N. 62° E   4½   miles to the enterance of a Small Creek on a bend to Lard
                            Side opposit to 3 Islands[1]   passed Several Small Islands
                            high lands on Std. a narrow bottom on the Lard side. Saw a
                            great Smoke in the R mts. S 20° W.[2]   the rock mts. Termo-
                            nate S 30° W.   a mtn. not So high at a long distance is S. 80°
                            E.—   7 ⟨6⟩ m

S. 78° E   2½   Miles to a bend to the Stard. Side passing Several Islands.
                            river pass under a high ruged hill on the Lard side   bad
                            road—   4 ms.

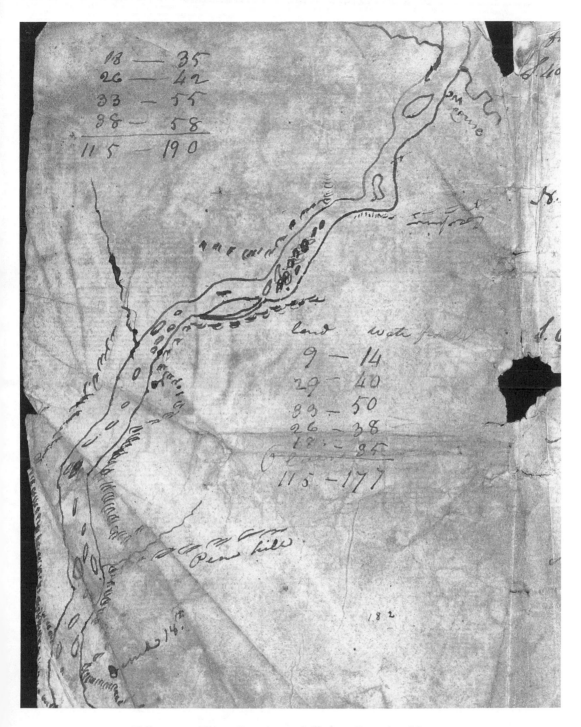

5. Yellowstone River, Sweetgrass-Stillwater Counties, Montana,
July 17–18, 1806, Voorhis First Draft

East	3½	miles to a Stard Bend passing a High point at 2 miles on the Lard Side a narrow bottom on the Stard Side High hills on each Side partially Covered with pine. Country ruged and Stoney. halted in a bottom to dine. 6 ms.
N. 20° E	2	Mile to a Lard. Bend river passing under the high land on the Stard Side at 1 mile the bottom on Lard Side ¼ of a mile wide. 3½ ms.
N. 72° E	3½	miles to a bend[3] [tear] ⟨passd.⟩ enterance a large dr[tear] [illegible, crossed out] [tear] ⟨S 45°⟩ to an Indian fort on [tear] an Island divided [tear] by a narrow Chann [tear] under the Stard. Hills
S. 45° E	6	miles to a high pine hill ⟨at⟩ [tear] Side at the foot of which the riv[er] [pass]es haveing made Several shot bends in which there is Several Islands Bottoms ½ m. wide on the Lard Side a good propotion of Cotton & Willow on the borders of the river— 10 m
S. 82° E	1	miles to the head of a Small Isld. Close to the Lard Shore and incamped river makeing a bend to the right and passing under high lands on the Stard. Side. Killed a Buffalow— 2 ⟨½⟩

[Clark]   *Friday 18th July 1806*

as we were about Setting out this morning two Buffalow Bulls came near our Camp   Several of the men Shot at one of them.   their being near the river plunged in and Swam across to the opposit Side and there died. Shabono was thrown from his horse to day in pursute of a Buffaloe, the hose unfortunately Steping into a Braroe[4] hole fell and threw him over his head.   he is a good deel brused on his hip Sholder & face.   after brackfast I proceeded on as usial, passd. over points of ridges So as to cut off bends of the [*NB: river*]   crossed a Small Muddy brook[5] on which I found great quantities of the Purple, yellow & black currents[6] ripe.   they were of an excellent flavour. I think the purple Superior to any I have ever tasted. The river here is about 200 yards wide   rapid as usial and the water gliding over corse gravel and round Stones of various sizes of an excellent grite for whetestones.   the bottoms of the river are narrow.   the hills are not exceeding 200 feet in hight   the sides of them are generally rocky and composed of rocks of the same texture of a dark

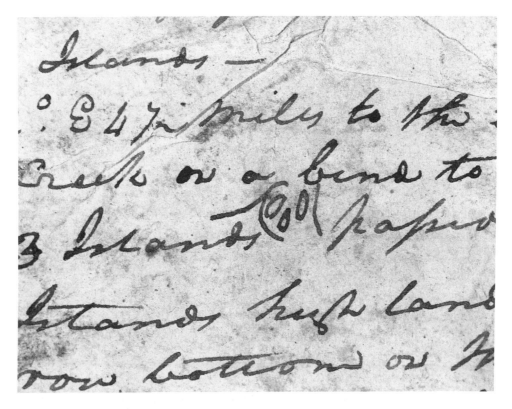

6. Islands on the Yellowstone River, Stillwater County, Montana,
July 18, 1806, Voorhis First Draft

Colour of Grit well Calculated for grindstones &c. The high bottoms is composed of gravel and Stone like those in the Chanel of the river, with a mixture of earth of a dark brown colour[7]   The Country back from the river on each Side is generally open wavering plains. Some pine is to be Seen in every direction in those plains on the Sides of hills &c.   at 11 A. M. I observed a Smoke rise to the S. S. E in the plains towards the termonation of the rocky mountains in that direction (which is Covered with Snow) this Smoke must be raisd. by the Crow Indians in that direction as a Signal for us, or other bands. I think it most probable that they have discovered our trail and takeing us to be Shoshone &c. in Serch of them the Crow Indians [*WC: now at peace with them*] to trade as is their Custom, have made this Smoke to Shew where they are—or otherwise takeing us to be their Enemy made this Signal for other bands to be on their guard. I halted in a bottom of fine grass to let the horses graze.

Shields killed a fat Buck on which we all Dined.   after dinner and a delay of 3 hours to allow the horses time to feed, we Set out at 4 P. M. I set out and proceeded down the river through a butifull bottom, passing a Indian fort on the head of a Small island near the Lard Shore and Encamped on a Small Island Seperated from the Lard Shore by a very narrow Chanel.[8] Shields killed a Buffalow this evening which Caused me to halt sooner than Common to Save Some of the flesh which was So rank and Strong that we took but very little. Gibson in attempting to mount his horse after Shooting a deer this evening fell and on a Snag and sent it nearly [*NB: two*] inches into the Muskeler part of his thy.   he informs me this Snag was about 1 inch in diamuter burnt at the end.   this is a very bad wound and pains him exceedingly. I dressed the wound.

Course Distance & remarks July 18th 1806

			Ms. by water
East	3	Miles to a Stard. Bend passing at the foot of a high pine hill rocky and Steep on the Lard. Side. passed several Islds.	4½
N. 62° E	4½	Miles on the course to the enterance of a *Small Creek* in a Lard. Bend opposit to three Islands passing Several Small Islands, high lands on the Stard. Side bottoms narrow on the Lard Side (Saw a smoke S. 30° W.[)] discover the Big horn mountain which is low at S. 80° E.	7
S. 78° E.	2½	Miles on the Course to a bend on the Stard Side passed Several Islands. river washing the base of a high ruged Stoney hill on the Lard Side	4
East	3½	Miles on the course to a Stard. Bend passing a high point at 2 Miles on the Lard. Side a narrow bottom on the Stard. Side. the hills are high on each Side partially covered with pine. Country ruged and Stoney emence qtty of Prickley pears[9]	6
N. 20° E.	2	Miles on the Course to a Lard Bend. river washing the base of the high land on the Starboard Side at one mile. the bottoms on the Larboard side a quarter of a mile wide—	3½

N. 72° E. 3½ | Miles on the Course to a Lard Bend   passd. the enterance of a *large dry Creek* & 3 islands an old indian fort on an Island close to the Lard Shore.   river washing the foot of the Stard. Hills } 5

S. 45° E. 6 | Miles on the course to a high hill on the Stard. Side at the foot of which the river passes, haveing made Several Short bends in which there is Several islands.   the bottoms ½ a mile wide on the Stard Side.   a good proportion of Cotton wood and willow on the borders of the river on each Side. } 11

S. 82° E. 1 | Mile to the head of a Small island close to the Lard Shore.   river makeing a bend to the Stard. under the high lands which is ruged and Stoney en- camped on the Island   Gibson Snaged his thye } 2

Ms. 26 by land   *by water* Ms. 43

1. At this point in the first draft Clark has inserted a small sketch map (fig. 6) showing the three islands. They were in Stillwater County, Montana, at the mouth of present White Beaver Creek, Clark's "Muddy Creek" ("Small Creek muddy" on *Atlas* map 115). *Atlas* map 107.

2. Clearly "S 20° W." here in the first draft, but "S. S. E" in the text of the Codex M entry and "S. 30° W." in the codex courses and distances. To the southwest would lie the Absaroka Range, the Beartooth Mountains, the Granite Range, and other highlands in the vicinity of the Yellowstone Plateau. The mountains to the east at a long distance would be the Pryor Mountains.

3. Part of this page in the first draft version is missing, resulting in gaps in the courses for this day and for July 19, 1806. See the Codex M entries for missing information.

4. A badger, *Taxidea taxus;* Clark's term is from the French *blaireau;* see July 30, 1804.

5. After passing Monument Butte, he reached White Beaver Creek, in Stillwater County. *Atlas* maps 104, 115.

6. The purple and yellow currants are genetic variants of golden currant. The black currant is probably the wild black currant, *Ribes americanum* Mill. See April 30, 1805, for a discussion of regional currants.

7. The high bottoms are Yellowstone River terraces of sand, gravel and cobbles. The dark soil is either organic-rich material or is derived from weathering of the dark-colored Tertiary-Cretaceous Livingston Formation.

8. In Stillwater County, some three miles west of Columbus and the mouth of the Still- water River (Clark's "Rose bud R"). A mile or so below the camp is the mouth of Huntley Creek, which does not appear on *Atlas* maps 108 or 115. The "Indian fort" appears on

Atlas maps 107 and 115 a little above a dry brook which is apparently present Berry Creek.

9. The species that Lewis noticed on July 10: brittle prickly pear and plains prickly pear.

[Clark]   (19)[1]

N. 72° E	2	miles to a bend on the Lard Sid lower part of a low Clift of rocks. large timbered bottom opposit and a large Creek Comes out of the hills opposit which I call. The [*blank*] river haveing made a bend to the Stard Side to the hills. above the Creek. 3 ms [*tear*] [p]assed Some high land [*tear*] [wh]ich the river passed [*tear*] miles on the Lard Sid and [*tear*] on the Stard Side. river [*tear*] genl. bends to the Stard. Side [*tear*]
[East	9]	[*tear*] Islands of various Sizes. passd. an old Indian fort at 2 miles in a Small Island near the Lard Shore (19)
North	1½	miles to a Lard Bend high Clift on the Stard. Side opsd. an Island— 1½
N 60° E	1	mile to the point of a high Clift on the Stard. Bend river makes a round bend to the Lard. Side 3 m
N. 50° E	1½	ms. to a point of high bluff on the Stard. Side passing a bend to Lard. an Island. High Bluffs on the Stard. Side— 3 m
East	3	miles to Some large trees in the Lard. bend passing Several Islands river very much divided and crooked Camped and killed 7 Elk and 4 Deer and a Antelope and wounded 4½ miles—

[Clark]   *Saturday 19th July 1806.*

I rose early and dressed Gibsons wound.   he Slept but very little last night and complains of great pain in his Knee and hip as well as his *thy*.   there being no timber on this part of the Rochjhone sufficintly large for a Canoe and time is pracious as it is our wish to get to the U States this Season, conclude to take Gibson in a litter if he is not able to ride on down the river untill I can find a tree Sufficently large for my purpose. I had the Strongest and jentlesst Horse Saddled and placed Skins & blankets in Such a manner that when he was put on the horse he felt himself in as easy a position as when lying.   this was a fortunate circunstance as he

Could go much more at his ease than in a litter.   passed Rose bud river[2] on Sd Side   [*NB: So called by Indians; i. e. Itch-ke-pe (Rose) ar-ja (rivr) about 40 yds. saw many rs. bds., a beautiful*]   I proceeded on about 9 miles, and halted to let the horses graze and let Gibson rest.   his leg become So numed from remaining in one position, as to render extreemly painfull to him. I derected Shields to keep through the thick timber and examine for a tree sufficently large & Sound to make a Canoe, and also hunt for Some Wild Ginger[3] for a Poltice for Gibsons wound.   he joined me at dinner with 2 fat Bucks but found neither tree or Ginger.   he informed me that 2 white bear Chased him on horsback, each of which he Shot from his horse &c. Currents are ripe and abundant, i, e, the Yellow, black & purple spcies.   we passed over two high points of Land from which I had a View of the rocky Mounts. to the W. & S. S. E. all Covered with Snow. I also Saw a low mountain in an Easterly direction.[4]   the high lands is partially Covered with pine and form purpendcular Clifts on either side.   afer dinner I proceeded on   the high lands become lower on either Side and those of the Stard Side form Bluffs of a darkish yellow earth;[5] the bottom widens to Several Ms. on the Stard Side.   the timber which cotton wood principally Scattered on the borders of the river is larger than above. I have Seen Some trees which would make very Small Canoes. Gibsons thy became So painfull that he could not Set on the horse after rideing about 2 hours and a half   I directed Sergt Pryor and one man to continue with him under the Shade of a tree for an hour and then proceed on to the place I Should encamp which would be in the first good [*NB: timber for canoes*] for the below. (It may be proper to observe that the emence Sworms of *Grass hoppers*[6] have distroyed every Sprig of Grass for maney miles on this Side of the river, and appear to be progressing upwards.[)]   about 4 Miles below the place I left Sergt. Pryor with Gibson   found some large timber near which the grass was tolerably good   I Encamped under a thick grove of those trees[7] which was not Sufficiently large for my purpose, tho' two of them would mak small Canoes. I took Shields and proceeded on through a large timbered bottom imediately below in Serch of better trees for Canoes, found Several about the Same Size with those at my Camp.   at dark I returned to Camp

Sergt. Pryor had arived with gibson. after my arival at this place the hunters killed Seven Elk, four Deer, and I wounded a Buffalow very badly near the Camp imediately after I arived. in the forepart of the day the hunters killed two deer an Antelope & Shot two Bear. Shabono informed me that he Saw an Indian on the high lands on the opposit Side of the river, in the time I was absent in the woods. I saw a Smoke in the Same direction with that which I had Seen on the 7th inst.[8] it appeared to be in the Mountains.

Course Distance Computed & remarks July 19th.

ms. by water

N. 72° E	2	ms. on the Course to a bend on the Larbd. Side at the lower point of a low Clift of rocks of ¼ of a mile in extent. a large Creek entering the bottom on the Stard Side nearly opposit which I call *rose bud River*[9] the river having made a bend to the Stard Side to the high land above the Creek an extensive timbered bottom on the Stard. Side	3
East	9	ms. on the course to a high point in a Stard Bend passed an old indian fort[10] on an island at 2 miles, the river passing under Some high lands on the Lard Side from 3 to 5 miles, and under high land from 6 miles on the Stard. Side. the river haveing made two genl. bends to the Stard Side passed Several of various Sizes and forms river about 200 yds wide	19
North	1½	ms. to a Lard Bend passing an island. high Clifts on the Starboard Side	1½
N. 60° E	1	me. on a direct course to a point of a high Clift in the Stard. Bend, river making a round bend bend to the Lard Side & then to the clift above point 1 ml.—	3
N. 50° E	1½	ms. on a direct course to a point of the high clift on the Stard. Side passing a Lard Bend in which there is an island high Clifts Continue on the Stard. Side	3

East   _3_   ms. on the course to a clump of a large Cotton wood trees in a Lard Bend passing several Islands river much divided and Crooked. high Yellow Bluff on the Stard. Side under which part of the river passes. The bottoms wide and extensive on the Lard. Side. Encamped—   }   _5 ½_

miles   *18*   *by land*   *by water miles—*   35

1. The first draft courses and distances break after this day, since Clark's party did not move again until July 24, when they resume. Preceding the entry for July 24, 1806, and upside down on the page facing the entry for July 19, appear the following columns of figures. They represent mileages for the Yellowstone trip, although Clark has made errors in addition, in spite of attempts to correct. The final total should probably be 827. They cover mileages for July 13–19 and July 24–August 2, 1806. Clark deducted the 48 miles he covered from the Three Forks of the Missouri to the point where he reached the Yellowstone (July 13–15, 1806) to give him the number of miles he traveled down that river.

191	48	
189	58	
80	55	
73	43	
41	_35_	dedut
_48_	239	= 48 = 191
622	69	
66	58	
_48_	62	
735	80	
_86_	73	
829	41	
	48	
	66	
	45	
	86	
	_8_	
	636	
	_191_	
	837	

2. Present Stillwater River, meeting the Yellowstone River opposite Columbus, Stillwater County, Montana. Presumably the captains obtained the name from the Mandans

or Hidatsas, although it does not appear in the lists of Yellowstone tributaries in the Fort Mandan Miscellany (vol. 3, pp. 365, 374). The term appears to be a Hidatsa name, *mickapa aaši,* "rosebud creek." The name should not lead to confusion with the present Rosebud Creek, in Rosebud County, Montana, the captains' "Mar-shas-kap river" (see below). *Atlas* maps 108, 115.

3. Wild ginger is not known from this region of Montana; the search may have proven fruitless. Booth & Wright, 34. See June 27, 1806, for a medicinal use of wild ginger.

4. The mountains to the south-southeast would be the Pryor Mountains. The low mountain in the east may be the area around Stratford Hill, from nine to seventeen miles south of Billings, Montana.

5. Clark has reached the northwestern flank of the Bighorn-Pryor uplift. The uplift here brings easily eroded Niobrara and Carlile shale of the Cretaceous Colorado Group to the surface. The yellow bluffs on the south side of the river are principally formed of the Virgelle Member of the Upper Cretaceous Eagle Sandstone.

6. Perhaps either the migratory grasshopper, *Melanoplus saguinipes,* or the Rocky Mountain locust, *M. spretus;* the latter is considered extinct from about the beginning of this century. It was probably Biddle who drew a red vertical line through part of this passage.

7. Clark camped on the north side of the Yellowstone River in Stillwater County, south of present Park City, where he remained until July 24; the so-called Canoe Camp. *Atlas* maps 108, 115.

8. The number here may be "17." The smoke was seen on July 18, 1806; see n. 2 for that date.

9. The words "rose bud River" appear to have been added to a blank space, perhaps by Clark. In the left margin are the words "Mands. call," the first word representing Mandans.

10. The "Indian fort" was just east of Columbus, in Stillwater County, near the town's airport. *Atlas* maps 108, 115.

[Clark]   *Sunday 20th July 1806*

I directed Sergt. Pryor and Shields each of them good judges of timber to proceed on down the river Six or 8 miles and examine the bottoms if any larger trees than those near which we are encamped can be found and return before twelve oClock.   they Set out at daylight. I also Sent Labech Shabono & hall to Skin & some of the flesh of the Elk Labeech had killed last evening   they returned with one Skin the wolves haveing eaten the most of the other four Elk. I also Sent two men in Serch of wood Soutable for ax handles.   they found some choke cherry[1] which is the best wood which Can be precured in this Country. Saw a Bear on an Island opposit and Several Elk. Sergt. Pryor and Shields returned at half

past 11 A M. and informed me that they had proceeded down the timbered bottoms of the river for about 12 miles without finding a tree better
than those near my Camp. I deturmined to have two Canoes made out of
the largest of those trees and lash them together which will Cause them to
be Study and fully Sufficient to take my Small party & Self with what little
baggage we have down this river. had handles put in the 3 Axes and
after Sharpening them with a file fell the two trees which I intended for
the two Canoes. those trees appeared tolerably Sound and will make
Canoes of 28 feet in length and about 16 or 18 inches deep and from 16
to 24 inches wide. the men with the three axes Set in and worked untill
dark. Sergt. Pryor dressed Some Skins to make him Clothes. Gibsons
wound looks very well. I dressed it. The horses being fatigued and their
feet very Sore, I Shall let them rest a fiew days. dureing which time the
party intended for to take them by land to the Mandans[2] will dress their
Skins and make themselves Clothes to bare, as they are nearly naked.
Shields killed a Deer & Buffalow & Shannon a faun and a Buffalow &
York an Elk one of the buffalow was good meat. I had the best of him
brought in and cut thin and Spread out to dry.

1. Choke cherry; for a previous use of the wood as axe handles, see July 10, 1805.
2. For this party and its purpose, see July 23 and 24, 1806.

[Clark]   *Monday 21st July 1806*[1]

This morning I was informed that Half of our horses were absent. Sent
out Shannon Bratten, and Shabono to hunt them. Shabono went up the
river Shanon down and Bratten in the bottom near Camp, Shabono and
Bratten returned at 10 A M and informed me that they Saw no Signs of
the horses. Shannon proceeded on down the river about 14 miles and did
not return untill late in the evening, he was equally unsuckcessfull. Shannon informed me that he Saw a remarkable large Lodge[2] about 12 miles
below, covered with bushes and the top Deckorated with Skins &c and
had the appearance of haveing been built about 2 years. I Sent out two
men on hors back to kill a fat Cow which they did and returned in 3
hours the men work very diligiently on the Canoes one of them nearly
finished ready to put in the water. Gibsons wound is beginning to heal. I
am in great hope that it will get well in time for him to accompany Sgt.

Pryor with the horses to the Mandans. This evening late a very black Cloud from the S. E. accompanied with Thunder and lightning with hard winds which Shifted about and was worm and disagreeable. I am apprehensive that the indians have Stolen our horses, and probably those who had made the Smoke a fiew days passed towards the S. W. I deturmined to have the ballance of the horses guarded and for that purpose sent out 3 men, on their approach near the horses were So alarmed that they ran away and entered the woods and the men returned— a Great number of Geese which raise their young on this river passed down frequently Since my arival at this place. we appear to be in the beginning of the buffalow Country. the plains are butifull and leavel but the Soil is but thin Stoney[3] and in maney parts of the plains & bottoms there are great quantity of prickly pears. Saw Several herds of buffalow Since I arived at this Camp also antilops, wolves, pigions, Dovs, Hawks, ravins, Crows, larks, Sparrows, Eagles & bank martins[4] &c. &c. The wolves which are the constant attendants of the Buffalow are in great numbers on the Scerts of those large gangues which are to be Seen in every direction in those praries

1. An asterisk is placed in the margin to the right of this dateline; its purpose is unknown.

2. Probably a Crow sun-dance lodge, where the traditional sun-dance was performed. Clark's party was now well within the Crow homeland; the lodge was probably a few miles southwest of present Billings, Yellowstone County, Montana. See Clark's description below, July 24, 1806. Voget, 93–101, 106–7, 112–13.

3. Semiarid climate, steep slopes, and wind combine to retard soil formation. The stones are Yellowstone River terrace gravel.

4. Probably the bank swallow, *Riparia riparia* [AOU, 616]. Holmgren, 32.

[Clark]   *Tuesday 22nd of July 1806.*

The wind continued to blow very hard from the N. E. and a little before day light was moderately Cool. I Sent Sergt. Pryor and Shabono in Serch of the horses with directions to proceed up the river as far as the 1st narrows[1] and examine particularly for their tracks, they returned at 3 P M and informed me that they had proceeded up the distance I derected them to go and could See neither horses nor tracks; the Plains imediately out from Camp is So dry and hard that the track of a horse

Cannot be Seen without close examination. I therefore derected Sergt. Pryor Shannon Shabono & Bratten to incircle the Camp at Some distance around and find the tracks of the horses and prosue them, they Serched for tracks all the evening without finding which Course the horses had taken, the plains being so remarkably hard and dry as to render it impossible to See a track of a horse passing through the hard parts of them. begin to Suspect that they are taken by the Indians and taken over the hard plains to prevent our following them. my Suspicions is grounded on the improbility of the horses leaveing the grass and rushes of the river bottoms of which they are very fond, and takeing imediately out into the open dry plains where the grass is but Short and dry. if they had Continued in the bottoms either up or down, their tracks Could be followed very well. I directed Labeech who understands traking very well to Set out early in the morning and find what rout the horses had taken if possible

1. Perhaps the area, in Stillwater County, Montana, between the present camp and the camp of July 18, where the bluffs close in on the Yellowstone River.

[Clark]   *Wednesday 23rd July 1806.*

last night the wolves or dogs came into our Camp and eat the most of our dryed meat which was on a scaffold   Labeech went out early agreeable to my directions of last evening. Sergt. Pryor and Windser also went out. Sgt. pryor found an Indian Mockerson and a Small piece of a roab, the mockerson worn out on the bottom & yet wet, and have every appearance of haveing been worn but a fiew hours before.   those Indian Signs is Conclusive with me that they have taken the 24 horses which we lost on the night of the 20th instant, and that those who were about last night were in Serch of the ballance of our horses which they could not find as they had fortunately got into a Small Prarie Serounded with thick timber in the bottom. Labeech returned haveing taken a great Circle and informed me that he Saw the tracks of the horses makeing off into the open plains and were by the tracks going very fast. The Indians who took the horses bent their course reather down the river.   the men finished both Canoes by 12 oClock to day, and I sent them to make Oars & get poles after which I sent Shields and Labeech to kill a fat Buffalow out of a gangue which has been in a fiew miles of us all day. I gave Sergt Pryor his instructions[1] and a letter to Mr. Haney[2] and directed that he G. Shannon & Windser take the remaining horses to the Mandans, where he is to enquire for Mr. H. Heney if at the establishments on the Assinniboin river[3] to take 12 or 14 horses and proceed on to that place and deliver Mr. Heney the letter which is with a view to engage Mr. Heney to provale on some of the best informed and most influential Chiefs of the different bands of Sieoux to accompany us to the Seat of our Government with a view to let them See our population and resourses &c.   which I believe is the Surest garentee of Savage fidelity to any nation that of a Governmt. possessing the power of punishing promptly every aggression. Sergt. Pryor is directed to leave the ballance of the horses with the grand Chief of the Mandans untill our arival at his village   also to keep a journal of the of his rout courses distances water courss Soil production, & animals to be particularly noted.[4] Shields and Labeech killed three buffalow two of them very fat   I had as much of the meat Saved as we could Conveniently Carry.   in the evening had the two Canoes put into the water and lashed together   ores and everything fixed ready to Set out early in the morning, at which time I have derected Sergt. Pryor to Set out with the horses and proceed on to the enterance of the big horn river [*NB: which we suppose to be at no great distance*][5] at which place the Canoes will meat him and Set him across the Rochejhone below the enterance of that river.

1. See Clark to Nathaniel Pryor, July 25 [23], 1806, Jackson (LLC), 1:313–14.

2. Hugh Heney, the North West Company trader whom the captains met at Fort Mandan; see December 16, 1804. For Clark's message to him now, see Clark to Heney, July 20, 1806, Jackson (LLC), 1:309–13.

3. The North West Company posts at Assiniboine House or Montagne à la Bosse, on the Assiniboine River in Manitoba. See vol. 2, p. 226 nn.

4. No journal by Pryor is known; see Appendix B, vol. 2. *Atlas* maps 116 and 117 show his route as a dotted line, perhaps based on information after Pryor rejoined Clark on August 8, 1806, or on his hypothetical journal.

5. The mouth of the Bighorn River, on the Treasure-Bighorn county line, Montana, was some ninety miles below Clark's camp of July 19–24, 1806, in Stillwater County, Montana. For Clark's confusion of the Bighorn with Clarks Fork Yellowstone River, see July 24, 1806.

[Clark]   [Speech for Yellowstone Indians, undated][1]

Children. The Great Spirit has given a fair and bright day for us to meet together in his View that he may inspect us in this all we say and do.

Children   I take you all by the hand as the children of your Great father the President of the U. States of America who is the great chief of all the white people towards the riseing sun.

Children   This Great Chief who is Benevolent, just, wise & bountifull has sent me and one other of his chiefs (who is at this time in the country of the Blackfoot Indians) to all his read children on the Missourei and its waters quite to the great lake of the West where the land ends and the sun sets on the face of the great water, to know their wants and inform him of them on our return.

Children   We have been to the great lake of the west and are now on our return to my country. I have seen all my read children quite to that great lake and talked with them, and taken them by the hand in the name of their great father the Great Chief of all the white people.

Children   We did not see the [*blank*] or the nations to the North. I have [come] across over high mountains and bad road to this river to see the [*blank*]

Natn. I have come down the river from the foot of the great snowey mountain to see you, and have looked in every derection for you, without seeing you untill now

Children   I heard from some of your people [*blank*] nights past by my horses who complained to me of your people haveing taken 4 [24] of their cummerads.

Children   The object of my comeing to see you is not to do you injurey but to do you good the Great Chief of all the white people who has more goods at his command than could be piled up in the circle of your camp, wishing that all his read children should be happy has sent me here to know your wants that he may supply them.

Children   Your great father the Chief of the white people intends to build a house and fill it with such things as you may want and exchange with you for your skins & furs at a very low price.   & has derected me [to] enquire of you, at what place would be most convenient for to build this house. and what articles you are in want of that he might send them imediately on my return

Children   The people in my country is like the grass in your plains noumerous   they are also rich and bountifull. and love their read brethren who inhabit the waters of the Missoure

Children   I have been out from my country two winters, I am pore necked and nothing to keep of the rain.   when I set out from my country I had a plenty but have given it all to my read children whome I have seen on my way to the Great Lake of the West.   and have now nothing.

Children   Your Great father will be very sorry to here of the [*blank*] stealing the horses of his Chiefs warrors whome he sent out to do good to his red children on the waters of Missoure.

[*two lines illegible*] their ears to his good counsels he will shut them and not let any goods & guns be brought to the red people.   but to those who open their Ears to his counsels he will send every thing they want into their country. and build a house where they may come to and be sup- plyed whenever they wish.

Children   Your Great father the Chief of all the white people has de- rected me to inform his red children to be at peace with each other, and the white people who may come into your country under the protection of the Flag of your great father which you.   those people who may visit you under the protection of that flag are good people and will do you no harm

Children   Your great father has derected me to tell you not to suffer your young and thoughtless men to take the horses or property of your neighbours or the white people, but to trade with them fairly and hon- estly, as those of his red children below.

Children   The red children of your great father who live near him and have opened their ears to his counsels are rich and hapy have plenty of horses cows & Hogs fowls bread &c.&c. live in good houses, and sleep sound.   and all those of his red children who inhabit the waters of the Missouri who open their ears to what I say and follow the counsels of their great father the President of the United States, will in a fiew years be a[s] hapy as those mentioned &c.

Children   It is the wish of your Great father the Chief of all the white people that some 2 of the principal Chiefs of this [*blank*] Nation should Visit him at his great city and receive from his own mouth. his good counsels, and from his own hands his abundant gifts, Those of his red children who visit him do not return with empty hands, he send them to their nation loaded with presents

Children   If any one two or 3 of your great chiefs wishes to visit your great father and will go with me, he will send you back next Summer loaded with presents and some goods for the nation. You will then see with your own eyes and here with your own years what the white people can do for you.   they do not speak with two tongues nor promis what they can't perform

Children   Consult together and give me an answer as soon as possible your great father is anxious to here from (& see his red children who wish to visit him)   I cannot stay but must proceed on & inform him &c.

1. This speech appears on two sheets in the Voorhis Collection. Clark obviously prepared it while he still expected to meet the Crows on the Yellowstone. The reference to the theft of his horses (see July 21, 1806) places its composition at this canoe-making camp or later.

[Clark] [1]

Set out July 24 1806 at 8 a. m in a 2 Canoes tied togethe.

S E.	1	mile to a Bluff on Std. bend
N. 70° E.	2	ms. under a bluff on Std. Side psd. an Island on the Lard.
N. 20° E.	4	m. to a Lard Bend passed ⟨an⟩ 4 Island on Stard. Side high bluff on Std. low prarie on Lard Side
⟨N.⟩ East	½	m to a large Island in the river of wood
N. 20° E.	½	m. to main Lard Shore
S. 18° E.	½	m. to an Island on Std. ⟨pass lower pt. of one in the⟩
N. 40° E.	1½	m. to a Lard. Bend, timber on both sides
S. 75° E	2	ms passed the lower pt. of the large island upper pt. I and 2 other Islands.
North	1½	ms. to the main Lard. Shore psd th Isld
N. 65° E.	2½	ms. to a bluff bank on the Std. Side passed Some high waves river 200 yds wide

N. 12° E.   1 ½   mile to a bend on the Lard.   passed a Small Island   low bottom on Stard Side

East   2   miles to a high black bluff on Stard.[2]

N. 20° E   3   m. to a bend on the Lard.   psd. 2 Islds. St. to the lower part of a Isd. Close to Lard. at Some high waves

N. 60° E   2 ½   ms. to the upper part of Timber in a bottom Lard Bend
               (25)   passed a Small Isd.

East   ⟨2⟩ 4   miles to the enteranc of Big horn R 100 yds wide & muddy on the Stard Side   Passed a riffle at 3 mile a Small Isd. in the mouth of the river.   passd. 5 Isds.

N.   2   mile to a Lard. bend   river 300 yds wide

N. 58° E ⟨2⟩ 4   ms. to a Stard. bend   passed ⟨4⟩ 5 Small islands   Some prarie on each Side.   and large Island on the Lard. Seperated from the main Shore by a narrow Channel on which there is a large lodge.   halted & Dined.

N 46° E   3   ms. to a bluffs in a Stard bends opposite to an Island passed one in the middle of the rive

N. 36° E   1 ½   mile to a large Brook in a bend to the Stard. Side.   passed a gravely riv

N. 25° W.   1 ½   mils to the enteranc of a [blank] in a bend to the Larbed. passed the lower point of 2 Islands near Ld.

N. 60° W.   3 ½   m. to a wood in the Std bend   passed 4 Islands.

North   1 ½   m. to open Plain in Lard bend   Some large timber in the
               21   bottom on the [tear] [starboard side?]

N. 60° E   3 ½   m. to a point on the Lard Side opposit a large Island in the middle of the river   passed Several Small Is.

North   1   m. to a Bend below   Som wood on the Lard Side

N 64° E   2 ½   m. to a Lard point   passed an Island and the lower part of the large Island

N E.   1   me. to the lower part of a timbered bottom on the Lard Side   Crossed Horss

East   2   miles to a high black bluff in a Stard. Bend   passed an Island Close under the Stard. Shore

N. 20° E   2   mile under a black bluff to the enterans of Brook on the Stard Sid under a high Clift of yellowish [rock?]

N. W.	2	miles to a bend on the Lard. passd. 2 Small Islands. High yellow bluff of excellent grit on the Stard Side round rocks of various Sizes.
North	4 / 18	miles to a Clif ⟨in a bend⟩ point on Lard Side high Clifts on Stard. under which there is a Cave passed the Clift on the Stard. Side at 2 miles Clifts low Lard Side— rock dark brown
N. 12° E	1½	miles to a low black low bluff on the Lard. Side opsd. a low bottom pd. 2 Small Islands of corse gravel
N. 55° E.	3½	miles to the upper point of an island in the Std. Bend passed a Creek at 3 miles on the Std Side

[Clark]   *Thursday 24th July 1806.*

had all our baggage put on board of the two Small Canoes which when lashed together is very Study and I am Convinced will the party I intend takeing down with me. at 8 A M. we Set out and proceeded on very well to a riffle about 1 mile above the enterance of Clarks fork or big horn river[3] [*NB: a river 150 yds. wide comes in from South, we thought it the B. H. but aftds when we found the B. H. we called it Clarks fork, a bold river washing plain. The Indians call this — or "The lodge where all danc"*] at this riffle the Small Canoes took in a good deel of water which obliged us to land a little above the enterance of this river which the [*blank*] has called Clarks fork to dry our articles and bail the Canoes. I also had Buffalow Skin tacked on So as to prevent the waters flacking in between the Two canoes. This last[4] River is 150 yards wide at it's Mouth and 100 a Short destance up the water of a light Muddy Colour and much Colder than that of the Roche-jhone a Small Island is Situated imediately in its mouth, the direction of this river is South and East of that part of the rocky mountains which Can be seen from its enterance and which Seem to termonate in that direction.—[5] [*NB: good place for fort &c— here* ⟨*inds*⟩ *the beaver country begins—best between this & Rochejhaune.*] I thought it probable that this might be the big horn river, and as the Rochejhone appeared to make a great bend to the N. I deturmined to Set the horses across on S. Side. one Chanel of the river passes under a high black bluff from one mile below the place we built the Canoes to within 3 miles of the enterance of Clarks fork[6] when the bottoms widen on each side those on the Stard

217

Side from ½ to a mile in width. river much divided by Islands. at 6 ms. below the fork I halted on a large Island[7] Seperated from the Stard. Shore by a narrow Channel, on this This being a good place to Cross the river I deturmined to wait for Sergt. pryor and put him across the river at this place. on this Island I observd a large lodge the Same which Shannon informed me of a fiew days past. this Lodge a council lodge,[8] it is of a Conocil form 6o feet diamuter at its base built of 20 poles each pole 2 ½ feet in Secumpheranc and 45 feet Long built in the form of a lodge & covered with bushes. in this Lodge I observed a Cedar bush Sticking up on the opposit side of the lodge fronting the dore, on one side was a Buffalow head, and on the other Several Sticks bent and Stuck in the ground. a Stuffed Buffalow skin was Suspended from the Center with the back down. ⟨on⟩ the top of those poles were deckerated with feathers of the Eagle & Calumet Eagle also Several Curious pieces of wood bent in Circleler form with sticks across them in form of a Griddle hung on tops of the lodge poles others in form of a large Sturrip. This Lodge was errected last Summer. It is Situated in the Center of a butifull Island thinly Covered with Cotton wood under which the earth which is rich is Covered with wild rye[9] and a Species of grass resembling the bluegrass,[10] and a mixture of Sweet grass[11] which the Indian plat and ware around their necks for its cent which is of a Strong sent like that of the Vinella after Dinner I proceeded on passed the enterance of a Small Creek[12] and Some wood on the Stard. Side where I met with Sergt. Pryor, Shannon & Windser with the horses they had but just arived at that place. Sergt. Pryor informed me that it would be impossible for the two men with him to drive on the horses after him without tireing all the good ones in pursute of the more indifferent to keep them on the Course. that in passing every gangue of buffalow Several of which he had met with, the loos horses as Soon as they Saw the Buffalow would imediately pursue them and run around them. All those that Speed suffient would head the buffalow and those of less Speed would pursue on as fast as they Could.[13] he at length found that the only practiacable method would be for one of them to proceed on and when ever they Saw a gang of Buffalow to Scear them off before the horses got up. This disposition in the horses is no doubt owing to their being frequently exercised in chasing different animals by their former owners the Indians as it is their Custom to chase every Speces of wild animal with horses, for which purpose they train all their horses. I had the horses drove across the river and Set Sergt. Pryor and his party across.[14] H. Hall who cannot Swim expressed a Willness to proceed on with Sergt. Pryor by land, and as another man was necessary to assist in driveing on the horses, but observed he was necked, I gave him one of my two remaining Shirts a par of Leather Legins and 3 pr. of mockersons which equipt him Completely and Sent him on with the party by land to the Mandans. I proceeded on the river much better than above the enterance of the Clarks fork[15] deep and [*NB: more navigable*] the Current regularly rapid from 2 to 300 yards in width where it is all together, much divided by islands maney of which are large and well Supplyed with Cotton wood trees, Some of them large, Saw emenc number of Deer Elk and buffalow on the banks. Some beaver. I landed on the Lard Side walked out into the bottom and Killd the fatest Buck I every Saw, Shields killed a deer and my man York killed a Buffalow Bull, as he informed me for his tongue and marrow bones. for me to mention or give an estimate of the differant Spcies of wild animals on this river particularly Buffalow, Elk Antelopes & Wolves would be increditable. I shall therefore be silent on the Subject further. So it is we have a great abundance of the best of meat. we made 70 ms. to day Current rapid and much divided by islands. Campd a little below Pryers river of 35 yds. on S E.[16]

Course Distance & remarks July 24th 1806

		miles
S E.	to a Bluff in a Stard Bend passed Lower point of an Isld.	1
S. 70° E[17]	under the Stard. Bluff passed an Island on the Lard Side	2
S. 20° E.	to a Lard Bend pasd. 4 Islands near the Lard Side. a high bluff on the Stard Side Low leavel plain on Lard Side	4
East	to a large Island Covered with wood middle of the river	½

N. 20° E	to the main Larboard Shore passing on the left of the Island	½
S. 18° E.	to a bend on the left Side of the island	½
N. 40° E	to a Lard. Bend. timber on both Sides of the river	1½
S. 75° E	Passing the lower point of an island at 2 miles opposit to the upper point of another island	2
North	to the main Lard Shore passed the island	1½
N 65° E.	to a Bluff bank on the Stard. Side. passed Some rough waves. the river about 200 yards wide	2½
N. 12° E	to a Lard. Bend passing a small island. low bottoms on Std.	1½
East	to a high bluff on the Stard. Side	2
N. 20° E.	to a Lard Bend. passed 2 islands, near the Stard shore ⟨pass⟩ to the lower point of an Island close on Lard. small rapid	3
N. 60° E.	to the upper part of a wood in a Lard Bend. low bottoms passed a Small Stoney Island	2½
East	to the enterance of Clarks fork 100 yds wide. passing a bad rapid at 3 miles. passed 5 Small islands	4
		29
North	to a Lard Bend. river near 300 yards wide	2
N. 58° E	to a Stard Bend passing 5 Small islands. passed an old indian fort of logs and bark on a Island Close to Lard Side	4
N. 46° E	to a Bluff in a Stard. Bend opsd. an Isld. passed one in Midl. R.	3
N. 36° E.	to a *large brook* [18] *in a Stard. Bend* opposit a Stony bar	1½
N 25° W.	to a Lard. Bend passed the lower point of 2 islands	1½
N. 60° W.	to a wood in the Stard Bend passed 4 islands	3½
North	to a Lard Bend opposit some large timber on Stard. Side	1½
N. 60° E.	to a point on the Lard Side opposit to a large island in the middle of the river. passed Several small islands	3½

North	to a bend below Some wood in the Lard Bend & low bottoms on either Side Horse Creek falls in on Std.	1
N 64° E.	to a Lard. point passing an Island and the lower point of a large Island.	2½
N. 45° E	to the lower part of a timbered bottom on the Lard Side (here I had the horses Crossed 26 in number &c.)	1
East	to a high Bluff bank in a Stard. Bend passed an Isld.	2
N. 20° E.	to the enterance of a *brook* [19] on the Stard. Side. passing at the foot of a high black bluff bank on the Stard. Side	2
N. W.	to a bend on the Lard. passed 2 small islands. a high clift of yellowish Gritty Stone [20] on the Stard Side	2
North	to a low clift of dark rock [21] on the Lard. Side. the high clift continue on the Stard. for 2 miles	4
N. 12° E.	to a low black Bluff [22] on the Lard. Side opsd. to a low bottom. 2 Small Stoney islands	1½
N. 55° E	to the upper point of an island in a Stard Bend ⟨opposd.⟩ passed a Creek on the Stard side at 3 miles Pryors river	3½

Miles 69

1. The first draft courses and distances resume here, where Clark again started traveling. The number "36" appears to the left of the heading, in an unknown hand.

2. The many black bluffs along this area near Clarks Fork Yellowstone River are composed of the Niobrara and Carlile Shale of the Colorado Group.

3. Clarks Fork Yellowstone River still bears the name from the expedition. As Biddle notes, Clark first took it to be the Bighorn River. The words "Clarks fork or" are interlined and may be a later addition. Clarks Fork Yellowstone reaches the Yellowstone in Yellowstone County, Montana, a few miles southeast of present Laurel. It rises in the Beartooth Mountains in southeast Park County, Montana, curves through a small portion of northwest Wyoming, then returns to Montana. Clark may have obtained the name "The Lodge where all dance" (which he gave Biddle for the interlineation) from the Mandans or Hidatsas on returning to their villages in August 1806. It does not appear in the lists of Yellowstone affluents in the Fort Mandan Miscellany, vol. 3. *Atlas* maps 108, 115.

4. The word may have been substituted for an erasure.

5. The Absaroka and Beartooth ranges.

6. "Clarks fork" appears to substitute for some erasures.

7. An unnamed island in the Yellowstone River, in Yellowstone County, some five miles due east of present Laurel. The island and lodge, which Shannon reported on July 21, 1806, appear plainly on *Atlas* maps 108 and 116. The reference to the starboard side is puzzling, since from the maps the island is closer to the larboard side, assuming that Clark assigned these bearings according to the direction of travel (here down the Yellowstone), following the captains' usual practice.

8. Compare the following with descriptions and pictures of the modern Crow Sun dance lodge in Frey, 101–9, 119, and Voget, 93–101.

9. Based on the habitat description, the wildrye is either the western species, basin wildrye, which reaches its eastern limit in Rosebud County, Montana, or possibly the more common eastern species, Canada wildrye, *Elymus canadensis* L. Barkley, 575, 489; Hahn, *Elymus* map.

10. Possibly fowl bluegrass, *Poa palustris* L., or the unnamed *P. glaucifolia* Scribn. & Will., both of which occur in meadows and moist places as described by Clark. The occurrence of Kentucky bluegrass as a native species of North America is uncertain. However, references by Lewis and Clark throughout the expedition to species "resembling the bluegrass" gives strong indication of the presence of bluegrass in the East, and may support the theory that populations of Kentucky Bluegrass were native to North America. Barkley, 517–18; Hitchcock & Chase, 1:124–25, 116; Boivin & Lôve.

11. Sweetgrass (and other vernacular names), *Hierochloe odorata* (L.) Beauv. This may be the easternmost limit for sweetgrass along the Yellowstone River at this low elevation. Hahn, *Hierochloe odorata* map; Hitchcock & Chase, 1:547–48; Barkley, 497; Cutright (LCPN), 334.

12. Perhaps Blue Creek in Yellowstone County, reaching the Yellowstone River south of present Billings; "Horse Creek" on *Atlas* map 108 and "Horse Brook" on map 116.

13. Obviously these horses had been trained, as Clark notes, by their Indian owners to hunt buffalo.

14. The horses crossed the Yellowstone south of Billings, in Yellowstone County, a mile or two below the mouth of Blue Creek (Clark's Horse Creek). *Atlas* map 116 shows "Sargent Pryors route with the Horses" as a dotted line.

15. Another substitution for apparent erasures.

16. After Sergeant Nathaniel Pryor of the party, in this entry and on *Atlas* maps 108 and 116, is present Dry Creek in Yellowstone County. It should not be confused with "Pryors Creek" of July 25. The camp of July 24 was just below the mouth of Dry Creek and on the opposite side of the river in Yellowstone County. Clark has greatly exaggerated the bend of the Yellowstone on all the *Atlas* maps.

17. There is a discrepancy in this course and the next with the draft copy courses of this day. The first version appears to be correct.

18. Apparently Duck Creek, reaching the Yellowstone in Yellowstone County, a few miles southwest of Billings. It does not appear on *Atlas* maps 108, 116.

19. Bitter Creek, entering the Yellowstone just opposite Billings. It is unnamed on *Atlas* maps 108 and 116.

20. The Virgelle Member of the Eagle Sandstone at Sacrifice Cliff, directly east of and opposite Billings. *Atlas* maps 108, 116.
21. A small outcrop of Claggett Shale.
22. Another small outcrop of Claggett Shale.

[Clark]   (25 July)

N. 20° W.	2	mile to the head of a large Isd. in the middle of the river passed an Island
East	2	miles to a low clift in the Lard Side ps a large Island
N. 25° E.	1	mile under a Bluff passed a Creek at ¼ a mile I call rock creek a Ld.
N. E	5	miles to ⟨th⟩ a high point of [*blank*] on the ⟨passed⟩ Stard. Side passed the large Island at 1 mile and Islands passed a Small river
N 20° W	2	miles to a Lard. Clift on the Lard Side passeded 3 islands
N. 25° E	4	m to the head of a Island in a Stard. bend passed 4 islands
N. 15° W.	3	m to a Low black Bluff on the Lard Side passed a large Brook on Lard. Side
N 60° East	1	mile to a ⟨Stard Side⟩ Lard. Point Bluff [on larboard side?]
N E	10	mile to a point of wood on the Stard Side opposit a Black bluff a high pt. of rocks a little [banks?] about 70 feet high Passing under a Black Bluff on ⟨for 3 miles⟩ the Lard Side passed a large Brook at ¼ of a mile on the Lard Side one at 5 mils one at 7 mils and a Small one at 8½ mils ⟨to a point of wood⟩ the Countrey to the Stard. open enterance leavel plain for 6 miles & then riseing gradually to about 300 feet passed 6 islands & several gravelly bars
N. 65° E.	3	mils to Stard. Bend passed the pt of an Island at 2 miles
North	1	mile to Lard Bluffs below the Island
N. 70° E	2½	mils to a point of the Bluff which has ⟨felled in⟩ Sliped in and filled up ⅓ of the Chanel on the top of this is a yellowish Stone of 20 feet thick Passed a Brook and an island
N. 80° E	3	miles to the point of a Bluff on the Lard. Side passd. Several Bars

East	2 ⟨3⟩	miles to a Bluff laterly Sliped in on the Lard Side opsd. the head of an Isld.
South	1	mile to th lower point of a Isld on the Stard. Side
N. 62° E	3 ⟨5⟩	miles to a point of a Lard Bluff passed Lower point of the Island.
East	3	miles to Pompys Tower 200 feet high and 400 yards in Se-cumfrance Situated in a low bottom on the Std. Side [*blank*] Paces from the river which is imediately between this Tower & the hight on the Lard Side— from the top of this Tower the river as far as Can be seen is N. 66° E ⟨4⟩ 5 miles to Clift point on the Lard Side passed a point of Clift at 2 miles on Lard. Side. passed the Enterance of [*illegible*] Creek at 9 Ms. This valley of a Baptiests Creek which falls in ⟨4?⟩ miles below is S 25° East a Low Mountain is S. 15° E about 40 miles. The Rock mountans covered with Snow is S W. The Little wolf mountaine which is but low is N. 55° W. about 45 m a large dry Creek falls in on the opposit Side opposit this Tower The Countrey to the N. is ruged near the river. a range of high hills which appear to run from South to North covered with pine at about 18 miles to the East to S. no timber. N. a few low pine
S 60° E	4	miles to the enterance of Baptiests Creek from the Stard. and Camped passed the Clieft, on the Lard at 3 miles, Several Gravelly

[Clark]   *Friday 25th July 1806.*

We Set out at Sunrise and proceeded on very well for three hours. Saw a large gange of Buffalow on the Lard Bank. I concluded to halt and kill a fat one, dureing which time Some brackfast was ordered to be Cooked. we killed 2 Buffalow and took as much of their flesh as I wished. Shields killed two fat deer and after a delay of one hour and a half we again proceeded on.   and had not proceeded far before a heavy shower of rain pored down upon us, and the wind blew hard from the S W.   the wind increased and the rain ⟨began⟩ continued to fall. I halted on the Stard. Side had Some logs set up on [end?] close together and Covered with deerskins to keep off the rain, and a large fire made to dry ourselves.

the rain continued moderately untill near twelve oClock when it Cleared away and become fair. the wind Contined high untill 2 P M. I proceeded on after the [*NB: rain*] lay a little and at 4 P M arived at a remarkable rock[1] Situated in an extensive bottom on the Stard. Side of the river & 250 paces from it. this rock I ascended and from it's top had a most extensive view in every direction. This rock which I shall Call Pompy's Tower is 200 feet high and 400 paces in secumphrance and only axcessable on one Side which is from the N. E the other parts of it being a perpendicular Clift of lightish Coloured gritty rock on the top there is a tolerable Soil of about 5 or 6 feet thick Covered with Short grass. The Indians have made 2 piles of Stone on the top of this Tower. The nativs have ingraved on the face of this rock the figures of animals &c. near which I marked my name and the day of the month & year. From the top of this Tower I Could discover two low Mountains & the Rocky Mts. covered with Snow S W. one of them appeard to be extencive and bore S. 15° E.[2] about 40 miles. the other I take to be what the indians Call the Little wolf Mtn. I can only see the Southern extremity of it which bears N 55° W about 35 Miles. The plains to the South rise from the distance of about 6 miles the width of the bottom gradually to the mountains in that derection. a large Creek[3] with an extencive Vally the direction of which is S. 25° E. meanders boutifully through this plain. a range of high land Covered with pine[4] appears to run in a N. & S. direction approaching the river below. on the Northerly Side of the river high romantic Clifts approach & jut over the water for Some distance both above and below. a large Brook[5] which at this time has Some running muddy water falls in to the Rochejhone imediately opposit Pompys Tower. back from the river for Some distance on that Side the hills are ruged & some pine back the plains are open and extensive. after Satisfying my Self Sufficiently in this delightfull prospect of the extensive Country around, and the emence herds of Buffalow, Elk and wolves in which it abounded, I decended and proceeded on a fiew miles, Saw a gang of about 40 Big horn animals fired at them and killed 2 on the Sides of the rocks which we did not get. I directed the Canoes to land, and I walked up through a crevis in the rocks almost inaxcessiable and killed 2 of those animals one a large doe and the other a yearlin Buck. I wished very much to kill a large buck, had there been one with the gang I Should have killd. him.   dureing the time the men were getting the two big horns which I had killed to the river I employed my Self in getting pieces of the rib of a fish which was Semented within the face of the rock   this rib is [*NB: about 3*][6] inchs ⟨diame⟩ in Secumpherance about the middle   [*NB: the fallen rock is near the water—   the face   of the rock where rib is is perpendr.—   4 is. lengthwise, a little barb projects*]   it is 3 feet in length tho a part of the end appears to have been broken off   I have Several peces of this rib   the bone is neither decayed nor petrified but very rotten.[7]   the part which I could not get out may be Seen, it is about 6 or 7 Miles below Pompys Tower in the face of the Lard. Clift about 20 feet above the water.   after getting the big horn on board &c I proceeded on a Short distance and encamped,[8] an earlyer than I intended on accout of a heavy cloud which was comeing up from the S. S W. and Some appearance of a Violent wind. I walked out and killed a Small Buck for his Skin which the party are in want of for Clothes.   about Sunset the wind blew hard from the W. and Some little rain. I encamped on the Stard. Side imediately below the enteranc Shannons River about 22 Yards wide, and at this time discharges a great portion of water which is very Muddy.   emence herds of Buffalow about our as it is now running time with those animals the bulls keep Such a grunting nois which is very loud and disagreeable Sound that we are compelled to Scear them away before we can Sleep.   the men fire Several Shot at them and Scear them away.

Course distance and remarks July 25th 1806[9]

		mils
N. 20° W.	to the head of a large Island in the middle of the river, haveing passed an island.	2
East	to a low Clift on the Lard. Side passed a large Island	2
N. 25° E.	passing under the Lard Bluff, passed rock Creek[10] (Small) on the Lard. Side but a Small quantity of water	1 ½

N. 45° E.	to a high point of land on the Stard. Side, passed a large island at 1 mile and Several Small islds. ⟨N 6 W⟩ passed the enterance of a small river [*EC: Pryor's Creek*][11] on Stard. Side	5
N. 20° W.	to a low Clift on the Lard. Side passed 3 islands	2
N. 25° E.	to the head of an Island in the Stard. Bend passed four islands	4
N. 15° W.	to a low black bluff on the Lard. Side,[12] haveing passed a large Brook[13] on the Lard Side	3
N. 60° E.	to a Lard point passing a Bluff on the Lard Side.	1
N. 45° E.	to a point of woodland on the Stard. Side opposite to a bluff bank which we passed under on the Lard Side passed a large brook at ¼ of a mile, one at 5 and one at 7 and a Small one at 8½ miles all on the Lard Side.[14] passed 6 islands and Several Stoney bars	10
N. 65° E.	to a Stard. Bend passing the head of an island at 2 miles	3
North	to a Larboard Bluff below the island	1
N 70° E.	to a Bluff on the Lard. Side which has Sliped into the river and filled up ⅓ of the river on the top a yellowish Gritty Stone of 20 feet thick[15]	2½
N. 80° E.	to the point of a Bluff on the Lard Side passed Several Stoney bars	3
East	to a rugid bluff latterly Slipped into the river on the Lard Side opposit to the head of an island	2
South	to the Lower point of an island on Stard. Side.	1
N. 62° E.	to the point of a Lard. Bluff passed the Island	3
East	to Pompys Tower. 200 feet high. 400 paces around from the top of which the rocky mountains Covered with Snow can be Seen S W. also two low mountains one S. 15 E. and the other N. 55° W this rock is Situated 250 paces from the water on the Stard Side of the river, and opposit to a large Brook on the Lard Side I call baptiests Creek	3

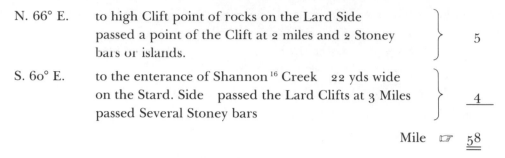

| N. 66° E. | to high Clift point of rocks on the Lard Side passed a point of the Clift at 2 miles and 2 Stoney bars or islands. | 5 |
| S. 60° E. | to the enterance of Shannon[16] Creek   22 yds wide on the Stard. Side   passed the Lard Clifts at 3 Miles passed Several Stoney bars | 4 |

Mile ☞ 58

[NB: See a description of the Country South in an appendex of the next book][17]

1. This sandstone formation is in Yellowstone County, Montana, one-half mile north of Interstate Highway 94, between the present villages of Nibbe and Pompeys Pillar, and about twenty-eight miles northeast of Billings. Pompeys Pillar is formed of the uppermost Cretaceous Hell Creek Formation (sometimes called Lance Formation). It has been isolated from the left bank of the river by meander development. The soil has formed on the top either because the rock there is more easily weathered or because it is protected from erosion. Apparently the first white man to see it was François-Antoine Larocque (see November 27, 1804) on his trip to the Yellowstone in September 1805, some ten months before Clark. Clark named the rock "Pompy's Tower" for little Jean Baptiste Charbonneau, whom he had nicknamed "Pomp." In the 1814 history Biddle altered this to a more classical "Pompey's Pillar," the name which has persisted. Clark's inscription of his name and date are still visible, the only surviving physical evidence of the expedition along its route. In 1876 a soldier participating in the campaign against the Sioux reportedly carved his name over the "k," and when reprimanded declared that he did not believe that there had been a white man in the country seventy years earlier. The inscription has since been deepened and is now protected by shatterproof glass. *Atlas* maps 110, 116; Appleman (LC), 322–25; Wood & Thiessen, 194 & n. 80; Bradley (MMC), 64–66.

2. The same bearing appears in Biddle's history. On *Atlas* map 110, however, "S. 15° W. 40 m" is noted by Pompys Tower. On *Atlas* map 116 no bearing is given, but a straight, dotted line runs from the tower southwesterly in the general direction of the Pryor Mountains in Big Horn County, Montana, which are in fact southwest of Pompeys Pillar. The Bighorn Mountains lie southeast of the position. The mountains to the northwest are the Bull Mountains, the "Southern extremity" of which would be Dunn Mountain.

3. Fly Creek, "Shannons River" after George Shannon of the party on *Atlas* maps 110 and 116, meeting the Yellowstone River from the south in Yellowstone County.

4. Pine Ridge in Big Horn County, just west of the Bighorn River, "Pine hills" on *Atlas* maps 110 and 117.

5. Clark's "River Baptieste," present Pompeys Pillar Creek, which meets the Yellowstone in Yellowstone County directly opposite Pompeys Pillar. *Atlas* maps 110, 116.

6. Biddle inserted the words over a blank space.

7. Clark found the fossilized rib in the uppermost Cretaceous Hell Creek Formation;

the rib probably came from a terrestrial dinosaur. The most common terrestrial dinosaurs of that period in this area were Hadrosaurus, Triceratops, Albertosaurus, and Tyrannosaurus, many examples of which have been found in the Hell Creek Formation in northern Garfield County and west-central McCone County, Montana.

8. Clark's camp was on the south side of the Yellowstone in Yellowstone County, just below the mouth of Fly Creek (Shannons River) and about two miles northeast of the present village of Pompeys Pillar. *Atlas* maps 110, 117.

9. Clark's route maps, *Atlas* maps 108, 109, 116, show great distortion of the Yellowstone River bend between present Billings and Pompeys Pillar, in Yellowstone County, a distortion repeated in his Western map of 1810 (*Atlas* map 125) and its published version of 1814 (*Atlas* map 126). This distortion appears also in the courses and distances for the day, notably the first, which should be more nearly due north. There is much underlining in this table in pencil (probably by Coues) and in red ink (probably by Biddle); these are not shown in this printing.

10. Present Five Mile Creek, which now meets the Yellowstone in northeast Billings, in Yellowstone County. *Atlas* maps 108, 116.

11. Present Pryor Creek, still bearing Nathaniel Pryor's name, meets the Yellowstone in Yellowstone County, just southwest of Huntley. *Atlas* maps 109, 116.

12. This is an outcrop of Upper Cretaceous Bearpaw Shale.

13. Probably present Crooked Creek, entering the Yellowstone in Yellowstone County, a few miles northeast of Huntley. *Atlas* maps 109, 116.

14. The first two are apparently Razor and Cabin creeks and the other two unnamed streams in Yellowstone County. *Atlas* maps 109, 116.

15. Clark's "Tumbling Bluff" (see Chapter 41); another outcrop of uppermost Hell Creek Formation.

16. "Shannon" appears to be a substitution for an erasure.

17. Perhaps a reference to Clark's "Notes of Information I believe Correct" and "Misselanious Notes Given by a Trader," in Codex N, pp. 122–37, reading backwards, much of which Clark must have obtained in later years. Not printed in this edition, it may be found in Thwaites (LC), 6:266–68.

[Clark]   (July 26th)

N. 18° E	6	Miles to a Point on the Std. Side passed a long narrow Island on Std. and Som bars, a high Clift on Lard.
N 57° E.	5	miles to a point on the Stard. Side Passed an Island and 4 Bars. a large Creek 40 yds wide ⟨Little Wolf⟩ Creek on Lard. Side at 4 miles
East	4	miles to a Clift a high Pine land on the Stard. Side passed a Small Creek on the Std. at 1 mile the head of an Island below the Lard. Clifts at 2 miles

N. 12° E	3½	miles to a Clift of rocks on the Sard. Side passed the Island and 2 Stoney bars white Clifts
East	5	miles to a Clift of rocks on the Std passed Several Stoney Islands.
N E.	2½	miles to a high Clift on the Lard Side opposit several Small Islands the Chanel much divided passed 2 Small Islands. low bottom on Stard. Side.
East	2½	miles to a Stard. Bend psd. an Island and Stoney bar
N. 10° E	1	mile to a Clift on the Lard. Side Islands on Stbd.
N. 54° E	1½	mile to the lower point of the near the Stard Side passed the upper point of an Island
North	4	miles to a high white clif on the Lard Side passed 2 Stony Islands
East	6	mils to the ⟨lower part of a large Island Seperated from the Stard. Shore by a narrow Chanel⟩ Enteranc of a Small brook Std Sd. Passed three Islands and the upper part of the 4th near th Lard.
North	4	miles to the ⟨upper⟩ lower pts of an Island close to the Lard Side. behind which a large Creek falls in on the Lard Side
N. 60° E	3	miles to a tree ⟨on⟩ und. the Lard. Clifts a Clift on th Lard Sid
East	4	miles to a large tree in a Std Bend
N. 35° E	4 ⟨5?⟩	miles to Lard. Bend passed a Clift on the Stard. at 2 mile. Small Bays Ld.
East	1½	miles to the lower pt. of an Isld.
N. 35 E.	2½	mils to a Clift in the Lard. bend
East	½	a mile to enterance of Big horn river on the Stard Side 220 yards wide from 5 to 7 feet deep quite across.

I walked up the bighorn and took the following Courses   viz.

S. 35° E	3	miles to a low cliff on the right passed a point on the right at 1½ miles a island close to the left side
S. 61° E	3	miles to a high band of a 2d Bottom in a left hand bend passed Some high waves on the right hand Side

S. 38° W.   4   miles to a right hand Bend   passed a large Creek of very Muddly water from the left at one mile.

The bottoms of this river wide and Covered with timber. The current Swift and tareing away its bank in each bend with extensive Sand points. less ⟨gravel⟩ large gravle than the rochejhone

[Clark]   *Saturday 26th July 1806.*

Set out this morning very early   proceeded on   Passed Creeks [*NB: Hall's N. Side*][1] very well. the Current of the river reagulilarly Swift much divided by Stoney islands and bars also handsome Islands Covered with Cotton wood the bottoms extensive on the Stard. Side on the Lard.   the Clifts of high land border the river, those clifts are composed of a whitish rock of an excellent grit for Grindstones.[2] The Country back on each Side is wavering lands with Scattering pine.   passed 2 Small Brooks on the Stard. Side and two large ones on the Lard. Side.[3] I shot a Buck from the Canoe and killed one other on a Small Island. and late in the evening passed a part of the river which was rock under the Lard. Clifts   fortunately for us we found an excellent Chanel to pass down on the right of a Stony Island half a mile below this bad place, we arived at the enterance of Big Horn River on the Stard. Side.[4]   here I landed imediately in the point which is a Sof mud mixed with the Sand[5] and Subject to overflow for Some distance back in between the two rivers. I walked up the big horn ½ a mile and crossed over to the lower Side, and formed a Camp on a high pcint.[6] I with one of my men Labeech walked up the N E Side of Big horn river 7 miles to th enterance of a Creek which falls in on the N E. Side and is 28 yds wide   Some running water which is very muddy this Creek I call Muddy Creek[7] Some fiew miles above this Creek the river bent around to the East of South.[8] The Courses as I assended it as follows   Viz:

S 35° E.   3   miles to a low Clift on the right   passed a point on the right at 1½ Ms. an island Situatd. close to the left hand Shore. under this Clift is Some Swift rapid water and high waves

S. 61° E.   3   miles to a high bank of a Second bottom in the left hand bend   passed head of the isld.

S. 38° W.   4   miles to a right hand bend, passing a large Creek of muddly water on the left side at 1 mile, opposit a Sand bar from the right.

The bottoms of the Big Horn river are extencive and Covered with timber principally Cotton.   it's Current is regularly Swift, like the Missouri, it washes away its banks on one Side while it forms extensive Sand bars on the other. Contains much less portion of large gravel than the R: Rochjhone and its water more mudy and of a brownish colour, while that of the rochejhone is of a lightish Colour.[9]   the width of those two rivers are very nearly the Same imediately at their enterances the river Rochejhone much the deepest and contain most water. I measured the debth of the bighorn quit across a ½ a mile above its junction and found it from 5 to 7 feet only while that of the River [NB: roche jaune] is in the deepest part 10 or 12 feet water   on the lower Side of the bighorn is extencive boutifull and leavil bottom thinly covered with Cotton wood under which there grows great quantities of rose bushes.[10] I am informed by the Menetarres Indians and others that this River takes its rise in the Rocky mountains with the heads of the river plate and at no great distance from the river Rochejhone and passes between the Coat Nor or Black Mountains and the most Easterly range of Rocky Mountains.[11]   it is very long and Contains a great perpotion of timber on which there is a variety of wild animals, perticularly the big horn which are to be found in great numbers on this river.   [NB: 2 large forks come in on Sth. & 1 on North][12]   Buffalow, Elk, Deer and Antelopes are plenty and the river is Said to abound in beaver.   it is inhabited by a great number of roveing Indians of the Crow Nation, the paunch Nation [NB: a band of Crows][13] and the Castahanas [NB: a band of Snake In.][14]   all of those nations who are Subdivided rove and prosue the Buffalow of which they make their principal food, their Skins together with those of the Big horn and Antilope Serve them for Clothes. This river is Said to be navagable a long way for perogus without falls and waters   a fine rich open ⟨200 yds wide⟩ Country.   it is 200 yds water & ¼ of a Me. wd. I returned to Camp a little after dark, haveing killed one deer, finding my Self fatigued went to bead without my Supper. Shields killed 2 Bull & 3 Elk.

Courses distances & remarks July 26th 1806

		M
N. 18° E.	to a point on the Stard. Side, passed a low narrow island on the Stard. and Som bars near the Lard. Side	6
N. 57° E.	to a point on the Stard Side. passed an island and 4 Stoney bars. also a large Creek 40 Yds wide I call Halls R [15] on the Lard. Side at 4 miles. but little water	6
East	4 Miles to a Clift under a high pine hill on the Stard. Side. passed a Small Creek on the Stard. at 1 mile and the Lard Clift opsd. the head of an Isld. at 2 Miles on this course	4
N. 12° E.	to a clift of white rocks on the Lard. Side,[16] passed the island and 2 Stoney bars	3½
East	to clift of rocks on the Stard. Side passed several bars or islands	5
N. 45° E.	to a high clift on the Lard. Side opposit Several Small islands. Chanel of the river much divided. passed 2 Small Islands. low bottoms on the Stard Side rocky Clifts on Lard side	2½
East	to a Stard. Bend passed an island & a Stony bar	2½
N. 10° E.	to a clift on the Lard Side Island on Stard. Side	1½
N. 54° E.	to the lower point of the island near the Stard. Side. passed the upper point of an island	1½
North	to a high White Clift on the Lard. Side haveing passed two Stoney Islands	4
East	to the enterance of a Small brook on the Stard. passed 3 islands and the upper point of the 4th near Lard.	6
North	to the lower point of an island Close to the lard. Side back of which a large Creek falls in on the Lard Side Island brook [17]	4
N. 60° E.	to a tree under a Lard. Clift passed a Std. Clift	3
East	to a large tree in the Stard. Bend	4
N. 35° E.	to a Lard. Bend passed the Stard. Clift at 2 Miles.	4
East	to the lower [SW?] point of an island	1½

233

N. 35° E.	to a clift in a lard. Bend under which there is a rapid. a gravelly bar opposit on the S. E of which there is a good Chanel.	2 ½
East	to the junction of *Big horn* River on the Stard. 220 yards wide from 5 to 7 feet deep quit across, and encamped on the lower side bottom subject to floods	½

Miles   62

1. Given as both "Halls ⟨dry⟩ River" and "Little Wolf C" on *Atlas* map 110, and "Halls creek" on *Atlas* map 117, after Hugh Hall of the party. It is present Cow Gulch, meeting the Yellowstone River in Yellowstone County, Montana, some five miles northeast of the village of Pompeys Pillar.

2. Again, the light-colored, silty sandstone in the Hell Creek Formation.

3. There are several small streams on the starboard (south) side of the Yellowstone in this area, some now having names, some not. The first, unnamed and a little beyond "Halls River" on the opposite side on *Atlas* maps 110 and 117, may be present Kaiser Creek in Yellowstone County. The second, also unnamed and a little upstream from "Island Brook" on the *Atlas* maps, is perhaps Sand Creek in Yellowstone County above Buffalo Creek. The first large creek, which does not appear on the *Atlas* maps, may be Hibbard Creek, in Yellowstone County. The second, Clark's "Island Brook," would be Buffalo Creek in Yellowstone County.

4. The Bighorn River forms the Yellowstone-Treasure county line where it reaches the Yellowstone River, a mile or so above the present village of Bighorn. *Atlas* maps 110, 117, 118.

5. The Bighorn River flows across a large exposure of shales of the Colorado Group after leaving Bighorn Canyon. These shales provide the dark color and mud to the river. The sand is all that remains of the rock transported beyond the mouth of the canyon.

6. The camp was above the junction of the Bighorn River with the Yellowstone and on the stream's east side in Treasure County. *Atlas* maps 110, 118.

7. This stream is Tullock Creek, entering the Bighorn from the southeast in Treasure County; on *Atlas* maps 110 and 117 it is "Muddy Creek" as in the journal entry, but on Clark's map of 1810 (*Atlas* map 125) it is "Horse River."

8. The general course of the Bighorn River going upstream is south or southwesterly; the bend that Clark seems to be talking about is a small one.

9. Clark here describes a typical fluvial cut and fill process. The water of the Bighorn River is more muddy near its mouth than is the water of the Yellowstone because the Bighorn flows across a large exposure of shales of the Colorado Group after leaving Bighorn Canyon. These shales provide most of the dark color and mud to the river.

10. Western wild rose.

11. Both main branches of the Platte rise in the Colorado Rockies; some tributaries of

the North Platte, such as the Sweetwater River, are relatively close to the upper Bighorn River in Wyoming. Some tributaries of the Bighorn rise in the Absaroka Range, which is east of the upper Yellowstone. The "Black Mountains" in this case may be the Big Horn and Rosebud mountains, in agreement with Lewis and Clark's grouping of various outlying ranges of the Rockies as part of the Black Hills.

12. The two southern (more properly eastern) branches of the Bighorn are probably the Little Bighorn River, always associated with Custer's defeat by the Sioux and other Indians in 1876, in Big Horn County, Montana, and Nowater Creek in Big Horn County, Wyoming. The principal tributaries on the western side are Shoshone River and Greybull River in Big Horn County, Wyoming, and Wind River in Fremont County, Wyoming.

13. The Hidatsas referred to the Crows as "the people who refused the paunch." The "Paunch tribe" are No. 96 in the Estimate of the Eastern Indians in vol. 3. See also November 12, 1804. Hodge, 1:44–45.

14. The Castahanas are No. 34 in the Estimate of the Eastern Indians in vol. 3, where they are described as speaking the same language as the "Me na ta re (or big belly)" and are also called "Gens des Vache." The latter term commonly referred to the Arapahoes, who spoke an Algonquian tongue. The captains used "Minitare," "Big Belly," and "Gros Ventre" to refer either to the Hidatsas or to the Atsinas. The latter are linguistically related to the Arapahoes. If their principal hunting ground was on the upper Bighorn River, we might assume them to be a division of the Crows, whose Siouan language was similar to that of the Hidatsas. "Gens des Vache" might be a mistake for "Gens de Panse" or Paunch Indians, which would make them Crows (see earlier note in this entry). Since Clark did not meet them, his information may have derived either from Sacagawea or from his sources for the Estimate of Eastern Indians, that is, from the Mandans, Hidatsas, and white fur traders. Hyde (IHP), 184–85, speculates that they were a Shoshonean group (hence "Snakes") who had been driven from the upper Bighorn by the time of Lewis and Clark, and identifies them with the Kwahari, or Kwahadi, Comanches. Hodge, 1:44–45, 212.

15. "I call Halls R" may be a later addition, interlined by Clark.

16. This is a light-colored, silty sandstone in the Hell Creek Formation.

17. "Island brook" may be a later addition by Clark.

[Clark]   [July 27, 1806]

from the Bighorn

N. 45° E   6   miles to a Brook in a Std. bend.   high sand [land?]   Passed a Island on which there is wood at 2 miles and one near the Stard. at 6 ms.

N. 45° W.   3   miles to Lard Bend   passed a point of a high Clift on the Stard Side at 2 miles   passed 2 Islands

N. 25° E	1½	miles to a high point on Stard.
N. 60° E	4½	miles to the lower part of a bluff on the Stard. Side passed a large Creek on the Lard Side behind a large ⌊island?⌋ creek 40 yds wide
N. 20° E	4	miles to the ⟨lower⟩ upper pt. of an Island near the Stard Side. passd. 3 islands low bottoms on each Side rivr wide and Current jentle. passed Little wolf river 60 yds. wid Scercely any water in on the Lard. at 1 mile.
N. 15° E.	5	miles to a black bluff in the Lard Bend passed the enterance of a river 50 yds wide but little water at 3 miles on the Lard Side. passed an Island close to the Stard Shore and ⟨one⟩ a bar below the river std.
N. 66° E	4	miles to Bluff in Lad bend a Low bottom on Stard. and a bluff about 60 feet high on the Lard. psd. 2 brooks Lard. no water
East	3	miles to a point of the Lard. Bluff. a low bottom on Stard.
N. 65° E.	5	miles to the head of an Island in the middle of the river passed 2 islands and 3 bars.
East	5	miles to the lower part of a wood on the Stard Side passed 1 large & 4 Small Islands. Extensive bottom both Sides
N. 45 E	2	miles to a [w?] tree in the Lard bend
S 15 E.[1]	2	miles to the enteranc of a Small river 60 yds wide little water on Std. opsd. an Isd. on Std.
N. 60° E	3½	miles to the a woon [wood] in the Lard Bend passed 2 small Isds.
S. 80° E	1½	miles to the Island on the Std. Side
North	½	mile to the Lard. main Shore
S. 18° E.	½	mile to the island on the Std. Side.
N. 30 E.	1	mile to the enteranc of a large Brook in the Lard. Bend abov a low Clift.
S. 45° E	1	mile to the lower point of the Isld. low bluff on the Lard Side
S. 76° E	4 ⟨7?⟩	miles to a point of wood on the Stard. Side passed an island. low white Clifts on the Lard Side

S. 82° E.	5 ⟨6?⟩	miles to a the Lower point of an Island near Std. Passed one near the Lard. Shore at 3 ms. and the upper pt. of an Isld. on Lard. side
N. 62° E	2½	miles to a point on the Stard Side opposit a Lard Bluff passed the Isd. Ld.
S W.	2	miles to the enteranc of a Brook 20 yds wide in a Stard. Bend an Island near Lard. high lands border the Lard Shore
N 80 E.	2½	miles to a Stard. point opposit a remakable conocal moun on the top of which a rock resembles a house with Chimnys.
S. 75 E	3½	miles to the point of an Island. passed the upper point of one on each Side at 2½ miles. passed a brook 20 yds wide on the Stard Side
N. 65° E	½	a mile to a point of the Lard ⟨Island⟩ Side opsd. lower point of the Stard. Island.
N. E.	3½	miles to the lower point of one island Close to the Lard Shore passed 2 islands
S. 60° E	1	mile to the upper part of a large Island
N.	2	miles to a point of the Island on the right passed a chanel at ¼ ms

[Clark]   *Sunday 27th July 1806*

I marked my name with red paint on a Cotton tree near my Camp, and Set out at an early hour and proceeded on very well   the river is much wider from 4 to 600 yards much divided by Islands and Sand bars, passed a large dry Creek [*NB: call Elk creek*][2] at 15 miles and halted at the enterance of River 50 yards wide on the Lard Side   I call R. Labeech[3] killed 4 Buffalow and Saved as much of their flesh as we could Carry took brackfast. The Buffalow and Elk is estonishingly noumerous on the banks of the river on each Side, particularly the Elk which lay on almost every point in large gang and are So jintle that we frequently pass within 20 or 30 paces of them without their being the least alarmd.   the buffalow are Generally at a greater distance from the river, and keep a continueing bellowing in every direction, much more beaver Sign than above the bighorn. I Saw Several of those animals on the bank to day.   the antilopes are Scerce as also the bighorns and the deer   by no means So plenty as they were near the Rocky mountains.   when we pass the Big horn I take my leave of the view of the tremendious chain of Rocky Mountains white with Snow   in view of which I have been Since the 1st of May last.

about Sunset I Shot a very large fat buck elk from the Canoe near which I encamped,[4] and was near being bit by a rattle Snake. Shields killed a Deer & a antilope to day for the Skins which the party is in want of for Clothes.   this river below the big horn river resembles the Missouri in almost every perticular ⟨its⟩ except that it's islands are more noumerous & Current more rapid, it's banks are generally low and falling in the bottoms on the Stard. Side   low and exteneive and Covered with timber near the river such as Cotton wood willow of the different Species rose bushes and Grapevines[5] together with the red berry or Buffalow Grees[6] bushes & a species of shoemake with dark brown[7]   back of those bottoms the Country rises gradually to about 100 feet and has Some pine.   back is leavel plains.   on the Lard Side the river runs under the clifts and Bluffs of high which is from 70 to 150 feet in hight and near the river is Some Scattering low pine   back the plains become leavel and extencive.   the Clifts are Composed of a light gritty Stone which is not very hard.   and the yound stone [NB: ⟨large gravel⟩ *round stones*] which is mixed with the Sand and formes bars is much Smaller than they appeared from above the bighorn, and may here be termed Gravel.[8]   the Colour of the water is a yellowish white and less muddy than the Missouri below the mouth of this river.

Course Distance & Remarks July 27th 1806.
from the Big Horn[9]

		M
N. 45° E.	to a Brook in a Stard. Bend.[10] passed an Island at 2 miles and one near the Stard Side at 6 miles	6
N. 45° W.	to a Lard Bend passing the point of a high clift on the Stard. at 2 miles. passed 2 islands	3
N. 25° E.	to a high point on the Stard. Side	1½
N. 60° E.	to the lower part of a Bluff on the Stard. Side, passed a large Elk Creek on the Lard. Side, back of an Isld.	4½

N. 20° E.	to the upper point of an island near the Stard. Side. passed 3 islands. a low bottom on each Side passed a river 50 yds wide on the Lard Side which contains but little water nearly dry Windsors River	4
N. 15° E.	to a black Bluff in the Lard. Bend. passed an Island close to the Stard. Shore, and a gravelly bar below	5
N. 66° E.	to a bluff in the Lard. Bend. a low bottom of wood on the Stard. Side. passing a Clift of 60 feet in hight on the Lard. and 2 dry Brooks on the same side.	4
East	to a point of the Lard Bluff. bottom low on Stard.	3
N. 65° E.	to the head of an island in the middle of the river. passed 2 islands and 3 bars	5
East	to the lower point of a wood on the Stard. Side passed 1 large and 4 Small islands. an extenive bottoms on both Sides	5
N. 45° E.	to a Tree in the Larboard Bend	2
N. 15° E.	to the enterance of a large Creek 60 yards wide on the Stard Side Containing but little water Labeichs R[11]	2
N. 60° E.	to a wood in the lard Bend. passed 2 Small islands	3½
S. 80° E.	to the island on the Stard. Side	1½
North	to the Lard. main Shore.	½
S. 18° E.	to the Lard. Side of the island	½
N. 30° E.	to the enterance of a large brook in the Lard bend above low clift white Creek[12]	1
S 45° E	to the lower point of the island. Low bluff on Lard.	1
S. 76° E.	to a point of wood on the Stard. Side, passed an island. low white Clifts on the Lard Side.	4
S. 82° E.	to the lower point of an island near the Stard. Side. passed one near the Lard. at 3 miles	5
N. 62° E.	to a point on the Stard side opposit to a low bluff passed the Lard Island	2½
S. 45° W.	to the enterance of a brook 20 yds wide[13] in the Stard. Bend an Island near the Lard. high lands border the Larboard Shore	2

N 80° E.	to a Stard. point opposit a Conic Mound on the top of which is a rock resembling a house & Chimney.[14]	2½
S. 75° E.	to the point of an island passed the upper pt. of one on each Side at 2½ miles. passed a brook on Sd Side 20 yds wide.[15]	3½
N. 65° E.	to a point of the Lard Side opsd. a low bottom	½
N. 45° E.	to the lower point of an Island. passed 2 islands	3½
S. 60° E	to the upper part of a large island	1½
North	to a point of the Island and Camped on the island	2
	Miles	80½

1. The course in Codex M is "N. 15° E." It appears that Clark had first written "25" rather than "15."

2. Alkali Creek, meeting the Yellowstone River in Treasure County, Montana. *Atlas* maps 110, 118. Someone, probably Coues, has circled in pencil "a large dry Creek at 15 miles."

3. "Little wolf or Winsors Creek" on *Atlas* map 110, and "Winsors dry Creek" on *Atlas* map 118, present Muggins Creek in Treasure County. It was probably Biddle who crossed through the words, "I call R. Labeech" in red ink; see later note in this entry.

4. Clark's camp was in Rosebud County, Montana, about two miles above the mouth of Big Porcupine Creek ("Little Wolf River" on *Atlas* map 119) and about eight miles west of present Forsyth; the course of the Yellowstone has evidently shifted since 1806, so that the campsite is some distance north of the present river. *Atlas* map 111.

5. River-bank grape, *Vitis riparia* Michx. Barkley, 220.

6. Buffaloberry again; see Lewis's entries of July 17 and 19, 1806.

7. Aromatic sumac or skunkbush, also known as squawbush, *Rhus aromatica* Ait. var. *trilobata* (Nutt.) Gray. It is significant that the common species of the riparian floodplain are being described here together. The deeply rooting skunkbush is characteristic of riparian streambanks and terraces of the arid West. Barkley, 223; Welsh et al., 47. The missing word may be "leaves."

8. In general, Clark is describing the Hell Creek Formation, but the Bearpaw Shale is exposed for a considerable distance on today's travels, and the Judith River Formation touches the north bank of the river a few miles upstream from his evening's camp. The decreased size of the stones or cobbles in the river bed results both from the continual striking of pebble against pebble as they are transported downstream and from the reduced transporting power of the river after it emerges into the plains country—the large cobbles are left farther upstream.

9. Many of the items are underlined in this table, some in lead pencil, some in blue pencil, perhaps by Coues. The underlining is not shown in this printing.

10. Apparently Unknown Creek, meeting the Yellowstone in Treasure County; it does not appear on *Atlas* maps 110, 111, or 118.

11. Sarpy Creek, meeting the Yellowstone west of present Sanders, clearly located on *Atlas* maps 111 and 118. In the journal narrative above Clark apparently misapplied the name to Muggins Creek ("Little Wolf or Winsors Creek") and Biddle crossed the name out. Thwaites (LC), 5:302, did not note the crossing out, which has caused some confusion to those seeking to locate "Labiechs R."

12. Starved to Death Creek enters the Yellowstone in Treasure County, east of Sanders. *Atlas* maps 111, 118.

13. Apparently Hay Creek, meandering near the Treasure-Rosebud county line, Montana. It is the first of two twenty-yard brooks on *Atlas* map 111; it is "Brook 20 yards wide" on *Atlas* map 118.

14. Shown as "Chimney Bluffs" on *Atlas* maps 111 and 119, opposite present Reservation Creek in Rosebud County.

15. Reservation Creek in Rosebud County, the second twenty-yard brook in succession on *Atlas* map 111; it is unlabeled on *Atlas* map 119, but below and across from "Chimney Bluffs."

[Clark]   (28 July)

N. 65° W	½	mile to a Lard. Bend.
S. E.	1 ⟨2⟩½	miles to a St. Stard. Side at a Sluce through the Island
East	1 ½	miles to the Lower point of the large Island. passed the ⟨enteranc of a large dry Creek on the Lard Side⟩
N. 80° E	1	mile to Lard Bend passed the upper point of an Island
N. 40° W.	2 ½	miles to ⟨Stard.⟩ Lard. Side. passed the enterance of a river 80 yds wide ⟨littl wate⟩ on the Lard Side.
S. 35° E	2	miles to a Stard Bend passed Isld.
N. 52° E	1 ½	miles to a Lard Side
S. 64° E.	1	mile to the Stard Side
N. 40° E	1 ¼	miles to the Lard Side passed a Crek on the Stards. Side 30 yds wide wth wate
East	1	mile to Stard Side
North	¾	of a mile to the Lard Side
N. 35° E.	2 ½	miles to a Stard. Bend opsd. an Isld.
N. 20° W	½	a Mile to a yellow bluff on Lard Sid
N. 60° E	2	miles to Lard Bend of a low Prarie no wood

South	3	miles to a high Bluff below a brook low naked bottom on Lard Side—
S. 45° E	2½	miles to a Stard. point below a Bluff yellow Stone opsd. an Island opsd. some remakable tables in the Lard. plains
S. 70° E.	3½	miles to upr. pt. Isd. in the Stard Bend high Bluff on the Stard. Side.
N. E	2	miles to the enteranc of Table Creek 30 yds wide on the Lard Side nearly dry
East	7	miles to a Stard Bluff ⟨passed⟩ high passed 3 Island and a river of 70 yd wide on the Lard. Side but little wate in it. buttle little timber.
East	2	mils to the enteranc of little horn R. from the S S. E 100 yds wide and Contain a great portion of water. but little wood a Small Island opposite
N. 55° E.	4½	Miles to the Center of a Lard Bend passd a Brook on Stard. Side at 3 miles psd. I
N. E	5½	miles to the Center of a Lard.
S. 45° E	1½	miles to the lower part of a Bluff in which there is 2 Stratias of Stone cole in Strates of from 4 to 8 feet thick about 30 feet above the water. Horozontially. pd. an Island a large Creek on Lard at 1 mile
East	8	Miles to a high Coal Bluff on the Stard Side. passed a large Creek at 6 miles on the Stard. Side Passed 2 Islands.[1]
N 60° E.	4½	Miles to a Cluster of large trees in the Stard Bend in an open Plain passed 5 Islands and Sevral bars
N. 10° W.	1½	mils to a Lard. Bluff a vain of Coal in this Bluff about 30 feet above the water Stard. bottoms an enteranc. a brook on Lard—
N. 73° E	6 ⟨4?⟩	miles to a [coal?] Point of the Lard. Bluff in which there is 5 Stratas of Coal psd. an island Close to the Lard Side river having made a deep ben Std.
S. 75° E.	2 ——— 71	miles to the Enterance of a Brook in the Stard. Bend passed the head of an Island close to Lard Shore Encamped on Stard Side—

[Clark]   *Monday 28th July 1806.*

Set out this morning at day light and proceeded on glideing down this Smooth Stream passing maney Isld. and Several Creeks and brooks   at 6 miles passed a Creek or brook of 80 yards wide [*NB: called by Indns—or Little Wolf river*][2]   on the N W. Side Containing but little water.   6 miles lower passed a small Creek 20 yds wide on the Stard Side[3]   18 Miles lower passed a large dry creek on the Lard Side[4]   5 Miles lower passed a river 70 yards wide Containing but little water on the Lard Side which I call Table Creek[5] from the tops of Several mounds in the Plains to the N W. resembling a table.[6]   four miles Still lower I arived at the enterance of a river 100 yards wide back of a Small island on the South Side.   it contains Some Cotton wood timber and has a bold Current, it's water like those of all other Streams which I have passed in the Canoes are muddy. I take this river to be the one the Indians Call the Little Big Horn river.[7] The Clifts on the South Side of the Rochejhone are Generally compd. of a yellowish Gritty Soft rock, whilest those of the N. is light Coloured and much harder   in the evening I passd. Straters of Coal in the banks on either Side   those on the Stard. Bluffs was about 30 feet above the water and in 2 vanes from 4 to 8 feet thick, in a horozontal position.   the Coal Contained in the Lard Bluffs is in Several vaines of different hights and thickness.   this Coal or Carbonated wood is like that of the Missouri of an inferior quallity.[8]   passed a large Creek[9] on the Stard. Side between the 1st and 2nd Coal Bluffs   passed Several Brooks the chanel of them were wide and contained but little running water, and encamped on the upper point of a Small island opposit the enterance of a Creek 25 Yards wide [*NB: Inds Call Ma Shas-kap riv.*] on the Stard. Side with water.[10]

Courses distance and Remarks July 28th 1806[11]

		Miles
N. 65° W.	½ to a Stard.[12] Bend	½
S. 45° E.	to the island at the enterance of a Small Sluice	1 ½
East	to the lower point of the island	1 ½
N. 80° E.	to the Lard. Bend passed the upper point of an island	1

N. 40° W.	to the Lard. Side. passed the enterance of river partly dry 80 yards wide on the Lard Side little wolf River	2 ½
S. 35° E.	to a Stard. Bend passed an island	2
N. 52° E.	to the Larboard Side	1 ½
S. 64° E.	to the Starboard Side	1
N. 40° E.	to the Lard Side passed a Creek 30 yards wide on the Starboard Side but little water in it	1 ¼
East	to the Stard. Side	1
North	to the Lard Side	¾
N. 35° E.	to a Stard. Bend opposit to an island	2 ½
N. 20° W.	to a yellow bluff on the Lard. Side [13]	½
N. 60° E.	to a low prarie in a Lard. Bend	2
South	to a high bluff below a Brook.[14] low open botton on Std.	3
S. 45° E.	to a Stard. point below a Clift of yellowish Stone [15] opsd. to an island. Some remarkable mounds in the plains on Lard Side	2 ½
S. 70° E.	to the upper point of an island in the Stard. Bend high Bluffs on the Stard. Side	3 ½
S. 45° E.	to the enterance of Table Brook 30 Yds wide on the Lard Side nearly dry	2
East	to a Stard. Bluff passed 3 islands and Table river on the Lard. Side 70 yards wide Some water	7
S. 86° E	to the enterance of *Little Horn* river [*EC: Mashaskup of Clarke's map*] [16] from the S. S. E. 100 yards wide with a Considerable portion of running water. Scattering timber on its borders a Small Island opposit its enterance. water Muddy	2
N. 55° E	to the Centr. of a Std. Bend passd. a brook on Std.[17] at 3 miles	4 ½
N. 45° E.	to the Center of a Lard. Bend	5 ½
S 45° E.	to the lower part of a Bluff in which there is 2 Stratias of Stone Coal on Std Side.[18] passed a Creek on Lard.[19]	1 ½

East	to a high Coal Bluff on the Lard Side passed a large Creek at 6 miles on the Stard. Side & 2 Islds	8
N. 60° E.	to a cluster of large trees in the Lard. Bend. passed 5 islands and Several bars	4½
N. 10° W.	to a Lard. Bluff a vein of Coal in this bluff about 30 feet above the water. bottoms low on the the Stard.	1½
N. 73° E.	to a Coal point of the Lard Bluff in which there is 5 Stratias of Coal at different hights all Horozon-tal. an island Close to the Lard Side the river have-ing made a deep bend to Stard. Side	6
S. 75° E.	to the enterance of a Brook in the Stard bend behind an island. passed an island Close the Lard Shore. encamped on the Small Isld.	2
	Miles	73

The Elk on the banks of the river were So abundant that we have not been out of Sight of them to day. J Shields killed 2 deer & Labeech killed an Antilope to day.   the antilopes and deer are not Abundant. Beaver plenty

1. The following figures preceded by the word "mils" appear as a column between courses at right angles to the other material on the page: 58, 55, 43, 35. They are Clark's mileage totals for July 16 through 19, 1806.

2. Not to be confused with the "Little wolf or Winsors Creek" of July 27, 1806, on *Atlas* map 110, which is present Muggins Creek. The present stream is Big Porcupine Creek in Rosebud County, Montana, reaching the Yellowstone River a few miles west of present Forsyth. Clark's original route map for July 28–August 1, 1806, is missing, but the map prepared for Prince Maximilian in 1833 (*Atlas* map 119) shows "Little Wolf River" clearly

3. Armells Creek meets the Yellowstone in Rosebud County a few miles below the mouth of Big Porcupine Creek on the opposite side. It is unnamed on *Atlas* map 119.

4. This is the "Table Brook" of the courses and distances, below, which is not the "Table Creek" of the journal narrative; it is now Little Porcupine Creek in Rosebud County, several miles downstream from Forsyth. It is "Table Creek" on *Atlas* map 119.

5. Horse Creek in Rosebud County, not far below the mouth of Little Porcupine Creek. On *Atlas* map 119 it is a large, unnamed stream below Little Porcupine Creek (Clark's "Table Creek" on the map).

6. These formations in Rosebud County extend from two to four miles northeast of Forsyth on the north side of the Yellowstone River, but are not noted on *Atlas* map 119.

7. Not the present Little Bighorn River, a tributary of the Bighorn River in Big Horn

County, Montana (see July 26, 1806). This stream is Rosebud Creek, meeting the Yellowstone in Rosebud County a mile or so above present Rosebud. It is a large, nameless stream on the south side of the Yellowstone on *Atlas* map 119.

8. By early afternoon Clark left the uppermost Cretaceous Hell Creek Formation (Lance) behind and entered the area underlain by the coal-bearing Tertiary (Paleocene) Tullock Member of the Fort Union Formation. This member is exposed on both sides of the river, but the colors may result either from the effect of sun and shadow on the rock or from differences in weathering caused by exposure. The coal is ranked as lignite. The beds here are too thin and discontinuous for anything but local use.

9. Sweeney Creek in Rosebud County, not named on *Atlas* map 119. The coal bluffs do not appear on the *Atlas* map.

10. Graveyard Creek, in Rosebud County just west of the Custer County line, meeting the Yellowstone a little below present Hathaway; "Mar shas kap River" on *Atlas* map 120. The camp, as Clark notes, was opposite the creek mouth in Rosebud County. The Indian name would have been obtained from the Mandans or Hidatsas, but Clark may have misidentified it, since the actual Mar-shas-kap appears to have been Rosebud Creek; see Fort Mandan Miscellany, vol. 3 of this edition. The term appears to be a Hidatsa name, *mickapa aaši*, "rosebud creek" (see July 19, 1806).

11. Again, underlining in both lead and blue pencil throughout this table, probably Coues's doing; it is not given here.

12. It is given as "Lard." in the draft version.

13. The Hell Creek Formation just northwest of Forsyth about where U.S. Highway 12 crosses the Yellowstone River.

14. Either Smith or Slaughterhouse creeks in Rosebud County joining the Yellowstone on either side of Forsyth; on *Atlas* map 119 it is the second nameless stream below "Little Wolf River" on the opposite side.

15. Again, the Hell Creek Formation, here just downstream from Forsyth.

16. Apparently this is Coues's notation; if so, the reference must be to Clark's published map of 1814 (*Atlas* map 126), but the "Mar shar kop" of that map cannot be either the "Little Horn" (clearly shown on the map), or "Table River" of the previous course, which was on the opposite side of the Yellowstone. The stream shown on the 1814 map seems to be in the right location for Graveyard Creek, which Clark identifies by the name "Mar shas Kap" in the journal.

17. Presumably Butte Creek in Rosebud County, entering the Yellowstone just below present Rosebud; a small unnamed stream just below the large, also unnamed river (present Rosebud Creek) on *Atlas* map 119, on the south side of the Yellowstone.

18. The strata of coal mentioned through this area are in the Tullock Member of the Fort Union Formation. This formation approaches the river at the town of Rosebud about midway between Clark's morning camp and his evening camp.

19. Sand Creek in Rosebud County joins the Yellowstone from the north a little above later Thurlow Siding; it does not appear on *Atlas* map 119.

[Clark]   [July 29, 1806]

N. 25° W.	5	miles to the enteranc of a dry Brook in a Lard. bend near the high land. passed 8 islands & 3 br
East	3	miles to a the enterance of a Brook in the Stard. Bend below an Island
N. 10° W.	1 ½	miles to a Lard. bend
East	1 ½	miles to a ⟨Clift⟩ Bluff on Stard. Side[1]
N. 40° E	4 ½	miles to a lower part of a Std. Bluff bluff low. wind high from N.
N.	1 ½	miles to a few trees in a Lard Bend
East	6	miles to a low bluff on the Stard. Side passed an Island and a large dry Brook at 5 miles & Som wood [on Std.?]
N. 76° E.	3	miles to a Coal Bluff on Stard passed an Isld. and a dry Brook on Stard. sd.
N. 40° E.	1	mile under the Coal Bluff Std.
North	4	miles to the upper part of the Lard. Bluff. passed an Island and a large Brook on the Stard. Side. and a low dry Brook or bead on the Lard.
N. 55° E	2 ⟨3⟩ ½	Miles to a Lard. point (dined) low bottom on each Side killed a Black Tail deer
N. 20° E	1 ⟨2⟩ ½	Miles to a Lard. Bluff Several Strates of Coal in the hills 1 mile back
N. 60° E	1 ½	Miles to a point of rocks on the Lard. Side passed a bar Ld.
N. 30° E	3 ⟨1 ½⟩	miles to a point on Std. Side pd a Sand near which the [*blank*] River comes near the Stard Shore
N. 45° E	2	miles to the enterance of [*blank*] 150 yds. Passed an isld. and 2 bars wate ¼ of a mile banks. Bluffs on Lard. wate of R muddy & worm
N. 32° E.[2]	2 ½	mile to the lowr part of the wood in the Stard. bend opsd. the head of an island
	44 ½	

[Clark]   *Tuesday 29th July 1806*

a Slight rain last night with hard thunder and Sharp lightening accompanied with a violent N. E. wind. I Set out early this morning   wind So hard a head that w made but little way.   in the fore part of the day, I saw great numbers of Buffalow on the banks.   the country on either Side is like that of yesterday.   passed three large dry Brooks on the Stard. Side[3] and four on the Lard Side.[4]   great quantities of Coal in all the hills I passed this day.[5]   late in the evening I arived at the enterance of a River which I take to be [*NB: called by Indians*] the *Lazeka* or Tongue River[6]   it discharges itself on the Stard. Side and is 150 yards wide of water   the banks are much wider. I intended to encamp on an eligable Spot imediately below this river, but finding that its' water So muddy and worm as to render it very disagreeable to drink, I crossed the rochejhone and encamped on an island close to the Lard. Shore.[7] The water of this river is nearly milk worm very muddy and of a ⟨dark⟩ lightish brown Colour. the Current rapid and the Chanel Contains great numbers of Snags. near its enterance there is great quantities of wood Such as is common in the low bottoms of the Rochejhone and Missouri.   [*NB: it heads in Cote Noir ⟨with⟩   has 2 branches   1 heads with the Chayenne & 1 with one of the Big H's branches*][8] tho' I believe that the Country back thro' which this river passes is an open one where the water is exposed to the Sun which heats it in its passage.   it is Shallow and throws out great quantities of mud and Some cors gravel.[9]   below this river and on the Stard Side at a fiew Miles from the Rochejhone the hills are high and ruged Containing Coal in great quantities.[10] Beaver is very plenty on this part of the Rochejhone. The river widens   I think it may be generally Calculated at from 500[11] yards to half a mile in width   more Sand and gravelly Bars than above. cought 3 cat fish.   they wer Small and fat.   also a Soft Shell turtle.[12]

Course Distance & Remarks July 29th

		M
N. 25° W.	to the enterance of a dry Brook [*EC: Bull*][13] in a Lard. Bend near the high lands. passed 8 islands & three Sand and gravelly bars	5
East	to the enterance of a brook[14] [*EC: Teepee*] in the Stard. Bend below a Small island	3

N. 10° W.	to a Larboard Bend	1 ½
East	to a Bluff on the Stard. Side	1 ½
N 40° E	to the lower part of a Stard. Bluff	4 ½
North	to a fiew trees in a Lard Bend	1 ½
East	to a low Bluff on the Stard. Side passed an island. also a large dry Brook Turtle Creek[15] at 5 Miles on the Stard Side on which there is Some wood	6
N. 76° E.	to a Coal Bluff on thc Stard Side[16] passed an island and a dry brook[17] on Stard Side	3
N. 40° E	under the Coal Bluff on Stard. Side	1
North	to the upper part of a Lard. Bluff passed an island and a large brook on the Stard. Side & a large Bead or dry brook on the Lard Side[18]	4
N. 55° E.	to a lard. point low bottom on each Side	2 ½
N 20° E.	to a Lard. Bluff (coal to be Seen in the hills 1 m from R.[)]	1 ½
N 60° E.	to a point of rocks on the Lard. Side passed a Sand bar	1 ½
N. 30° E	to a point on Stard Side near which the river is within 100 paces of Tongue river[19]	3
N. 45° E.	to the enterance of Le-ze-ka[20] or Tongue river on the Stard. Side 150 yds wide. passed an island	2
	Miles	4̲1̲

1. The following figures appear as a column at the top of a page in the draft version and following this entry; they are written at a right angle to the rest of the text: 58, 55, 43, 35, (191), 69, 58, 62, (189), 80, 73, 44, 17, 694. The numbers in parentheses are sub-totals and the final figure a grand total. The final total should be 594. The column apparently represents mileages on the Yellowstone starting July 16, 1806, but the last two do not match any known day's total.

2. In Codex M this appears as the first course of July 30, 1806.

3. Cottonwood, Moon, and either Snell, Lignite, or Coal creeks, all in Custer County, Montana, on the south side of the Yellowstone River. One of them would presumably be the "Dry Brook" below the "Mar shas kap River" and the camp of July 28 on *Atlas* map 120.

4. Probably Bull, Wilson, Whitetail, and Steiger or Reservation creeks in Custer County

on the north side of the Yellowstone. Two unnamed streams appear on that portion of the river on *Atlas* map 120.

5. The Tullock Member of Fort Union Formation. Although there are numerous beds of coal, the beds generally are thin, discontinuous, and of low quality.

6. Tongue River meets the Yellowstone in Custer County; at its mouth today is Miles City. *Atlas* map 120. The Indian name is presumably from the Mandans or the Hidatsas; see Fort Mandan Miscellany, vol. 3. "*Lazeka* or Tongue River" may have been written in later over erasures. The term is a Mandan name, *résik*, "tongue." Besides his interlineation Biddle also put brackets in red ink around the words "which take to be."

7. As Clark indicates, his camp was on the north side of the Yellowstone, in Custer County, a little below Tongue River, opposite, and north of Miles City. On *Atlas* map 120 it seems to be incorrectly placed on the south side of the Yellowstone just below the Tongue.

8. One of these branches is probably Pumpkin Creek, which rises in Powder River County, Montana. The other would be Tongue River, which rises in the Big Horn Mountains (probably Biddle's "Cote noir" in this case), near the source of the Little Bighorn River in Sheridan County, Wyoming. Neither is close to the sources of the Cheyenne River in east-central Wyoming.

9. The gravel carried by the Tongue River is composed principally of clinker and of pebbles derived from higher terrace deposits along which the stream flows. Clinker is the common term for the burned, baked, or fused products of the combustion of the coal and the adjacent deposits—most commonly, the material directly above the coal bed.

10. Again, the Tullock Member of the Fort Union Formation.

11. "5" appears to have been written over "3."

12. Western spiny soft shell turtle, *Trionyx spiniferus hartwegi*. Benson (HLCE), 88.

13. Probably Wilson Creek; see a previous note in this entry. The interlined "Bull" is evidently Coues's guess at the creek. It was probably Coues who underlined many words in pencil in this table. The underlining is not done here.

14. Probably Theade Creek in Custer County, on the south side of the Yellowstone above Cottonwood Creek; it is "Dry Brook" on *Atlas* map 120. An interlineation by Coues, evidently "Teepee," must represent his guess at the creek's name. Coues (HLC), 3:1160 n. 21.

15. Apparently Moon Creek; see a previous note in this entry. It is "Turtle dry creek 40 yds wide" on *Atlas* map 120. "Turtle Creek" may be a later interlineation by Clark.

16. The Tullock Member of the Fort Union Formation at the mouth of Lignite Creek.

17. Probably Lignite Creek; see a previous note in this entry.

18. Coal Creek on the starboard and Reservation Creek on the larboard; see previous notes in this entry.

19. The words "of Tongue River" appear to have been added to a blank space.

20. "Le-ze-ka" seems to be a substitution for some erasures.

[Clark]   (30th July) 30th

N. 14° W.	3	miles to a Lard Bluff passed an Island and 2 gravelly bars
N. 40° E	6	miles to the enteranc of a dry Brook with Stard. Bend Passed the enteranc of a river 100 yds wide below the Lard. Bluff at 5 miles. Som wood on this River. (rained)
N. 30° W	1¾	miles to a tree in Lard bend
N 60° E.	1¼	miles to a Bluff in a Stard. bend passed a Shoal ⅔ across th river from the Lard. Side
North	1½	mile to 3 trees in a Lard. bend passed a large dry Creek on the Stard. at ½ a mile 80 yds
N 70° E	4	miles to the point of a Clift on the Stard. Side opposit to the great Shoal quite across the riv rock dark brown Sand. this may be run with ease and Safty in a large Canoe
N E.	3	mils to a bush in a naked point on the Lard Side passed a large dry brook on each Side low Bluff on the Stard. Side
N. 20° E	1	mile to the head of an Island low bluff on Std. no wood on either side Passed a Brook on Stard. Side
N. 10° W.	2½	miles to the enterance of a large dry Creek on the Lard Side above a bluff passed 1 on the Stard.
N 70° E	1	mile to Brook on the Stard Bend passed a high bluff on the Lard. for ½ ml.
North	1½	miles to the enteranc of a ⟨large⟩ small dry Creek in the Lard. Bend near a high Bluff
N. 20° E	1	mile to a large dry Brook in Std. bend
N. 5° W.	2	miles the Center Lard Bend rocks on both Sides in the bottom but little wood
N. 30° E.	2	miles to a Stard. point
East	2	miles to a Stard Bend passd. a Brook on each Side but little wood
N. 20° E.	1½	miles on the Stard. Bend passed a Brook on Stard Side low bluff Lard.
North	1 ⟨2⟩ ½	miles to a few bushes in a Lard Bend
N. E	1	mile to a Brook which discharges itself on the Stard. Side

		in the Center of a rapid I call Bear rapid not bad a god Chanel on the Lard. Side
N. W	¾	of a m. to a bluff in the Lard Bend passed a dry river 88 yds chanel and nearly ¼ of a mile when high—
N. E.	2 ⟨3⟩ ¼	miles to a Bluff in a Stard. Bend passed a bar on Stard. point
North	4 ⟨5⟩ ½	miles passed a low bluff on each Side a ⟨large Brook⟩ at
	45	3 River 100 yards wide Shallow & very muddy I take this to be the [*blank*] River, it discharges a great deel of mud and red stones has latterly been high— at 4 ms. passed large dry Brook a Lard. low bluff on each side.[1]

[Clark]   *Friday 30th July 1806*

Set out early this morning   at 12 miles arived at the Commencement of Shoals the Chanel on the Stard Side near a high bluff.   passed a Succession of those Shoals for 6 miles the lower of which was quit across the river and appeared to have a decent of about 3 feet.   here we were Compeled to let the Canoes down by hand for fear of their Strikeing a rock under water and Splitting. This is by far the wost place which I have Seen on this river from the Rocky mountains to this place   a distance of 694 miles by water.   a Perogu or large Canoe would with Safty pass through the worst of those Shoals, which I call the Buffalow Sholes[2] from the Circumstance of one of those animals being in them.   the rock which passes the river at those Sholes appear hard and gritty of a dark brown Colour.[3]   the Clifts on the Stard. Side is about 100 feet in hight, on the Lard Side the Country is low and the bottom rises gradually back.   here is the first appearance of Birnt hills[4] which I have Seen on this river they are at a distance from the river on the Lard Side. I landed at the enterance of a dry Creek[5] on the Lard side below the Shoals and took brackfast. Those Dry Rivers, Creeks &c are like those of the Missouri which take their rise in and are the Conveyance of the water from those plains.   they have the appearanc of dischargeing emence torrents of water.   the late rains which has fallen in the plains raised Sudenly those Brooks which receive the water of those plains on which those Suden & heavy Showers of rain must have fallen, Several of which I have Seen dischargeing those waters, whiles those below heading or takeing their rise in the Same neighbourhood, as I passed them appears to have latterly been high. those Broods discharge emencely of mud also, which Contributes much to the muddiness of the river. after Brackfast proceeded on the river much narrower than above from 3 to 400 yards wide only and only a fiew scattering trees to be Seen on the banks. at 20 miles below the Buffalow Shoals passed a rapid which is by no means dangerous, it has a number of large rocks in different parts of the river which Causes high waves a very good Chanel on the Lard. Side. this rapid I call Bear rapid[6] from the Circumstance of a bears being on a rock in the Middle of this rapid when I arived at it. a violent Storm from the N. W. obliged us to land imediately below this rapid, draw up the Canoes and take Shelter in an old Indian Lodge above the enterance of a river which is nearly dry it has laterly been very high and Spread over nearly ¼ a mile in width. its Chanel is 88 yards and in this there is not more water than could pass through an inch auger hole. I call it Yorks dry R.[7] after the rain and wind passed over I proceeded on at 7 Miles passed the enterance of a river[8] the water of which is 100 yds wide, the bead of this river nearly ¼ of a mile this river is Shallow and the water very muddy and of the Colour of the banks a darkish brown.[9] I observe great quantities of red Stone[10] thrown out of this river that from the appearance of the hills at a distance on its lower Side induced me to call this red Stone river. [*NB: By a coincidence I found the Indian name Wa ha Sah*][11] as the water was disagreeably muddy I could not Camp on that Side below its mouth. however I landed at its enteranc and Sent out and killed two fat Cows, and took as much of the flesh as the Canoes would conveniently Carry and Crossed the river and encamped at the enterance of a Brook on the Lard. Side under a large Spredding Cotton tree.[12] The river on which we passed to day is not So wide as above containing but fiew islands with a Small quantity of Cotton timber. no timber of any kind to be Seen on the high lands on either Side.

Course distance and Remarks 30th July

		M
N. 32° E.	to the lower part of a wood in the Stard. Bend opposit the head of an island near the Lard Side	2½
N. 14° W.	to a Lard. Bluff passed an island and 2 bars	3

N. 40° E.	to the enterance of a dry brook [13] in the Stard Bend passed the enterance of a [*EC: Dry*] [14] river below the Lard Bluff 100 yards wide nearly dry at 5 miles on this River there appears to be Some Cotton wood	6
N. 30° W.	to a tree in the Lard. Bend	1 ¾
N. 60° E.	to a Bluff in the Stard. Bend pass a rocky Shoal ⅔ of the river from the Lard Side	1 ¼
North	to 3 trees in the Lard Bend passed a large dry Creek 60 yards wide on the Stard. side [15]	1 ½
N. 70° E.	to the point of a clift on the Stard. Side opposit to the great Shoal. a dark brow rock quit across [16] passeable	4
N. 45° E.	to a bush on the Lard point passed a dry brook [*EC: Sand Cr.*] on each side. [17] a low bluff on the Stard. Side	3
N. 20° E.	to the head of an island. passed a brook [18] on the Stard. Side and a low bluff, no wood on either Side	1
N. 10° W.	to the enterance of a large dry Creek [*EC: Muster Cr.*] [19] on the Lard. Side above a bluff. passed one on the Stard. Side [20]	2 ½
N. 70° E.	to a Brook [21] in the Stard. Bend passed a high bluff on the Lard. Side for ½ a mile	1
North	to the enterance of a Small dry Creek [22] in the Lard Bend near a high bluff	1 ½
N. 20° E.	to a large dry brook [*EC: Cottonwood*] [23] in a Stard. Bend	1 ½
N. 5° W.	to the Center of a Lard. Bend rocks on both Sides	2
N. 30° E.	to a Stard. point	2
East	to a Stard. Bend passed a dry brook [*EC: Wolf Cr (N.)*] [24] on each Side	2
N. 20° E.	to a hollow in the Stard. Bend passed a Brook [25] on the Stard. Side. low bluffs [*EC: Devil's Backbone*] on the Lard. Side	1 ½

North	to a fiew bushes in a lard. Bend	1 ½
N. 45° E.	to a Brook[26] which discharges itself on the Stard. Side at white Bear island rapids. not bad	1
N. 45° W.	to a Bluff in the Lard. Bend, below the enterance of a dry river [*EC: York's*] 88 yard Chanel, and when it is high spreads over nearly ¼ of a mile in width York	¾
N. 45° E.	to a Bluff in the Stard. Bend passed a bar Std. pt.	2 ¼
North	to the Center of a Lard. bend low bluffs on each Side at 3 miles passed *redstone* river [*EC: Powder R.*] on the Stard. Side 100 yards water & near ¼ of a mile Chanel very muddy; at 4 Miles encamped at the enterance of a large dry brook on the Lard.	4 ½
	Miles	48

In the evening below the enterance of redstone river I observed great numbers of Buffalow feeding on the plains, elk on the points and antilopes. I also Saw Some of the Bighorn animals at a distance on the hills. Gibson is now able to walk, he walked out this evening and killed an antilope.

1. The following figures appear in a column in the right margin beside the last course of this day: 191, 189, 380, 80, 73, 44; the third figure is a sub-total. For the first two figures see the draft courses for July 27, 1806. The last three appear to be the mileages for July 27, 28, and 29, with discrepancies.

2. Buffalo Shoals are in Custer County, Montana, just below the mouth of Sand Creek, "Little dry River" on *Atlas* map 120.

3. The shoals are formed of more indurated sandstone or, possibly, concretions in the Tullock Member of the Fort Union Formation.

4. The Tongue River Member of the Fort Union Formation approaches the river near here, but caps the higher hills only. It contains thicker and more continuous coal beds than the Tullock Member, and many of these beds have been burned extensively forming red clinker.

5. Muster Creek in Custer County, meeting the Yellowstone River near Kinsey; on *Atlas* map 120 it appears as "Dry creek."

6. Bear Rapid is in Prairie County, Montana, a little above the mouth of Custer Creek. *Atlas* map 121.

7. The name, of course, derived from Clark's servant York; the stream is present Custer Creek in Prairie County. *Atlas* map 121. The words appear to be a later addition, interlined by Clark in a different shaded ink.

8. Powder River meets the Yellowstone in Prairie County; on *Atlas* map 121 it is "War har sah River red stone R." See an additional note below.

9. The color of the material in the banks is derived largely from coal detritus.

10. The red stone is clinker. Much of the clinker comes from the area along the Powder River nearly due east of Miles City.

11. The Indian name, presumably learned from the Mandans or Hidatsas, is "War-rah-sash" in Fort Mandan Miscellany, vol. 3. Biddle seems to imply here in this interjected sentence that the translation is "red stone river," but in the Fort Mandan document the implied meaning is Powder River, the source of the modern name. It is a Mandan term, $w^a ra\check{s}u\eta te$, "powder."

12. Clark's camp was in Prairie County, a little below and opposite the mouth of Powder River ("War har sah"), at the mouth of Crooked Creek, a nameless stream on *Atlas* map 121. The site is not marked on the *Atlas* map.

13. Jones Creek meets the Yellowstone in Custer County, just above Tusler; on *Atlas* map 120 it is a nameless stream nearly opposite the mouth of Sunday Creek ("Big dry River").

14. In addition to his penciled interlineations, Coues has underscored some words in pencil, but the underlinings are not shown here. The stream is Sunday Creek ("Big dry River") and given as one hundred and twenty yards wide on *Atlas* map 120.

15. This is difficult to identify with any known stream, unless Clark meant "larboard," in which case it could be Sand Creek in Custer County, just above Buffalo Shoals, evidently the "Little dry River" of *Atlas* map 120.

16. The shoals are formed of more indurated sandstone or, possibly, concretions in the Tullock Member of the Fort Union Formation.

17. Muster Creek on the larboard and Dixon Creek on the starboard, both in Custer County; they are "Dry creek 40 yards wide" and "dry brook," respectively, on *Atlas* map 120. The interlined "Sand Cr." is Coues's guess as to the larboard creek's identity.

18. Deep Creek in Custer County; a nameless stream meeting the Yellowstone from the south on *Atlas* map 120.

19. Harris Creek meets the Yellowstone in Custer County west of present Shirley; on *Atlas* map 120 it is a nameless stream just below an island in the river. The interlined "Muster Cr." is Coues's guess as to its identity.

20. Hay Creek in Custer County, opposite and a little above Harris Creek; it is nameless on *Atlas* map 120.

21. Dead Horse Creek in Custer County now empties into Buffalo Rapids Ditch which runs parallel to the Yellowstone; another small, nameless stream on the south side of the river on *Atlas* map 120.

22. Cabin Creek in Custer County, on the north side of the Yellowstone, nameless on *Atlas* map 120.

23. Cottonwood Creek, as Coues interlined, in Custer County, meeting the Yellowstone south of Bonfield, a nameless stream on *Atlas* map 120.

24. Mack Creek on the starboard and an unnamed creek on the larboard, both in Custer County, both nameless on *Atlas* map 120. "Wolf Cr (N.)" would be Coues's name for the larboard stream.

25. Williams Creek in Custer and Prairie counties, nameless on *Atlas* map 121. "Devils Backbone," interlined by Coues, is a name in use in his time for the larboard bluffs. Coues (HLC), 3 : 1162 n. 23. That name may have referred to an irregular hill about a mile west of the river across from the mouth of Williams Creek rather than to the bluffs.

26. Camp Creek in Prairie County, reaching the Yellowstone at "Bear Rapid," nearly opposite the mouth of Custer Creek ("Yorks dry River" on *Atlas* map 121).

[Clark]   (31st July)

S 80° E	1 ½	Miles to a Stard. Bluff in a bend low bluff on the Lard Side
N. 28° W.	½	a mile passed wolf rapid which is not bad high bluff on the Std side
N. 80° W.	2 ½	to a high bluff under very high hills or low mountains on the Lard Side opsd. a point on which there is wood
N. 10° E	1	mile to the enteran of a dry brook Lard. passing under a high Bluff of diferent Colour on th Lard Side high Prarie on Std.
East	1	to a Lard point at a fiew trees.
N. 55 E.	3	miles to a Lard. point passed a Std. point at 1 mile high cole blufs on [larboard?]
N E.	1 ½	miles to a red bluff on Lard Side passed Std point
East	6	miles to a Stard Bend passed 2 Lard. and a Stard point low bluff Std. passed a river 100 yards wide on the Lard Side. water Shallow & muddy—
N 60° E.	3 ⟨1 ½⟩	miles to an Isld. on a Stard point passed a ⟨brook in the Lard Bend⟩ a Stard. point and a Lard point
N. 30° E	2	miles to the enterance of a river in the Stard. Bend 40 yds wide deep *Coal R* [1] Banks of Coal below its enterance
N. 10° W.	1 ½	miles to a high bluff on Lard Side
East	2 ½	to the enterance of a Brook below a Lard. Bluff passed

a Std. point   passed under a high bluff Lard. Slipping in to R.

S. E.	1	mile to a Lard. point
N. E.	6 ⟨5?⟩	miles to the head of a Isld. near an Id. Std. Sid low Coal Bluff on Stard Side passed a Brook on Stard side
N. 20° E.	4	miles to the enterance of a brook in the Lard Bend opposit an island on the Stard Side
N. 70° E.	3	Miles to the lower part of Stard Bluff passed an Small island at the enterance of a river 60 yds. wide deep banks on each Side
N. 30° W	3	miles to a Lard. Bluff opposit a Stard. point.
N. 80° E	6 ⟨5?⟩	miles to the enterance of a Creek oppst on the Stard Side passed a brook below the Lard. Clifts at 1 mile one on the Std. at 3 miles. a Island Close to the Stard Side at 2 miles
N. 12° E	3	miles to the lower part of a Stard. Bluff in the bend opsd. an island
N. 70° W	1½	miles to the lower point of a Island passed a ⟨Creek on Lard.⟩ Several Sand bars. 1 single
N. 5° W.	2½	miles to a tree in the Lard Side on a low bluff opsd. to an a low timbered bottom below a Brook

[Clark]   *Saturday 31st of July 1806*

I was much disturbed last night by the noise of the buffalow which were about me.   one gang Swam the river near our Camp which alarmed me a little for fear of their Crossing our Canoes and Splitting them to pieces. Set out as usial about Sun rise   passed a rapid which I call wolf rapid[2] from the Circumstance of one of those animals being at the rapid. here the river approaches the high mountanious Country on the   N W. Side.[3]   those hills appear to be composed of various Coloured earth and Coal without much rock[4]   I observe Several Conical pounds [*NB: mounds*] which appear to have been burnt.[5]   this high Country is washed into Curious formed mounds & hills and is cut much with reveens.   the Country again opens and at the distance of 23 miles below the Redston or *War-har-*

sah[6] River I landed in the enterance of a Small river[7] on the Stard. Side 40 yards wid Shallow and muddy.   it has lately been very high.   haveing passed the Enterance of a River on the Lard Side 100 yards wide which has running water.[8]   this river I take to be the one the Menetarries Call little wolf or *Sa-a-shah* [*NB: Shah*] River[9]   The high Country is entirely bar of timber.   great quantities of Coal or carbonated wood is to be seen in every Bluff and in the high hills at a distance on each Side.[10]   Saw more Buffalow and Elk and antilopes this evening than usial.   18 Miles below the last river on the Stard. Side, I passed one 60 yards wide which had running water.   this Stream I call *oah tar-pon-er* or Coal ⟨R⟩ River[11] has very steep banks on each side of it.   passed Several large Brooks[12] Some of them had a little running water, also Several Islands   Some high black looking Bluffs and encampcd on the Stard. Side on a low point.[13]   the country like that of yesterday is open extencive plains.   as I was about landing this evening Saw a white bear and the largest I ever Saw eating a dead buffalow on a Sand bar.   we fired two Shot into him, he Swam to the main Shore and walked down the bank. I landed and fired 2 more Shot into this tremendious animal without killing him.   night comeing on we Could not pursue him he bled profusely. Showers all this day

Course distance and Remarks 31st July 1806

		M
N. 80° E.	to a Bluff in a Stard. Bend passed a Low Bluff on the Lard. Side	1 ½
N. 28° W.	to a high Bluff on the Stard Side. passed wolf rapid (not bad)	½
N. 80° W.	to a Bluff under a very high rugid hill or low Mtn. on the Lard. Side opposit a timbered point	2 ½
N. 10° E.	to the enterance of a dry brook[14] on Stard. Side passed under a high ⟨range⟩ Bluff of different coloured earth[15] on the Lard. Side. high prarie on the Stard. Side	1
East	to a Lard point at a fiew Cotton wood trees	1
N. 55° E.	to a Lard. point. passed a Stard. point at 1 mile high Coal bluffs on the Lard Side	3

N. 45° E.	to a red bluff on the Lard. Side. passed a Std. point	1 ½
East	to a Stard. Bend passed two Lard. and one Stard. point passed a river 100 yards wide on the Lard Side. Shallow and the water muddy. low Bluffs. Shabono R.[16]	6
N. 60° E.	to an island close to the Stard. point passed a Std point and a Lard point river narrow	3
N. 30° E.	to the enterance of a river in the Stard. Bend 40 yds. wide Steep Coal banks[17] on each Side of this little river. about 4 feet deep & muddy. *Coal river*[18]	2
N. 10° W.	to a high Bluff on Lard. Side (rugid)	1 ½
East	to the enterance of a brook[19] below the Lard. Bluff. passed a Stard point. also a high Bluff on the Lard. Side laterly Sliped into the river	2 ½
S. 45° E.	to a Lard. point	1
N 45° E.	to the head of an island near the Stard Side. low coal bluffs on Stard Side. passed a Brook[20] on Stard. Side	6
N. 20° E.	to the enterance of a brook[21] in the Lard Bend opposit to an island near the Stard. Side	4
N 70° E	to the lower part of a Stard. Bluff at the enterance of a river[22] 60 yards wide with deep banks on each Side gibsons R passed a Small island. river muddy & Shallow	3
N. 30° W.	to a Lard. Bluff opsd. a Stard point	3
N. 80° E.	to the enterance of a creek[23] below a Stard Bluff opposit to an island. passed a brook on Lard Side at 1 mile one on Stard at 3 miles and an island Close to the Stard Side at 2 miles	6
N. 12° E.	to the lower part of a Stard. Bluff in a bend opposit to an island	3
N. 70° W	to the lower point of an island psd. Sand bars in different parts of the river	1 ½

N. 5° W.	to a Single tree on a low Lard Bluff below the enterance of a Brook²⁴ on the Lard Side. Encampd opposit on the Stard Side	}	2 ½

Miles   66

1. The words "*Coal R*" may have been added to a blank space; it is O'Fallon Creek (see later note in this entry).

2. "Wolf rapid" is in Prairie County, Montana, near the mouth of Conns Coulee, some four miles southwest of present Terry. *Atlas* map 121.

3. Including Little Sheep and Big Sheep mountains and other high country in Prairie County. *Atlas* map 121.

4. The Tullock, Lebo, and Tongue River members of the Fort Union Formation all are exposed in vertical succession in the hills northwest of the river. The sediments are principally sandstone, mudstone, claystone, siltstone, and shale with coal beds. Most of these rocks are soft and easily eroded except for occasional lenses of indurated sandstone.

5. The conical mounds form where resistant sandstone caps less resistant materials, protecting them from erosion.

6. Clark apparently added this word later to a blank space. The stream is Powder River; see notes at July 30.

7. O'Fallon Creek enters the Yellowstone River about a mile west of present Fallon in Prairie County. Both creek and town bear the name of Benjamin O'Fallon, trader, Indian agent, and nephew of William Clark. The creek was apparently named by one of O'Fallon's later friends or associates in the fur trade, since neither Clark's journals nor *Atlas* map 121 give it that name. On the *Atlas* map it is "Oak Tar pon er River" and "Coal River"; the latter is the name used in both sets of courses and distances, but not in the journal text. "Poner" may be the Mandan term, *pasáŋh*, "creek," but the meaning of the first portion of the word is unknown (see Fort Mandan Miscellany, vol. 3). Wood & Moulton, 374–75.

8. Cherry Creek enters the Yellowstone from the north in Prairie County a little below Terry. On *Atlas* map 121 it is "Shabonas River" after Toussaint Charbonneau.

9. This cannot be the "Little Wolf mountain Creek" of the Fort Mandan Miscellany, vol. 3 of this edition, although the name, as Clark indicates, would have been learned from the Hidatsas at Fort Mandan. Clark may have added the name to a blank space. The term is Hidatsa, *ceeša*, "wolf."

10. The coal is in the Ludlow Member of the Fort Union Formation near the river and in the Tongue River Member at a short distance from the river.

11. Not the stream that bears those names in the courses and distances or on *Atlas* map 121; this is Cabin Creek in Prairie County, "Gibsons deep river" on the *Atlas* map, after George Gibson of the party. The words "*Oak-tar-pon-er* or Coal ⟨R⟩" may have been added later to a blank space and partly interlined.

12. Including Cherry, Cabin, and Cedar creeks. *Atlas* map 121.

13. The camp was in Dawson County, Montana, some seven miles southwest of pres-

ent Glendive. *Atlas* map 121. The high, black-looking bluffs most likely are composed of the Pierre Shale near the center of the Cedar Creek anticline about ten miles southwest of Glendive.

14. This is hard to identify unless Clark means "larboard," as he has it in the Voorhis version, in which case it could be Lost Boy Creek, which joins the Yellowstone from the northwest in Prairie County, some five miles west of Terry; on *Atlas* map 121 a nameless stream is shown among the "High broken Hills" below Wolf Rapid.

15. The Tullock, Lebo, and Tongue River members of the Fort Union Formation are exposed in vertical succession on this hill at the mouth of Lost Boy Creek. Each member has slightly different coloration and composition.

16. "Shabono R" may have been added to a blank space.

17. Ludlow Member of the Fort Union Formation at the mouth of O'Fallon Creek.

18. In the courses and distances and on *Atlas* map 121 "Coal River" and "Oak Tar pon er" are O'Fallon Creek; in the journal narrative (see earlier note in this entry) they are Cabin Creek.

19. Perhaps Hatchet Creek in Prairie County; "Dry Brook" on *Atlas* map 121.

20. The most prominent stream on this course is Bad Route Creek on the larboard side, in Prairie County. However, a "Dry Brook" appears on the starboard side on *Atlas* map 121.

21. Evidently Cracker Box Creek in Dawson County; the island appears on *Atlas* map 121, but not the stream.

22. Cabin Creek (see earlier note in this entry), the "Oak-tar-pon-er or Coal River" of the journal narrative.

23. Cedar Creek in Dawson County, "Cat fish Creek" on *Atlas* map 121.

24. Whoopup Creek in Dawson County, a nameless stream opposite the camp of July 31 on *Atlas* map 121.

[Clark]   [*Weather, July 1806*][1]

Day of the month	State of the weather at Sun rise	Wind at Sun rise	State of the weather at 4 P. M	Wind at 4 P M.
1st	c a f	N W	f.	N W
2cd	f.	S E	f	N. W
3rd	f.	S E	f	S W
4th	f.	S W	f.	S W
5th	f.	N. E.	f.	S W.
6th	f.	S W.	c. a. r. T. & L	S W
7th	c. a. r	W.	f. a. r	S W by W
8th	f. a. r	W.	f.	S W
9th	c.	S W.	f.	S W

10th	f.	S. E.	f.	S W.
11th	f.	S E	f.	N N E
12th	f.	S E.	f.	N W
13th	f.	S S E	f.	N E
14th	f.	N W	f.	N W
15th	f.	S E. by E	f.	N E
16th	c.	N E	c.	N. E
17th	f. a. r. h. T. & L.	S E	f.	S W
18th	f.	S W	f.	S E
19th	f.	N W	f.	S E
20th	f.	N F.	f.	N E
21st	f.	N E	c.	N. E.
22nd	f. a. T. L & r	N E	c.	N. E
23rd	f.	N. E.	c.	S E
24th	f.	S W	r.	S W.
25th	c.	E	c. a r	S W
26th	c.	S S W	f a. r.	N W.
27th	f.	N. E.	f.	S W.
28th	C a f r	N E	f.	N. W.
29th	c. a. r. T. & L	N. E	f.	N.
30th	f. a. r. T. L	N. W.	f. a. r.	S. E
31st	f.	N W.	c. a. r	N E

[Remarks][2]

1st   a Species of wild Clover in blume

2nd   Musquetors very troublesom

3rd   Cap L. & my Self part at Travellers rest.

4th   a worm day. I saw a Speces of Honeysuckle[3] with a redish brown flower in blume

5th   Cool night. Some dew this morning[4] the nights are Cool. the musquetors are troublesome untill a little after dark when the air become Cool and Musquetoes disappear.

6th   cold night with frost. I slept cold under 2 blankets on head of Clarks river. I arived in an open plain in the middle of which a violent Wind from the N W. accompanied with hard rain which lasted from 4 untill half past 5 P. M.   quawmash in those plains at the head of wisdom River is just begining to blume and the grass is about 6 inches high.

7th   Saw a blowing Snake.[5]   a violent rain from 4 to ½ past 5 last evening & Some rain in the latter part of last night.   a small Shower of rain at 4 this morning accompanied with wind from the S. S. W.

8th   a Small Shower of rain a little after dark   a heavy rain and wind from S W. at 4 P. M yesterday[6]   a heavy Shower of rain accompanied with rain from the S W. from 4 to 5 P M.   passed the boiling hot Springs emerced 2 peces of raw meat in the Spring and in 25 Minits the Smallest pece was sufficiently cooked and in 32 the larger was also sufficiently cooked

9th   Hard frost. Some ice this morning.   last night was very Cold and wind hard from the N E. all night. The river is 12 inches higher than it was last Summer when we made the deposit here and portage from this place.   more Snow on the adjacent mountains than was at that time.

10th   white frost this morning.   ice ¾ of an inch thick on Standing water.   grass killd by the frost.   river falling proceviable.   a large white frost last night.   the air extreemlly Cold. Ice ¾ of an inch thick on Standing water.

11th   frost this morning.   goslins nearly grown   fishing hawks[7] have their young   The yellow Current nearly ripe.   a Slight frost last night.   the air Cool.   the Musquetors retired a little after dark, and did not return untill about an hour after Sunrise.

12th   wisdom river is high but falling. Prickly pears in blume

14th   Saw a Tobaco worm[8] shown me by *York*

15th   Struck the river Rochejhone 120 yds wide   water falling a little

16th   Saw the wild indigo & common sunflower

17th   Heavy showers of rain   Hard Thunder & Lightning last night   a heavy Shower of rain accompanied with hail Thunder and

Lightning at 2 a. m. with hard wind from the S W.   after the Shower was over it Cleared away and became fair.

18th   yellow, purple, & black Currents ripe and abundant

19th   Saw the lst Grape vine[9] of the dark purple kind   the grape nearly grown

20th   Sworms of grass hoppers have eaten the grass of the plains for many miles. The River Rochejhone falls about ½ an in in 24 hours and becoms much Clearer than above. The Grass hoppers are emencely noumerous and have distroyed every Specics of grass from one to 10 Miles above on the river & a great distance back.

21st   river falls a little and the water is nearly Clear

22nd   raind Slightly last evening about dark with hard winds Thunder & lightning   a fiew drops of rain last night at dark.   the Cloud appd. to hang to the S W, wind blew hard from different points from 5 to ⟨7⟩ 8 P M which time it thundered and Lightened. The river by 11 a. m. to day had risen 15 inches, and the water of a milky white Colour.

23rd   violent wind last night from S W. The river has fallen within the last 24 hours 7 inches.   the wind was violent from the S W for about 3 hours last night from the hours of 1 to 3 A. M.

24th   Violent wind last night.   river falling a little   Since the last rise it had fallen 13 inches.   river falling a little   it is 6 feet lower than the highest appearance of it's rise. Rained from 3 to 4 P M but Slightly.   the wind violent from the S. W. (Sgt. Pryor crossd and Set out for the Mandans.[)]

25th   rained from 3 to 4 P M yesterday but Slight.   rained Several Showers   Several Showers of rain with hard winds from the S and S W the fore part of the day.   the brooks on each Side are high and water muddye.

26th   a Slight Shower this morning with hard wind from the S. W. The river falling, but very Slowly 1 inch in 24 hs.

27th   Saw a flight of gulls,[10] a Small rattle Snake[11] Several flocks of Crows & black burds.[12]

28th   a fiew drops of rain this morning a little before day light.   river Still falling a little   Bratten Coet [caught] a beaver   Labeech Shot 2 last evenig. I saw a wild Cat[13] lying on a log over the water.

29th[14]   a fiew drops of rain accompanied with hard Claps of Thunder and Sharp lightning last night   wind hard from the N. E.

30th   Great number of Swallows,[15] they have their young. Killed 1s black tail deer.   young gees beginning to fly   a Slight Shower of rain accompanied with thunder and lightning. Several Showers in the course of this day.   it cleared away in the evening and became fair   river falling a little. Great quantities of Coal appear in the bluffs on either Side. Some appearance of Burnt hills at a distance from the river.[16]

31st   rained only a fiew drops last night.   a Small Showers to day. wind hard from the N E   The wind blew hard and it was Showery all day tho not much rain.   the clouds came up from the W. and N W frequently in course of the day.

1. Clark's weather table for July 1806 appears in Codex M, pp. 147–49 (reading backwards). Since he and Lewis separated on July 3 there is no relationship with Lewis's weather notes for the rest of the month, so the table and remarks appear here with no notice of discrepancies.

2. Clark has remarks in both the margin of his weather table and separately. There is an unusual amount of repetition between the two sets of remarks, as the reader will note. Some duplication has been omitted without comment.

3. Perhaps orange honeysuckle.

4. The separate remark begins "a dew this morning.   the nights are Cool," then continues with "the musquetors."

5. Perhaps western hog-nosed snake, *Heterodon nasicus*. Burroughs, 276–77; Coues (HLC), 2:435 n. 23.

6. Clark's marginal comments for July 8 and 9 run together and are separated at what appears to be a logical point.

7. Osprey, *Pandion haliaetus* [AOU, 364].

8. Probably tobacco hornworm, *Manduca sexta*.

9. Some unknown wild grape, *Vitus* sp.

10. Any of several species of *Larus*.

11. Probably the prairie rattlesnake.

12. The common, or American, crow, *Corvus brachyrhynchos* [AOU, 488]. Without the size given, the blackbirds are not identifiable.

13. Probably the bobcat, *Lynx rufus*.

14. The marginal remark reads, "rain Slightly with Thunder and lightning."

15. Probably the barn swallow, *Hirundo rustica* [AOU, 613]. Holmgren, 33.

16. Geology notes to these references are found under Clark's entry of this date, July 30, 1806.

[Clark] (August 1st)

N. E.	2½	miles to a tree below a large Brook in a ⟨Lard⟩ Stard Bend opposit the head of an Island
North	5	miles to the head of an isld passed 2 islands and a large Brook on the Lard Side
N E.	1½	to the Stard. Shore at a tree passed a Brook Stard
N. W.	2½	to the lower point of an Isld. Close to the Lard Side passed an [isd?] on the Stard Side
N. 40° E	2½	miles to a Stard. bend pds an Island
N 15° E.	3	miles to a Lard. point
North	1½	to a wood on the Stard. Side Passed a small Island
N. 24° W.	2	miles to Some wood on Lard Side
N. 20° E.	1	m to the head of an island
N. 10° E.	1	m to a Bluff on the Lard Side
N. 46° E.	1½	m. to a wood on Lard. Side
North	2	m to a wood on Lard Side
N 80° E.	1½	m to a wood on the Stard. Sid
N. 50° W.	1	m. to deep bend on Lard Side Passed a Coal Bluff on the Stard. Side
N. 40° E.	1	mile to the Center of the Lard. Bend
S 50° E.	1	mile to a wood in the Std. bend
N. 28° E	1½	miles to an Island near the Stard.
N 10° E.	1	miles to the interance of a larg dry Creek on the Lard Side
N. 70° E.	2	miles to the lower point of a wood in a Stard Bend

⟨S⟩ N. 20° E   6   miles to a Lard point opsd a high bluff.   passed an Island

North   1 ½   miles to the Center of a Stard. Bend opposit an island.

N. 50° E   2 ½   miles to the interanc of a [*blank*] on the Stard side

               <u>43</u>

[Clark]   *Sunday 1st of August 1806.*

We Set out early as usial the wind was high and ahead which caused the
water to be a little rough and delayed us very much   aded to this we
had Showers of rain repeetedly all day at the intermition of only a fiew
minits between them. My Situation a very disagreeable one.   in an open
Canoe wet and without a possibility of keeping my Self dry.   the Country
through which we passed is in every respect like that through which I
passed yesterday. The brooks have all Some water in them from the rains
which has fallen.   this water is excessively muddy. Several of those brooks
have Some trees on their borders as far as I can See up them. I observe
Some low pine an cedar[1] on the Sides of the rugid hills on the Stard. Side,
and Some ash timber[2] in the high bottoms.   the river has more Sand
bars today than usial, and more Soft mud.   the current less rapid.   at
2 P. M. I was obliged to land to let the Buffalow Cross over.   not withstanding an island of half a mile in width over which this gangue of
Buffalow had to pass and the Chanel of the river on each Side nearly ¼ of
a mile in width, this gangue of Buffalow was entirely across and as thick
as they could Swim.   the Chanel on the Side of the island the went into
the river was crouded with those animals for ½ an hour.   [*NB: I was
obliged to lay to for an hour*] the other Side of the island for more than ¾ of
an hour. I took 4 of the men and killed 4 fat Cows for their fat and what
portion of their flesh the Small Canoes Could Carry   that which we had
killed a few days ago being nearly Spoiled from the wet weather.   encamped on an Island Close to the Lard Shore.[3]   two gangues of Buffalow
Crossed a little below us, as noumerous as the first.

Course distance and Remarks Augt. 1st 1806[4]
                                                                    M

N. 45 E.   to a Single tree below a large brook in a Stard. Bend   2 ½
               opposit to the head of an island Pine brook[5]

North	to the head of an island. passed 2 islands, also a large Brook[6] on the Lard Side	5
N. 45° E.	to a tree on the Stard. Shore, passed a Brook Std.[7]	1 ½
N. 45° W.	to the lower point of an island close to the Lard Side. passed an island close to the Stard. Side	2 ½
N. 40° E.	to a Stard. Bend passed an island	2 ½
N. 15° E.	to the Lard. point	3
North	to a wood on the Stard. Side passd. a small island	1 ½
N 24° W.	to Some timber on the Lard Side	2
N. 20° E	to the head of an island	1
N. 10° E.	to a Bluff on the Lard Side	1
N. 46° E.	to a wood on the Lard Side	1 ½
North	to a wood on the Lard Side	2
N. 80° E.	to a wood on the Stard Side	1 ½
N. 50° W.	to a deep bend on the Lard Side passed a Coal Bluff[8] for ½ a mile on the Stard Side low and leavel	1 ½
N. 40° E.	to the Center of a Lard. Bend	1
S. 50° E.	to a wood in a Stard Bend psd. Buffalow Crossing C[9]	1
N. 28° E.	to the head of an island near the Stard Side	1 ½
N. 10° E.	to the enterance of a dry Creek[10] on the Lard. Side	1
N. 70° E.	to the lower point of a wood in the Stard Bend	2
N. 20° E.	to a Lard point opposit to a high bluff passed an island	6
North	to the center of a Stard. Bend opposit to an island	1 ½
N. 50° E.	to the enterance of a Small brook[11] on Stard. Side passed Several Sand bars & opposit to an Isld.	2

Miles 45

[Clark]   Augut 1st[12]

Sunrise

1.	wind N W.—	c. a. r.—	N.—	r.—	{	rained last night rained
2.	N.	c. a. r.—				all day at intervales

1. Limber pine and probably Rocky Mountain juniper, or possibly creeping juniper. Both limber pine and Rocky Mountain juniper are commonly found together along the low-elevation foothills of the Montana Rockies and in isolated populations on the eastern Great Plains.

2. Green ash as noticed by Lewis on August 7.

3. The island on which Clark camped is in Dawson County, Montana, just below the mouth of Cottonwood Creek in Wibaux County, a nameless stream on *Atlas* maps 112 and 122.

4. It was probably Coues who underlined in pencil some words in this table; the underlinings have not been kept.

5. "Pine Brook" on *Atlas* map 121, present Sand Creek entering the Yellowstone from the east in Dawson County.

6. Upper Sevenmile Creek meets the Yellowstone in Dawson County a mile or so above present Glendive; it is nameless on *Atlas* map 121.

7. Cains Coulee in Dawson County at Glendive, a nameless stream just below the "High black hills" on *Atlas* map 121. Clark apparently missed the more prominent Glendive Creek a few miles ahead.

8. The Ludlow Member of the Fort Union Formation at the mouth of Morgan Creek.

9. The buffalo crossing appears to be misplaced on *Atlas* maps 112 and 122; it should be at the bend above "Buffalow Creek," present Thirteenmile Creek, in Dawson County.

10. Thirteenmile Creek; see earlier note in this entry. *Atlas* maps 112, 122.

11. Cottonwood Creek; see earlier note in this entry.

12. A weather observation at the end of Clark's Codex M, placed here by date.

[Clark]   [August 2, 1806]

N. 20° E.	6	miles to a Bluff Point on the Stard. Side passed 3 islands and Sevr. Sand bars. a large Creek on the Lard. at 4 miles.
N 40° E.	2½	miles to the head of an Isld. passed the lower point of one
N. 10° E.	4	miles to the lower part of a low bluff on Stard Side passed a Small island and Several Sand bers
North	2	miles to a Small island near the Lard Shore low leavel Plain on Lard.
N. 70° ⟨W⟩ E	1½	to ⟨lower⟩ a Stard. Bend at the interanc of ⟨Jo. Feilds⟩ a Creek of steep banks about 30 yards wide a large Island opposit
North	1	mile to a point on the Stard Side Passed under a large Stard Bluff

N. 20° E.	1 ½	to a point of a large Isd. on the Is Std
N. 70° E	1	miles to a lower part of a low bluff on Std. main Shore
N. 26° E	1 ⟨2⟩ ½	miles some wood below a high Bluff. passed the lower Point of the large island at ½ a mile. Several Sand bars.
N. 12° W.	6 ⟨7⟩	to point on the Stard Side passed 2 island and Several Sand bars on muddy islands river wide
N 20° E	7	Miles to a point of wood on ⟨the Stard Side⟩ upper Island passed an Isd. on Std. Several mud islands rive wide
N 60° E	13 ⟨14⟩	miles to a Stard. Bluff in a bend passes ⟨the head of an⟩ 2 island in the middle of the river. Several Sand Islds. Islands thickly Covered with wood & above an island close to the Lad. Side in a bend.
North	9	miles to Stard point. passed a Bluff on Std. at 4 miles. an island & 3 Sand bars
N. E.	5	miles to an object in the Std. Bend low bottoms on both Sides. passed Sands Killed a white Bear
*N. 10° E.[1]	3	miles to Stard. point of wods extinsive bar on the Lard pont
N. 20° E.	2	miles on the Stard point river one mile wide low bluff on Lard. extincve bar from the Stard.
N. 35° E.	4	miles to a thick wood on the Center of the Stard. Bend rive more than 1 mile wide Several Sand bars a Brook on the Std. side Clifts at a [*word unclear*] discharges on Std side
N 60° W.	4 ½	miles to a Stard point a Sand or mud bar on each side
N. 10° E	1 ½	miles to a tree in the Ld. bend ⟨passed⟩ Mud bar on Std. pt.
N. 80° E	4	Mile to a ⟨gully⟩ Point ⟨in⟩ a Stard. Bluff Som yellow rock abv th wtr. passed extince timber bottoms on each Side rive about 300 yds wide only
⟨N. 30° E	2 ⟨1⟩ ½	miles to the Comencment of a wood on the Stard.

Side op opossd. a Creek on Std. at ½ a mile & a
Brook just below.⟩

North   6   Miles to a high bluff below the interanc of Jo Fields
River 35 yds wide on Stard. Side   river widen to ¾
of a mile

26   (2d Aug)

[Clark]   *Monday August 2nd 1806.*

Musquetors very troublesom this morning   I Set out early   river wide
and very much divided by islands and Sand and Mud bars.   the bottoms
more extencive and contain more timber Such as Cotton wood ash willow
&c. The Country on the N W. Side rises to a low plain and extends leavel
for great extent. Some high rugid hills in the forepart of this day on the S
E. Side on which I saw the big horns but could not get near them. Saw
emence numbers of Elk Buffalow and wolves to day.   the wolves do catch
the elk. I saw 2 wolves in pursute of doe Elk which I beleive they Cought
they very near her when She entered a Small wood in which I expect they
cought her as She did not pass out of the small wood during my remaining in view of it which was 15 or 20 minits &c.   passed the enterance of
Several brooks on each Side,[2] a Small river 30 yds wide with Steep banks
on the Stard. Side, which I call *Ibex* River[3]   the river in this days decent is
less rapid crouded with Islds and muddy bars and is generally about one
mile in wedth.   as the islands and bars frequently hide the enterance of
Brooks &c. from me as I pass'd maney of them I have not noticed.   about
8 A. M this morning a Bear of the large vicious[4] Species being on a Sand
bar raised himself up on his hind feet and looked at us as we passed down
near the middle of the river.   he plunged into the water and Swam towards us, either from a disposition to attack't or from the Cent of the
meat which was in the Canoes.   we Shot him with three balls and he returned to Shore badly wounded.   in the evening I saw a very large Bear
take the water above us. I ordered the boat to land on the opposit Side
with a view to attack't him when he Came within Shot of the Shore.   ⟨I let
swim⟩ when the bear was in a fiew paces of the Shore I Shot it in the
head.   the men hauled her on Shore and proved to be an old Shee which
was so old that her tuskes had worn Smooth, and Much the largest

feemale bear I ever Saw. after taking off her Skin, I proceeded on and encampd[5] a little above the enterance of Jo: Feilds Creek on Stard. Side in a high bottom Covered with low Ash and elm. the Musquetors excessively troublesom.

I have noticed a great preportion Buck Elks on this lower part of the river, and but very few above. those above which are emencely noumerous are feemales Generally. Shields killed a Deer this morning dureing the time we were at Brackfast. we were very near being detained by the Buffalow today which were Crossing the river we got through the line between 2 gangues.

Cours distance and remarks Augt. 2d 1806[6]

		M
N. 20° E.	to a bluff point on the Stard. Side passed 3 islands and Several Sand bars. also a large Creek[7] on the *Lard.* at 4 M.	6
N. 40° E.	to the head of an island, haveing passed the Lower pt. of one	2 ½
N. 10° E.	to the lower part of a low bluff on the Stard. Side passed a Small island and Several Bars.	4
North	to a Small island near the lard. Shore a low leavel extencive plain on the Lard Side	2
N. 70° E.	to the enterance of a Creek 30 yards wide in a Stard. Bend opposit to a large island Ibex Creek	1 ½
North	to a point on the Stard Side passing under a low bluff.	1
N. 20° E	to a point of a large island on the Stard Side	1 ½
N. 70° E	to the lower part of a low bluff on Stard Main Shore	1
N. 26° E	to Some wood below a high bluff Stard. Side. passd. the lower point of the large island at ½ a mile and Several Sand bars or reather mud islands	1 ½
N. 12° W.	to a Stard. point passed two islands and Several muddy & gravelly bars. river about 1 mile wide	6
N. 20° E.	to a wood on the upper point of an island passd. an island near the Std. and Several bars. river 1 M. wide	7

N. 60° E.	to a Stard. Bluff in a bend above the Buffalow Crossings[8] passed 2 islands in the middle of the river hickly covered with wood. also passed the head of a 3rd island close to the Stard Side in the bend. passed Several bars river wide &c.	13
North	to a Stard. point passed a Stard. Bluff at 4 miles passed an island and three Bars	9½
N. 45° E.	to an object in a Stard. Bend passed Several sand bars, low timbered on each Side (killed a white Bear or one of that Specis)	5
N. 10° E.	to a Stard. point of woods, an extenciv bar on the Lard. Side	3
N. 20° E.	along the ⟨Lard.⟩ Stard. point, low bluffs on Lard. an extencive bar from the Stard. river more than 1 mile	2
N. 35° E.	to a thick wood in the Center of a Stard Bend passed Several bars. a brook on the Stard. Side bottoms narrow on Stard. river more than 1 mile wide	4
N. 60° W.	to a Stard. point. psd. a mud bar on each Side of the Rivr	4½
N. 10° E.	to a tree in the Lard. Bend. mudy bar on Stard	1½
N. 80° E.	to a Bluff Point on the Stard. bend Some yellow rock[9] just above the water. passed extencive timbered bottoms on each Side. river only 300 yds wide	4
North	to a high Bluff imediately belowe the enterance of Jo. Field's Creek on the Stard. Side 35 yds wide river about ¾ of a mile wide. encamped short of the distance 2 miles on the Stard side—	6

Miles 86

1. The meaning of the asterisk is unknown.

2. Including Burns, Lone Tree, Shadwell, Fox, O'Brien, and Bennie Peer creeks, few of which appear on *Atlas* maps 112 and 122.

3. "*Ibex*" may have been written in later; the name refers to the bighorn sheep. On *Atlas* map 112 it seems likely that the name "Ibex river" was also written in later, the earlier name being "Jo. F. Creek River." In the draft courses "Jo Feilds" is crossed out. Clark must at first have thought the stream to be the Joseph Fields Creek of *Atlas* maps 48

and 56 (see April 26, 1805), present Charbonneau Creek in McKenzie County, North Dakota, indicating that he thought himself much nearer the mouth of the Yellowstone than was the case. Ibex River is apparently Smith Creek in Richland County, Montana, reaching the Yellowstone near present Savage on the opposite side. *Atlas* map 122.

4. Apparently the "v" was written over an "f," "ferocious" being the word Clark perhaps first intended. There is no doubt that the animal was a grizzly.

5. Clark camped just above the mouth of Charbonneau Creek in McKenzie County; the site is shown on *Atlas* map 56.

6. There is some red underlining of words in this table; it is not repeated here.

7. Burns Creek in Richland County, meeting the Yellowstone from the west about a mile north of the Wibaux County line. This is the "Samuels Creek" of *Atlas* maps 112 and 122. "Samuel" may have been the same person for whom Point Samuel in Oregon was named on November 26, 1805. Coues (HLC), 2:721 n. 3, speculates, without evidence, that he may have been Samuel Lewis, copyist for Clark's map of 1814 (*Atlas* map 126), whom he further theorizes to have been a relative of Meriwether Lewis.

8. The lower "Buffalow Crossings" on *Atlas* maps 112 and 122, in Richland County, some eight miles southwest of present Sidney.

9. This is a sandstone in the Tongue River Member of the Fort Union Formation at the mouth of Horse Creek, McKenzie County, North Dakota.

[Clark]   [August 3, 1806] [1]

West	¼	along the Std. Bluff
North	1¾	to the Lowr pat of the Std. Bluff. Comincment of a large timbered bottom Std Passed an Island
N. 20° W.	3½	m. to a Lard point passed a Sand bar on Lard. and one below the Std. pont. Bottoms of wood extince
N. 40° W.	2	miles to a Stard. point passed a Deep bend to the Stard. an extincve Sand bar from the Lard
N. W. Point	1½	miles to the Point at the junction of the Missouri an extence Sand bar opposit on the Std sd

[Clark]   *Tueday August 3rd 1806.*

last night the Musquetors was so troublesom that no one of the party Slept half the night.   for my part I did not Sleep one hour.   those tormenting insects found their way into My beare and tormented me the whole night.   they are not less noumerous or troublesom this morning.   at 2 miles passed the enterance of Jo. Field's Creek [2] 35 yds wide imediately above a high bluff which is falling into the river very fast.   on the Side of this bluff I saw Some of the Mountain Bighorn animals. I assended the hill below the Bluff. the Musquetors were So noumerous that I could not Shute with any Certainty and therefore Soon returned to the Canoes. I had not proceeded far before I saw a large gangue of ewes & yearlins & fawns or lambs of the bighorn, and at a distance alone I saw a ram. landed and Sent Labeech to kill the ram, which he did kill and brought him on board. this ram is not near as large as maney I have Seen. however he is Sufficiently large for a Sample I directed Bratten to Skin him with his head horns & feet to the Skin and Save all the bone. I have now the Skin & bone of a Ram a Ewe[3] & a yearlin ram of those big Horn animals. at 8. A. M. I arived at the Junction of the Rochejhone with the Missouri, and formed my Camp imediately in the point between the two river at which place the party had all encamped the 26th of April—1805.[4] at landing I observed Several Elk feeding on the young willows in the point among which was a large Buck Elk which I shot & had his flesh dryed in the Sun for a Store down the river. had the Canoes unloaded and every article exposed to dry & Sun. Maney of our things were wet, and nearly all the Store of meat which had been killed above Spoiled. I ordered it to be thrown into the river. Several Skins are also Spoiled which is a loss, as they are our principal dependance for Clothes to last us to our homes &c.

Course distance & Remarks Augt. 3rd 1806.

West	along the Stard. Bluff to a point opposit to a low extencive timbered bottom on the Lard Side	¼
North	to the lower part of the Stard. Bluff at the Commencement of a large timbered bottom. passed an island	1¾
N. 20° W.	to a Lard point passed a large bar on the Lard Side, and one below the Stard. point bottoms on each Side extenciv & covered with wood	3½
N. 58° W.	to the junction of the Rochejhone with the Missouri, passed a Stard. point at 1½ miles above which there is a deep bend to the Std. and an extenciv Sand bar from the above Lard. point. also an extencive Sand bar below the Stard. point	2½

Miles 8

The distance from the Rocky Mountains at which place I struck the River Rochejhone to its enterance into the Missouri 837 Miles 636 Miles of this distance I decended in 2 Small Canoes lashed together in which I had the following Persons. John Shields, George Gibson, William Bratten, W. Labeech, Toust. Shabono his wife & child & my man York. The Rochejhone or Yellow Stone river is large and navagable with but fiew obstructions quite into the rocky mountains. and probably ⟨to head⟩ near it's source. The Country through which it passes from those Mounts. to its junction is Generaly fertile rich open plains the upper portion of which is rolcing and the high hills and hill Sides are partially covered with pine and Stoney. The middle portion or from the enterance of Clarks Fork as low as the Buffalow Shoals the high lands Contain Some Scattering pine on the Lard. Side. on the Stard. or S. E. Side is Some hills thickly Supplied with pine. The lower portion of the river but fiew pines are to be Seen the Country opens into extencive plains river widens and Contains more islands and bars; of corse gravel sand and Mud. The Current of this river may be estimated at 4 Miles and ½ pr. hour from the Rocky Mts. as low as Clarks Fork, at 3½ Miles pr. hour from thence as low as the Bighorn, at 3— Miles pr. hour from thence as low as the Tongue river, at 2¾ Miles pr. hour from thence as low as Wolf rapid and at 2½ miles pr. hour from thence to its enterance into the Missouri

The Colour of the Water differs from that of the Missouri it being of a yellowish brown,[5] whilst that of the Missouri is of a deep drab Colour containing a greater portion of mud than the ⟨Missouri⟩ Rochejhone.[6] This delighfull river from indian information has it's extreem sources with the North river in the Rocky mountains on the confines of New Mexico.[7] it also most probably has it's westerly sources connected with [NB: *those of*] the Multnomah and those the main Southerly branch of Lewis's river while it's Easterly branches head with those of Clark's R.[8] the bighorn and River Platte and may be said to water the middle portion of the Rocky Mountains from N W to S. E. for several hundred miles. the indians inform us, that a good road passes up this river to it's extreem source from whence it is buta short distance to the Spanish settlements.[9] there is also a considerable fall on this river within the mountains [NB: *no*] but at what distance from it's source we never could learn[10] like all other branches of the Missouri which penetrate the Rocky Mountains all that portion of it lying within those mountains abound in fine beaver and Otter, it's streams also which issuing from the rocky mountain and discharging themselves above Clark's fork inclusive also furnish an abundance of beaver and Otter and possess considerable portions of small timber in their vallies.   to an establishment on this river at clarks Fork the Shoshones both within and West of the Rocky Mountains would willingly resort for the purposes of trade as they would in a great measure be relived from the fear of being attacked by their enimies the blackfoot Indians and Minnetares of fort de Prarie, which would most probably happen were they to visit any establishment which could be conveniently formed on the Missouri.[11] I have no doubt but the same regard to personal safety would also induce many numerous nations inhabiting the Columbia and Lewis's river West of the mountains to visit this establishment in preference to that at the entrance of Maria's river, particularly during the first years of those Western establishments.   the Crow Indians, Paunch Indians Castahanah's and others East of the mountains and south of this place would also visit this establishment; it may therefore be looked to as one of the most important establishments of the western fur trade.   at the entrance of Clark's fork there is a sufficiency of timber to support an establishment, an advantage that no position possesses from thence to the Rocky Mountains. The banks of the yellowstone river a bold not very high yet are not subject to be overflown, except for a few miles immediately below where the river issues from the mountain. the bed of this river is almost entirely composed of loose pebble, nor is it's bed interrupted by chains of rock except in one place and that even furnishes no considerable obstruction to it's navigation.   as you decend with the river from the mountain the pebble becomes smaller and the quantity of mud increased untill you reah Tongue river where the pebble ceases and the sand then increases and predominates near it's mouth.[12] This river can be navigated to greater advantage in perogues than any other craft yet it possesses suficient debth of water for battauxs[13] even to the mountains; nor is there any of those moving sand bars so formidable to the navigation of many parts of the Missouri. The Bighorn R and Clark's fork may be navigated a considerable distance in perogues and canoes. Tongue river is also navigable for canoes a considerable distance.

1. With this entry the draft courses and distances for the Yellowstone journey end. From here Clark was traversing familiar territory. The last two courses are not repeated in the codex entry but are replaced by a single course that is somewhat different than either of these.

2. Charbonneau Creek, McKenzie County, North Dakota. *Atlas* maps 48, 56.

3. Perhaps it was Biddle who placed brackets around and underlined the words "a Ewe," all in red ink.

4. The camp was in McKenzie County, as Clark notes, at the campsite of April 26, 1805. *Atlas* maps 35, 48, 56.

5. The color of the water in the rivers is derived largely from the formations through which they pass. The many yellow-colored rocks of the Fort Union Formation give some of their color to the water of the Yellowstone River.

6. The Missouri River passes through more varied formations than the Yellowstone and passes through a long stretch of shale of the Colorado Group, Claggett Shale, and Bearpaw Shale after it emerges into the plains. These shale formations, being more easily eroded, impart more mud and dark color to the Missouri than is found in the Yellowstone. From here the remainder of the description of the Yellowstone under this date is in Lewis's hand, obviously inserted by him after the reunion of the two captains on August 12, 1806. Since there is no break in the writing nor any added pages, Clark must have written up this journal, at least from August 4 on, after the reunion. This would mean that more than a week's worth of entries would have had to have been added and there are no known draft entries from this period.

7. The North River is the Rio Grande del Norte, whose sources in Colorado are hundreds of miles southeast of those of the Yellowstone and the Snake (the southerly branch of Lewis's River) in northwest Wyoming. The Willamette (Multnomah) heads in western Oregon. Biddle took extra notes on the Yellowstone's sources in conversation with Clark after the expedition. Biddle Notes [ca. April 1810], Jackson (LLC), 2:521–22.

8. Clarks Fork Yellowstone River; see July 24, 1806. It was probably Biddle who inserted brackets in red ink from "the Multnomah" to "branch of."

9. The Spanish settlements in New Mexico, a good deal farther from the sources of the Yellowstone than Lewis seems to have imagined.

10. The Falls of the Yellowstone are within present Yellowstone National Park in northwest Wyoming, south of where Clark's party struck the river. It was probably Biddle who inserted brackets in red ink from "there is" to "learn." If he was denying the existence of the falls he was misinformed.

11. A Missouri Fur Company party led by Manuel Lisa built Fort Raymond at the Yellowstone-Bighorn confluence in 1807, the first of various posts on the Yellowstone dealing with the Crows and the mountain tribes. The Missouri Fur Company's attempt to

establish a post at the Three Forks in 1810 was defeated by the intense hostility of the Blackfeet (see July 28, 1805), who indeed feared that such a post would furnish guns and ammunition to the mountain tribes. When the American Fur Company finally established Fort McKenzie on the Missouri near the mouth of the Marias in 1831, it was for the purpose of trading with the Blackfeet themselves. Oglesby, 54–59, 93–115; Ewers (BRNP), 50–52, 60; Chittenden, 1 : 141–44, 333–36.

12. The Yellowstone River has a much steeper gradient than the Missouri and is thus able to transport cobbles and gravel farther downstream. Also, unlike the Missouri River, glaciers did not force the Yellowstone River from its course between its present junction with the Missouri and the mountains. Therefore the Yellowstone River in this stretch has had a longer period of time to grade its bed and remove falls and major rapids along its course.

13. The French *bateau* refers to various wooden boats, generally larger and heavier than canoes, used by Anglo-Americans and Canadians for river travel. They might be propelled by oars, poles, or sails. The name was used especially for a keelless, flat-bottomed, plank craft with ends tapered to points, which was more mobile and lighter than a pirogue. Forty feet seems to have been a common length. Criswell, 11; Baldwin (KA), 42; McDermott (GMVF), 20.

[Clark]   *Wednesday 4th August 1806*

Musquetors excessively troublesom So much So that the men complained that they could not work at their Skins for those troublesom insects. and I find it entirely impossible to hunt in the bottoms, those insects being So noumerous and tormenting as to render it imposseable for a man to continue in the timbered lands and our best retreat from those insects is on the Sand bars in the river and even those Situations are only clear of them when the Wind Should happen to blow which it did to day for a fiew hours in the middle of the day. the evenings nights and mornings they are almost indureable perticelarly by the party with me who have no Bears to keep them off at night, and nothing to Screen them but their blankets which are worn and have maney holes. The torments of those Missquetors and the want of a Sufficety of Buffalow meat to dry, those animals not to be found in this neighbourhood induce me to deturmine to proceed on to a more eliagiable Spot on the Missouri below at which place the Musquetors will be less troublesom and Buffalow more plenty. [(]I will here obseve that Elk is Abundant but their flesh & fat is hard to dry in the Sun, and when dry is much easir⟨ly⟩ Spoiled than either the Buffalow or Deer) I ordered the Canoes to be reloaded with our baggage & dryed meat which had been Saved on the Rochejhone together with the Elk killed at this place. wrote a note to Capt Lewis informing him of my intentions and tied it to a pole which I had Stuck up in the point. At 5 P. M Set out and proceeded on down to the 2d point which appeared to be an eligable Situation for my purpose killed a porcupine[1] on this point the Musquetors were So abundant that we were tormented much worst than at the point. The Child of Shabono has been So much bitten by the Musquetor that his face is much puffed up & Swelled. I encamped on this extensive Sand bar which is on the N W. Side.[2]

1. Yellow-haired porcupine, *Erethizon dorsatum epixanthum*. Burroughs, 119–20.

2. Clark's campsites from his leaving the Yellowstone-Missouri junction on August 4, 1806, until his reunion with Lewis on August 12 are difficult to locate because of the lack of information in his journal and on his maps. The August 4 camp was in the "2d point" below the Yellowstone, a somewhat ambiguous reference since the points are formed by the river bends, and the river has shifted over the years. This may be the camp Lewis passed on August 7, which he judged to be seven miles below the mouth of the Yellowstone. This would be in McKenzie or Williams County, North Dakota, perhaps in the vicinity of the party's camp of April 25, 1805. *Atlas* map 35; MRC map 59.

[Clark]   *Thursday 5th August 1806.*

The Musquetors was So troublesom to the men last night that they Slept but very little. indeed they were excessive troublesom to me. my Musquetor Bear has a number of Small holes worn through they pass in. I Set out at an early hour intending to proceed to Some other Situation. I had not proceded on far before I Saw a ram of the big horn Animal near the top of a Lard. Bluff I assended the hill with a view to kill the ram. the Misquetors was So noumerous that I could not keep them off my gun long enough to take Sight and by thair means missed. at 10 a. m. the wind rose with a gentle breeze from the N. W. which in Some measure thinned the Misquetors. I landed on a Sand bar from the South Point intending to form a Camp at this place and Continue untill Capt Lewis Should arive. and killed two Buck Elks and a Deer the best of their flesh & fat I had Saved. had all the dryed meat & fat put out to Sun and continued at this place untill late in the evening finding that there were no buffalow or fresh Sign I dcturmined to proceed on accordingly Set out at 4 P. M and proceeded on but a fiew miles eeir I saw a Bear of the white

Species walking on a Sand bear. I with one man went on the Sand bear and killed the Bear which proved to be a feemale very large and fat. much the fattest animale we have killed on the rout as this bear had got into the river before we killed her I had her toed across to the South Side under a high Bluff where formed a Camp,[1] had the bear Skined and fleaced. our Situation was exposed to a light breeze of wind which continued all the forepart of the night from the S W. and blew away the misquetors.

1. This camp had to be above Little Muddy River (Lewis and Clark's White Earth River), which reaches the Missouri at Williston, Williams County, North Dakota, since Clark passed the stream the next day. It was probably in McKenzie County. *Atlas* maps 35, 47, 56; MRC map 59.

[Clark]   *Friday 6th August 1806*

I rose very wet. about 11 P M last night the wind become very hard for a fiew minits Succeeded by Sharp lightning and hard Claps of Thunder and rained for about 2 hours very hard after which it continued Cloudy the balance of the night. as we were about Setting out a female Big horn animal came on the bluff imediately above us and looked down. I derected Labeech to Shoot it which he did, after Skinning this animal we Set out and proceeded on to a Sand bar on the S W. Side below the enterance of White earth river where I landed and had the meat Skins and bedding all put out to dry.[1] wind hard from the N W. I halted on the N W. Side of this river in the bend above the white earth river, where I saw where the Indians had been digging a root which they eate and use in Seup [*NB: Soup*],[2] not more than 7 or 8 days past. This morning a very large Bear of white Specis, discovered us floating in the water and takeing us, as I prosume to be Buffalow imediately plunged into the river and prosued us. I directed the men to be Still. this animal Came within about 40 yards of us, and tacked about. we all fired into him without killing him, and the wind So high that we could not pursue hi[m], by which means he made his escape to the Shore badly wounded. I have observed buffalow floating down which I suppose must have been drounded in Crossing above. more or less of those animals drown or mire in passing this river. I observed Several floating buffalow on the R. Roche-

282

jhone imediately below where large gangues had Crossed. The wind blew hard all the after part of the day. I derected the men to dress their Skins except one which I took with me and walkd. through the bottom to the foot of the hills   I killed five deer and the man with me killed 2.   four others were killed in the Course of the day by the party only 2 of those deer were fat owing as I suppose to the Musquetors which are So noumerous and troublesom to them that they Cannot feed except under the torments of millions of those Musquetors.

1. Clark does not say how far below the mouth of Little Muddy River (White Earth River) this camp was; it was probably in McKenzie County, North Dakota, on a site now submerged by Garrison Reservoir, somewhere above Tobacco Creek (see August 9, 1806).
2. Breadroot, scurf pea, pomme blanche, prairie turnip, *Psoralea esculenta* Pursh. See Lewis's description at May 8, 1805. This ethnobotanical observation documents an early August harvest of breadroot. At this time the Indians would have been able to locate the roots before the above-ground stem had abscised and broken away from the storage root, and it would have been at a most nutritious stage, after the spring flowering and carbohydrate storage period. Booth & Wright, 137; Barkley, 181; Wedel (NPT).

[Clark]   *Saturday 7th August 1806*

Some hard rain this morning after daylight which wet us all. I formed a Sort of Camped and delayed untill 11 a. m. when it Stoped raining for a short time. I directed every thing put on board and proceeded on down. the rain Continued at intervales all day tho' not hard in the evenig Saw a Bear on the bank but Could not get a Shoot at it.   at 6 P M I landed on a Sand bar on the South Side and Campd.[1] Soon after we landed the wind blew very hard for about 2 hours, when it lulled a little.   the air was exceedingly Clear and Cold and not a misquetor to be Seen, which is a joyfull circumstance to the Party.

1. The site of this camp, where Clark's party remained until August 9, is particularly difficult to locate because of the lack of information from Clark. It must still have been above Tobacco Creek (see August 9, 1806), in McKenzie County, North Dakota, the place now being under Garrison Reservoir.

[Clark]   *Sunday 8th August 1806*

A cool windey morning   I derected Shields and Gibson to turn out and hunt this morning.   at 8 A. M. Sergt. N. Pryor Shannon, hall &

Windsor Came down the river in two Canoes made of Buffalow Skins.[1] Sergt. Pryor informed me that the Second night after he parted with me[2] on the river Rochejhone he arived about 4 P M on the banks of a large Creek which contained no running water.[3] he halted to let the horses graze dureing which time a heavy Shower of rain raised the Creek so high that Several horses which had Stragled across the Chanel of this Creek was obliged to Swim back. here he deturmined to Continue all night it being in good food for the horses. In the morning he could See no horses. in lookg about their Camp they discovered Several tracks within 100 paces of their Camp, which they pursued found where they had Caught and drove off all the horses. they prosued on five miles the Indians[4] there divided into two parties. they Continued in pursute of the largest party five miles further finding that there was not the Smallest Chance of overtakeing them, they returned to their Camp and packed up their baggage on their backs and Steared a N. E. course to the River Rochejhone which they Struck at *pompys Tower,* there they killed a Buffalow Bull and made a Canoe in the form and shape of the mandans & Ricares [*NB: Shannon killed Buf. & made Canoe*] (the form of a bason) and made in the following manner. Viz: 2 Sticks of 1¼ inch diameter is tied together So as to form a round hoop of the Size you wish the canoe, or as large as the Skin will allow to cover, two of those hoops are made one for the top or brim and the for the bottom the deabth you wish the Canoe, then Sticks of the Same Size are Crossed at right angles and fastened with a throng to each hoop and also where each Stick Crosses each other. then the Skin when green is drawn tight over this fraim and fastened with throngs to the brim or outer hoop So as to form a perfect bason. one of those Canoes will carry 6 or 8 Men and their loads. Those two Canoes are nearly the Same Size 7 feet 3 inches diamieter & 16 inchs deep 15 ribs or Cross Sticks in each. Sergt. Pryor informs me that the Cause of his building two Canoes was for fear of ones meating with Some accedent in passing down the rochejhone a river entirely unknown to either of them by which means they might loose their guns and amunition and be left entirely destitute of the means of precureing food. he informed me that they passed through the worst parts of the rapids &

Shoals in the river without takeing a drop of water, and waves raised from the hardest winds dose not effect them. on the night of the 26th ulto: the night after the horses had been stolen a Wolf bit Sergt. Pryor through his hand when asleep, and this animal was So vicious as to make an attempt to Seize Windsor, when Shannon fortunately Shot him.[5] Sergt. Pryers hand has nearly recovered. The Country through which St. Pryor Passed after he parted with me is a broken open Country. he passed one Small river which I have Called Pryors river which [*NB: rises*] in a Mtn. to the South of Pompys tower.[6] The note I left on a pole at the Mouth of the River Rochejhone Sergt. Pryor concluding that Capt. Lewis had passed took the note and brought it with him. Capt. Lewis I expect will be certain of my passing by the Sign which I have made and the encampment imediately in the point. Sergt. Pryor bing anxious to overtake me Set out Some time before day this morning and forgot his Saddlebags which contains his papers &c.[7] I Sent Bratten back with him in Serch of them. I also Sent Shannon over to hunt the bottom on the opposit Side. Shields and Gibson returned at 10 A. M. with the Skins and part of the flesh of three deer which they had killed in this bottom. I derected them to take one of the Skin Canoes and proceed down to the next bottom and untill my arival which will be this evening if Sergt. Pryor returns in time. My object is to precure as many Skins as possible for the purpose of purchaseing Corn and Beans of the Mandans. as we have now no article of Merchindize nor horses to purchase with, our only resort is Skins which those people were very fond the winter we were Stationed near them. after dark Sergt. Pryor returned with his Saddlebeggs &c. they were much further up than he expected.

1. Probably bullboats, which Pryor and his companions would have seen among the Mandans and Hidatsas; see October 6, 1804.

2. Pryor parted with Clark on July 24, 1806, above present Billings, Montana; see the first part of his route on *Atlas* maps 108, 116. The incident he now tells of would have occurred on the night of July 25–26.

3. Pryor's route probably roughly paralleled present Interstate Highway 90, headed easterly; he may have camped on Fly Creek in Bighorn County, Montana, several miles west of present Hardin.

4. Pryor and his men were in the country of the Crows, or Absaroke (see November 12, 1804), who were renowned as horse thieves.

5. The wolf's behavior suggests rabies, but neither Pryor nor Windsor contracted the disease, as far as is known.

6. Present Pryor Creek (see July 25, 1806), which rises in the Pryor Mountains in Big Horn and Carbon counties, Montana. *Atlas* maps 109, 116.

7. There is no indication of what the "papers &c." consisted of, but this is the only hint that Pryor may have been keeping a journal, as the sergeants supposedly were required to do. However, the papers may simply have been the letters he was supposed to deliver. Since the entry makes it clear that the papers were recovered, this is not the explanation of Pryor's journal not being available.

[Clark]   *Monday 9th August 1806*

a heavy dew this morning. loaded the Canoes and proceeded on down about 6 miles and landed at the Camp of the 2 hunters Shields and Gibson whome I had Sent down to hunt last evening, they had killed five deer two of which were in good order which they brought in. here I took brackfast and proceeded on a fiew miles and I walked on Shore across a point of near 10 miles in extent in this bottom which was mostly open I saw Some fiew deer and Elk. I killed 3 of the deer which were Meagure the Elk appeared fat. I did not kill any of them as the distance to the river was too great for the men to Carry the meat   at the lower part of this bottom a large Creek of runnig water 25 yds wide[1] falls in which meanders through an open roleing plain of great extent.   in the low bottoms of this Creek I observed Some timber Such as Cottonwood, ash & Elm.   on my arival at the lower part of the bottom found that the canoes had been in waiting for me nearly two hours. The Squar brought me a [*NB: 1800 Miles up the Missouri I found a*] large and well flavoured Goose berry[2] of a rich Crimsin Colour, and deep purple berry of the large Cherry of the Current Speces[3] which is common on this river as low as the Mandans, the engagees Call it the Indian Current. I landed opposit to a high plain on the S. E. Side late in the evening and walked in a Grove of timber where I met with an Elk which I killed.   this Elk was the largest Buck I ever Saw and the fattest animal which have been killed on the rout. I had the flesh and fat of this Elk brought to Camp[4] and cut thin ready to dry.   the hunters killed nothing this evening.

1. This stream could be Tobacco Creek, in Williams County, North Dakota (the captains' "Halls Strand Creek"), or Tobacco Garden Creek in McKenzie County (their "Pumic Stone Creek"). *Atlas* maps 47, 56; MRC maps 57, 58.

2. Either hawthorn gooseberry, *Ribes oxyacanthoides* L., or bristly gooseberry, *R. setosum* Lindl., both of which seem to reach their southern distributional limit along the Missouri River near this area of North Dakota. Barkley, 135–36. It was probably Biddle who drew a red vertical line through most of this botanical passage.

3. Probably the golden currant again.

4. Biddle locates this area as being 1800 miles up the Missouri. One of Clark's statements of creeks and rivers places "Halls Strand Creek" (present Tobacco Creek in Williams County, North Dakota, see Chapter 41) 1790 miles up the river; thus the camp would be approximately ten miles above that stream, in McKenzie County. Biddle has also added the phrase "1800 miles up the Missouri" next to the August 10 entry's dateline. The site is probably now inundated by Garrison Reservoir. This was the camp Lewis passed on August 11, after his wounding by Cruzatte, which probably occurred nearby. *Atlas* maps 34, 47, 56; MRC map 58.

[Clark]   *Tuesday 10th August 1806*[1]

had the flesh of the elk hung on poles to dry, and Sent out the the hunters. wind blew hard from the East all day. in the after part of the day it was [*NB: Cloudy*] & a fiew drops of rain. I finished a Copy of my Sketches of the River Rochejhone.[2] Shields killed a black tail deer & an antilope. the other hunters killed nothing. deer are very Scerce on this part of the river. I found a Species of Cherry[3] in the bottom the Srub or bush which are differant from any which I have ever Seen and not very abundant even in this Small tract of country to which it Seems to be confined. the Stem is compound erect and subdivided or branching without any regular order. it rises to the hight of 8 or 10 feet Seldom putting out more than one Stem from the Same root not growing in cops as the Choke Cherry does. the bark is Smooth and of a dark brown colour. the leaf is petialate, oval accutely pointed at it's apex, from 1 and a ¼ to one and a ½ inch in length and from a half to ¾ of an inch in wedth, finely or manutely Serrate, pale green and free from bubessance. The fruit is a globular berry about the Size of a buck Shot of a fine Scarlet red; like the cherries cultivated in the U. States each is supported by a Seperate Celindric flexable branch peduncle which issues from the extremities of the boughs. the peduncle of this cherry Swells as it approaches the fruit being largest at the point of insertion. the pulp of this fruit is of an agreeable ascid flavour and is now ripe. the Style and Stigma are permanent. I have never Seen it in blume. it is found on the high Stiff[4] lands or hill Sides—. the men dug great parcel of the root which the Nativs call Hankee[5] and the engagees the white apple which they boiled and made use of with their meat. This is a large insipid root and very tasteless. the nativs use this root after it is dry and pounded in their Seup.

1. Next to this dateline are Biddle's words in red ink, "1800 miles up Missouri."

2. Probably the following maps plus others now lost: *Atlas* maps 105–12. See also *Atlas*, 11; Wood & Moulton, 379, 383–84.

3. This description of the pin cherry is largely copied from Lewis's description of August 12, 1806; see a note at August 3 on Clark's journal-keeping during this period. It was apparently Biddle who drew a red vertical line through the passage.

4. An adjective applied to soil which is not friable but heavy, dense, and hard to work.

5. Breadroot; see August 6, 1806. Clark's term "white apple" is a translation of the French *engagés'* word for the plant, pomme blanche, and now a common name for it.

[Clark]   *Wednesday 11th August 1806*

I set out early this morning. at 10 A. M. landed on a Sand bar and brackfast dureing brackfast and my delay at this place which was 2 hours had the Elk meat exposed to the Sun. at Meridian I set out and had not proceeded more than 2 miles before I observed a Canoe near the Shore. I derected the Canoes to land here I found two men from the illinoies Jos. Dixon, and [*blank*] Handcock[1] those men are on a trapping expedition up the River Rochejhone. They inform me that they left the Illinois in the Summer 1804. the last winter they Spent with the Tetons in Company with a Mr. *Coartong* [*NB: Qu: Coautoin*][2] who brought up goods to trade The tetons robed him of the greater part of the goods and wounded this Dixon in the leg with a hard wad.[3] The Tetons gave Mr. *Coartong* Some fiew robes for the articles they took from him. Those men further informed me that they met the Boat and party we Sent down from Fort Mandan near the Kanzas river on board of which was a Chief of the Ricaras,[4] that he met the Yankton Chiefs with Mr. Deurion,[5] McClellen[6] & Several other traders on their way down. that the Mandans and Menitarrais wer at war with the Ricaras and had killed two of the latter. the

Assinniboins were also at war with the Mandans &c and had prohibited the N W. traders from Comeing to the Missouri to trade.[7] they have latterly killed one Trader near the Mous River[8] and are now in wait for Mr. McKenzey[9] one of the Clerks who have been for a long time with Menetarias. Those dificulties if true will I fear be a bar to our expectations of having the Mandan Minetarra & Ricara Chief to acompany us to the U. States. Tho we Shall endeaver to bring abot a peace between Mandans Mennetaries & Ricaras and provail on Some of their Cheifs to accompany us to the U. States. proceeded on to a point on the S W Side nearly opposit the entrance of Goat pen creek and encamped[10] found the Musquetors excessively troublesom.

1. For Dickson and Hancock see Lewis's entry for August 12, 1806, in Chapter 37.

2. This could be Charles Courtin, whom the party apparently met on September 14, 1806. Clark may have added his name here and below to blank spaces. See also August 2 and September 15, 1804.

3. A plug or patch of leather, paper, or other material might be used to pack the ball in a muzzle-loading rifle or musket more tightly. Somehow Dickson was struck by one of these instead of a ball, hard enough to cause some injury.

4. The party sent back in the keelboat under Corporal Richard Warfington; see April 7, 1805. For the Arikara chief, see October 9, 1804.

5. For Pierre Dorion see June 12, 1804.

6. For Robert McClellan see September 12, 1806.

7. For North West Company troubles with the Assiniboines in 1805, see Wood & Thiessen, 162, 199, 242.

8. The Souris River in Saskatchewan, North Dakota, and Manitoba; see December 26, 1804.

9. Charles McKenzie of the North West Company; see November 27, 1804.

10. "Goat pen Creek," which the party passed going west on April 15, 1805, is the present Little Knife River in Mountrail County, North Dakota. Clark's camp would have been in McKenzie County, near where North Dakota Highway 23 crosses the Missouri; the site would now be inundated by Garrison Reservoir. *Atlas* maps 34, 47, 56; MRC map 56.

[Clark]   *Thursday 12th August 1806*

I set out early this morning and had not proceeded on far before Shannon discovered he had lost his Tomahk. I derected him to land his Skin Canoe and go back to our Camp of last night in Serch of it, and proceeded on my self with the two wood and one Skin Canoe to a large bottom on the N. E Side above the head of Jins [*NB: Qu: an*] island[1] and landed to take brackfast as well as to delay untill Shannon & Gibson Should arive. Sent out Shields & Labiech to hunt deer in the bottom, at 2 ⟨a⟩ P m. Shannon and gibson arived having found the tomahawk at our camp they killed 3 Elk &c. one of the Canoes of Buffalow Skin by accident got a hole peirced in her of about 6 inches diamuter. I derected two of the men to patch the Canoe with a piece of Elk skin over the hole, which they did and it proved all Sufficient, after which the Canoe did not leak one drop. The two hunters returned without haveing killed any thing. at meridian Capt Lewis hove in Sight with the party which went by way of the Missouri as well as that which accompanied him from Travellers rest on Clarks river; I was alarmed on the landing of the Canoes to be informed that Capt. Lewis was wounded by an accident—. I found him lying in the Perogue, he informed me that his wound was slight and would be well in 20 or 30 days this information relieved me very much. I examined the wound and found it a very bad flesh wound the ball had passed through the fleshey part of his left thy below the hip bone and cut the cheek of the right buttock for 3 inches in length and the debth of the ball. Capt L. informed me the accident happened the day before by one of the men Peter Crusat misstakeig him in the thick bushes to be an Elk. Capt Lewis with this Crusat and Several other men were out in the bottom Shooting of Elk, and had Scattered in a thick part of the woods in pursute of the Elk. Crusat Seeing Capt L. passing through the bushes and takeing him to be an Elk from the Colour of his Cloathes which were of leather and very nearly that of the Elk fired and unfortunately the ball passed through the thy as aforesaid. Capt Lewis thinking it indians who had Shot him hobbled to the canoes as fast as possible and was followered by Crusat, the mistake was then discovered. This Crusat is near Sighted and has the use of but one eye, he is an attentive industerous man and one whome we both have placed the greatest Confidence in dureing the whole rout.— After Capt. Lewis and my Self parted at Travellers rest,[2] he with the Indians proceeded down the West Side of Clarks river Seven miles and crossed on rafts 2 miles below the East fork 120 yards wide, after Crossing the river he proceeded up the North Side of the east fork and encampd.   here the Indians left him and proceeded down Clarks river in Serch of the *Tushepaws*.   an Indian man Came up with Cap L. from the W. of the mountains and proceeded on with those who had accompanied us. Capt. L. proceeded up the E. fork of Clarks river 17 ms. to the enterance of Cokahlarishkit river or the river to buffalow, he proceeded up on the North Side of this river which is 60 yards wide crossing Several Small Streams and the N. fork, and passing over part of the dividing mountain onto the waters of Deabourns river in the plains and in a Derection to the N. extremity of Easte range of rocky mountains which pass the Missouri at the pine Island Rapid.   from thence he bore his Course to the N E untill he Struck Meadcin river near where that river Enters the rocky Mts. and proceeded down Medicine river to the Missouri at the white bear Islands at the upper part of the portage.   this rout is a very good one tho not the most derect rout, the most derect rout would be to proceed up the Missouri above Dearborns river and take a right hand road & fall on a South branch of the Cokatlarishkit R. and proceed down that river to the main road   but the best rout would be from the falls of the Missouri by fort mountain and passing the N. extremity of that range of the Rocky Mountains which pass the Missouri at the pine Island rapid Course nearly S. W. and to the gap through which the great road passed the dividing mountain the distance from the falls to this gap about 45 miles through a tolerable leavel plain on an old indian road.   and the distance from thence to Clarks river is 105 miles. The total distance from the falls of the Missouri to Clarks river is only *150* miles of a tolerable road—   Capt L. arived at the white Bear Islands and encampd. on the West Side of the Missouri and in the morning he discovered that the Indians had taken of Seven of his best horses, drewyer prosued the indians two day's on the rout towards Clarks river.   he Saw their camp on Dearborns river near the road on which Capt. Lewis & party Come on a by place where they had left only one or two day at this encampment he Saw great appearanc of horses—   on the return of Drewyer Capt L. took Drewyer & the 2 fieldses & proceeded on his intended rout up Marias river leaving Sergt. Gass, Thompson, Frazier, Werner, McNeal & Goodrich at the portage to prepare Geer and repar the wheels & Carrage against the arival of the Canoes and he also left 4 horses for the purpose of hauling the Canoes across. The Canoes arrived on the 16th, and on the 26th they had all except one across, the Plains becom So muddy from the emence rains which had fallen, that they Could not get her over the portage. on the 28th they joined Capt Lewis at the Grog Spring a fiew miles above the enterance of Marias river—. From the Falls of Missouri Capt. L. proceeded on with Drewyer & the 2 fieldses Courss[3]

17th July

N. 10° W.   20   miles from the Great falls of the Missouri to rose river through an open fertile plain.

18th July

N. 25° W.   7   miles to the Sourse of Buffalow Creek, passing a dividing ridge dividing the waters of Mairias river from rose river at 6 miles   Country hilly &c.

N. 15° W.   12   Miles down Buffalow Creek   here the timber Commences Creek 25 Yds wide   no running water.

North   5   miles to Marias river 130 yards wide 3 feet deep.   here Capt Lewis encamped the 18th July 1806

N. 80° W.   20   miles up Marias river on its North Side   passed a large Creek on the South Side with Some timber in it's vally at 8 miles   also another large Creek on the N. Side at 15 miles 30 yards wide with but little water—.

July 20th

S. 80° W.   28   Miles with the river in it's course upwds.   on it's N. Side river 120 yds wide, passed a Creek on South Side at 6 miles, one at 22 miles on the N. Side the last has no water, Some little timber, the genl. course of this river is very Streight its vally ½ m. wide.

July 21st

S. 80° W.   15   Miles to the forks of the river the Main Southern branch bears S. 75° W. about 30 miles to the rocky Mountains.

N. 40° W.　6　miles up the North branch 30 yds wd. confined close between clifts of rocks, Shallow, rapid and not navagable.

N. 25° W.　7　Miles up the North fork, hills broken & pore.

N. 30° W.　7　M. up the river, water transparent.

S. 80° W.　10　M. through the plains　the river maeking a considerable bend to the right or N W.

S. 75° W.　11　M. through the plains on the N. Side of the river which here made a considerable bend to the left or S. haveing passed the river twice.

here Capt Lewis Continued the 23rd 24th & 25th of July to make Some celestial observations but the weather proved So Cloudy that he only made the following observations on the 23rd of July ⟨which gave⟩

Observed Meridian Altd. of ☉'s L. L. with Octant by the back observation—
}　62° 00′ 00″

Latitude deduced from this observation [*blank*]
observed equal altitudes of the Sun with the Sextant.

		h	m	s			h	m	s	
A	M	7	40	57	P	M	4	32	40	Altitude of ☉
	″		42	30		″		33	13	56° 8′ 45″
	″		43	5		″		34	43	

On the 26th of July Capt Lewis Set out on his return to the enterance of Marias river to meet with the party with, the Canoes from the falls. his course was through the plains

　S. E.　5　Miles—　passing a Small Creek from the mts—

　S. 70° E.　9　Miles to a principal branch of Marias River 65 yards wide not very deep at 7 mile.　this last branch is Shallow and rapid about the Size of the former from the ⟨N W⟩ S W. both of those Streams Contain a great preportion of timber—　here we find the 3 Specis of Cotton before mentioned

　N 80° E.　4　miles down Marias river and met with 8 Indians of the Blackfoot nation with about 30 horses, those Indians professed friendship and Set out with him and encamped together the night of the 26th of July, thy informed him that there was two large bands of their nation in that quarter one of which would be at the enterance of Marias river in a fiew days. they also informed that a french Trader was with one of those bands, that they traded with the white people on the Suskashwen River at 6 easy days march or about 150 miles distant from whome they precured Guns Powder Lead blankets &c. in exchange for wolf and beaver Skins. Capt Lewis gave them a Flag Meadel & Handkerchief Capt. L. informed those Indians where he was from & where he had been and his objects & friendly views &c. of which they appeared to be well Satisfied.

"on the morning of the 27th at day light the indians got up and crouded around the fire, Jo. Field who was on post had carelessly laid his gun down behind him near where his brother was Sleeping. one of the Indians Slipd. behind him and took his gun and that of his brother unperceived by him, at the Same instant two others advanced and Seized the guns of Drewyer and Capt Lewis who were yet asleep. Jo. Fields Seeing this turned about to take his gun and Saw the fellow running off with his and his brothers, he called to his brother who instantly jumped up and prosued the indian with him whome they overtook at the distance of 50 or 60 paces Siezed their guns and rested them from him and R. Field as he Seized his gun Stabed the indian to the heart with his knif who fell dead; (this Cap L. did not know untill Some time after.[)] drewyer who awoke at the first alarm jumped up and Seized & rested his gun from the indian &c. Capt L. awoke and asked what was the matter Seeing Drewyer in a Scuffle for his gun he turned to get his gun and found her gorn, he drew a pistol from his holsters and prosued the Indian whom he Saw in possession of his gun making off he presented the pistol and the indian lay down the gun. the two Fields Came up and drew up to Shoot the Indian which Capt L. forbid the indians then attempted to drive off all the horses. Capt L. derected the men to fire on them if they attempted to drive off the horses, and prosued two fellows who Continued to drive of his horses he Shot the indian who had taken his gun and then in possession of his horse through the belly, he fell and raised on his elbow and fired at Capt L. the other made his escape into a nitch out of Sight with his bow and arrows and as Capt L. guns was empty and he without his

Shot pouch he returnd. to the Camp where the 2 fields and Drewyer joind him having prosued the indians across the river   the were now in possession of the most of their own as well as the indian horses and a gun Several bows & arrows and all the indians baggage the gun & Some feathers and flag they took and burnt all the ⟨rest⟩ other articles.   and Saddled up a many of the best horses as they wished with Some Spear horses, and Set out for to intersept the party at Marias river and proceded on a little to the S. of East *112* Miles to the Missouri at the Grog Spring.   here they met with Canoes and party decending joined them leaving their horses on the river bank, and proceeded on to the enterance of Marias river opened the deposits, found Several articles damaged.   3 Beaver traps could not be found, the red perogue unfit for Service, from thenc they proceeded without delay to the River Rochejhone   See cources of Capt Lewis rout in next book.["]⁴

at 2 P. M. Shannon & Gibson arived in the Skin Canoe with the Skins and the greater part of the flesh of 3 Elk which they had killed a fiew miles above.   the two men Dixon & Handcock the two men we had met above came down intending to proceed on down with us to the Mandans.   at 3 P M we proceded on all together ⟨after⟩ having left the 2 leather Canoes on the bank.   a little below the enterance of ⟨Jos⟩ Shabonos Creek we Came too on a large Sand point from the S. E. Side and Encamped.⁵   the wind blew very hard from the S W. and Some rain. I washed Capt L. wound which has become Sore and Somewhat painfull to him.

1. The party first passed this island on April 15, 1805, on the outbound journey, but did not refer to it by any name. It is nameless on *Atlas* maps 34 and 47 and would be the "Knife R. Towhead" of MRC map 56, between Mountrail and McKenzie counties, North Dakota, or near it. The meeting place of Lewis and Clark northeast of the head of the island would be in Mountrail County, some six miles south of present Sanish, now be under Garrison Reservoir. Mattison (GR), 48–50. The letters after Biddle's "Qu:" are not distinct.

2. For Lewis's narrative of his exploration after the captains' separation on July 3, 1806, see Chapter 37 in this volume.

3. The courses and distances match Lewis's (see Chapter 37), but the dates and separations are somewhat incorrect.

4. A reference to Clark's copy of Lewis's courses from Travelers' Rest to the Great Falls in Codex N. It is placed after Lewis's entry of July 10, 1806, in Chapter 37. Clark is summarizing Lewis's remarks for July 27 and 28.

5. "Shabonos Creek," which they passed going west on April 14, 1805, is now Bear Den Creek in McKenzie County. The camp would be near the McKenzie-Mountrail county line, on a site now inundated by Garrison Reservoir. Mattison (GR), 48–49; *Atlas* maps 34, 47, 56; MRC map 56.

Chapter Thirty-Nine

From the Little Missouri to White River

August 13–31, 1806

[Clark]   ⟨Wednesday⟩ Friday 13th August 1806 [EC: Friday correct]

the last night was very Cold with a Stiff breeze from the N. W.   all
hands were on board and we Set out at Sunrize and proceeded on very
well with a Stiff breeze astern the greater part of the day.   passed the
enterance of the Little Missouri river at 8 A. M. and arived at the Enterance of Myry river at Sun Set and encamped on the N E Side[1] haveing
came by the assistance of the wind, the Current and our oars 86 miles.
below the little bason[2] I with Drewyer walked through the N. E point.
we Saw an Elk and Several deer. Drewyer wounded the Elk but could not
get him. I joined the perogus & party again in the bend below and proceeded on. Some indians were Seen in a Skin Canoe below, they were decending from an old Camp of theirs on the S. W. Side, those I Suppose to
be Some of the Minetaras who had been up on a hunting expedition, one
Canoe was left at their Camp.   we had not proceeded far before I discovered two indians on a high hill.   nothing very remarkable took place.
the Misquetors are not So troublesom this evening as they have been.
the air is cool &c.

1. "Myry Creek," which the party first passed on April 9, 1805, is now Snake Creek in McLean County, North Dakota. The campsite, which must now be under Garrison Reservoir, would be in McLean County northeast of present Riverdale. Mattison (GR), 7, 27; *Atlas* maps 33, 46, 55; MRC map 52.

2. The "little bason" in Mercer and McLean counties, North Dakota, first passed on April 10, 1805, appears on *Atlas* maps 33, 46, 55; MRC map 53.

[Clark]   *Thursday [X: Saturday] 14th August 1806*[1]

Set out at Sunrise and proceeded on. when we were opposit the Minetares Grand Village[2] we Saw a number of the Nativs viewing of we derected the Blunderbuses fired Several times, Soon after we Came too at a Croud of the nativs on the bank opposit the Village of the Shoe Indians or *Mah-har-ha's* at which place I saw the principal Chief of the Little Village of the Menitarre[3] & the principal Chief of the *Mah-har-has*.[4] those people were extreamly pleased to See us. the Chief of the little Village of the Menetarias cried most imoderately, I enquired the Cause and was informed it was for the loss of his Son who had been killed latterly by the Blackfoot Indians. after a delay of a fiew minits I proceeded on to the *black Cats* [NB: *Mandan*] Village[5] on the N. E. Side of the Missouri where I intended to Encamp but the Sand blew in Such a manner that we deturmined not to continu on that Side but return to the Side we had left. here we were visited by all the inhabitants of this village[6] who appeared equally as well pleased to See us as those above. I walked up to the Black Cats village & eate some Simnins[7] with him, and Smoked a pipe this Village I discovered had been rebuilt Since I left it and much Smaller than it was; on enquirey into the Cause was informed that a quarrel had taken place and [NB: *a number of*][8] Lodges had removed to the opposd Side. I had Soon as I landed despatched Shabono to the Minetarras inviting the Chiefs to visit us, & Drewyer down to the lower Village of the Mandans[9] to ask Mr. Jessomme[10] to Come and enterpret for us. Mr. Jessomme arived and I spoke to the chiefs of the Village[11] informing them that we Spoke to them as we had done when we were with them last and we now repeeted our envitation to the principal Chiefs of all the Villages to accompany us and to the U States &c. &c. the Black Cat Chief of the Mandans, Spoke and informed me that he wished to Visit the United States and his Great Father but was afraid of the *Scioux* who were yet at war with them and had killed Several of their men Since we had left them, and were on the river below and would Certainly kill ⟨this⟩ him if he attempted to go down. I indeavered to do away with his objections by informig him that we would not Suffer those indians to hurt any of our red Children who Should think proper to accompany us, and on their return they would be equally protected, and their presents which would be very liberal, with themselves, Conveyed to their own Country at the expence of the U. States &c. &c. The chief promised us Some corn tomorrow. after the Council I directed the Canoes to cross the river to a brook opposit where we Should be under the wind and in a plain where we would be Clear of musquetors &[12] after Crossing the Chief of the *Mah har has* told me if I would Send with him he would let me have some corn. I directed Sergt Gass & 2 men to accompany him to his Village, they Soon returned loaded with Corn. the Chief and his wife also came down. I gave his wife a fiew Needles &c.— The Great Chif of all the Menitarres the one eye[13] Came to Camp also Several other Chiefs of the different Villages. I assembled all the Chiefs on a leavel Spot on the band and Spoke to them & see next book.[14]

1. This entry ends the daily entries in Codex M. There follows (reading backwards) Clark's weather diaries for June, July, and August 1806, and then some miscellaneous notes on the back flyleaf. One of the items is a weather observation from August 1, 1806, and is placed at that date. Another item reads: "From the head of Jeffersons River through Snake Mountain is North 12 miles thence to Wisdom river is N. 20° E." Assuming the "head of Jefferson river" to be the forks of the Beaverhead in Beaverhead County, Montana, "Snake Mountain" is probably the Rattlesnake Cliffs. Wisdom River is the Big Hole River. See August 3 and 10, 1805. *Atlas* maps 65, 66. A final miscellaneous item reads:

Memorandom

1st. Complete the maps
2. copy of Sketch of the rochejhone
3. a Copy of Courses & distances
4. to fill up vacinces in my book

Clark obviously intended to remind himself of tasks needed to complete the record of the expedition. "Complete the maps" may refer to maps begun at Fort Clatsop; see *Atlas,* 12, 19 n. 129. "Copy a Sketch of the rochejhone" obviously refers to maps of the Yellowstone River, which helps to date the memorandum after the completion of that stage of the journey, though which maps are meant is not clear; see *Atlas,* 11, 19 n. 119. "A copy of the Courses & distances" may be a reminder to copy the draft material giving courses and distances for July 13–19 and July 24–August 3, 1806. "To fill up vacinces in my book" may refer to some sort of blanks in Clark's journals; see Introduction to the Journals, vol. 2, p. 31.

2. For these Hidatsa and Mandan villages in Mercer and McLean counties, North Dakota, see October 26 and 27, 1804. *Atlas* maps 29, 33, 46, 55; MRC map 52.

3. Black Moccasin; see October 29, 1804. Biddle, in later conversations with Clark, expands on Black Moccasin's recollection of his son's death. Biddle Notes [ca. April 1810], Jackson (LLC), 2:522.

4. White Buffalo Robe Unfolded; see October 29, 1804.

5. For Black Cat, see October 29, 1804. It was probably Biddle who underlined his name with red ink.

6. Evidently Rooptahee, or Ruptare, village in McLean County. *Atlas* map 29.

7. Summer squashes; see October 8, 1804.

8. Biddle placed the words at a blank space.

9. Matootonha, or Mitutanka, village in Mercer County. *Atlas* map 29.

10. For René Jusseaume, see October 27, 1804.

11. Black Cat. What seems to be the number "63," perhaps in Clark's hand, appears above the word "spoke," but its purpose is unclear.

12. This would seem to place the camp on the west side in Mercer County, considerably below Matootonha village. *Atlas* map 29; MRC maps 51, 52.

13. For Le Borgne, or One Eye, see March 9, 1805.

14. The next book, Codex N, begins with the date August 15, 1806, but continues with the same conference with the chiefs, and is clearly about events of the same day as the end of Codex M. It is impossible to say where August 14 actually ends and the fifteenth begins. Presumably the material covering these days was written later and the heading for August 15 was misplaced. Coues (HLC), 3:1182 n. 10, believes most of the events given under August 14 belong to the fifteenth. Ordway notes on this date that "Capt Lewis fainted as Capt Clark was dressing his wound, but Soon came too again."

[Clark]   Thursday August 15th 1806 Continued Mandans Vilg[1]

after assembling the Chiefs and Smokeing one pipe, I informed them that I Still Spoke the Same words which we had Spoken to them when we first arived in their Country in the fall of 1804.   we then envited them to visit their great father the president of the U. States and to hear ⟨their⟩ his own Councils and receive his Gifts from his own hands as also See the population[2] of a government which Can at their pleasure protect and Secur you from all your enimies, and chastize all those who will Shut their years to ⟨their⟩ his Councils.   we now offer to take you at the expense of our Government and Send you back to your Country again with a considerable present ⟨of⟩ in merchendize which you will recive of your great Father. I urged the necessity of their going on with us as it would be the means of hastening those Supples of Merchindize which would be Sent to their Country and exchanged as before mentioned for a moderate price in Pelteries and furs &c. the great Chief of the Menetaras Spoke, he Said he wished to go down and See his great father very much, but that the Scioux were in the road and would most certainly kill him or any others who Should go down they were bad people and would not listen to any thing which was told them. when ⟨we⟩ he Saw us last we told him that we had made peace with all the nations below, Since that time the Seioux had killed 8 of their people and Stole a number of their horses. he Said that he had opened his ears and followed our Councils, he had made peace with the Chyennes and rocky mountains indians, and repieted the same objecctions as mentioned. that he went to war against none and was willing to receive all nations as friends. he Said that the Ricaras had Stolen from his people a number of horses at different times and his people had killed 2 Ricaras. if the Sieoux were at peace with them and Could be depended on he as also other Chiefs of the villages would be glad to go and See their great father, but as they were all afraid of the Sieoux they Should not go down &c.

The Black Cat ⟨sent⟩ Chief of the Mandans Village on the North Side of the Missouri Sent over and requested me to go over to his village which envertation I axceptd and crossed over to his village. he had a parcel of Corn about 12 bushuls in a pile in his lodge. he told me that his people had but little corn part of which they had given me. after takeing a Smoke he informed me that as the Sieoux were very troublesom and the road to his great father dangerous none of this village would go down with us. I told the Cheifs and wariers of the village who were there present that we were anxious that Some of the village Should go and See their great father and hear his good words & recve his *bountifull gifts* &c. and told them to pitch on Some Man on which they could rely on and Send him to See their Great father, they made the Same objections which the Chief had done before. a young man offered to go down, and they all agreeed for him to go down the charector of this young man I knew as a bad one and made an objection as to his age and Chareckter at this time

Gibson who was with me informed me that this young man had Stole his knife and had it then in his possession, this I informed the Chief and directed him to give up the knife he delivered the knife with a very faint apology for his haveing it in his possession. I then reproached those people for wishing to Send Such a man to See and hear the words of So great a man as their great father; they hung their heads and Said nothing for Some time when the Cheif Spoke and Said that they were afraid to Send any one for fear of their being killed by the Sieux. after Smoking a pipe and relateing Some passages I recrossed to our Camp—.[3] being informed by one of our enterpreters that the 2d Chief of the Mandans Comonly Called the little Crow[4] intended to accompany us down, I took Charbono and walked to the Village to See this Chief and talk with him on the Subject. he told me he had deturmined to go down, but wished to have a council first with his people which would be in the after part of the day. I smoked a pipe with the little Crow and returned to the boat. Colter one of our men expressed a desire to join Some trappers [*NB: the two Illinois Men we met, & who now came down to us*] who offered to become Shearers with and furnish traps &c. the offer a very advantagious one, to him, his Services Could be dispenced with from this down and as we were disposed to be of Service to any one of our party who had performed their duty as well as Colter had done, we agreed to allow him the prvilage provided no one of the party would ask or expect a Similar permission to which they all agreeed that they wished Colter every Suckcess and that as we did not wish any of them to Seperate untill we Should arive at St. Louis they would not apply or expect it &c.[5] The Maharha Chief brought us Some Corn, as did also the Chief of the little village of the Menetarras on mules of which they have Several. [*NB: bought from the Crow Inds. who get or Steal them from the Spaniards*][6] The evening is Cool and windy. great number of the nativs of the different villages Came to view us and exchange robes with our men for their Skins— we gave Jo Colter Some Small articles which we did not want and Some powder & lead. the party also gave him Several articles which will be usefull to him on his expedittion.— This evening Charbono informed me that our back was scercely turned before a war party from the two menetarry villages followed on and attacked and killed the Snake Indians whome we had Seen and in the engagement between them and the Snake indians they had lost two men one of which was the Son of the principal Chief of the little village of the menitarras.[7]   that they had also went to war from the Menetarras and killed two Ricaras.   he further informed me that a missunderstanding had taken place between the Mandans & minetarras and had verry nearly come to blows about a woman, the Menitarres at length presented a pipe and a reconsilliation took place between them

1. Codex N begins with a list, about a page and a half long, of items sent to Washington from St. Louis; it has been placed in Chapter 41 in this volume. The first dated entry is for August 15, 1806, but as noted for August 14, there is in fact considerable doubt where the events of August 14 leave off and those of August 15 begin. This confusion is most unusual in the journals.

2. The sheer numbers of whites in the East often impressed Western Indian chiefs more than anything else on their travels to Washington.

3. For reflections on these negotiations, see Ronda (LCAI), 245–48.

4. For Little Crow, or Little Raven, see October 29, 1804.

5. Colter spent another four years in the Rockies and on the upper Missouri. In his wanderings he had various hairbreadth escapes from the Blackfeet and considerably increased white knowledge of the region, especially the area of the Yellowstone Plateau and Jackson Hole. See Appendix A, vol. 2, p. 515. Biddle added some reflections of his own to his account of this incident, which he thought "shows how easily men may be weaned from the habits of civilized life to the ruder but scarcely less fascinating manners of the woods." Coues (HLC), 3:1182; Harris.

6. Whether the Crows went as far as New Mexico to steal mules from the Spanish settlements, or obtained them from other tribes closer to New Mexico, is not clear. The former is by no means impossible.

7. Black Moccasin of the Awatixa Hidatsa village Metaharta.

[Clark]   *Friday 16th August 1806*

a cool morning. Sent up Sergt. Pryor to the mandan village, for Some Corn which they offered to give us.   he informed that they had more Corn collected for us than our Canoes Could Carry Six load of which he brought down. I thanked the Chief for his kindness and informed him that our Canoes would not Carry any more Corn than we had already brought down.   at 10 A. M the Chiefs of the different villages came to See us and Smoke a pipe &c.   as our Swivel[1] Could no longer be Serveceable to us as it could not be fireed on board the largest Perogue, we Concluded to make a present of it to the Great Chief of the Menetaras (the One Eye) with a view to ingratiate him more Strongly in our favour I had the Swivel Charged and Collected the Chiefs in a circle around it and adressed them with great ceremoney. told them I had listened with much attention to what the One Eye had Said yesterday and beleived that he was Sincere & Spoke from his heart. I reproached them very Severely for not attending to what had been Said to them by us in Council in the fall of 1804 and at different times in the winter of 1804 & 5, and told them our backs were Scercely turned befor a party followed and killed the pore defenceless snake indians whom we had taken by the hand & told them not to be afraid that you would never Strike them again &c. also mentioned the ricers &c. The little Cherry[2] old Chief of the Mene-tarras Spoke as follows Viz: "Father we wish to go down with you to See our Great Father, but we know the nations below and are afraid of the Scioux who will be on the river and will kill us on our return home. The Scioux has Stolen our horses and killed 8 of our men Since you left us, and the Ricaras have also Struck us. we Staid at home and listened to what you had told us. we at length went to war against the Scioux and met with Ricaras and killed two of them, they were on their way to Strike us. We will attend to your word and not hurt any people all Shall be Wel-com and we Shall do as you direct—.["] The One Eye Said his ears would always be open to the word of his great father and Shut against bad Council &c. I then a good deel of Ceremony made a preasent of the Swivel to the *One Eye* Chief and told him when he fired this gun to re-member the words of his great father which we had given him. this gun had anounced the words of his great father to all the nations which we had Seen &c. &c. after the council was over the gun was fired & deliv-ered, they Chief appeared to be much pleased and conveyed it imme-diately to his village &c. we Settled with and discharged Colter. in the evening I walked to the village to See the little Crow and know when he would be ready, took with me a flag intending to give him to leave at his lodge but to my astonishment he informed me he had declined going down the reason of which I found was through a jellousy between himself and the principal Chief he refused a flag & we Sent for Mr. Jessomme and told him to use his influn to provail on one of the Chiefs to acompany us and[3] we would employ him. he informed us soon after that the big

white Chief [4] would go if we would take his wife & Son & Jessoms wife &
2 children   we wer obliged to agree to do

1. The party's small cannon, recently recovered from the cache at the Great Falls of
the Missouri; see May 29, 1804.

2. Cherry Grows on a Bush of Menetarra village; see October 29, 1804.

3. From about here the remainder of the entry appears to be an afterthought, crowded
into the bottom of one page and the top of the next in Codex N.

4. Big White, or Sheheke, of Mitutanka village; see October 29, 1804.

[Clark]   *Saturday* 17th *of August 1806*

a Cool morning   gave some powder & Ball to Big White Chief   Settled
with Touisant Chabono for his Services as an enterpreter the pric of a
horse and Lodge [1] purchased of him for public Service in all amounting
to 500$ 33 ⅓ cents.   derected two of the largest of the Canoes be fas-
tened together with poles tied across them So as to make them Study for
the purpose of Conveying the Indians and enterpreter and their families
we were visited by all the principal Chiefs of the Menetarras to take
their leave of us   at 2 oClock we left our encampment after takeing leave
of Colter who also Set out up the river in Company with Messrs. Dickson
& Handcock.   we also took our leave of T. Chabono, his Snake Indian
wife and their Son Child who had accompanied us on our rout to the pacific Ocean in the Capacity of interpreter and interpretes. T. Chabono
wished much to accompany us in the Said Capacity if ⟨he⟩ we could have
provailed the Menetarre Chiefs to dcend the river with us to the U.
States, but as none of those chiefs of whoes ⟨set out⟩ language he was
Conversent would accompany us, his Services were no longer of use to
the U' States and he was therefore discharged and paid up. [2]   we offered
to convey him down to the Illinois if he Chose to go, he declined proceeding on at present, observing that he had no acquaintance or prospects of
makeing a liveing below, and must continue to live in the way that he had
done. I offered to take his little Son a butifull promising Child who is 19
months old to which they both himself & wife wer willing provided the
Child had been weened.   they observed that in one year the boy would
be Sufficiently old to leave his mother & he would then take him to me if
I would be so freindly as to raise the Child for him in Such a manner as I

thought proper, to which I agreeed &c.—[3] we droped down to the *Big white Cheifs* Mandan Village ½ a mile below on the South Side,[4] all the Indians proceeded on down by land.   and I walked to the lodge of the Chief whome I found Sorounded by his friends the men were Setting in a circle Smokeing and the womin Crying.   he Sent his bagage with his wife & Son, with the Interpreter Jessomme & his wife and 2 children to the Canoes provided for them.   after Smoking one pipe, and distributing Some powder & lead which we had given him, he informed me that he was ready and we were accompd to the Canoes by all the Village   Maney of them Cried out aloud.   as I was about to Shake with the Grand Cheifs of all the Villages there assembled they requested me to Set one minit longer with them which I readily agreed to and directed a pipe to be lit.   the Cheifs informed that when we first came to their Country they did not beleive all we Said we then told them.   but they were now Convinced that every thing we had told them were true, that they Should keep in memory every thing which we had Said to them, and Strictly attend to our advice, that their young men Should Stay at home and Should no go again to war against any nation, that if any atacted them they Should defend themselves, that we might depend on what they Said, and requested us to inform their great father.   the also requested me to tell the Ricaras to Come and See them, not to be afraid that no harm Should be done them, that they were anxious to be in peace with them.

   The Seeoux they Said they had no dependance in and Should kill them whenever they Came into their Country to do them harm &c. I told them that we had always told them to defend themselves, but not to Strike those nations we had taken by the hand, the Sieoux with whome they were at war we had never Seen on our return we Should inform their great fathe of their conduct towards his faithfull red Children and he would take Such Steps as will bring about a lasting peace between them and his faithfull red children. I informed them that we should inform the ricaras what they had requested &c. The Grand Chief of the Mineterres Said that the Great Cheif who was going down with to see their great father was a well as if he went also, and on his return he would be fully informed of the words of his great father, and requested us to take care of this Gt. Chief.   we then Saluted them with a gun and Set out and proceeded on to *Fort Mandan*[5] where I landed and went to view the old works the houses except one in the rear bastion was burnt by accident, Some pickets were Standing in front next to the river.   we proceeded on to the old Ricara village the S E wind was so hard and the ⟨wind⟩ waves So high that we were obliged to Come too, & Camp on the S W Side near the old Village.   (18 mils)[6]

1. Probably the tipi, or "leather lodge," which the captains, Charbonneau, Sacagawea, and Jean Baptiste used after leaving Fort Mandan until it became too rotten to be habitable. See April 7, 1805.

2. Charbonneau's discharge, made out at about this date, is in the Academy of Natural Sciences in Philadelphia.

3. Clark repeated these offers to Charbonneau, with additional offers of employment or financial assistance and a warm expression of regard for Charbonneau, Sacagawea, and Jean Baptiste, in a letter written from the Arikara villages a few days later. Clark to Toussaint Charbonneau, August 20, 1806. Jackson (LLC), 1:315–16. For Jean Baptiste Charbonneau's later career, see February 11, 1805, and sources listed there.

4. Mitutanka village in Mercer County, North Dakota, at later Deapolis. *Atlas* map 29; MRC map 52.

5. For the site of Fort Mandan, in McLean County, North Dakota, see November 2, 1804. *Atlas* map 29; MRC map 51.

6. The camp would be near one of the old Arikara villages in Oliver County, North Dakota, near present Hensler, first noted on October 24 and 25, 1804. *Atlas* map 29; MRC map 51.

[Clark]   *Monday 18th August 1806.*

moderate rain last night, the wind of this morning from the S. E. as to cause the water to be So rough that we Could not proceed on untill 8 a. m. at which time it fell a little & we proceeded on tho' the waves were yet high and the wind Strong. Saw Several Indians on either Side of the river.   at 9 A. M. I saw an Indian running down the beech and appd. to be anxious to Speak to us I derected the Canoes to land.   this Indian proved to be the brother of the Chief we had on board and Came down from his Camp at no great distance to take his leave of his brother.   the Chief gave him a par of Legins and took an effectunate leave of his brother and we procedeed on haveing previously Sent on 2 canoes with hunters to kill Some meat at 2 P. M we overtook the Canoe hunters, they had killed three deer which was divided and we halted and Cooked Some dinner on the Sandbar. wind Still high and from the Same point. The Chief pointed out Several places where he Said ⟨their⟩ his nation formerly lived and related Some extroadinary Stories of their tredition. after Dinner we proceeded on, to a point on the N E. Side opposit the remains of an old Mandan village a little below the enterance of *Chiss-che tor* River and the place we Encamped as we assended this river 20th of October 1804 haveing come 40 miles to day.[1] after landing which was a little before night the hunters run out into the bottom and Killed four deer. The winds blew hard from the S. E. all day which retarded our progress very much after the fires were made I set my self down with the big white man Chiefe and made a number of enquiries into the tredition of his nation as well as the time of their inhabiting the number of Villages the remains of which we see on different parts of the river, as also the cause of their evacuation. he told me his nation first Came out of the ground where they had a great village. a grape vine grew down through the Earth to their village and they Saw light Some of their people assended by the grape vine upon the earth, and Saw Buffalow and every kind of animal also Grapes plumbs &c. they gathered Some grapes & took down the vine to the village, and they tasted and found them good, and deturmined to go up and live upon the earth, and great numbers climbed the vine and got upon earth men womin and children.[2] at length a large big bellied woman in climbing broke the vine and fell and all that were left in the Village below has remained there ever Since (The Mandans beleive when they die that they return to this village) Those who were left on earth made a village on the river below and were very noumerous &c. he Said that he was born [*NB: about 40 years*] in the Village Opposit to our Camp and at that time his nation inhabited 7 villages as large as that and were full of people, the Sieoux and Small pox killed the greater part of them and made them So weak that all that were left only made two Small villages when Collected, which were built near the old Ricaras village above. their troubles with the Scioux & Pawnees or Ricaras Compelled them to move and build a village where they now live.

[*NB: Qu:*] he Said that the Menitarras Came out of the water to the East and Came to this Country and built a village near the mandans from whome they got Corn beens &c. they were very noumerous and resided in one village a little above this place on the opposit Side. they quarreled about a buffalow, and two bands left the village and went into the plains, (those two bands are now known bye the title Pounch, and Crow In- dians.[)][3] the ballance of the Menetaras moved their village to where it now Stands where they have lived ever Since—[4]

[*NB: The Village of the Mandans on the North East side was formed of two villages formerly lived on the East side opposite the 7. War & Small pox reduced them to one vill. which crossed & joined the 2 vills. near ricaras (having first settled (before the ⟨two⟩ 7 came into 2) on East Side—[)] Then this moved with the 2 to where they now live, So that[5] the vills originally was of 9 vills (See Note)*]

1. The camp would be in Burleigh County, North Dakota, a little south of Bismarck and below the mouth of the Heart (Chiss-che-ter) River and the camp of October 20, 1804, on the opposite shore. *Atlas* map 28; MRC map 49; MRY map 137. The old Man- dan villages are in Morton and Burleigh counties. See October 21 and 22, 1804.

2. Clark's Biblical phrasing here suggests that he recognized the religious nature of this origin story, and its kinship to Genesis.

3. A traditional account of the separation of the Hidatsas and the Crows into two peoples.

4. The following paragraph, beginning with a bracket not printed, was an addition by Biddle (but not in his usual red ink) squeezed in at the bottom of a page. It apparently grew out of conversations with Clark in 1810. The "Note" to which Biddle refers is proba- bly that found in Biddle Notes [ca. April 1810], Jackson (LLC), 2:522.

5. The rest of the sentence actually appears at the head of the paragraph, but this would appear to be the intended order.

[Clark]   *Tuesday 19th of August 1806*

Some rain last night and this morning the wind rose and blew with great Violence untill 4 P. M and as our camp was on a Sand bar we were very much distressd with the blows of Sand. I directed the hunters to pro- ceed on down the bottom and kill and butcher Some meat and if the wind Should lie that I should proceed on down to their Camp &c. Capt. Lewis'es wounds are heeling very fast, I am much in hope of his being able to walk in 8 or 10 days—. at 4 P. M the wind Seased to blow with that violence which it had done all day we Set out and proceeded on down. the hunt- ers which was Sent out this morning killed 4 Elk & 12 deer near the river we came too and brought in the most of the flesh and proceeded on to a Sand on the N E Side and Encamped.[1] the wind rose and become very

Strong from the S. E. and a great appearance of rain. Jessomme the Interpreter let me have a piece of a lodge and the Squars pitched or Stretched it over Some Sticks, under this piece of leather I Slept ⟨under⟩ dry, it is the only covering which I have had Suffecient to keep off the rain Since I left the Columbia. it began to rain moderately Soon after night. The indians appear well Satisfyed with the party and mode of proceedure. we decended only *10 miles* to day Saw Some Elk and buffalow on the Shore near where we Encamped. the Elk beginning to run. the Buffalow are done running & the bulls are pore.

1. As Clark notes, their camp was some ten miles below the previous night's camp, in Burleigh County, North Dakota, probably near the camp of October 19, 1804, on the opposite side. The site is probably now inundated by Oahe Reservoir. *Atlas* map 28; MRC map 49.

[Clark]   *Wednesday 20th of August 1806*

a violent hard rain about day light this morning. all wet except myself and the indians. we embarked a little after Sun rise wind moderate and ahead. we proceeded on at meridn. passed the enterance of Cannonball river[1] imediately above is the remains of a large Sieoux encampment which appears to have been made this Spring. at 3 P M passed the enterance of Wardepon River[2] [*NB: Scioux boundary to which they claim the country*] Saw great number of wolves on the bank Some Buffalow & Elk, tho' not so abundant as near the River Rochejhone. passed the place where we left the last encampment of Ricaras in the fall 1804 and encamped on a Sandbar from the N. E. Side,[3] having made 81 miles only, the wind blew hard all day which caused the waves to rise high and flack over into the Small Canoes in Such a manner as to employ one hand in throwing the water out. The plains begin to Change their appearance the grass is turning of a yellow colour. I observe a great alteration in the Corrent course and appearance of this pt. of the Missouri. in places where there was Sand bars in the fall 1804 at this time the main Current passes, and where the current then passed is now a Sand bar— Sand bars which were then naked are now covered with willow Several feet high. the enteranc of Some of the Rivers & Creeks Changed owing to the mud thrown into them, and a layor of mud over Some of the bottoms of 8 inches thick.

1. The Cannonball River on the Morton-Sioux county line in North Dakota, first passed on October 18, 1804. *Atlas* map 27; MRC map 48.

2. Clark called this "War-re-Con nee" River when they passed it on October 16, 1804; it is now Beaver Creek in Emmons County, North Dakota. Possibly Clark has confused the name with the "Eă-Neăh Wáu-de-pón," or Little Sioux River in Harrison County, Iowa; see August 8, 1804. *Atlas* map 27; MRC map 47.

3. The camp was in Campbell County, South Dakota, probably below the mouth of Spring Creek, on *Atlas* map 26 a nameless stream flowing from a lake; see October 13, 1804. The site would now be inundated by Oahe Reservoir. MRC map 46.

[Clark]   *Thursday 21st August 1806*

Musquetors very troublesom in the early part of last night and again this morning   I directed Sergt. Ordway to proceed on to where there was Some ash and get enough for two ores which were wanting. Men all put their arms in perfect order and we Set out at 5 a. m.   over took Sergt. ordway with wood for oars &c.   at 8 A. M. Met three french men Comeing up, they proved to be three men from the Ricaras two of them Reevea & Greinyea[1] wintered with us at the mandans in 1804   we Came too, those men informed us that they were on their way to the Mandans, and intended to go down to the Illinois this fall.   one of them quit a young lad requested a passage down to the Illinois, we concented and he got into a Canoe to an Ore.[2] Those men informd us that 700 Seeoux had passed the Ricaras on their way to war with the Mandans & Menitarras and that their encampment where the Squaws and Children wer, was Some place near the Big Bend of this river below.   no ricaras had accompanied them but were all at home, they also informed us that no trader had arived at the Ricaras this Season, and that they were informed that the Pania or Ricara Chief who went to the United States last Spring was a year, died on his return at Smoe place near the Sieoux river &c.[3] ⟨after⟩ those men had nether [*NB: powder*] nor lead we gave them a horn of powder and Some balls and after a delay of an hour we parted from the 2 men Reevey & Grienway and proceeded on.   the wind rose and bley from the N. W.   at half past 11 a. m. we arived in view of the upper

Ricara villages,[4] a Great number of womin Collecting wood on the banks, we Saluted the village with four guns ⟨on St⟩ and they returned the Salute by fireing Several guns in the village, I observed Several very white Lodges on the hill above the Town which the ricaras from the Shore informed me were Chyennes who had just arived—. we landed opposit to the 2d Village[5] and were met by the most of the men women and children of each village as also the Chyennes they all appeared anxious to take us by the hand and much rejoiced to See us return. I Steped on Shore and was Saluted by the two great Chiefs, whome we had made or given Medals to as we assend this river in 1804, and also Saluted by a great number both of Ricaras & Chyennes, as they appeared anxious to here what we had done &c. as well as to here Something about the Mandans & Minetarras. I Set my self down on the Side of the Bank and the Chiefs & brave men of the Ricaras & Chyennes formed a Cercle around me.[6] after takeing a Smoke of Mandan tobacco which the Big white Chief who was Seated on my left hand furnished, I informed them as I had before informed the Mandans & Menitarras, where we had been what we had done and Said to the different nations in there favour and envited Some of their Chiefs to accompany us down and See their great father and receve from his own mouth his good Councils and from his own hands his *bountifull* gifts &c. telling pretty much the Same which I had told the mandans and men-itarras. told them not to be afraid of any nation below that none would hurt them &c. a man of about 32 years of age was intreduced to me as 1st Chief of the nation this man they Call the grey eyes[7] or [*blank*] he was absent from the Nation at the time we passed up, the man whome we had acknowledged as the principal chief[8] informed me that the Grey eyes was a greater Chief than himself and that he had given up all his pretentions with the Flag and Medal to the Grey eyes— The principal chief of the Chyenne's [*NB: Ricaras*][9] was then introduced he is a Stout jolley fellow of about 35 years of age whome the Ricaras Call the *Grey Eyes* I also told the ricaras that I was very Sorrey to here that they were not on friendly terms with their neighbours the Mandans & Menetarras, and had not listened to what we had Said to them but had Suffered their young men to join the Sieoux who had killed 8 Mandans &c. that their young men had Stolen the horses of the Minetarras, in retaliation for those enjories the Mandans & Menetarras had Sent out a war party and killed 2 ricaras. how could they expect other nations would be at peace with them when they themselves would not listen to what their great father had told them. I further informed them that the Mandans & ⟨Ricaras⟩ Menetaras had opened their ears to what we had Said to them but had Staid at home untill they were Struk that they were Still disposed to be friendly and on good terms with the ricaras, they then Saw the great Chief of the Mandans by my Side who was on his way to see his great father, and was derected by his nation & the Menetaras & Maharhas, to Smoke in the pipe of peace with you and to tell you not to be afraid to go to their towns, or take the Birds in the plains that their ears were open to our Councils and no harm Should be done to a Ricara. The Chief will Speak presently—. The Grey eyes Chief of the ricaras made a very animated Speach in which he mentioned his williness of following the councels which we had given them that they had Some bad young men who would not listen to the Councels but would join the Seioux, those men they had discarded and drove out of their villages, that the Seioux were the Cause of their Missunderstanding &c. that they were a bad peoples. that they had killed Several of the Ricaras Since I Saw them. That Several of the chiefs wished to accompany us down to See their great father, but wished to see the Chief who went down last Sumer return first, he expressed Some apprehention as to the Safty of that Chiefs in passing the Sieoux. that the Ricaras had every wish to be friendly with the Mandans &c. that every mandan &c. who chose to visit the ricares should be Safe that he Should Continue with his nation and See that they followed the Council which we had given them &c.— The Sun being very hot the Chyenne Chief envited us to his Lodge which was pitched in the plain at no great distance from the River. I accepted the invitation and accompanied him to his lodge which was new and much larger than any which I have Seen   it was made of 20 dressed Buffalow Skins in the Same form of the Sceoux and lodges of other nations of this quarter. about this lodges was 20 others Several of them of nearly the Same Size. I enquired for the ballance of the nation and was informed that they were near at hand and would arive on tomorrow and when all together amounted to 120 Lodges—. after Smokeing I gave a medal of the Small size to the Chyenne Chief &c.

which appeared to alarm him, he had a robe and a fleece of fat Buffalow meat brought and gave me with the meadel back and informed me that he knew that the white people were all *medecine* and that he was afraid of the midal or any thing that white people gave to them.[10] I had previously explained the cause of my gveing him the medal & flag, and again told him the use of the medal and the caus of my giveing it to him, and again put it about his neck delivering him up his preasent of a roab & meat, informing him that this was the medecene which his Great father directed me to deliver to all the great Chiefs who listened to his word and followed his councils, that he had done So and I should leave the medal with him as a token of his cincerity &c.   he doubled the quantity of meat, and received the medal

The Big White chief of the Mandans Spoke at some length explainin the Cause of the misunderstanding between his nation and the ricaras, informing them of his wish to be on the most freindly termes &c.   the Chyennes accused both nations of being in folt. I told to them all that if they eve wished to be hapy that they must Shake off all intimecy with the Seioux and unite themselves in a Strong allience and attend to what we had told them &c. which they promesed all to do and we Smoked and parted on the best terms, the Mandan Chief was Saluted by Several Chiefs and brave men on his way with me to the river—   I had requested the ricaras & Chyennes to inform me as Soon as possible of their intentions of going down with us to See their great father or not.   in the evening the Great Chief requested that I would walk to his house which I did, he gave me about 2 quarts [*NB: carrots*] of Tobacco, 2 beaver Skins and a trencher of boiled Corn & beans to eat (as it is the Custom of all the Nations on the Missouri to give Something to every white man who enters their lodge Something to eat)   this Chief informed me that none of his Chiefs wished to go down with us they all wished to See the cheif who went down return first, that the Chyennes were a wild people and were afraid to go.   that they Should all listen to what I had Said. I gave him Some ribon to Suspend his Medal to and a Shell which the Snake indians gave me for which he was very much pleased.

The interpreter informed me that the Cheifs of those villages had no intention of going down.   one the Cheifs of the Village on the island talkd. of going down. I returned to the boat where I found the principal Chief of the lower vilege who had Cut part of his hair and disfigured himself in Such a manner that I did not know him, he informed me the Sieux had killed his nephew and that Was in tears for him &c. we detur-mind to proceed down to the Island and accordingly took the chief on board and proceeded on down to the 1sd village[11] at which place we arived a little before dark and were met as before by nearly every individ-ual of the Village, we Saluted them and landed imediately opposit the town. The one arm 2d Cheif of this village whome we had expected to accompany us down Spoke to the mandan Cheif in a loud and thretening tone which Caused me to be Some what alarmed for the Safty of that Cheif, I inform the Ricaras of this village that the Mandans had opened their ears to and fold. our Councils, that this Cheif was on his way to see their Great Father the P. of U S. and was under our protection that if any enjorey was done to him by any nation that we Should all die to a man. I told the Ricaras that they had told us lies, they promised to be at peace with the mandans & Menetarras. that our back was Scrcely turned be-fore they went to war & Killd. them and Stole their horses &c— The Cheif then envited me & the Mandan Chief to his house to talk there. I accompanied him, after takeing a very Serimonious Smoke the 2d Cheif informd. me that he had opened his ears to what we had Said to him at the time we gave him the medal that he had not been to war against any Natn. Since, that once been to See the mandans and they were going to kill him, they had not killed the Mandans, it was the Seeoux who killed them and not the ricaras, he Said that the Mandan Cheif was as Safe as if he was in his own Vilg that he had opened his ears and Could here as well as the mandans. I then informd them what I had told the upper villages and we all become perfectly reconsiled all to each other and Smoked in the most perfect harmony we had invatations to go into their lodges and eate. I at length went to the grand Chiefs Lodge by his particelar invita-tion, the Mandan Chief Stuck close to me the Chief had prepd. a Supper of boiled young Corn, beens & quashes of which he gave me in Wooden bowls. he also gave me near 2 quarts of the Tobacco Seed, & informed me he had always had his ears open to what we had Said, that he was well convinced that the Seeoux was the caus of all the trouble between the

Mandans & them the Ricars had Stolen horses from the Mandan which had been returned all except one which could not be got, this mischief was done by Some young men who was bad. a long Conversation of explanations took place between the Ricara & mandan Chiefs which appeared to be Satisfactory on both Sides. the Chief gave a pipe with great form and every thing appeared to be made up. I returned to the river & went to bead.[12] the Indians contd on board. made 22 miles to day only.

1. The first of these may be François Rivet, one of the expedition *engagés* of 1804. The identity of "Greinyea" is uncertain, but he is thought to be a man named Grenier, an employee of Joseph Gravelines and probably one of the two men the party met on October 18, 1804, who had been robbed by the Mandans. Ordway says that they had been trapping as far as the "river Roshjone" (Yellowstone). For Rivet, see Appendix A, vol. 2.

2. Gass, in his entry for this day, says the young man had formerly worked for the North West Company.

3. In fact, this chief died in Washington. The Arikaras' suspicions as to the cause of his death led to hostilities with the Americans. On the question of his identity, see October 9 and November 6, 1804. Jefferson to the Arikaras, April 11, 1806, Jackson (LLC), 1:306 and n. 2.

4. The Arikara villages, shown on *Atlas* map 25, were in Corson and Campbell counties, South Dakota, above the mouth of Grand River; see October 8, 1804. The sites are now inundated by Oahe Reservoir. MRC map 45.

5. Since the first village, in the captains' reckoning, was that on Ashley Island (see October 8, 1804), the second was presumably on the north bank of the Missouri River in Corson County. There exists some confusion as to whether the captains viewed the Arikaras in that vicinity as living in one village or two (see October 9, 1804), but this probably does not affect the general location of the "2d Village" in this instance. However, whether the party landed at this village, or villages, in Corson County, or opposite in Campbell County, may be questioned since Clark's use of the word "opposite" is not always clear.

6. Apparently Clark was speaking for both captains, as among the Mandans and Hidatsas, indicating that Lewis was still unable to move about because of his wound.

7. Grey Eyes evidently took precedence over the other Arikara chiefs, whether or not he was "principal chief" in the white man's sense of the term. In 1807 Nathaniel Pryor, on his unsuccessful mission to return Big White to his people, gave Grey Eyes a large government peace medal. In 1811 the chief was trading with Wilson Price Hunt, leader of the overland Astorians, and with Manuel Lisa. In 1823 his son was killed in a skirmish with Missouri Fur Company traders. The same year the Arikaras attacked William Ashley's trapping brigade at the tribe's villages; in this battle John Collins, of the Corps of Discovery, died. This prompted a punitive expedition of U.S. troops from Fort Atkinson led by

Colonel Henry Leavenworth. When Leavenworth's artillery bombarded the villages on August 10, 1823, Grey Eyes was killed. Pryor to Clark, October 16, 1807, Jackson (LLC), 2 : 434, 438 n. 5; Bradbury, 130–31; Meyer, 48–49, 54; Chittenden, 2 : 589; Berry, 26, 40, 43–45, 55; Ronda (LCAI), 249; Ney, 173–80.

8. This was Kakawissassa, or Lighting Crow; see October 9, 1804.

9. Biddle's later interpolation would appear to be an error, induced by the Arikaras' calling this Cheyenne by the Arikara chief's name. The two may have exchanged names, thus establishing a ritual brotherhood.

10. Alexander Henry found that the Hidatsas had a similar attitude toward the medals and flags given out by Lewis and Clark, preferring to give these articles to their enemies in hopes the bad medicine would fall upon them. At this early stage of Indian-white contact special powers were often attributed to whites, which could be beneficial or malign according to the intentions of the giver. Coues (NLEH), 1 : 349–50. The chief was probably given the 55 mm Jefferson medal.

11. The village of Sawa-haini on Ashley Island, above the mouth of Grand River; see October 8, 1804. *Atlas* map 25; MRC map 45.

12. Apparently at Ashley Island, between Campbell and Corson counties, now under Oahe Reservoir. *Atlas* map 25; MRC map 45.

[Clark]   *Friday 22nd August 1806.*

rained all the last night   every person and all our bedding wet, the Morning cloudy, at 8 A M. I was requested to go to the Chiefs, I walkd up and he informed me that he Should not go down but would Stay and take Care of the village and prevent the young men from doing rong and Spoke much to the Same porpt of the Grey Eyes, the 2d Chief Spoke to the Same and all they Said was only a repitition of what they had Said before.   the Chief gave me some Soft Corn and the 2d Chief Some Tobacco Seed—   the Interpreter Garrow[1] informed me that he had been Speeking to the Chiefs & warriers this morning and assured me that they had no intention of going down untill the return of the Cheif who went down last Spring was a year. I told the Cheifs to attend to what we had Said to them, that in a Short time they would find our words tru and Councils good.   they promised to attend Strictly to what had been Said to them, and observed that they must trade with the Sieoux one more time to get guns and powder; that they had no guns or powder and had more horses than they had use for, after they got guns and powder that they would never again have any thing to do with them &c. &c. I returned the Canoes & derected the men to prepare to Set out. Some Chyennes from two Lodges on the Main ⟨N⟩ S E. Shore Came and Smoked with me and at 11 A. M we Set out haveing parted with those people who appeared to be Sorry to part with us.   at this nation we found a french man by the name of Rokey[2] who was one of our Engagees as high as the Mandans this man had Spend all his wages, and requested to return with us— we agreed to give him a passage down. I directed 2 guns to be fired.   we proceeded on   passed the Marapa and the *We ter hoo* Rivers,[3] ⟨to a⟩ and landed to dry our bedding and robes &c which were all wet.   here we delayed untill 6 P M. and dryed our things which were much Spoiled.

I derected 5 of the hunters to proceed on to Grouse Island a fiew miles below and hunt on that island untill we arived, we proceded on to the main N E Shore below the Island and encamped,[4] the hunters joined us without any thing.   they Saw no game on the island.   we made only 17 Miles to day.   below the ricaras the river widens and the Sand bars are emencely noumerous much less timber in the bottoms than above—.

The Chyenne's[5] are portly Indians much the complections of the Mandans & ricaras high Cheeks, Streight limbed & high noses the men are large, their dress in Sumner is Simpelly a roab of a light buffalow Skin with or without the hair and a Breach clout & mockerson Some ware leagins and mockersons, their ornaments are but fiew and those are composed principally of Such articles as they precure from other indians Such as blue beeds, Shell, red paint rings of brass broaches &c.   they also ware Bears Claws about their necks, Strips of otter Skin (which they as well as the ricaras are excessively fond of) around their neck falling back behind.   their ears are cut at the lower part, but fiew of them were ornements in them, their hair is generally Cut in the forehead above their eyes and Small ornimented plats in front of each Sholder the remainder of the hair is either twisted in with horse ⟨of⟩ or buffalow hair divided into two plats over the Sholder or what is most common flow's back, Their women are homely, corse feetured wide mouthes they ware ⟨on⟩ Simpially a leathe habit made in a plain form of two pieces of equal length and equal weadth, which is sewen together with Sinues from the tail to about half way from the hip to the arm, a String fastens the 2 pieces together over the Sholders leaveng a flap or lapells which fall over near half way ther body both before and behind. those dresses usially fall as low as mid leg, they are frequently ornemented with beeds and Shells & Elk tuskes of which ⟨they⟩ all Indians are very fond of. those dresses are als frequently Printed ⟨into⟩ in various regular figures with hot sticks which are rubed on the leather with Such velosity as to nearly burn it this is very handsom. they were their hair flowing and are excessively fond of ornimenting their ears with blue beeds— this nation peacbly disposed they may be estimated at from 350 to 400 men inhabetig from 130 [120?] to 150 Lodges, they are rich in horses & Dogs, the dogs Carry a great preportion of their light baggage. they Confess to be at war with no nation except the Sieoux with whome they have ever since their remembranc been on a difencive war, with the Bands of Sieoux. as I was about to leave the Cheifs of the Chyennes lodge he requested me to Send Some traders to them, that their country was full of beaver and they would then be encouraged to Kill beaver,[6] but now they had no use for them as they could get nothing for their skins and did not know well, how to catch beaver. if the white people would come amongst them they would become acquainted ⟨with them⟩ and the white people would learn them how to take the beaver—. I promised the Nation that I would inform their Great father the President of the U States, and he would have them Supplied with goods, and mentioned in what manner they would be Supplied &c. &c.—

I am happy to have it in my power to Say that my worthy friend Capt Lewis is recovering fast, he walked a little to day for the first time. I have discontinud the tent in the hole the ball came out—

I have before mentioned that the Mandans Maharhas Menetarras & Ricarras, keep their horses in the Lodge with themselves at night.

1. For Joseph Garreau, see October 8, 1804, March 16, 1805.

2. Ordway refers to him in his entry of August 21, 1806; in Quaife (MLJO), 392, the name is given as "Ross," but in Ordway's manuscript it could easily be "Roie." This would be the *engagé* Peter (or Pierre) Roi, whose name Clark at least once (see July 4, 1804) spells "Roie." See Appendix A, vol. 2.

3. The first stream is Rampart Creek, the second Grand River, both in Corson County,

South Dakota; the party first passed these streams on October 8, 1804. Mattison (OR), 87–88; *Atlas* map 25; MRC map 45; MRY map 107.

4. Grouse Island is later Blue Blanket Island, which the party passed on October 7, 1804. The camp was below the island in Walworth County, South Dakota, some six miles southeast of present Mobridge; the site would now be inundated by the Oahe Reservoir. Mattison (OR), 83–84; *Atlas* map 25; MRC map 45; MRY map 105.

5. For the Cheyennes, see October 12, 1804.

6. The words "Kill beaver" and the next use of the word "beaver" appear to be substitutions for erasures.

[Clark]   *Saturday 23rd August 1806*

We Set out very early, the wind rose & became very hard, we passed the Sar-war-kar-na-har river[1] at 10 A. M and at half past eleven the wind became So high and the water So rough that we were obliged to put to Shore and Continue untill 3 p. M. when we had a Small Shower of rain after which the wind lay, and we proceeded on. Soon after we landed I Sent Shields & Jo. & Reubin Fields down to the next bottom of timber to hunt untill our arival.   we proceeded on Slowly and landed in the bottom.   the hunters had killed three Elk and 3 Deer the deer were pore and Elk not fat   had them fleece & brought in.   the Musqueters large and very troublesom.   at 4 P. M a Cloud from the N W with a violent rain for about half an hour   after the rain we again proceeded on. I observe great quantities of Grapes and Choke Cheries, also a Speces of Currunt[2] which I had never before observed the leas is larger than those above, the Currt. black and very inferior to either the yellow, red, or perple—   at dark we landed on a Small Sand bar under a Bluff on the S W. Side and encamped,[3] this Situation was one which I had Chosen to avoid the Musquetors, they were not very troublesom after we landed.   we Came only *40* Miles to daye

My Frend Capt Lewis is recoverig fast   the hole in his thy where the Ball passed out is Closed and appears to be nearly well.   the one where the ball entered discharges very well—.

1. The "Sur-war-kar-ne" of October 7, 1804, present Moreau River in Dewey County, South Dakota. *Atlas* map 25; MRC map 44.

2. The currant is the wild black currant again. See April 30, 1805, for a discussion of regional currants.

3. This camp would be in Potter County, South Dakota, probably below the present crossing of U.S. Highway 212 and above the camp of October 4, 1804, on Dolphees Island. The site would now be inundated by Oahe Reservoir. Mattison (OR), 63–64; *Atlas* map 24; MRC map 43.

[Clark]   *Sunday 24th August 1806*

a fair morning   we Set out as usial about Sunrise and proceeded on untill 2 P M when the wind blew So hard from the N. W. that we could not proceed   came too on the S W. Side where we continued untill 5 P. M. when the wind lay a little and we again proceeded on.   at 8 a M. we passed La-hoo-catts Island,[1] opposit the lower point of this Island on the S. W. Side near the top of the Bluff I observed a Stratea of White stone   I landed and examined it found it to be a Soft White Stone containing very fine grit, when expd. to the Sun and become Dry this Stone will Crumble   the Clay of this bluff to the above and below is remarkably Black.[2]   at half past 9 a. m. passed Good hope Island[3] and at 11 a. m passed Caution Island[4] a Short distance below this Island we came too. Sent out a hunter he Saw Several deer they were very wild and he returned without haveing killed any, the deer on this pt. of the Missouri is mostly the Mule or black tail Species.   we Saw only 6 buffalow to day the Sicoux have been laterly encamped on the river and have Secured the most of the game opp. a large trail has passed on a derection to the enterance of the Chyenne this probably is the trail of a war party.   at 5 P. M. we proceeded on a fiew miles and Encampd. on the gouge of the lookout bend[5] of 20 miles around and ¾ through, a little above an old tradeing house and 4 miles above of our outward bound encampment of the 1st of October 1804, haveing made *43* miles to day.

1. Later Dolphees Island, between Dewey and Potter counties, South Dakota, where the party camped on October 4, 1804. Mattison (OR), 63; *Atlas* map 24; MRC map 43.

2. This strata of soft white stone is a layer of bentonite—a clay derived from volcanic ash—contained within the Upper Cretaceous Pierre Shale.

3. Later Pascal Island, between Potter and Dewey counties; see October 3, 1804. Mattison (OR), 63; *Atlas* map 24; MRC map 43.

4. Later Plum Island, between Dewey and Sully counties, South Dakota; see October 2, 1804. Mattison (OR), 62; *Atlas* map 24; MRC map 42.

5. Clark locates this camp above Jean Vallé's trading post and the camp of October 1,

1804. This places it near the upper end of Lookout Bend, in Dewey County, on a site now inundated by Oahe Reservoir. Mattison (OR), 60; *Atlas* map 24; MRC map 42.

[Clark]   *Monday 25th August 1806*

a cool clear morning a Stiff breeze ahead   we Set out at the usial hour and proceeded on very well. I derected Shields Collins Shannon and the two fieldses to proceed on in the two small Canoes to the Ponia Island[1] and hunt on that Island untill we came on, they Set out before day light— The Skirt of timber in the bend above the Chyenne is not very Considerable the timber is Scattered from 4 to 16 miles on the S W Side of the river, and the thickest part is at the distance of 6 & 10 miles from the Chyenne, a narrow bottom of Small Cotton trees ⟨& willow⟩ is also on the N E pt. at the distance of from 4 to 4½ miles above the Chyenne   imediately at the enterance of that river I observe but fiew large trees Some Small Growth and willows on the lower Side bottom on the Missouri about ½ a mile and extends up the Chyen 1 mile   about a quarter of a mile above is a 2d bottom of Cotton timber, in the point above the Chyenne there is a considerable bottom of about 2 miles on that river and a large timbered bottom a Short distance above.   at 8 A. M. we Came to at the mouth of the Chyenne[2] to delay untill 12 to make a meridian observation and derected 3 hunters to proced up this river and hunt its bottoms untill twelve at which hou we Shall proceed on.   the hunters returned with 2 deer   the Chyenne discharges but little water which is much the colour of the missouri tho not So muddy   I observe a very eligable Situation on the bank of the Chyenne on it's lower Side about 100 paces from it's enterance.   this Situation is above the high floods and has a perfect Command of each river we obtained a Meridian altitude with the Sextt. and artificial Horizon *112° 50'00"*—   after which we proceeded on   passed the pania Island and came up with Shields and Collins they had killed two deer only at 3 P M we passed the place where we Saw the last encampement of Troubleson Tetons below the old ponia village[3] on the S W Side.   a very large timbered bottom on the N. E. Side imedialely below the Pania Island. Latd. of Chyenne is [*blank*] North.   at Sunset we landed about the Center of a large bottom on the N E Side a little below the enterance of No timber Creek and below our Encamp-

ment of 29th of Septr. 1804.[4]   dreyer killed a deer after we encamped.
a little above our encampmt. the ricaras had formerly a large village on
each Side which was destroyed by the Seioux.   there is the remains of 5
other villages on the S W. Side below the Chyenne river and one on Le ho
catts Isld.[5]   all those villages have been broken up by the Seioux. This
day proved a fine Still day and the men played their oars and we made *48*
miles to day. The 2 fields and Shannon did not join this evening which
caused me to encamp earlier than usial for them.   we Saw no game on
the plains today.   the Tetons have been on the river not long Since—.

1. "Pania Island," on or near which the party camped on September 30, 1804, is the
later Cheyenne Island, just below the mouth of the Cheyenne River in Sully County,
South Dakota. Mattison (OR), 56–57; *Atlas* map 23; MRC map 42.

2. They first passed the mouth of the Cheyenne River on October 1, 1804; it reaches
the Missouri on the boundary between Dewey and Stanley counties, South Dakota. *Atlas*
map 23; MRC map 42.

3. They had passed this Sioux village in Stanley County on September 30, 1804.
Atlas map 23; MRC map 41.

4. "No Timber Creek" is present Chantier Creek in Stanley County; the camp of September 29, 1804, does not appear in its correct position on *Atlas* map 23 (see under that
date). The present camp was apparently in Hughes County, South Dakota, below the entrance of Chantier Creek. Cf. Mattison (OR), 38–39; MRC map 41. The word "below"
appears to be a substitution for an erasure.

5. Some of these villages, in Stanley County, appear on *Atlas* map 23; see September
29, 1804.

[Clark]   *Tuesday 26th of August 1806*

   a heavy dew this morning   the hunters or Shannon & the 2 fields
came up at Sunrise and we Set out, they had killed only 2 Small deer one
of which they had eat   at 8 passed the place the Tetons were encamped
at the time they attempted to Stop us in Septr. 1804,[1] and at 9 A. M.
passed the enterance of Teton River.[2] Saw Several black tail or Mule deer
and Sent out to kill them but they were wild and the hunters Could not
get a Shot at either of them.   a fiew miles below the Teton river I observed a buffalow Skin Canoe lying on the S Shore and a Short distance
lower a raft which induces me to Suspect that the Tetons are not on the
Missouri at the big bend as we were informed by the Ricaras, but up the
Teton river.   at Meridn. we halted on the N E. Side opposit a handsom

leavel plain in which there is great quantities of plumbs[3] which are not yet ripe. we passed the enteranc of Smoke Creek[4] and landed and Continued two hours to Stop a leak in the perogue and fix the Stearing oare, Saw great quantities of Grapes,[5] they are black tho' not thurerly ripe. at 5 P M. we landed a Louisells fort on Ceder Island,[6] this fort is entire and every part appears to be in the Same state it was when we passed it in Septr. 1804. I observed the appearance of 3 fires in the houses which appeared to have been made 10 or 12 days past. we proceeded on about 10 miles lower and encamped on the S. W. Side opposit our outward bound encampment of the 21st of Septr. 1804, a fiew miles above Tylors River.[7] we had a Stiff breeze from the S. E. which continued to blow the greater part of the night dry and pleasant. as we were now in the Country where we were informed the Sceoux were assembled we were much on our guard deturmined to put up with no insults from those bands of Seioux, all the arms &. in perfect order. Capt. L. is Still on the mending hand he walks a little. I have discontinued the tent in the hole where the ball entered, agreeable to his request. he tells me that he is fully Convinced that the wound is sufficiently heeled for the tents to be discontinued. we made *60* miles to day with the wind ahead greater part of the day—

1. This area is in Stanley County, South Dakota, above the mouth of Bad "Teton" River. See the description of this episode in the entries for September 26, 27, and 28, 1804. Mattison (OR), 30–33; *Atlas* map 23; MRC maps 40, 41.

2. The party first reached the Bad "Teton" River on September 24, 1804. *Atlas* map 23; MRC map 40.

3. The wild plum, *Prunus americana* Marsh., does not ripen until September. Barkley, 146.

4. Smoke Creek is now La Chapelle, or Chapelle Creek, in Hughes County, South Dakota. The party first passed it on September 23, 1804. Mattison (BB), 263–65; *Atlas* map 22; MRC map 39.

5. River-bank grape again.

6. Régis Loisel's Fort aux Cedres, on the later Dorion Island No. 2; see May 25 and September 22, 1804. Mattison (BB), 261–63; *Atlas* map 22; MRC map 39; MRY map 62.

7. The camp of September 21, 1804, was in Hughes County, at or just below the "Mock Island" of *Atlas* map 22; the present camp was opposite in Lyman County, South Dakota, some four miles above the mouth of Medicine River, or Creek (Lewis and Clark's

"Tylors River"). The site would now be inundated by Lake Sharpe (Big Bend Reservoir). Mattison (BB), 260–61; MRC map 39.

[Clark]   *Wednesday 27th Augt. 1806*

Set out before Sunrise   a Stiff breeze a head from the East proceeded to the enterance of Tylors river on the S W Side and landed on a Sand bar and Sent out the hunters to kill Some meat, our Stock of meat being now exousted and this the most favourable place to precure a fresh Supply, the hunters returned in 3 hours without haveing killed any thing. they informed me that the bottoms were entirely beaten up and the grass laid flat by the emence number of Buffalow which had been here a Short time past.   the deer had left the bottom.   they Saw several Buffalow Bulls which they did not think proper to kill as they were unfit for use. here we discover the first Signs of the wild turkey.[1]   at 1 P M we halted in the big bend[2] and killed a fat buck elk near the river, which was very timely as our meat was entirely exhosted.   at 2 P. M we again proceeded on down saw Several Buffalow Bulls on each Side of the river also Some deer of the Common kind.[3]   at 6 P. M. we herd the bellowing of the Buffalow Bulls in the lower Isld. of the Big bend below the Gouge[4] which induced a belief that there was Some fat Cows, 5 men went out from the 2 Small Canoes which was a little a head, and killed two Cows one Bull and a Calf nether of them wer fat we droped the Perogue & Canoes to the lower part of the Island near to where the buffalow was killed and incamped haveing Come 45 Miles only to day.   had the buffalow butched and brought in and divided. My friend Capt Lewis hurt himself very much by takeing a longer walk on the Sand bar in my absence at the buffalow than he had Strength to undergo, which Caused him to remain very unwell all night.

1. The wild turkey, *Meleagris gallopavo* [AOU, 310].
2. The Big Bend, or Grand Detour, of the Missouri River, enclosing land in Lyman County, South Dakota, appears prominently on *Atlas* map 22; Lewis and Clark first passed it on September 20 and 21, 1804. Mattison (BB), 258; MRC map 38.
3. The white-tailed deer of the eastern United States.
4. The nameless island at the lower end of the Big Bend on *Atlas* map 22, also un-

named on MRC map 38, perhaps the Brule Island of Mattison (BB), 252. Now under Lake Sharpe (Big Bend Reservoir), between Lyman and Buffalo counties, South Dakota, it was the site of their camp for this day. For the problem of identifying the "Lower Island Creek" of the *Atlas* map, opposite whose mouth the island lies, see September 19, 1804. MRY maps 53, 54.

[Clark]   *Thursday 28th of August 1806*

Capt Lewis had a bad nights rest and is not very well this morning.   we Set out early and proceded on very well, Saw a number of Buffalow bulls on the banks in different places.   passd the 3 rivers of the Seioux pass[1] at 9 A. M.   a Short distance below on the S W Side Sent out Reubin & Joseph Feild to hunt for the Mule deer or the antilope neither of which we have either the Skins or Scellitens of,[2] we derected those two men to proceed on down to the places we encamped the 16th & 17th of Septr. 1804 and which place the party had called pleasant Camp from the great abundance of Game Such as Buffalow Elk, antilopes, Blacktail or mule deer, fallow deer, common deer wolves barking Squirels, Turkies and a variety of other animals, aded to which there was a great abundance of the most delicious plumbs and grapes.   this Situation which is a Short distance above the enterance of Corvus Creek we are deturmined to delay one day for the purpose of prcureing the sceletins of the Mule deer & antilope, and Some barking Squirels.   a fiew miles below the place the 2 Fields were Set on Shore we Set Drewyer and Labeech on Shore with the Same directions which had been given to the 2 field's   at 12 oClock we Landed on the S W. Side at the Same Spot which we had encamped on the 16th and 17th of September 1804, and formed a Camp,[3] Sent out Serjt. Pryor, Shields, Go. Gibson, Willard and Collins to hunt in the plains up Corvus Creek for the Antilope and Mule deer   Sent out Bratten and Frazier to kill the barking Squirel,[4] and Gave directions to all of them to kill the Magpye[5] if they Should See any of them Several of the men and the Squaws of the enterpreter Jessomme and the Mandan Chief went to Some plumb bushes in the bottom and geathered more plumbs than the party Could eate in 2 days, those blumbs are of 3 Speces,[6] the most of them large and well flavored.   our Situation is pleasent a high bottom thinly timbered and covered with low grass without misquitors.   at 3 P. M Drewyer and Labeech arived, the latter haveing killd. a Deer of the

Common Speceis only.   in the evening late all the hunters returned without any Speces of animal we were in want of, they killed 4 Common deer and two buffalow a part of the best of the meat of those animals they brought in.   we precured two of the barking Squirels only.   as we Could not precere any Mule deer or antelope we concluded to Send the hunters on a head early in the morning and delay untill 10 A. M to give them time to hunt. I derected Shannon & Collins to go on the opposit Side, and Labeech and Willard to proceed down on this Side at Some distance from the river and join the party at the round Island[7] &c. and R. Field to proceed on Slowly in the Small Canoe to that place and take in any thing which the hunters might kill. Made 32 miles to day

The hunters informed me that they Saw great numbers of Buffalow in the plains. I Saw Several herds of those animals on either Side to day at a distance.

1. The party first passed this area in Lyman and Buffalo counties, South Dakota, on September 19, 1804. *Atlas* map 22; MRC map 37.

2. Skins and skeletons of the pronghorn, and antlers, ears, and tail of the mule deer were shipped back to Jefferson from Fort Mandan in April 1805, providing for the identification of two new species. Lewis to Jefferson, April 7, 1805, Jefferson to Charles Willson Peale, October 9, 1805, Jackson (LLC), 1:234–35, 263.

3. Clark called this camp "Plumb Camp" on September 17, 1804, but here refers to it as "Pleasant Camp," a name confirmed by Gass and Ordway. It was near present Oacoma, in Lyman County. Corvus Creek is now American Creek in Lyman County. Mattes (FR), 521–22; *Atlas* maps 20, 21, 22; MRC map 37.

4. Prairie dog.

5. The black-billed magpie, first described on September 16 and 17, 1804, in this same locality.

6. There is only one plum in this region, the wild plum. Again, genetic variation accounts for the size and flavor differences.

7. Below White River in Brule County, South Dakota; see the next entry, August 29, 1806.

[Clark]   *Friday 29th August 1806*

a cloudy morning   the hunters proceeded on agreeable to their orders of last night. I Sent out two men to the village of barking Squirels with directions to kill Some of them.   they after 2 hours returned and informed me that not one of those Squirels were to be Seen out of their the Skins of the party which they had been dressing Since yesterday being now ⟨nearly⟩ completely dressed I derected all loose baggage to be put on board the Canoes and at 10 A. M. Set out and proceeded on   passed the white river[1] at 12 oClock and halted below the enterance of Shannons Creek[2] where we were joined by Labeech Shannon and Willard, they had killed 2 common der but no Mule deer or antilopes. Willard informed me that he Saw 2 antilopes but Could not get near to them. Willard and Labiech waded white river a fiew miles above its enterance and inform me that they found it 2 feet water and 200 yards wide. the water of this river at this time nearly as white as milk.   put Drewyer out to hunt on the S W. Side and proceeded on below the round Island[3] and landed on the N. E. Side   I with Several of the men went out in pursute of Buffalow.   the men killed 2 Bulls near me they were very por   I assended to the high Country and from an eminance, I had a view of the plains for a great distance.   from this eminance I had a view of a greater number of buffalow than I had ever Seen before at one time. I must have Seen near 20,000 of those animals feeding on this plain. I have observed that in the country between the nations which are at war with each other the greatest numbers of wild animals are to be found—   on my return to the river I killed 2 young deer.   after Dinner ⟨I⟩ we proceeded down the river about 3 mile to the Camp of Jo. & Rubin fields and Collins, and encamped on the S W. Side a little below our encampment of 13th Septr. 1804,[4] haveing made 20 Miles only.   neither of the hunters killed either a Black tail deer or an antilope. Jo. Fields & Shields each killed a porcupin and two others of the hunters Killed Deer, Drewyer did not join us untill 10 P. M.   he informed that he Saw some antilopes and Mule deer but Could kill none of them. Jo. Field informed that he wounded female of the Mule deer a little below our Camp late in the evening and could not prosue her I directed him to Set out with 3 others and follow the Deer and get her if possible early in the morning.

1. White River, joining the Missouri River in Lyman County, South Dakota, first passed on September 15, 1804. *Atlas* maps 20, 21, 22; MRC map 36.

2. Present Ball or Bull Creek, in Lyman County, at whose mouth they camped on September 14, 1804. *Atlas* maps 20, 21, 22; MRC map 36.

328

3. Evidently later Dry Island, in Brule County, South Dakota, first passed on September 14, 1804. *Atlas* maps 20, 21, 22; MRC map 36.

4. This camp was in Lyman County, a little below the Round Island and the camp of September 13, 1804. Mattes (FR), 512; *Atlas* maps 20, 21, 22; MRC map 36.

[Clark] *Saturday 30th of August 1806*

Capt. Lewis is mending Slowly.   we set out at the usial hour and proceeded on very well a fiew miles   Jo Field who was on the Shore being behind I derected one of the Small Canoes with R. Fields & Shannon to continue on the point of a Sand bar untill he coms up. I took 3 hunters and walked on the N E Shore with a view to kill Some fat meet.   we had not proceeded far before Saw a large plumb orchd of the most deelicious plumbs, out of this orchard 2 large Buck Elks ran the hunters killed them. I Stoped the Canoes and brought in the flesh which was fat and fine.   here the party Collected as many plumbs as they could eate and Several pecks of which they put by &c.   after a delay of nearly 2 hours we again proceeded on downwards   passed 3 Small Islands and as we were about to land at the place appointed to wait for the 2 fields and Shannon, I saw Several men on horseback which with the help of a Spie glass I found to be Indians on the high hills to the N E   we landed on the S. W. Side and I sent out two men to a village of Barking Squirels to kill Some of those animals imedeatily after landing about 20 indians was discovered on an eminanc a little above us on the opposite Side.   one of those men I took to be a freinch man from his a blanket Capoe & a handkerchief around his head.   imediately after 80 or 90 Indian men all armed with fusees & Bows & arrows Came out of a wood on the opposite bank about ¼ of a mile below us.   they fired of their guns as a Salute we returned the Salute with 2 rounds.   we were at a loss to deturmin of what nation those indians were.   from their hostile appearance we were apprehensive they were Tetons.   but from the Country through which they roved we were willing to believe them eithe the Yanktons, Ponars or Mahars[1] either of which nations are well disposed towards the white people. I deturmined to find out who they were without running any resque of the party and indians, and therefore took three french men[2] who could Speak the Mahar Pania and some Seioux and in a Small canoe

I went over to a Sand bar which extended Sufficently near the opposite Shore to Converse.   imedeately after I Set out 3 young men Set out from the opposite Side and Swam next me on the Sand bar. I derected the men to Speak to them in the Pania and mahar Languages first neither of which they could understand   I then derected the man who could Speak a fiew words of Seioux to inquire what nation or tribe they belong to they informed me that they were Tetons and their Chief was *Tar-tack-kah-sab-bar* or the black buffalow[3]   This Chief I knew very well to be the one we had seen with his band at Teton river which band had attempted to detain us in the fall of 1804 as we assended this river and with whome we wer near comeing to blows. I told those Indians that they had been deef to our councils and ill treated us as we assended this river two years past, that they had abused all the whites who had visited them since. I believed them to be bad people & Should not Suffer them to cross to the Side on which the party lay, and directed them to return with their band to their Camp, that if any of them come near our camp we Should kill them certainly. I lef them on the bear and returned to th party and examined the arms &c.   those indians seeing Some Corn in the Canoe requested Some of it which I refused being deturmined to have nothing to do with those people. Several others Swam across one of which understood pania, and as our pania interpreter was a very good one we had it in our power to inform what we wished. I told this man to inform his nation that we had not forgot their treatment to us as we passed up this river &c.   that they had treated all the white people who had visited them very badly; robed them of their goods, and had wounded one man[4] whome I had Seen. we viewed them as bad people and no more traders would be Suffered to come to them, and whenever the white people wished to visit the nations above they would Come Sufficiently Strong to whip any vilenous party who dare to oppose them and words to the Same purpote. I also told them that I was informed that a part of all their bands were gorn to war against the Mandans &c, and that they would be well whiped as the Mandans & Menetarres & had a plenty of Guns Powder and ball, and we had given them a Cannon to defend themselves.   and derected them to return from the Sand bar and inform their Chiefs what we had Said to them, and to keep away from the river or we Should kill every one of them &c. &c.   those fellows requested to be allowed to Come across and make Cumerads which we positively refused and I directed them to return imediately which they did and after they had informed the Chiefs &c. as I Suppose what we had Said to them, they all Set out on their return to their Camps back of a high hill.   7 of them halted on the top of the hill and blackguarded us, told us to come across and they would kill us all &c. of which we took no notice.   we all this time were extreamly anxious for the arival of the 2 fields & Shannon whome we had left behind, and were Some what consd. as to their Safty.   to our great joy those men hove in Sight at 6 P. M. Jo. Fields had killed 3 black tail or mule deer.   we then Set out, as I wished to See what those Indians on the hill would act.   we Steared across near the opposit Shore, this notion put them Some agitation as to our intentions, some Set out on the direction towards their Camps   others walked about on the top of the hill and one man walked down the hill to meet us and invited us to land to which invitation I paid no kind of attention.   this man I knew to be the one who had in the fall 1804 accompaned us 2 days and is Said to be the friend to the white people.[5]   after we passd. him he returned on the top of the hill and gave 3 Strokes with the gun [*NB?: on the earth—this is swearing by the earth*] he had in his hand   this I am informed is a great oath among the indians.[6]   we proceeded on down about 6 miles and encamped on a large Sand bar in the middle of the river[7] about 2 miles above our encampment on Mud Island on the 10th Septr. 1804 haveing made 22 miles only to Day. Saw Several Indians on the hills at a distance this evening viewing us.   our ⟨camp⟩ encampment of this evening was a very disagreable one, bleak exposed to the winds, and the Sand wet. I pitched on this Situation to prevent being disturbed by those Scioux in the Course of the night as well as to avoid the Musquetors—. Killed 9 whistleing squirels.[8]

1. The last two would be Poncas and Omahas.
2. Two of them would surely be Pierre Cruzatte and François Labiche; the other might be Jusseaume, or perhaps Jean Baptiste Lepage could speak one of these languages. Ordway seems to indicate that Jusseaume's wife played an important part in this episode,

though it is hard to tell from the manuscript whether the husband or wife was involved. Ordway's words read, "Mrs Jessom could understand Some words they Said and he heared them Say that if we came on their Side of the river they would kill us & that we were good for to kill &c."

3. For Black Buffalo, see September 25–28, 1804.

4. Joseph Dickson; see Clark's entry, August 11, 1806, and Lewis's entry for August 12, 1806.

5. Buffalo Medicine; see September 24, 1804.

6. The earth was one of the four Superior Gods, together with the rock, the sky, and the sun. Hassrick, 207. Biddle underlined a few words in red ink in these passages about the oath; they are not so underlined here.

7. This camp was between Gregory and Charles Mix counties, South Dakota, in the vicinity of the later Hot Springs Island, probably the "Bull Island" of *Atlas* map 20; the camp of September 10, 1804, was on Pocahontas, or Toehead Island. The site would now be inundated by Fort Randall Reservoir. Cf. Mattes (FR), 505–6; MRC map 35.

8. "Whistling squirrel" seems to have been the captains' name for the Columbian ground squirrel of the Rocky Mountains. Here Clark means the prairie dog.

[Clark]   *Saturday 31st August 1806*

all wet and disagreeable this morning.   at half past 11 ⟨P. M.⟩ last night the wind Shifted about to the N. W. and it began to rain with hard Claps of thunder and lightning the Clouds passd over and the wind Shifted about to the S W. & blew with great violence So much So that all hands were obliged to hold the Canoes & Perogue to prevent their being blown off from the Sand bar, however a Suden Squal of wind broke the cables of the two Small Canoes and with Some dificuelty they were got to Shore Soon after the 2 Canoes in which Sergt. Pryor and the indians go in broke loose with wiser and Willard in them and were blown quite across the river to the N E. Shore where fortunately they arived Safe, I Sent Sergt. Jo Ordway with a Small perogue and 6 men to prosue the 2 Canoes and assist them in effecting a landing, those 2 Canoes being tied together 2 men could not manage them, the wind Slackened a little and by 2 A. M. Sergt Ordway with willard wiser and the 2 Canoes returned all Safe, the wind continud to blow and it rained untill day light all wet and disagreeable.   all the party examind their arms and put them in order and we Set out and proceeded on down. Saw Several Indians on the hills untill we passed the Island of Cedar[1] 9 A. M   the morning Cloudy and wind down the the river at 4 P. M. passed the doome[2] and lowest village of Barking Squirels. this is also the highest up the river where I observed the fox Squirel[3] in the bottom above the doome on N. E Side I killed 2 fox Squirels. we Saw no game of any kind to day as the banks as usial. the Sun Shone with a number of flying Clouds. we encamped on the N. E. Side[4] a little below our Encampment of the 5th of Septr. on no preserve Island haveing Come 70 Miles.

1. The later Little Cedar Island between Gregory and Charles Mix counties, South Dakota, which the party first passed on September 10, 1804. *Atlas* maps 7, 20; MRC map 34; MRY maps 31, 32.

2. Clark means "dome." First noted on September 7, 1804, and then called a cupola, it was identified as the "Tower" in Boyd County, Nebraska; it is now called Old Baldy. It is the Steeple on *Atlas* map 19; the village of "barking squirrels" (prairie dogs) is shown just above it. MRC map 33.

3. Fox squirrel, *Sciurus niger*. Burroughs, 96.

4. The party camped in Charles Mix County, as Clark notes a little below their camp of September 5, 1804, which was on "no preserve Island," nameless on *Atlas* map 19. They were near the mouth of Chouteau Creek, "Goat Creek" on the *Atlas* map. MRC map 32.

[Clark]   [*Weather, August 1806*][1]

day of the Month	State of the weather at Sun rise	State of wind at Sunrise	State of the weather at 4 P. M.	Wind at 4 P. M.	State of river rise or fall	Inches &c.	part of Inches
1st	c. a. r	N. W.	r.	N.	ris	5	½
2nd	c. a. r.	N.	f. a. r.	N	r	3	
3rd	f.	S W	f.	S W.	rise	2	¼
4th		N W.	f.	N E	fal	6	½
5th	f.	N. F..	f	N. F..	fal	7	
6th	C a r T & L	S W.	f.	N E	fall	2	½
7th	r.	N. E.	c. a. r.	N.	fall	2	½
8th	f.	N.	f.	N. W.	fall	2	
9th	f.	N. E	f.	N. E.	fall	1	¼
10th	f.	E.	c.	E.	fall		¾
11th	f.	N. W.	f.	N. W	fall	2	
12th	f.	S. W.	c	S W.	fall	2	¼
13th	f. a. r.	S W	f.	S. W.	fall	2	½
14th	f	N. F.	f	S W	fall	3	½

15th	f.	N W	f.	N. W	f.	2	
16th	f.	N W	f	N. W	f.	3	½
17th	c.	S E	c.	S. E			
18th	C a r	S E	f.	S. E	f	1	½
19th	T. L. & r.	S E	c.—	S. E	f		¾
20th	C. a. T. L & r	S W.	f.	N. W	f	1	¼
21st	f.	S. E.	f.	N. W	f	2	½
22d	c. a. r	S W	f.	S E	f	4	
23rd	C	S E	r.	N. W	f	1	½
24th	f.	N E	f.	N W	f	2	
25th	f.	S W.	f.	N W	f	1	½
26th	f.	S. E	f.	S. E.	f		¾
27th	f.	S. E.	f.	S. E	f	1	¼
28th	f.	S. E	f.	N W			
29th	c.	N W	f. a. r.	S E	f		½
30th	c. a. r	S E	f.	S. E.			
31st	c. a. r. T & L. & w	S E	c. a. r	S E			

[Remarks][2]

1st   rained last night and all day to day at intervales

2nd   rained a little last night and Several Showers this morng

3d   Musquetors troublesom. I arive at the Missouri.   heavy dew.

4th   Rochejhone falling much faster than the Missouri

5th   Musquetors excessively troublesom   both rivers falling.

6th   rained hard last night with Thunder Lightning & hard wind from S. W.   killed a white Bear & Bighorn.

7th   Commenced raining at daylight and contined at intervals all day.   air Cool.

8th   air cool. Sergt. pryor arrive in Skin Canoes.

9th   a heavy dew.   air cool and clear   found red goose berries[3] and a dark purple current & Service's

10th   found a Species of Cherry[4] resembling the read Heart cherry of our country.

11th   sarvis berries in abundance & ripe.

12th   Capt. Lewis overtake me with the party

13th   a fiew drops of rain last night at 8 P. M with hard S W wind

14th   Mandan Corn ⟨is r[ipe?]⟩ now full and beginning to harden

16th   Northern lights[5] Seen last night which was in Streaks

17th   leave the Mandans.

18th   raincd moderately last night in forpart of the night.

19th   Comenced raining at 5 A. M and Continued with a hard wind untill [*blank*]

21st   rained a little in the course of the night.   at day a violent hard Shower for ½ an hour

22nd   rained the greater part of last night.   grape and plums ripe.[6] The rains which have fallen in this month is most Commonly from flying Clouds which pass in different directions, those Clouds are always accompanied with hard winds and Sometimes accompanied with thunder and lightning— The river has been falling moderately Since the third of the month.   the rains which has fallen has no impression on the river than Causing it to be more muddy and probably prevents its falling fast.—.

23d   rained at 10 A M. & 4 P M   hard wind

24th   wind blew hard all day   grapes in abundance.

26th   Heavy dew this morning. Saw a pilecan

27th   first Turkeys at Tylor River above the big bend

29th   Some rain this morning only a fiew drops and at 10 A. M.

30th   a fiew drops of rain last night   I Saw the Tetons.

31st   rained most of last night with T. Li. & a hard wind from the S. W. some rain to day.

1. Clark's weather table for August 1806 appears in Codex M, pp. 146–47 (reading backwards). Lewis's weather table is placed after his last entry for the month (August 12) at the end of Chapter 37.

2. Clark has a number of remarks in the margin of his weather table for this month. There is only one separate remark for the month, on the twenty-second. See note for that date.

3. See botanical notes for August 9, 1806

4. Pin cherry. The "read Heart" cherry is probably the black cherry; see Lewis's entry of August 12, 1806.

5. Aurora borealis.

6. Clark's only separate remark for the month begins here with "The rains."

Chapter Forty

The Home Stretch

September 1–26, 1806

[Clark]   *Monday 1st of September 1806*

Musquitors very troublesom last night, we set out at the usial hour and had not proceeded on far before the fog became So thick that we were oblige to come too and delay half an hour for the fog to pass off which it did in Some measure and we again proceded on   R. Jo. Fields and Shannon landed on an Ponceras Island[1] to try to kill Some deer which was Seen on the beech and the ⟨remainder of the⟩ Canoes all passed them at 9 A. M we passed the enterance of River *Quiequur*[2] which had the Same appearance it had when we passed up water rapid and of a milky white Colour   about two miles below the Quicurre, 9 Indians ran down the bank and beckened to us to land, they appeared to be a war party, and I took them to be Tetons and paid no kind of attention to them further than an enquirey to what tribe they belonged, they did not give me any answer, I prosume they did not understand the man who Spoke to them as he Spoke but little of their language.   as one Canoe was yet behind we landed in an open Commanding Situation[3] out of Sight of the indians deturmined to delay untill they Came up.   about 15 minits after we had landed Several guns were fired by the indians, which we expected was at the three men behind. I calld out 15 men and ran up with a fill deturmination to Cover them if possible let the number of the indians be what they might. Capt Lewis hobled up on the bank and formed the remainder of the party in a Situation well calculated to defend themselves and the Canoes &c.   when I had proceeded to the point about 250 yards I discovered the Canoe about 1 mile above & the indians where we had left them. I then walked on the Sand beech and the indians came down to meet me   I gave them my hand and enquired of them what they were Shooting at, they informed me that they were Shooting off their guns at an old Keg which we had thrown out of one of the Canoes and was floating down.   those Indians informed me they were Yanktons,[4] one of the men with me knew one of the Indians to be the brother of young Durion's wife.[5]   finding those indians to be Yanktons I invited them down to the boats to Smoke.   when we arived at the Canoes they all eagerly Saluted the Mandan Chief, and we all Set and Smoked Several pipes. I told them that we took them to be a party of Tetons and the fireing I expected was at the three men in the rear Canoe and I had went up with a full intention to kill them all if they had been tetons & fired on the Canoe as we first expected, but finding them Yanktons and good men we were glad to See them and take them by the hand as faithfull Children who had opened their ears to our Councils.   one of them Spoke and Said that their nation had opened their years, & done as we had directed them ever Since we gave the Meadel to their great Chief, and Should Continue to do as we had told them we enquired if any of their Chiefs had gone down with Mr. Durion,[6] the answered that their great Chief and many of their brave men had gone down, that the white people had built a house near the Mahar village where they traded.[7]   we tied a piec of ribon to each mans hair and gave them Some Corn of which they appeared much pleased. The Mandan Cheif gave a par of elegant Legins to the principal man of the indian party, which is an indian fashion. [*NB: to make presents*][8]   the Canoe & 3 men haveing joined us we took our leave of this party telling them to return to their band and listen to our councils which we had before given to them. Their band of 80 Lodges were on plum Creek[9] a fiew miles to north.   those nine men had five fusees and 4 bows & quivers of arrows.   at 2 P. M. we came too on the upper point of bon homme[10] opposit the antient fortification and Sent out men to hunt on each Side and on the island.   and the canoes on each Side of the island to receive any meat might be killed   I walked on the N. E. main Shore found the bottom rich and thickly covered with Peavine rich weed[11] grass interwoven in Such a manner with grape vines that I could not get through and was obliged to assend a high plains the passing through which I also found

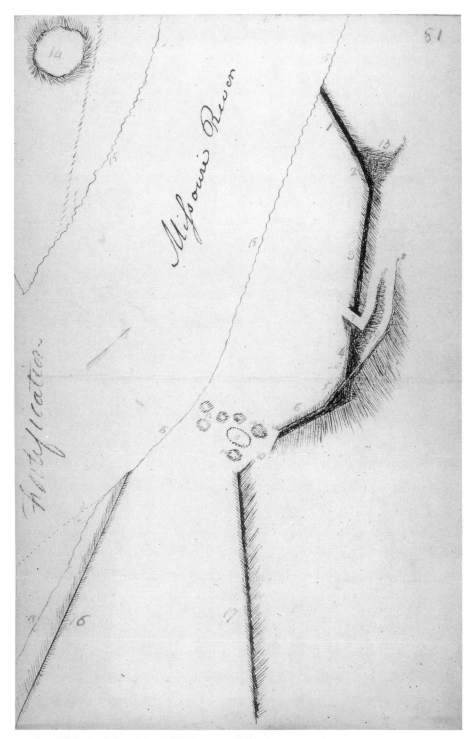

7. Bon Homme Island on the Missouri River, Bon Homme County, South Dakota, and Knox County, Nebraska, September 1, 1806, Codex N, p. 81

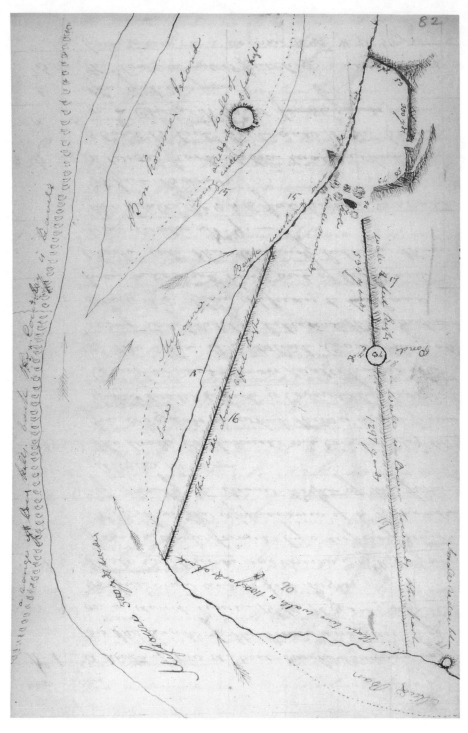

8. Bon Homme Island on the Missouri River, Bon Homme County, South Dakota, and Knox County, Nebraska, September 1, 1806, Codex N, p. 82

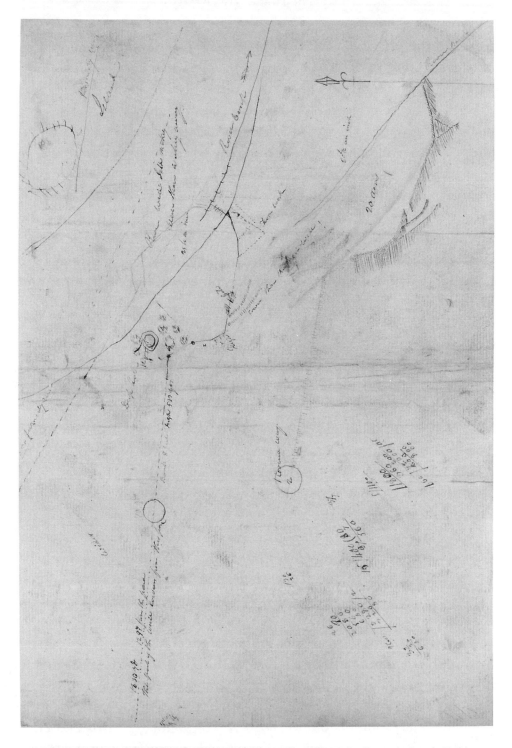

9. Bon Homme Island on the Missouri River, Bon Homme County, South Dakota, and Knox County, Nebraska, September 1, 1806, Estimate of Western Indians

tiresom.   the grass was nearly as high as my head and the musquitors excessively bad.   at the lower point of the Island all the Canoes & hunters Came together. Labeech killed an Elk only the flesh of which was brought on in the perogue.   at this island we brought 2 years together or on the 1st of Septr. 1804[12] we Encamped at the lower point of this Island.   after we all Came together we again proceeded on down to a large Sand bar imediately opposit to the place were we met the Yanktons in Council at the Calumet Bluffs and which place we left on the 1t of Septr. 1804. I observed our old flag Staff or pole Standing as we left it.   the musquitors excessively troublesom untill about 10 P. M. when the S W wind became Strong and blew the most of them off.   we came 52 miles to day only with a head wind.   the Country on either Side are butifull and the plains much richer below the Queiquer river than above that river.—

[Clark]   [*undated, ca. September 1, 1806*][13]

No. 1.—   a wall of the Antient brook Commincing on the bank of the River and running on a direct line S. 76° W. 96 yard, about 75 feet baece and 8 feet high

2.—   Wall Continued and Course S. 84° W. 53 yards from an angle formed by a Slopeing decent No. 13.   has the appearance of a horn-work of nearly the Same hight of the former Angle No. 1—

3.—   the Wall Continued on a Course N. 69° W. for 300 yards in which there is a low part of the wall which is Covered by two Circular and lower walls one back of the other.   8 8   which Covers the gate way Completely, between those outer walls 8 8.   there appears to ⟨be⟩ have been a Covered way out of the Main work into the Vacaney between those two walls No. 9.—   This wall No. 2 is 8 feet high and about 75 feet Bace

4.—   a wide port of the wall wich is about 12 feet high and 105 feet base on ⟨a⟩ the Course Continued N. 69° W. ⟨for 56 yards⟩ from the gateway

5.—   The Wall about 15 feet high and about 90 feet bace on a course N. 32° W. for 56 yds.

6.—   the Wall Continus on a Course N. 20° W for 73 yards and ends abruptly near a whole near Several mounds prismiscutly in the Gorge of the work between this and the river

10. N. 32° W. 96 yards across a low place much lower than the Common leavel of the plain to the Commencement of a Wall of 8 feet high— this is an open Space from whence there is Some appearance of a Covered way to the Water

10   is a large hollow place much lower then the plain

12 12.—   Several little mounds in the gouge

7.   the gateway to the Stong work

14.—   a redoubt Situated on an Island   Which makeing on the Side next to the main work, the wall forming this reboubt is 6 feet high

15 15.—   The river banks at the waters edge

16.—   a thick wall of about 6 feet high passing from the Rivers edge at the gouge of the work perfectly Strieght ⟨and ? self⟩ to the bend of the River above and there ends abruptly where the Missouri is under mineing its banks— on this wall maney large Cotton Trees of two & 3 feet ⟨thi⟩ diamieter   this Bank passes thro a wood in it's whole Couse

No. 17 19.—   a Streaght wall of 1830 yard extending from the Gorge of the Strong work on a Course N. 80° W. This wall is 8 feet high to a round pon (No. 18)   from then it becoms lower and Strikes the Missouri at a place where that river has the aptr. of haveing incroached on its banks for a great distance.   this wall passes in it's whole Course thro a leavel plain.

18.—   a Deep pond of 73 yards diamieter in the Wall, perfectly round

20—   This from the extremity of one wall to the other 1100 yards.

21—   a Small redoubt on the bank of the river

The Strong part of this work which must be about ⅔ of it's original Size Contains Twenty acres.—

The part Contained between the two walls is about 500 acres and is Certain that those walls have been longer and must have contained a much greater space—

1. Between Bon Homme County, South Dakota, and Knox County, Nebraska, at the mouth of Ponca Creek in Nebraska; "Poncar I." on *Atlas* map 19, evidently the later Pawnee Island. They first passed it on September 5, 1804. *Atlas* map 19; MRC map 32.

2. The Niobrara River, which joins the Missouri in Knox County, first passed on September 4, 1804. *Atlas* map 19; MRC map 32.

3. Apparently this was on the Bon Homme County side, since the village of the Indians (see below) was on Emanuel Creek. *Atlas* map 19; MRC maps 31, 32.

4. For the Yanktons, see August 28–31, 1804.

5. "Young Durion" was probably Pierre Dorion, Jr.; see August 29, 1804. His wife among the Yanktons was named Holy Rainbow; she was apparently not the same woman who was the only survivor of an 1812 massacre of Astorians on the Boise River in Idaho, in which Pierre died. Speck, 165, 183–85; Irving (Astor), 446–48; Munnick (PD).

6. Pierre Dorion, Sr.; see June 12, 1804. For his assignment to conduct the Yankton delegation to Washington, see August 31, 1804.

7. Presumably the Omaha village near Homer, in Dakota County, Nebraska; see August 13, 1804. *Atlas* map 16.

8. Biddle added underlining in red ink to "par of elegant Legins . . . of the indian."

9. Emanuel Creek in Bon Homme County, near present Springfield, first passed on September 3, 1804. *Atlas* maps 7, 19; MRC map 31.

10. Bon Homme Island, now inundated by Lewis and Clark Lake, was between Bon Homme County and Knox County. The party first reached it on September 1, 1804. The "antient fortification" consisted of natural sand ridges which Clark sketched and described on September 2, 1804. On this date, September 1, 1806, Clark again made sketches (figs. 7, 8) and descriptive notes on pp. 81–85 of Codex N. The notes are included as the second entry for this date. Another drawing of the area appears in the Estimate of Western Indians (fig. 9) and may have been inserted there at about this time.

11. Peavine is probably hog peanut, *Amphicarpa bracteata* (L.) Fern., and richweed is *Pilea pumila* (L.) Gray.

12. On August 28–September 1, 1804, they had camped at the Calumet Bluff in Cedar County, Nebraska, just below the present Gavins Point Dam, and had councilled with the Yanktons. Now they camped opposite in Yankton County, South Dakota. Mattison (GP), 53–55; *Atlas* map 18; MRC map 30.

13. These notes accompany Clark's drawings of the "fortification" on Bon Homme Island in Codex N (figs. 7, 8); see previous notes.

[Clark]   *Tuesday 2nd of September 1806*

Set out at the usial hour   passed the River Jacque[1] at 8 A. M.   in the first bottom below on the N E. Side   I observed the remains of a house which had been built since we passed up, this most probably was McClellins tradeing house with the Yanktons in the Winter of 1804 & 5.[2] the wind was hard a head & continued to increas which obliged us to lay by nearly all day.   as our Store of meat, I took with me 8 men and prosued a Small Gang of Cows in the plains 3 miles and killed two which was in very good order, had them butchered and each man took a load as much as he Could Carry and returned to the Canoes, the wind Still high and water rough we did not Set out untill near Sun Set   we proceded to a Sand bar a Short distance below the place we had Come too on account of the wind and Encamped ⟨the⟩ on a Sand bar,[3] the woods being the harbor of the Musquetors and the party without the means of Screaning themselves from those tormenting insects.   on the Sand bars the wind which generaly blows moderately at night blows off those pests and we Sleep Soundly. The wind Continued to blow hard from the Same point S. E untill 3 P. M   I saw in my walk to day Lynn and Slipery Elm.[4]   the plains are tolerably leavel on each Side and very fertile. I saw 4 prarie fowls Common to the Illinois,[5] those are the highest up which have been Seen, white Oak[6] is very Common also white ash[7] on the riveens and high bottoms.   two turkys killed to day of which the Indians very much admired being the first which they ever Saw. Capt L. is mending fast— we made only 22 Miles to day.

1. The James River, first passed on August 27, 1804, meets the Missouri in Yankton County, South Dakota. *Atlas* map 18; MRC map 30; MRR maps 82, 83.

2. For Robert McClellan see September 12, 1806. The trading house would have been in Yankton County, a little below the mouth of the James River. *Atlas* map 18; MRC map 30.

3. They camped a few miles below the mouth of the James River; it is not really clear whether this was in Yankton County, South Dakota, or in Cedar County, Nebraska. *Atlas* map 18; MRC map 30.

4. American linden, *Tilia americana* L., and slippery elm, *Ulmus rubra* Muhl. This observation of the linden and elm together is significant since the trees reach their distributional limit on the Missouri River in this area. Barkley, 87, 33; Little (CIH), 193-E, 198-E.

5. The greater prairie-chicken. In fact, its range extends north to southern Manitoba and Saskatchewan. Burroughs, 211.

6. Bur oak, *Quercus macrocarpa* Michx., belongs to the larger taxonomic group of white oak species. True white oak, *Q. alba* L., occurs farther down the Missouri River. Clark did not distinguish between the two species even though the acorn is significantly different. Apparently, he was using the general name to identify the oak from a distance. Barkley, 38–39.

7. Green ash, *Fraxinus pennsylvanica* Marsh. var. *subintegerrima* (Vahl) Fern., is the species noted here. White ash, *F. americana* L., is not found this far north. Again, Clark may have sighted the tree from a distance since the leaves of the two species are distinguishable. Barkley, 298–99; Little (CIH), 130-E, 126-E.

[Clark]   *Wednesday 3rd of September 1806*

Wind Continued to blow very hard this morning.   it Shifted last night
to the S. W. and blew the Sand over us in Such a manner as to render the
after part of the night very disagreeable.   the wind luled a little and we
Set out and proceeded on with the wind a head   passed the enterance of
redstone River[1] on the N E. Side at 11 A M. and at half past 4 P. M we
Spied two boats[2] & Several men, our party peyed their Ores and we Soon
landed on the Side of the Boats   the men of these boats Saluted us with
their Small arms I landed & was met by a Mr. James Airs[3] from Mack-
anaw by way of Prarie Dechien and St. Louis.   this Gentleman is of the
house of Dickson & Co: of Prarie de Chian who has a Licence to trade
for one year with the Sieoux   he has 2 Batteaux loaded with Merchendize for that purpose. This Gentleman receved both Capt. Lewis and my
Self with every mark of friendship he was himself at the time with a chill
of the agu on him which he has had for Several days.   our first enquirey
was after the President of our country and then our friends and the State
of the politicks of our country &c. and the State Indian affairs to all of
which enquireys Mr. Aires gave us as Satisfactory information as he had it
in his power to have Collected in the Illinois which was not a great deel.
soon after we Landed a violent Storm of Thunder Lightning and rain
from the N W. which was violent with hard Claps of thunder and Sharp
Lightning which continued untill 10 P M after which the wind blew hard.
I set up late and partook of the tent of Mr. Aires which was dry. Mr. Aires
unfortunately had his boat Sunk on the 25 of July last by a violent Storm
of Wind and hail by which accident he lost the most of his usefull articles
as he informd. us.   this Gentleman informed us of maney Changes &
misfortunes which had taken place in the Illinois amongst others the loss
of Mr. Cady Choteaus house and furniture by fire.[4]   for this misfortune
of our friend Choteaus I feel my Self very much Concernd &c.   he also
informed us that Genl. Wilkinson[5] was the governor of the Louisiana and
at St. Louis.   300 of the american Troops had been Contuned on the
Missouri a fiew miles above it's mouth, Some disturbance with the Spaniards in the Nackatosh Country[6] is the Cause of their being Called down
to that Country, the Spaniards had taken one of the U, States frigates in
the Mediteranean,[7] Two British Ships of the line had fired on an Ameri-

can Ship in the port of New York, and killed the Capts. brother.[8]   2 Indians had been hung in St. Louis for murder and several others in jale.[9] and that Mr. Burr & Genl. Hambleton fought a Duel, the latter was killed &c. &c.[10] I am happy to find that my worthy friend Capt L's is so well as to walk about with ease to himself &c., we made *60* Miles to day   the river much crowded with Sand bars, which are very differently Situated from what they were when we went up.

1. Vermillion River, first reached on August 24, 1804, joins the Missouri in Clay County, South Dakota, southeast of present Vermillion. Clark called it the "White Stone River" on the westbound trip. *Atlas* map 17; MRC map 29.

2. This location, where they apparently camped for the night, is particularly vague. From the mileage given below it would seem to have been in Union County, South Dakota, or Dakota County, Nebraska, some miles up the Missouri from present Sioux City.

3. James Aird, a Scotsman, had been a trader at Mackinac by 1779 and one of the earliest settlers at Prairie du Chien, in modern Wisconsin, where he was employed by Robert Dickson, one of the leading traders on the upper Mississippi. He is described as a large man, much respected by the Indians. Technically, he declared himself an American citizen for trading purposes in 1805. He seems to have made more than one trip up the Missouri; John Bradbury met him in St. Louis and again at the Omaha village in 1810. During the War of 1812 he served as a British agent, encouraging the Indians of the upper Mississippi to fight against the Americans. After the war he remained at Prairie du Chien, where he died in 1819, apparently working for the American Fur Company. Thwaites (LC), 5:374 n. 2; Bradbury, 87 and n. 50; Cruikshank, 137, 151, 154; Lavender (FW), 58–62, 65–67, 285–86, 290, 439–40 n. 2, 444 n. 13, and passim.

4. This was the house of Jean Pierre Chouteau, the St. Louis fur trader and friend and host of the captains; see March 21, May 3 and 20, 1804. His house burned on the night of February 15, 1805. Thwaites (LC), 5:375 n. 1, erroneously identified the man as Pierre Chouteau, Jr. Such confusion is understandable since family members at various times called both Jean Pierre and his son, Pierre, Jr., by the name Cadet, a French term occasionally used for a younger or second-born son. Foley & Rice, 44, 114, 211.

5. James Wilkinson, after serving in the Revolutionary War, moved to Kentucky in 1784 and became active in politics and in business at New Orleans. He entered the regular army in 1791 and soon became a brigadier general, serving in Anthony Wayne's campaign against the Northwest Territory Indians, during which time Clark served under him and apparently admired him. After Wayne's death in 1796 he became the ranking officer in the U.S. Army; at the same time he was a secret agent in the pay of the Spanish governor of Louisiana. During his service in the West he was engaged in various intrigues in the Spanish borderlands which have never been entirely unraveled. He was governor of Louisiana Territory from 1805 to 1807. He was involved with Aaron Burr in whatever conspiracies Burr had in progress, but when Burr was tried for treason in 1807 Wilkinson

was the chief witness against him, narrowly escaping indictment himself. Wilkinson held an important command on the Canadian border in the War of 1812 and was notably unsuccessful. He died in Mexico in 1825 and was remembered as the general who never won a battle or lost a court martial. Hay & Werner; Weems.

6. The region between Natchitoches, Louisiana, which became part of the United States by the Louisiana Purchase, and Nacogdoches, in eastern Texas, still Spanish territory, was an area of political intrigues, smuggling, and illegal border crossings. In February 1806 American troops took over a Spanish post a few miles west of Natchitoches in Louisiana; the following July a Spanish force of 400 men moved across the Sabine River boundary into the area northwest of Natchitoches. General Wilkinson's mission was to expel the intruders, but the Spanish governor of Texas withdrew his forces west of the Sabine, and he and Wilkinson negotiated an agreement recognizing a "neutral ground" east of the river. Expansionists like Aaron Burr, who had hoped for war as an opportunity to seize Texas and West Florida for the United States, were greatly disappointed. Cook, 476, 486, and passim; Nasatir (BR), 128–29.

7. The U.S. frigate *President* was fired on by Spanish gunboats near Algeciras, Spain, in the fall of 1804, but was not captured.

8. The British warship *Leander* fired on the American merchant ship *Richard* off New York on April 25, 1806, killing one seaman. This was one of the various incidents arising from Britain's policy of impressment of American seamen and seizure of American ships during the Napoleonic wars which eventually led to the War of 1812.

9. The two Indians were probably the Kickapoos called Ouabesca and Ouifumcaka (variously spelled) who were accused of murdering an unidentified white man on December 30, 1805, in Louisiana territory on a prairie opposite the Osage River. In June 1806 a jury found them guilty, and on the following day the two men were sentenced to be hanged by the neck on June 10 "until they be dead, dead, dead." The two men were executed, but Governor Wilkinson pardoned a third Kickapoo, Hononquise, who was implicated in the crime. Information provided by William E. Foley, December 1991.

10. Aaron Burr, Jefferson's vice president, and Alexander Hamilton, the Federalist leader and Washington's Secretary of the Treasury, fought the most famous duel in American history on July 11, 1804, at Weehawken, New Jersey. Hamilton died of his wound.

[Clark]   *Thursday 4th September 1806*

The Musquitors became troublesom early this morning   I rose at the usial hour found all the party as wet as rain could make them.   as we were in want of Some tobacco I purposed to Mr. Airs to furnish us with 4 Carrots for which we would Pay the amount to any Merchant of St. Louis he very readily agreed to furnish us with tobacco and gave to each man as much as it is necessary for them to use between this and St. Louis, an instance of Generossity for which every man of the party appears to ac-

knowledge. Mr. Airs also insisted on our accepting a barrel of flour—
we gave to this gentleman what Corn we Could Spear amounting to about
6 bushels, this Corn was well Calculated for his purpose as he was about
to make his establishment and would have it in his power to hull the Corn
& The flower was very acceptable to us.   we have yet a little flour part of
what we carried up from the Illinois as high as Maria's river and buried it
there untill our return &c.   at 8 A. M   we took our leave and Set out,
and proceeded on very well, at 11 A. M. passed the Enterance of the big
Sieoux River[1] which is low, and at meridian we came too at Floyds Bluff
below the Enterance of Floyds river[2] and assended the hill, with Capt
Lewis and Several men, found the grave had been opened by the nativs
and left half Covered.[3]   we had this grave Completely filled up, and returned to the Canoes and proceeded on to the Sand bar on which we encamped from the 12th to the 20th of August 1804[4] near the Mahar Village,[5] here we came to and derected every wet article put out to dry, all
the bedding of the party and Skins being wet.   as it was late in the evening we deturmined to continue all night.   had issued to each man of the
party a cup of flour.   we See no Species of Game on the river as usial
except wild geese and pelicans. I observed near Sergt Floyds Grave a
number of flurishing black walnut trees,[6] these are the first which I have
seen decending the river.   a little before night Several Guns were heard
below and in a direction towards the Mahar village which induced us to
suspect that Mr. McClellin who we was informed was on his way up to
trade with the Mahars had arived at the Creek below and that those reports of Guns was Some of his party out hunting.   every thing being dry
we derected the Perogue & Canoes to be loaded and in readiness to Set
out in the morning early.   at dark the Musquetors became troublesom
and continued So all night the party obtained but little Sleep—   we
made *36* miles only to daye.

1. The Big Sioux River reaches the Missouri between Union County, South Dakota,
and Woodbury County, Iowa, at Sioux City; the party first passed it on August 21, 1804.
Atlas maps 16, 17; MRC map 28.
2. Floyd River in Woodbury County, passed the day Sergeant Charles Floyd died and
was buried at Sioux City, August 20, 1804. *Atlas* map 16; MRC map 27.
3. In 1810 Clark told Biddle that a Sioux chief encamped near the gravesite had lost a

son and had opened the grave and placed the son's body with Floyd's, "for the purpose of accompanying him to the other world believing the white man's future state was happier than that of the Savages." It is not clear whether the opening of the grave Clark refers to here was this second burial, or whether that was done some time after the party's return. Clark could easily have learned of a later disturbance of the site through his fur trade contacts. It raises the question of whether all the bones buried under the present Sergeant Floyd Monument at Sioux City actually belonged to the sergeant. Biddle Notes [ca. April 1810], Jackson (LLC), 2:541–42; Appleman (LC), 285–87.

4. They camped here again, in either Woodbury County, or in Dakota County, Nebraska, but Clark is mistaken about the date they first came there, which was August 13, 1804. They called it the "Fishing Camp."

5. The Omaha village noted on August 13, 1804, situated just north of Homer in Dakota County, Nebraska. *Atlas* map 16.

6. Black walnut, *Junglans nigra* L., actually extends farther up the Missouri River than Clark allows. However, the walnut probably existed in sheltered ravines and would be noticed only well back from the Missouri floodplain and beyond Clark's view. Barkley, 38; Little (CIH), 134-E.

[Clark]   *Friday 5th September 1806*

The Musquetors being So excessively tormenting that the party was all on board and we Set out at day light and proceeded on very well. here the river is bordered on both [sides?] with timber &c becoms much narrower more Crooked and the Current more rapid and Crouded with Snags or Sawyers than it is above, and continus So all day. We did not meet with McClellen as we expected at the Creek.[1] the report of the guns which was heard must have been the Mahars who most probably have just arrived at their village from hunting the buffalow. this is a Season they usialy return to their village to Secure their Crops of Corn Beens punkins &c &c. proceeded on very well passd. the blue Stone bluff[2] at 3 P. M here the river leaves the high lands and meanders through a low rich bottom. Encamped on the S W Side on a Sand bar at a cut off a little below our Encampment of the 9th of August 1804.[3] haveing made *73* Miles to day— Capt. Lewis still in a Convelesent State. We Saw no game on the Shores to day worth killig only Such as pelicans Geese ducks, Eagles and Hawks &c.—

1. Presumably Omadi Creek in Dakota County, Nebraska, nameless on *Atlas* map 16. They did not meet McClellan until September 12, 1806. MRC map 27.

2. Bluestone Bluff is composed of the light- to dark-gray, sandy, carbonaceous shale of the middle unit of the Lower and Upper Cretaceous Dakota Group. At 3:00 p.m., the sun would have had an azimuth of about 245° and would have been almost directly behind the bluffs; additionally, at that time the sun would have had an altitude of about 35° above the horizon. The bluffs, thus, would have been partly in shadow, a condition which would have enhanced the sensation of a blue coloration. *Atlas* map 15; MRC map 26.

3. This camp would be in Monona County, Iowa, a few miles south of present Onawa, near the southern end of Guard Lake, the old river course. *Atlas* map 15; MRC map 26.

[Clark]   *Saturday 6th of September 1806*

The Musquetors excessively troublesom   we Set out early at the great Cut off[1] Saw a herd of Elk, we landed and Sent out Several hunters to kill Some of the Elk, they returnd. without killing any as the Elk was wild and ran off much fritened. I Sent the two Small Canoes on a head with derections to hunt in two bottoms below, and after a delay of half an hour proceeded on wind-hard a head at the lower point 7 of Pelecan Island a little above the Petite River de Seeoux[2] we met a tradeing boat of Mr. Ag. Choteaux[3] of St Louis bound to the River Jacque to trade with the Yanktons, this boat was in Care of a Mr. Henry Delorn,[4] he had exposed all his loading [*NB: to dry*] and Sent out five of his hands to hunt they Soon arived with an Elk.   we purchased a gallon of whiskey of this man [*NB: promised to pay Choteau who would not receive any pay*] and gave to each man of the party a dram which is the first Spiritious licquor which had been tasted by any of them Since the 4 of July 1805. Several of the party exchanged leather for linen Shirts and beaver for Corse hats. Those men Could inform us nothing more than that all the troops had movd. from the Illinois and that Genl. Wilkinson was prepareing to leave St. Louis. We advised this trader to treat the Tetons with as much Contempt as possible and Stated to him where he would be benefited by such treatment &c &c. and at 1 P. M Set out   those men gave us 2 Shots from a Swivell they had on the bow of their boat which we returned in our turn.   proceeded on about 3 miles and Came up with two of the hunters, they had not killd. any thing.   at 5 miles we over took the Canoe of the other hunters with Shannon in it floating down, the two fields being in the woods behind we Came too on a Sand bar on the N. E. Side[5] and delayed all the after part of the [day?] for the two Fields, Sent out 3 men to hunt

in the bottom up the river and observe if they Saw any Sign of the hunters.   the evening proved Cloudy and the wind blew hard   two pelicans
were killed to day.   we came *30* Miles only to day   the 2 fieldses did not
join us   I think they are below. The Chief & the Squaws & children are
awarey of their journey. Children cry &c.

1. This large cut-off of the Missouri River in Monona County, Iowa, first noticed on
August 8, 1804, appears conspicuously on *Atlas* map 15. MRC map 25.

2. The Little Sioux River in Harrison County, Iowa, first passed on August 8, 1804.
Atlas map 14; MRC map 25.

3. René Auguste Chouteau; see December 11, 1803.

4. Perhaps a relative of David Delaunay; see May 20, 1804. Conceivably the Joseph, or
Pierre, Delaunay who was later an overland Astorian, or Jean Baptiste Delorme, another
Astorian. Lavender (FW), 168–69; Irving (Astor), 273; Ronda (AE), 90, 177, 279. On the
other hand, he may have been a member of the De Laurier family which was prominent
in early Ste. Genevieve and vicinity. Houck, 1 : 343, 2 : 2, 90. Thwaites (LC), 5 : 378, has
"Delorn," but "Delorie" or "Deloree" seem equally valid versions of Clark's script.

5. The camp would be in Harrison County, or in Burt or Washington County, Nebraska, between Little Sioux and Soldier rivers. *Atlas* map 14; MRC map 25.

[Clark]   *Sunday 7th September 1806*

as we were doubtfull that the two fieldses were behind I derected
Sergt. Ordway with 4 men to Continue untill Meridian and if those men
did not arive by that hour to proceed on.   if we met with them at any
Short distance a gun Should be fired which would be a Signal for him to
proceed on.   we had proceeded on about 8 miles by water and the distance through not more than 1 mile when we Saw the fire of those 2 men,
I derected a gun fired as a Signal for Sergt. ordway to proceed on, and
took the boys on board.   they had killed nothing & informed me they
had been Somewhat almd. at our delay, that the distance across from the
little Sieoux river was about 1½ miles only, the bottoms thick and Grass
very high.   we proceded on with a Stiff Breeze ahead   (*note* the *evaperation* on this portion of the Missouri has been noticed as we assended this
river, and it now appears to be greater than it was at that time. I am
obliged to replenish my ink Stand every day with fresh ink at least 9/10 of
which must evaperate.[)][1]   we proceded on to a bottom on the S W Side

352

a little above the Soldiers river² and Came too and Sent out all the hunters.   they killed 3 Elk which was at no great distance   we Sent out the
men and had the flesh brought in Cooked and Dined. Sergt. Ordway
Came up & after takeing a Sumptious Dinner   we all Set out at 4 P M
wind ahead as usial.   at Dusk we came too on the lower part of a Sand
bar on the S W side found the Musquetors excessively tormenting not
withstanding a Stiff breeze from the S. E.   a little after dark the wind
increased the Musquetors dispersed   our Camp of this night is about 2
miles below our Encampment of the 4th of august 1804 assending³   we
came *44* miles to day only—

1. Lewis called attention to evaporation on the upriver trip in his Weather Diary entry
for September 23, 1804.
2. Soldier River, first passed on August 6, 1804, meets the Missouri in Harrison
County, Iowa. *Atlas* map 14; MRC map 24.
3. They camped in either Harrison County, or in Washington County, Nebraska, near
present Blair, Nebraska. *Atlas* map 14; MRC map 24.

[Clark]   *Munday 8th September 1806*

Set out very early this morning, passed an old tradeing house¹ on the S
W Side a few miles above the Council bluffs, at 11 A M we Came too at
the bluffs² and Capt Lewis and myself walked up on the bluffs and
around to examine the Country and Situation more particularly, the
Situation appeared to us eaqually as eligable as when we passed up for an
establishment, the hill high and Commanding with a high rich bottom of
great extent below.   we proceeded on very well   all being anxious to get
to the River Platt to day they ply'd their orers very well, and we arived at
our old encampment at White Catfish Camp³ 12 miles above the river
platt at which place we lay from the 22th to the 26th of July 1804   here
we encamped haveing made 78 Miles to day. The Missouri at this place
does not appear to Contain ⟨as much⟩ more water than it did 1000 Miles
above this, the evaperation must be emence; in the last 1000 miles this
river receives the water 20 rivers and maney Creeks   Several of the
Rivers large and the Size of this river or the quantity of water does not
appcar to increas any—

1. The post first passed on August 4, 1804, south of Blair, Washington County, Nebraska, probably established by James Mackay in 1795; see January 10, 1804. *Atlas* map 14; MRC map 24.

2. The Council Bluff near Fort Calhoun, Washington County, where they camped from July 30 to August 3, 1804, and counciled with the Otos and Missouris. *Atlas* map 13; MRC map 24.

3. The party camped here July 22–27, 1804, near the Mills-Pottawatomie county line, in Iowa. They have now left the area of the large-scale *Atlas* maps. MRC map 23.

[Clark]   *Tuesday 9th September 1806*

Set out early at 8 A. M   passed the enterance of the great river Platt[1] which is at this time low the water nearly clear the Current turbelant as usial; the Sand bars which Choked up the Missouri and Confined the [river?] to a narrow Snagey Chanel are wastd a way and nothing remains but a fiew Small remains of the bear [bar] which is covered with drift wood, below the R. Platt the Current of the Missouri becomes evidently more rapid than above and the Snags much more noumerous and bad to pass   late in the evening we arived at the Bald pated prarie[2] and encamped imediately opposit our encampment of the 16th and 17th of July 1804.[3]   haveing made 73 miles only to day. The river bottoms are extencive rich and Covered with tall large timber, and the hollows of the reveins may be Said to be covered with timber Such as Oake ash Elm and Some walnut & hickory.[4]   our party appears extreamly anxious to get on, and every day appears produce new anxieties in them to get to their Country and friends. My worthy friend Cap Lewis has entirely recovered his wounds are heeled up and he Can walk and even run nearly as well as ever he Could.   the parts are yet tender &c. &.

The Musquetors are yet troublesom, tho' not So much So as they were above the River platt.   the Climate is every day preceptably wormer and air more Sultery than I have experienced for a long time.   the nights are now So worm that I sleep Comfortable under a thin blanket, a fiew days past 2 was not more than Sufficient

1. They first reached the Platte, which mouths between Cass and Sarpy counties in Nebraska, on July 21, 1804. MRC map 22.

2. Clark first noted the bald-pated prairie, in Fremont County, Iowa, and Atchison County, Missouri, on July 16, 1804. MRC map 21.

3. The camp would be in Nemaha County, Nebraska, or Atchison County, Missouri, northeast of Peru, Nebraska. MRC map 21; MRR map 58.

4. The tall and large timber of the bottoms is primarily plains cottonwood and sycamore, *Platanus occidentalis* L. Two common species of hickory, bitternut hickory, *Carya cordiformis* (Wang.) K. Koch, and shagbark hickory, *C. ovata* (Mill.) K. Koch, are associated with bur oak, green ash, American elm, and black walnut in the sheltered ravines as described. Barkley, 32, 36–37; Little (CIH), 147-E. Clark provides a description of the Missouri River vegetation of this general area in his entry for July 30, 1804.

[Clark]   *Wednesday 10th of September 1806*

we Set out very early this morning and proceeded on very well with wind moderately a head   at [*blank*] P M we met a Mr. Alexander La fass and three french men from St. Louis in a Small perogue on his way to the River Platt to trade with the Pania Luup or Wolf Indians.[1]   this man was extreemly friendly to us he offered us any thing he had, we accepted of a bottle of whisky only which we gave to our party, Mr. la frost informed us that Genl. Wilkinson and all the troops had decended the Mississippi and Mr. Pike and young Mr. Wilkinson had Set out on an expedition up the Arkansaw river or in that direction[2]   after a delay of half an hour we proceedd on about 3 miles and met a large perogue and 7 Men from St. Louis bound to the Mahars for the purpose of trade, this perogue was in Charge of a Mt. La Craw,[3] we made Some ficw enquiries of this man and again proceeded on through a very bad part of the river Crouded with Snags & Sawyers and incamped on a Sand bar about 4 miles above the Grand Nemahar.[4]   we find the river in this timbered Country narrow and more moveing Sands and a much greater quantity of Sawyers or Snags than above. Great caution and much attention is required to Stear Clear of all those dificuelties in this low State of the water.   we made 65 Miles to day.   we Saw Deer rackoons and turkies on the Shores to day one of the men killed a racoon[5] which the indians very much admired.

1. For the Wolf, Loup, or Skiri Pawnees, see April 12, August 3, 1804, and Fort Mandan Miscellany, vol. 3.

2. Zebulon Montgomery Pike, a young army officer, had carried out an expedition to the upper Mississippi in 1805. In July 1806 he set out with a small party to traverse the central Great Plains to the headwaters of the Arkansas River, with the intention of returning down the Red River. Unlike Lewis and Clark, his orders came not from President Jefferson but from General James Wilkinson, whose son Lieutenant James B. Wilkinson

accompanied the party part of the way. Pike followed the Arkansas to its upper reaches in present Colorado, discovered but did not climb Pike's Peak, and apparently became lost in the mountains. He was captured by the Spanish authorities of New Mexico, who claimed the territory he had entered and who feared he might be the vanguard of an American army of invasion. Historians now believe that General Wilkinson did indeed have some ulterior purpose, which Pike may or may not have been aware of, but no solid proof has come to light. The Spanish conveyed Pike and his men through northern Mexico and Texas before returning him to the United States in 1807. Some people accused Pike of involvement in Aaron Burr's conspiracies but he was able to continue his army career. He became a brigadier general in the War of 1812, led an invasion into Canada, and was killed there in 1813. Hollon; Jackson (JP); Nasatir (BR), 141–43.

3. This party was bound for the Omaha village in Dakota County, Nebraska. The man in charge was probably Joseph La Croix, an Englishman in spite of his name, who perhaps worked for James Aird. He reportedly cut prices greatly, defeated his competitor Robert McClellan, and even so did not make a profit. Lavender (FW), 66, 74.

4. The camp on the sandbar would have been in either Richardson County, Nebraska, or Holt County, Missouri, above the Big Nemaha River near Rulo, Nebraska. MRC map 19.

5. *Procyon lotor*.

[Clark]   *Thursday 11th Septr. 1806*

a heavy Cloud and wind from the N W. detained us untill after Sunrise at which time we Set out and proceeded on very well, passed the nema-har[1] which was low and did not appear as wide as when we passed up. Wolf river[2] Scercely runs at all, at 3 P. M we halted a little above the Nadawa river[3] on the S. Side of the Missouri to kill Some meat that which we killed a fiew days past being all Spoiled. Sent out 6 hunters they killed and brought in two Deer only, we proceeded on a fiew miles below the Nadawa Island and encamped on a Small Isld. near the N. E. Side,[4] have-ing Came 40 Miles only to day, river rapid and in maney places Crouded with Snag's. I observe on the Shores much deer Sign— the [mosqui-toes?] are no longer troublesome on the river, from what cause they are noumerous above and not So on this part of the river I cannot account. Wolves were howling in different directions this evening after we had en-camped, and the barking of the little prarie wolves resembled those of our Common Small Dogs that ¾ of the party believed them to be the dogs of Some boat assending which was yet below us. the barking of those little wolves I have frequently taken notice of on this as also the other Side of the Rocky mountains, and their Bark so much resembles or Sounds to me like our Common Small Cur dogs that I have frequently mistaken them for that Speces of dog— The papaws nearly ripe—.

1. The Big Nemaha River, which the party reached on July 11, 1804, joins the Missouri in Richardson County, Nebraska. MRC map 19.

2. Wolf Creek in Doniphan County, Kansas, first passed on July 9, 1804. MRM map 51.

3. The party first reached the Nodaway River on July 8, 1804; the mouth, which may have shifted since Lewis and Clark's time, now lies between Holt and Andrew counties, Missouri. On this occasion the party apparently halted on the Doniphan County side of the Missouri. MRC map 18.

4. Nodaway Island was first noted on July 8, 1804; the camp would probably be in either Andrew or Buchanan County, Missouri, most likely the former. MRC map 18.

[Clark]   *Friday 12th of September 1806*

a thick fog a litile before day which blew of[f] at day light. a heavy Dew this morning. we Set out at Sunrise the usial hour and proceeded on very well about 7 miles met 2 perogues from St. Louis one contained the property of Mr. Choteau bound to the panias on River Platt, the other going up trapping as high as the Mahars. here we met one of the french men who had accompanied us as high as the Mandans he informed us that Mr. McClellen was a fiew miles below the wind blew a head Soon after we pased those perogues, we Saw a man on Shore who informed us that he was one of Mr. McClellens party and that he was a Short distance below, we took this man on board and proceeded on and Met Mr. McClellin[1] at the St. Michl. Prarie[2] we came too here we found Mr. Jo. Gravelin[3] the Ricaras enterpreter whome we had Sent down with a Ricaras Chief in the Spring of 1805 and old Mr. Durion[4] the Sieux enterpreter, we examined the instructions of those interpreters and found that Gravelin was ordered to the Ricaras with a Speach from the president of the U. States to that nation[5] and some presents which had been given the Ricara Cheif who had visited the U. States and unfortunately died at the City of Washington, he was instructed to teach the Ricaras agriculture & make every enquirey after Capt Lewis my self and the party— Mr. Durion was enstructed to accompany Gravelin and through his influence pass him with his presents & by the tetons bands of Sieux, and to provale on Some of the Principal chiefs of those bands not exceeding six to Visit the Seat of the Government next Spring he was also enstructed to make every enquirey after us. we made Some Small addition to his instructions by extending the number of Chiefs to 10 or 12 or 3 from each band including the Yanktons &c. Mr. McClellin receved us very politely, and gave us all the news and occurrences which had taken place in the Illinois within his knowledge the evening proveing to be wet and Cloudy we Concluded to continue all night, we despatched the two Canoes a head to hunt with 5 hunters in them[6]

1. Robert McClellan was already known to Lewis and Clark. He served from 1790 to 1795 as a scout with the U.S. Army in Anthony Wayne's campaigns against the tribes of the Northwest Territory, during which time he had a number of adventures, acquired a considerable reputation, and rose to the rank of lieutenant. For several years he engaged in rather unsuccessful trading ventures on the Missouri, becoming a bitter enemy of Manuel Lisa. In 1810 he joined the overland expedition of the Astorians and went with them to the Columbia. In 1812 he returned overland with Robert Stuart, in the first white party through South Pass in Wyoming. He died in 1815 in Saint Louis and was buried on the farm of his old comrade William Clark. Carter (RM); Irving (Astor), 114–15, and passim; Lavender (FW), 73–75, 88–90, 146–60, 170–77, 192–93, and passim; Oglesby, 32–33, 53, 80, 99–100, 104, 112–13.

2. The site of their camp for this day, St. Michael's Prairie in Buchanan County, Missouri, at present St. Joseph, was first noted on July 7, 1804. MRC map 17.

3. The captains met Joseph Gravelines at the Arikara villages on October 8, 1804, employed him during the winter at Fort Mandan, and sent him to Washington with the unfortunate Arikara chief in the spring of 1805.

4. Pierre Dorion, Sr., again.

5. By this message Jefferson attempted to reassure the Arikaras that there was no foul play in the chief's death and retain their friendship for the United States; he was not successful. Jefferson to the Arikaras, April 11, 1806, Jackson (LLC), 1:306.

6. The remaining half-page (p. 62 of Codex N) is blank after this entry. The entry of September 13 begins at the top of the next page.

[Clark]   *Saturday 13th September 1806*

rose early   Mr. McClellen [*NB: an old acquaintance in the army*] gave each man a Dram[1] and a little after Sunrise we Set out   the wind hard a head from the S E   at 8 A M we landed at the Camp of the 5 hunters ⟨which⟩ whome we had Sent a head, they had killed nothing, the wind being too high for us to proceed in Safty through the emecity of Snags which was imediately below we concluded to lye by and Sent on the Small Canoes a Short distance to hunt and kill Some meat, we Sent out 2 men in the bottom they Soon returned with one turky and informed that the rushes was so high and thick that it was impossible to kill any deer. I felt my Self very unwell and derected a little Chocolate which Mr. McClellen gave us, prepared of which I drank about a pint and found great relief at 11 A. M. we proceeded on about 1 mile and come up with the hunters who had killed 4 deer, here we delayed untill 5 P. M when the hunters all joined us and we again proceded on down a fiew miles and encamped on the N E Side of the Missouri haveing decended 18 Miles only to day.[2] the day disagreeably worm.   one man George Shannon left his horn and pouch with his powder ball and knife and did not think of it untill night. I walked in the bottom in the thick rushes and the Growth of timber Common to the Illinois Such as cotton wood, Sycamore, ash[3] mulberry,[4] Elm of different Species,[5] walnut, hickory, horn beem,[6] pappaw arrow wood[7] willow,[8] prickly ash,[9] &c and Grape vines,[10] pees of 3 species[11] &c &c. Birds most Common the buzzard Crow the hooting owl[12] and hawks, &c. &c.—

1. In conversations with Biddle in 1810 Clark commented under this date that some of the men had been weaned from liquor, others had not. But the former eventually "relapsed into their old habits." Biddle Notes [ca. April 1810], Jackson (LLC), 2:544.

2. This camp would be in Buchanan County, Missouri, or Doniphan County, Kansas, in the vicinity of the "yellow oaker" creek of July 5, 1804 (perhaps Brush Creek in Doniphan County), and the camp of that day. MRC map 17.

3. At this point on the Missouri, the ash could be either white ash or green ash.

4. Red mulberry, *Morus rubra* L. Little (CIH), 139-E.

5. Probably slippery elm and the more common American elm described from higher on the river. The rarer rock elm, *Ulmus thomasi* Sarg., is also known from the area. Barkley, 34.

6. American hornbeam, *Carpinus caroliniana* Walt. Little (CIH), 109-E.

7. Black haw, *Viburnum prunifolium* L. The term arrowwood is often used to refer to the whole genus *Viburnum*. Barkley, 330; Fernald, 1338–42.

8. Black willow, *Salix nigra* Marsh. Barkley, 104; Little (CIH), 190-E.

9. Prickly ash, *Zanthoxylum americanum* Mill. Barkley, 225.

10. Probably river-bank grape, but it could be any of several species of *Vitis* in the area. Barkley, 219–20.

11. Probably hog peanut, wild bean, *Strophostyles helvola* (L.) Ell., and possibly ground nut, *Apios americana* Medic. All are pea-like, are known from the area, and show pea-like fruits at this time of year. Barkley, 158, 183, 159.

12. Great horned owl, *Bubo virginianus* [AOU, 375]. Holmgren, 32.

[Clark]   *Sunday 14th Sept. 1806*

Set out early and proceeded on very well.   this being the part of the Missouri the Kanzas nation[1] resort to at this Season of the year for the purpose of robbing the perogues passing up to other nations above, we have every reason to expect to meet with them, and agreeably to their Common Custom of examining every thing in the perogues and takeing what they want out of them, it is probable they may wish to take those liberties with us, which we are deturmined not to allow of and for the Smallest insult we Shall fire on them.   at 2 P. M. a little below the lower of the old Kanzas Village[2] we met three large boats bound to the Yanktons and Mahars the property of Mr. Lacroy, Mr. Aiten & Mr. Coutau[3] all from St. Louis, those young men received us with great friendship and pressed on us Some whisky for our men, Bisquet, Pork and Onions, & part of their Stores, we continued near 2 hours with those boats, makeing every enquirey into the state of our friends and Country &c.   those men were much affraid of meeting with the Kanzas.   we Saw 37 Deer on the banks and in the river to Day 5 of which we killed[4] those deer were Meager.   we proceeded on to an Island near the middle of the river below our encampment of the 1st of July 1804 and encamped[5] haveing decended only 53 miles to day.   our party received a dram and Sung Songs untill 11 oClock at night in the greatest harmoney.

1. For the Kansa, or Kaw, Indians, see June 5, 1804. "The Kanzas" is written over some other word.

2. Probably the village noted on July 2, 1804, in northeast Leavenworth County, Kansas. They are now near present Fort Leavenworth. MRC map 16.

3. This may be Charles Courtin, first referred to on September 15, 1804. He traded with the Teton Sioux, the Arikaras, and the Poncas, and is believed to have reached the Three Forks of the Missouri and to have been killed in western Montana in 1809. Osgood (FN), 136 n. 6; Josephy, 660–63; Jackson (LLC), 2:437 n. 3.

4. Gibson shot one from a canoe, according to Ordway.

5. The camp of July 1, 1804, was on Leavenworth Island, opposite present Leavenworth, Kansas. MRC map 15.

[Clark]   *Monday 15th of September 1806*

we set out early with a Stiff Breeze a head   saw Several deer Swiming the river soon after we Set out.   at 11 A. M. passed the enterance of the Kanzas river[1] which was very low, about a mile below we landed and Capt Lewis and my Self assended a hill which appeared to have a Commanding Situation for a fort, the Shore is bold and rocky imediately at the foot of the hill,[2] from the top of the hill you have a perfect Command of the river, this hill fronts the Kanzas and has a view of the Missouri a Short distance above that river.   we landed one time only to let the men geather Pappaws or the Custard apple of which this Country abounds, and the men are very fond of.   we discovered a Buck Elk on a Small Island, and sent the 2 fields and Shannon in pursute of it   they Soon Came up with and killed the Elk, he was large and in fine order we had his flesh Secured and divided.   as the winds were unfabourable the greater part of the day we only decended <u>49</u> Miles and encamped a Short distance Above Hay Cabin Creek.[3]   we are not tormented by the Musquetors in this lower portion of the river, as we were above the river plat and as high up as the Rochejhone and for a fiew miles up that river, and above its' enterance into the Missouri.   we passd Some of the most Charming bottom lands to day and the uplands by no means bad, all well timberd.   the weather disagreeably worm and if it was not for the constant winds which blow from the S. and S E. we Should be almost Suficated Comeing out of a northern Country open and Cool between the Latd. of 46° and 49° North in which we had been for nearly two years, rapidly decending into a woody Country in a wormer Climate between the Latds. 38° & 39° North is probably the Cause of our experiencing the heat much more Senceable than those who have Continued within the parralel of Latitude.

1. The Kansas River was first reached on June 26, 1804; it joins the Missouri in Wyandotte County, Kansas. MRC map 14.

2. The hill would be in downtown Kansas City, in Jackson County, Missouri. MRC map 14.

3. As on other occasions on this downriver journey, Clark does not indicate which side of the river the camp was on; it would be in either Jackson or Clay County, Missouri. "Hay Cabin Creek," first passed on June 24, 1804, is the present Little Blue River in Jackson County. MRC map 13.

[Clark]   *Tuesday 16th September 1806*

we Set out early this morning and proceded on tolerably well   the Day proved excessively worm and disagreeable, So much So that the men rowed but little, at 10 A M we met a large tradeing perogue bound for the Panias we continued but a Short time with them.   at 11 A. M we met young Mr. Bobidoux[1] with a large boat of six ores and 2 Canoes, the licenes of this young man was to trade with the Panias Mahars and ottoes reather an extroadanary a license for [so] young a man and without the Seal of the teritory anexed, as Genl. Wilkensons Signeture was not to this instrement we were Somewhat doubtfull of it. Mr. Browns Signeture we were not acquainted with without the Teritorial Seal.   we made Some enquireys of this young man and Cautioned him against prosueing the Steps of his brother in attempting to degrade the American Charector in the eyes of the Indians.   we proceeded on to an Island a little above our encampment of the 16th & 17th of June 1804 haveing Came 52 miles only to day.[2]

1. Ordway and Gass both say that this party was bound to trade with the Kansa Indians. Several members of the Robidoux family of Saint Louis, over several generations, were leaders in the fur trade. Joseph Robidoux, probably the young man the party met here, had established a trading post at the site of St. Joseph, Missouri, in 1800 and is regarded as the founder of that city. His license to trade had apparently been issued by the territorial secretary, Joseph Browne, in the absence of the governor, General Wilkinson. Lewis, in an "Essay on an Indian Policy," later expressed further suspicions that the Robidoux family were fomenting disloyalty to the United States among the Indians, but Clark evidently changed his mind about them, since he granted trading licenses to them as superintendent of Indian affairs. Joseph Robidoux later operated his St. Joseph post for the American Fur Company and continued to play an important role in the western fur trade for many years. Mattes (JR); Lavender (FW), 78; Coues (HLC), 3:1236 and n.7, 1243.

2. The camp of June 16, 1804, was in Carroll County, Missouri, nearly opposite the present town of Waverly. The June 17 camp was about a mile above this. The island where they now camped would be between Carroll and Lafayette counties, a few miles up the Missouri from Waverly. MRC map 12.

[Clark]   *Wednesday 17th September 1806*

We Set out as usial early   pass the Island of the little Osage Village[1] which is considered by the navigater of this river to be the worst place in it.   at this place water of the Missouri is confined between an Island and the S E main Shore and passes through a narrow chanel for more than 2 miles which is crouded with Snags in maney places quite across obligeing the navigater to pick his passage between those Snags as he can, in maney places the current passing with great velocity against the banks which cause them to fall &c. at 11 A. M. we met a Captain McClellin[2] late a Capt. of Artily of the U States Army assending in a large boat. this gentleman an acquaintance of my friend Capt. Lewis was Somewhat astonished to See us return and appeared rejoiced to meet us. we found him a man of information and from whome we received a partial account of the political State of our Country, we were makeing enquires and exchangeing answers &c. untill near mid night. this Gentleman informed us that we had been long Since given out by the people of the U S Generaly and almost forgotton, the President of the U. States had yet hopes of us;[3] we received some civilities of Capt. McClellin, he gave us Some Buisquit, Chocolate Sugar & whiskey, for which our party were in want and for which we made a return of a barrel of corn & much obliges to him. Capt. McClellin informed us that he was on reather a speculative expedition to the confines of New Spain, with the view to entroduce a trade with those people. his plan is to proceede up this river to the Entcrance of the river platt there to form an establishment from which to trade partially with the Panas & Ottoes, to form an acquaintance with the Panias and provail Some of their principal Chiefs to accompany him to Santa Fee where he will appear in a stile calculated to atract the Spanish government in that quarter and through the influence of a handsome present he expects to be promited to exchange his merchindize for Silver & gold of which those people abound. he has a kind of introductory Speach from Govr. Wilkinson to the Panias and Ottoes and a quantity of presents of his own which he purposes distributing to the Panias and ELeatans[4] with a view to gain their protection in the execution of his plans, if the Spanish Governmt. favour his plans, he purposes takeing his merchendize on mules & horses which Can easily be procured of the panias, to Some point convenient to the Spanish Settlements within the Louisiana Teritory to which place the inhabitants of New mexico may meet him for the purpose of trade &c. Capt McClellins plan I think a very good one if strictly prosued &c.

we Sent 5 hunters a head with directions to halt below Grand river and hunt untill we arived which would be in the morning. This day proved worme.   we decended only 30 miles to day and encamped 4 miles above Grand river on S E. Side.[5]

1. Clark refers to the Little Osage village and the danger of the river in the vicinity on June 15, 1804. The village would have been in Saline County, Missouri, in the neighborhood of Malta Bend. MRC map 11.

2. John McClallen, or McClellan, who should not be confused with Robert McClellan, was a New Yorker. He entered the army in 1794 as a lieutenant of artillery, was promoted to captain in 1798, and resigned in January 1806, probably to undertake the venture Clark refers to here. He was an associate of General Wilkinson, who may have been a secret backer of his enterprise. His movements after meeting Lewis and Clark are mysterious, but it appears he did not make his way to New Mexico. The regular commerce between Missouri and Santa Fe did not begin until 1821. There is some evidence that McClallen continued on up the Missouri, wintered in South Dakota, then traveled on to the Three Forks and finally established a trading post in the Flathead country in western Montana. In 1807 David Thompson of the North West Company, operating on the upper Columbia River in British Columbia, received messages from an American who claimed to be a U.S. Army officer, giving the name of Pinch or Perch, who warned Thompson that he was trespassing on American territory, which was not true. This person has never been identified, but McClallen is as likely a candidate as any. It would also appear that he and his men became involved in hostilities between the Flatheads and the Blackfeet and were killed by the latter in 1810. It has been speculated that Pierre Cruzatte, Joseph Field, and John B. Thompson of Lewis and Clark's party returned up the Missouri after reaching St. Louis, joined McClallen, and were among those killed with him, although there is no clear evidence. See Appendix A, vol. 2. Heitman, 655; Majors; Josephy, 42, 657–60; Nasatir (BR), 142.

3. According to Sergeant Ordway, Robert McClellan told them on September 12 that "the people in general in the United States were concerned about us as they had heard that we were all killed   then again they heard that the Spanyards had us in the mines &C." The Spanish had, in fact, made attempts to stop the expedition. Spain still had a claim on the Pacific Northwest, and the Spanish government, like Lewis and Clark, believed the headwaters of the Missouri to be much closer to New Mexico than was actually the case. Between 1804 and 1806 the government of New Spain sent no less than four expeditions from New Mexico out onto the Great Plains to intercept the party, either going or coming back. The first three were led by the great trailblazer Pedro Vial and the last, the largest Spanish expedition to cross the plains, by Facundo Melgares. The first and the last came within several days' travel of the American party but were defeated by logistical problems and lack of Indian cooperation. Cook, 453–85; Loomis & Nasatir, xxi–xxii, 181–204, 428–30.

4. For the Eliatans, or Aliatans—in this case perhaps Comanches—see April 1, 1805.

5. The Grand River, first passed by the party on June 13, 1804, now meets the Missouri between Carroll and Chariton counties, Missouri; the mouth may have been farther upstream in 1806. The camp would have been in Saline County. MRC map 10. Following this entry is a blank page (p. 69 of Codex N).

[Clark]   *Thursday 18th of September 1806*

we rose early   Capt McClellin wrote a letter and we took our leave, and procceded on   passed the Grand river at 7 A M.   a Short distance below we came up with our hunters, they had killed nothing.   at 10 oClock we Came too and gathered pottows to eate   we have nothing but a fiew Buisquit to eate and are partly compelled to eate poppows which we find in great quantities on the Shores, the weather we found excessively hot as usial.   the lands fine particularly the bottoms.   a charming Oake bottom on the S E Side of the Missouri above the 2 Charletons rivers[1] we find the Current of this part of the Missouri much more jentle than it was as we assended, the water is now low and where it is much confin'd   it is rapid.   we saw very little appearance of deer, Saw one bear at a distance and 3 turkeys only to day.   our party   entirely out of provisions Subsisting on poppaws.   we divide the buiskit which amounted to nearly one buisket per man, this in addition to the poppaws is to last is down to the Settlement's which is 150 miles   the party appear perfectly contented and tell us that they can live very well on the pappaws.   we made 52 miles to day only.   one of our party J. Potts complains very much of one of his eyes which is burnt by the Sun from exposeing his face without a cover from the Sun. Shannon also complains of his face & eyes &c. Encamped on an Island nearly opposit to the enterance of Mine river[2]

1. The Chariton River meets the Missouri in Chariton County, Missouri; the party first passed it on June 10, 1804. MRC map 10.
2. The party first passed Lamine River on June 8, 1804; it joins the Missouri in Cooper County, Missouri, a few miles above Booneville. MRC map 9.

[Clark]   *Friday 19th of Sept. 1806*

Set out this morning a little after day & proceeded on very well   the men ply their oares & we decended with great velocity, only Came too once for the purpose of gathering pappows, our anxiety as also the wish of the party to proceed on as expeditiously as possible to ⟨get to⟩ the Illinois enduce us to continue on without halting to hunt. we Calculate on ariveing at the first Settlements on tomorrow evening which is 140 miles, and objecet of our party is to divide the distance into two days, this day to the Osarge River, and tomorrow to the Charriton a Small french Village—[1] we arived at the Enterance of Osage River at dark and encamped on the Spot we had encamped on the 1st & 2d of June 1804 haveing Came 72 miles.[2] a very singular disorder is takeing place amongst our party that of the Sore eyes. three of the party have their eyes inflamed and Sweled in Such a manner as to render them extreamly painfull, particularly when exposed to the light, the eye ball is much inflaimed and the lid appears burnt with the Sun, the cause of this complaint of the eye I can't [account?] for. from it's Sudden appearance I am willing to believe it may be owing to the reflection of the Sun on the water[3]

1. La Charette in Warren County, Missouri, which they did indeed reach the next day. Clark here confuses the name with that of the Chariton River.

2. Osage River mouths on the Osage-Cole county line, Missouri; the camp of June 1–3, 1804, and of this date, would be just above the river in Cole County, near Osage City. MRC map 6.

3. Chuinard (OOMD), 395, believes the symptoms strongly suggest infectious conjunctivitis. However, the problem may be related to the diet of pawpaws; handling the fruit can cause dermatitis, and if the men were wiping sweat from faces and eyes this might explain the inflammation. Rogers.

[Clark]   *Saturday 20th Septr. 1806*

as three of the party was unabled to row from the State of their eyes we found it necessary to leave one of our Crafts and divide the men into the other Canoes, we left the two Canoes lashed together which I had made high up the River Rochejhone, those Canoes we Set a drift and a little after day light we Set out and proceeded on very well. The Osage river very low and discharges but a Small quantity of water at this time for so large a river. at meridian we passed the enterance of the Gasconnade river[1] below which we met a perogue with 5 french men bound to the

Osarge Gd. village.² the party being extreemly anxious to get down ply their ores very well, we Saw Some cows on the bank which was a joyfull Sight to the party and Caused a Shout to be raised for joy at [*blank*] P M we Came in Sight of the little french Village called Charriton [*NB: Char-rette*]³ the men raised a Shout and Sprung upon their ores and we soon landed opposit to the Village. our party requested to be permited to fire off their Guns which was alowed & they discharged 3 rounds with a harty Cheer, which was returned from five tradeing boats which lay opposit the village. we landed and were very politely received by two young Scotch men from Canada one in the employ of Mr. Aird a Mr. [*blank*]⁴ and the other Mr. Reed,⁵ two other boats the property of Mr. Lacomb & Mr. [*blank*] all of those boats were bound to the Osage and Ottoes. those two young Scotch gentlemen furnished us with Beef flower and Some pork for our men, and gave us a very agreeable supper. as it was like to rain we accepted of a bed in one of their tents. we purchased of a Citizen two gallons of Whiskey for our party for which we were obliged to give Eight dollars in Cash, an imposition on the part of the Citizen. every person, both French and americans Seem to express great pleasure at our return, and acknowledged them selves much astonished in Seeing us return. they informed us that we were Supposed to have been lost long Since, and were entirely given out by every person &c.

Those boats are from Canada in the batteaux form and wide in perpotion to their length. their length about 30 feet and the width 8 feet & pointed bow & Stern, flat bottom and rowing Six ores only the Skeneckeity⁶ form. those Bottoms are prepared for the navigation of this river, I beleive them to be the best Calculated for the navigation of this river of any which I have Seen. ⟨not⟩ they are wide and flat not Subject to the dangers of the roleing Sands, which larger boats are on this river. the American inhabitants express great disgust for the govermt of this Teritory. from what I can lern it arises from a disapmt. of getting all the Spanish Grants Confirmed—.⁷ Came 68 ms. to day.

1. They first reached the Gasconade River on May 27, 1804; it enters the Missouri in Gasconade County, Missouri. MRC map 5.

2. For the Osages see May 31, 1804. Whether these traders were bound for the Osages on the Osage River or on the Arkansas River is not indicated.

3. La Charette, in Warren County, Missouri, has since been washed away by the Missouri; the party first passed it on May 25, 1804. MRC map 4.

4. This unnamed young man may have been Ramsay Crooks, then a nineteen-year-old Scottish immigrant working for Robert Dickson and James Aird. In the next few years he would be a partner of Robert McClellan in trading ventures on the Missouri, then in 1810 he joined the overland Astorians under Wilson Price Hunt and went to the mouth of the Columbia with them in 1811. In 1812–13 he returned east with Robert Stuart's overland party through South Pass. For over twenty years thereafter he was an executive with John Jacob Astor's American Fur Company, concentrating his activities in the upper Great Lakes region and becoming one of the major figures of the fur trade. When the Astor organization split up in 1834 Crooks became head of its successor company on the Lakes and continued in the trade in one way or another until his death in 1859. Carter (RC); Lavender (FW), 78, and passim; Irving (Astor), 108, 114, 126–27, and passim.

5. Reed's identity is not clear. David Lavender believes that he was named James and that he was, like Crooks, an employee of Robert Dickson and James Aird. Lavender also suggests that he might be the same as the John Reed who was with the overland Astorians on their journey to the Pacific. He was killed by Indians, with several other Astorians including Pierre Dorion, Junior, in Idaho in 1814. Lavender (FW), 71–72, 74–75, 78, 80–81, 93, 131, 160, 165–67, 170, 171, 174, 215, 445 n. 14, 449 n. 9; Irving (Astor), 130, 446–49, and passim.

6. Schenectady boats were first built in the city of that name and were used extensively on the rivers of western New York and the upper Saint Lawrence. Amos Stoddard judged them better for shallow water than keelboats. Long, 213 n. 105; Stoddard, 303.

7. Spain offered free land to attract Anglo-American settlers to Spanish Louisiana, but because of the abundance of land and the smallness of the region's population few residents attempted to follow the cumbersome process required for securing a completed title. Prior to 1804 local officials accepted uncompleted concessions as authorization to hold lands and raised no questions when they were sold or inherited. Some of the early French settlers and even more of the incoming Anglo-Americans simply squatted on the land without bothering to request a formal concession from the Spanish authorities. Following the Louisiana Purchase, many residents scurried to secure formal titles for their holdings. Reports of widespread fraud made Congress reluctant to authorize wholesale confirmation of the Spanish land titles of Upper Louisiana. A barrage of complaints from territorial residents led to the appointment of a commission to examine and adjust these claims. The controversies persisted for many years, and as territorial officials both Lewis and Clark subsequently found themselves embroiled in the contentious business. Foley, 99–100, 143–44, 148, 158, 170–74. This passage is struck through with vertical lines. Perhaps the captains wanted to distance themselves from the politically explosive matter.

[Clark]   *Sunday 21st Septr. 1806*[1]

rose early this morning   Colected our men   Several of them had accepted of the invitation of the Citizens and visited their families.   at half after 7 A. M we Set out.   passed 12 canoes of Kickapoos[2] assending on a hunting expedition. Saw Several persons also Stock of different kind on the bank which reviv'd the party very much.   at 3 P M we met two large boats assending.   at 4 P M we arived in Sight of St. Charles,[3] the party rejoiced at the Sight of this hospital village plyed thear ores with great dexterity and we Soon arived opposit the Town, this day being Sunday we observed a number of Gentlemen and ladies walking on the bank, we Saluted the Village by three rounds from our blunderbuts and the Small arms of the party, and landed near the lower part of the town.   we were met by great numbers of the inhabitants, we found them excessively polite.   we received invitations from Several of those Gentlemen a Mr. Proulx,[4] Taboe,[5] Decett,[6] Tice Dejonah & Quarie and several who were pressing on us to go to their houses, we could only visit Mr. Proulx and Mr. Deucett in the course of the evening. Mr. Querie under took to Supply our party with provisions &c.   the inhabitants of this village appear much delighted at our return and seem to vie with each other in their politeness to us all.   we Came only 48 miles today.   the banks of the river thinly Settled &c.   [NB: *some Settlements since we went up*]

1. Lewis apparently began a letter to Jefferson this day which he did not complete. Possibly it was misdated, since the dateline reads "St. Louis," but the poor hand suggests it was written in a boat. Lewis to Jefferson, September 21, 1806, Jackson (LLC), 1:317–19.

2. The captains had encountered Kickapoos in Illinois and Missouri at various times before the start of the expedition and in its early stages. See March 21, May 5, 17, and 22, 1804.

3. The party first arrived in St. Charles, in St. Charles County, Missouri, on May 16, 1804. MRC map 2.

4. Basil Proulx was an early inhabitant of St. Charles. Thwaites (LC), 5:392 n. 1.

5. This could be Pierre-Antoine Tabeau, whom the captains first met at the Arikara villages on October 9, 1804. There were other Tabeaus in Missouri, however, and Tibeau, Thibault, and Tabot were other surnames to be found in the region. Houck, 2:68–69.

6. Clark first met François Duquette on May 16, 1804.

[Clark]   *Monday 22nd of Sept. 1806*

This morning being very wet and the rain Still Continueing hard, and our party being all Sheltered in the houses of those hospitable people, we did not [think?] proper to proceed on untill after the rain was over, and continued at the house of Mr. Proulx. I took this oppertunity of writeing to my friends in Kentucky &c.[1]   at 10 A M. it seased raining and we Colected our party and Set out and proceeded on down to the Contonemt. at Coldwater Creek about 3 miles up the Missouri on it's Southern banks,[2] at this place we found Colo. Hunt[3] & a Lieut Peters[4] ⟨in Command of⟩ & one Company of Artillerists   we were kindly received by the Gentlemen of this place. Mrs. Wilkinson the Lady of the Govr. & Genl. we wer Sorry to find in delicate health.[5]

we were honored with a Salute of [*blank*] Guns and a harty welcom— at this place there is a publick Store kept in which I am informed the U. S have 60000$ worth of indian Goods[6]

1. Probably not the letter that was eventually sent to Clark's relatives in Kentucky; see September 24, 1806.

2. Fort Bellefontaine was in Saint Louis County, Missouri, near the mouth of Coldwater Creek. When established in 1805 by General Wilkinson, it was the first United States fort west of the Mississippi, and included a government Indian factory as well as a military post. The factory was moved to Fort Osage (see June 23, 1804) in 1808. The fort itself was moved to higher ground because of flooding in 1810, and was abandoned in 1826. Frazer, 68–70; Thwaites (LC), 5:392–93 n. 2.

3. Thomas Hunt of Massachusetts served in the Revolutionary War from the Battle of Lexington and Concord on, and was twice wounded; he rose to the rank of captain and resigned in 1784. In 1791 he was appointed captain in the Second Infantry Regiment, promoted to major in 1793, transferred to the First Infantry in 1796, became lieutenant colonel in 1802 and colonel in 1803. He died in 1808. Heitman, 557.

4. George Peter of Maryland was appointed second lieutenant in the Second Infantry Regiment in 1799 and discharged in 1800, rejoined the army as a lieutenant of artillery in 1801, was promoted to captain in 1807 and resigned in 1809. He died in 1861. Heitman, 786; Thwaites (LC), 5:393 n. 2.

5. Ann Biddle Wilkinson, a distant relative of Nicholas Biddle, died in February 1807.

6. The remaining half-page (p. 75 of Codex N) is blank.

[Clark]   *Thursday 23rd of Septr. 1806*

we rose early took the Chief to the publick store & furnished him with Some clothes &c.   took an early breckfast with Colo. Hunt and Set out decended to the Mississippi and down that river to St. Louis at which place we arived about 12 oClock.   we Suffered the party to fire off their pieces as a Salute to the Town.   we were met by all the village and re-

ceived a harty welcom from it's inhabitants &.[1] here I found my old acquaintance Majr. W. Christy[2] who had Settled in this town in a public line
as a Tavern Keeper. he furnished us with Store rooms for our baggage
and we accepted of the invitation of Mr. Peter Choteau[3] and ⟨par⟩ took a
room in ⟨the⟩ his house ⟨of Mr. Peter Cadeaus Choteaus⟩ we payed a
friendly visit to ⟨Mes. Choteau and⟩ Mr ⟨Ogustus⟩ August Chotau[4] and
Some of our old friends this evening. as the post had departed from St.
Louis Capt Lewis wrote a note to Mr. Hay[5] in Kahoka to detain the post at
that place untill 12 tomorrow which was reather later than his usial time
of leaveing it[6]

1. Ordway says, "the people gathred on the Shore and Huzzared three cheers."
2. William Christy, born in Pennsylvania, moved to Kentucky as a boy, where he was a
neighbor of Clark's family, and served in the campaigns against the Indians north of the
Ohio under Generals Arthur St. Clair and Anthony Wayne. He received a license to keep
a tavern in St. Louis in 1806. Later he was secretary of the land claims commission (see
September 20, 1806), fought Indians again in the War of 1812, and was the first auditor
of public accounts of the new state of Missouri. He died in 1837. Houck, 3:49, 60, 113,
146, 266.
3. Jean Pierre Chouteau; see March 21, 1804, September 3, 1806.
4. René Auguste Chouteau; see December 11, 1803.
5. For John Hay, the postmaster of Cahokia, see January 30, 1804.
6. The remaining half-page (p. 76 of Codex N) is blank.

[Clark]   *Wednesday 24th of September 1806*

I sleped but little last night however we rose early and Commencd
wrighting our letters Capt. Lewis wrote one to the presidend[1] and I
wrote Govr. Harrison[2] & my friends in Kentucky[3] and Sent of George
Drewyer with those letters to Kohoka & delivered them to Mr. Hays[4]
&. we dined with Mr. Chotoux to day, and after dinner went to a Store
and purchased Some Clothes, which we gave to a Tayler and derected to
be made. Capt Lewis in opening his trunk found all his papers wet, and
Some Seeds spoiled[5]

1. See Lewis to Jefferson, September 23, 1806, Jackson (LLC), 1:319–24.
2. William Henry Harrison, an old army comrade of Clark's and now governor of Indiana Territory.

3. Clark's letter to his relatives in Kentucky was probably intended for publication, and was in fact the first published report of the expedition. Lewis actually composed the first draft, which Clark copied. Clark to [George Rogers Clark?], September 23, 1806, Lewis's draft of Clark's Letter, September 24, 1806, Jackson (LLC), 1:325–35. In October 1990 the Filson Club of Louisville, Kentucky, received a number of Clark's letters written to his brother Jonathan. What had previously been suspected as a letter to George Rogers Clark on September 23, 1806, appeared among the new collection addressed to Jonathan. Jackson surmised that the letter might well have been intended for Jonathan when he gave George Rogers as the possible addressee.

4. Clark probably means Hay again.

5. The remaining half-page (p. 77 of Codex N) is blank.

[Clark]   *Thursday 25th of Septr. 1806*

had all of our Skins &c. Suned and Stored away in a Storeroom of Mr. Caddy Choteau.[1]   payed Some visits of form, to the gentlemen of St. Louis.   in the evening a dinner & Ball[2]

1. The storeroom of Jean Pierre Chouteau; see September 3, 1806.

2. The affair was held at William Christy's tavern. Eighteen toasts were drunk, starting with one to President Jefferson, "The friend of science, the polar star of *discovery*, the philosopher and the patriot," and ending with "Captains Lewis and Clark—Their perilous services endear them to every American heart."   Ronda (SLW).

[Clark]   *Friday ⟨25⟩th [EC: 26] of September 1806*[1]

a fine morning   we commenced wrighting &c.[2]

1. This is the last daily entry in Codex N and the last of the captains' daily journal entries for the expedition. Only a small portion of this page (p. 78) is taken up with text for September 25 and 26, the remainder is blank. The remainder of Codex N consists of blank pages (pp. 79–80, 86–121, 143), maps and notes of Bon Homme Island (pp. 81–85), and a number of miscellaneous notes (pp. 122–54, reading backwards), including Clark's weather diary for September 1806, Clark's summary of Lewis's journey from Travelers' Rest to the Great Falls of the Missouri, a map of that route, and several other items that are printed in Chapter 41 of this volume.

2. The nature of this "wrighting" is not clear. Some of the letters they had begun a few days earlier may not yet have been finished; see September 24, 1806. It is likely that they were writing other letters in the next few days; see Lewis to an Unknown Correspondent, September 29, 1806. Jackson (LLC), 1:335–43. It is possible that Clark still had some of his journals to complete, although there are objections to this supposition. See the Introduction to the Journals, vol. 2.

[Clark]

Date of the Month	State of the weather at Sun rise	Course of the wind at Sun rise	State of the weather at 4 oClock	Course of wind at 4 P. M
1st	fog	S. E.	f. a. r.	S. E.
2nd	f.	S E	f.	S E
3rd	f.	S W	f.	S W
4th	f. a. r. T & L	S. E	f.	S E
5th	f	S E	c	S W
6th	c.	S E	f.	S E
7th	f	S E	f.	S. E.
8th	f.	S E	f.	S E
9th	f.	S E	f.	S E
10th	f.	S E	f.	S E
11th	C. a. r.	S E	f. a r.	S E
12th	f.	S E	c a r	S E
13th	f.	S E	f.	S E
14th	f.	S E	c.	S E
15th	f.	S E	f.	S E
16th	f.	S E	f.	S E
17th	f.	S E	f.	S E.
18th	f.	S E	c.	S. E
19th	f.	S E	f.	S E
20th	f.	N. E	f.	S E
21st	C. a. r.	S. E.	c.	S E
22	r. a T. L & r.	S	C. a. r	S
23	c. & r.	N E	c. a. r	N E
24	r		c. a. r	
25th	c.	N E.	f.	
26th	f.	S E	f.	S. E
27th	f.	N E	f	S E
28th	f.	S E	f	S E
29th	f	S	f	S E
30th	f	S E	f	E

[*Remarks*][2]

1st a thick fog untill 8 A. M. a fiew drops of rain about 1 P. M.

2nd Hard wind all day. Saw the prarie fowl common in the Illinois plains. Saw Linn and Slipery elm

3d   a Stiff breeze from S E. untill 12 at night when it changed to S W. and blew hard all night

4th   at 6 P. M a violent Storm of Thunder Lightng and rain untill 10 P. M when it ceased to rain and blew hard from N W untill 3 A. M.

6th   heard the whipper will[3] Common to the u states at Soldiers river.

7th   Saw the whiperwill and heard the common hooting owl Musquetors very troublesom. killed 3 Elk.

8th   warmest day we have experienced in this year. passed River platt—

11th   a fiew drops of rain only a little before day and Some rain at 2 P M

12th   Heavy dew this morning and fog Some rain from 12 to 4 P M

15th   day very worm Smokey and worm

16th   this day very Sultry and much the hotest which we have experienced

17th   day worm, but fiew musquetors

19th   Saw a green Snake[4] as high up as Salt Rivr[5] on the missouri. the limestone bluffs[6] commence below Salt river on S. Side

21st   a Slight Shower of rain a little before day light this morning

22nd   at St Charles the raine commencd about 9 P. M and was moderate untill 4 A. M when it increased and rained without intermition untill 10 A M: Some Thunder and lightning about daylight. it Continued Cloudy with Small Showers of rain all day. we arived at the Mississippi

23rd   at St. Louis Several light Showers in the course of this day. we arrived at St Louis at 12 oClock.

24th   rained moderately this morning and continued Cloudy with moderate rain at intervales all day

26th   fair and worm

27th   emencely worm

28th   do

29th   do

30th   do

1. Only Clark has a weather table for September 1806; it appears in Codex N, pp. 151–52 (reading backwards).

2. Clark has remarks in the margin of his weather table; the only separate remarks are for the twenty-second, twenty-third, and twenty-fourth. The marginal remarks for the twenty-second are nearly duplicated in the separate remarks; we give only the latter here. The remarks for the twenty-third and twenty-fourth are separate only.

3. Whip-poor-will, *Caprimulgus vociferus* [AOU, 417].

4. Smooth green snake, *Opheodrys vernalis*. Benson (HLCE), 89.

5. Petite Saline Creek in Moniteau County, Missouri, previously mentioned on June 6, 1804.

6. Jefferson City limestone from the area of Cole and Moniteau counties.

Chapter Forty-One

Postexpeditionary Miscellany

Introduction

The following items represent another collection of miscellaneous documents comparable to the miscellany gathered at Fort Mandan (see Chapter 10) and at Fort Clatsop (see Chapter 30). Many of the items may have been started at Fort Clatsop or at Camp Chopunnish, but there is no way to positively date them. Certainly, some of them were completed near the end of or at the close of the expedition after reaching St. Louis. The fact that Clark's Estimated Distances include his trip on the Yellowstone River testifies to the late completion of that document. The documents in Part 2 particularly show the haste to finish up some summary-type lists and broad overviews of the new lands through which the party had passed. After reaching St. Louis in September 1806 the time for developing such tables, lists, and compilations would be scarce.

Part 1: Estimated Distances

Clark prepared this extensive list of estimated distances for the route from St. Charles, Missouri, to the Pacific Coast and the return as an apparent supplement to his route maps. This document is found in Codex N, pp. 128–42 (reading backwards). Some of the numbers under the last column ("Distances up the Missouri") have been lined through in the codex, but the marks appear to be more check-offs than actual strike outs. Since many are quite faint and questionable they are not shown here as strike outs. A similar list is in Voorhis No. 4; it has been compared to this one and significant variations have been noted. The table in the Voorhis notebook probably served as a duplicate to guard against loss or injury to the codex piece.

[Clark]   [undated]

A Summary Statement of the Rivers Creeks and most remarkable places, their distances from each other &c— their distances from the Mississippi assending the Missouri, across the Rocky Mountains and down the Columbia to the Pacific Ocian as was explored in the years of 1804, 5, and 6—by Capts. Lewis & Clark &—

Names of remarkable places	The width of rivers and Creeks in yds.	Side on which they are Situated	Distance from one place to another	Distances up the Missouri from the Mississippi[1]
	yards	⟨Ms⟩	Ms	Ms.
To the village of St. Charles	—	N. E.	21	21
" " Osage Womans River	30	N. E.	20	41
" " Chauretts Village & Creek	20	N. E.	27	68
" " Shepherds Creek		S W	15	83
" " Gasconnade River	157	S W	17	100
" " Muddy River	50	N. E	15	115
" Grand Osage River	397	S W.	18	133
" the Murrow Creek	20	S W.	5	138
" " Cedar Island & Creek	20	N. E.	7	145
" " Lead Mine Hill		S W.	9	154
" " Manitou Creek	20	S W.	8	162
" " Split rock Creek	20	N. E	8	170
" " Saline or Salt River	30	S W	3	173
" " Manitou River	30	N E	9	182
" " Good Womans River	35	N E	9	191
" " Mine River	70	S W	9	200
" " Arrow Prarie		S W	6	206

" Two Charliton Rivers	30/70	N. E.	14	220
" " antient village of the Missouri Nation near which place Fort Orleans Stood		N E	16	236
" Grand River	90	N E	4	240
" " Snake Creek	18	N E	6	246
" " Antient village of the little *Osage*—		S W	10	256
" " Tigers Island and Creek	25	N E	20	276
" " Eueberts Island and Creek[2]	—	S W	12	388
" " Fire prarie Creek	—	S W	12	300
" " Fort point	—	S W	6	306
" " Hay Cabin Creek	20	S W.	6	312
" " Coal bank		S W.	9	321
" " Blue water River	30	S W.	10	331
" Kanzas River	230	S W.	9	*340*
" the Little River Platt	60	N E	9	349
" " 1st Old Kanzas Village		S W	28	377
" " Independance Creek a mile below the 2d old Kanzas Village		S W	28	405
" " St. Michaels prarie		N E	25	430
" " Nodawa River	70	N E	20	450
" " Wolf or *Loup* River	60	S W	14	464
" Big *Ne-me-hur* River	80	S W	16	480
" the *Tar-ki-o* Creek	23	N E	3	483
" " *Neesh-nah-ba-to-no* River	50	N E	25	508
" " Little Ne ma har River	48	S W.	8	516
" " *Bald pated prarie* the Neesh-nahbatona within 150 yards of the Missouri		N. E.	23	539
" " Weeping water Creek	25	S W	29	568
" *River Platt* (or Shoal river[)]	600	S W	32	*600*

" " Butterfly or papelion Creek	18	S W.	3	—
" " Musquetor Creek	22	N. E.	7	610
" " Antiant Village of the Ottoes	—	S W.	11	—
" " antient Anawways village below a Bluff on the N E. Side		N E	6	—
" " Bowyers river	25	N E	11	—
" Councill Bluffs (establishnt)	—	S W	12	650
" Soldiers River	40	N E	39	689
" *Ea-neah, Wau-de-pon* (Little Sieux R.[)]	80	N E	44	733
" the *Wau-car-de* or bad Spirit Creek	—	S W.	55	788
around a bend of the river to the N E the Gorge of which is only 974 yards	—		21	809
To an Island 3 miles N E of the Mahar vilg.			27	836
" Floyds Bluff and River	35	N. E.	14	850
" the Big Sieoux River	110	N E	3	853
" " Commencement of the Copperas cobalt, pirites and alum bluffs	—	S W	27	880
To the Hot or burning Bluffs—	—	S W.	30	910
" " White Stone River	30	N E	8	918
" " Petite Arc an Old Mahar village at the mouth of little bow Creek	15	S W	20	938
" *River Jacque* or James river	90	N E	12	950
" the Calumet Bluff (of mineral)	—	S W.	10	960
" Antient fortification Good mans Isd.	—	S W.	16	976
" Plumb Creek	12	N E	10	986
" White paint Creek	28	S W	8	994
" Quicurre or rapid river	152	S W.	6	1000

" the poncar River & village	30	S W	10	1010
" " Dome and village of Burrowing or barking Squirels	—	S W.	20	1030
" " Island of Cedar		—	45	1075
" White River	300	S W.	55	1130
" the three Rivers of the Sieoux pass	350	N E	22	1152
" an Island in the Comencmt. of the big bend		N. E	20	1172
" upper part of the big bend, the gorge of which is 1¼ Ms.		S W.	30	1202
" Tylors river	35	S W	6	*1208*
" ⟨Lousells⟩ [*NB?: Loisel's*] Fort on Cedar island			18	1226
" Teton River	70	S W.	37	1263
" the upper of five old Ricara villages reduced by the Sieoux & abandoned	—	S W.	42	1305
" Chyenne River (place for an Esbmt)	400	S W.	5	1310
" an old ricara Village on *La-hoo-catts* Island	—	—	47	1357
" *Sar-war-kar-na* River	90	S W.	40	1397
" *We-tar-hoo* River	120	S W.	25	1422
" 1st Ricaras Village on an Island	—	S W.	4	
" 2d *Ricaras* 3 Villages		S W.	4	*1430*
" the Stone Idol Creek ⟨Ponia creek⟩	18	N E	18	—
" " *War-re-con-ne* River	35	N E	40	1488
" Cannon Ball River	140	S W	12	1500
" Chesschetar River near 6 old Mandan Vgs.	38	S W	40	1540
" the Old Ricara & Mandan Villages	—	S W	40	1580

" Fort Mandan (wintering post of ⟨pty⟩ 1804[)]		N E	20	*1600*
" Mandan Villages (on each Side[)]	—		4	1604
" Knife river on which the two Minetarre and the Maharhas villages are situated near the mouth	80	S W	2	1606
" the Island			11	—
" " Miry River	10	N E	16	1633
" " Island in the little bason	—	—	28	—
" Little Missouri River	134	S W.	29	1690
" " Wild onion Creek	16	N E	12	—
" " Goose egg Lake	300	N E	9	—
" " Shabonos Creek	20	S W	16	1727
" " Goat pen Creek (Mouse River waters of Lake Winnipick near the Missouri[)]	20	N E	16	1743
" " Halls Strand Lake & Creek	—	N. E	47	1790
" *White earth* River	60	N E	50	1840
Rochejhone or *Yellow Stone* River	858	S W.	40	*1880*
to Marthys River	50	N E	60	1940
" Porcupine River	112	N E	50	1990
" the little Dry Creek	25	S W	40	2030
" " Big Dry Creek	100	S W	9	—
" " Little Dry River	200	S W	6	2045
" " Gulf in a Stard. Bend			32	—
" *Milk River*	150	N. E	13	2090
" Big Dry River	400	S W	25	—
" Werners run	10	N E	9	—
" Pine Creek	20	N E	36	2160
" Gibsons River	35	N E	17	2177
" Brown Bear defeeted Creek	40	S W	12	—
" Brattens River	100	N E	24	2213

" Burnt Lodge Creek	50	S W	6	
" Wisers Creek	40	N E	14	2233
" Muscle Shell River	110	S W	37	2270
" Growse Creek	20	N E	30	—
" North Mountain Creek	30	N E	36	2336
" South Mountain Creek	30	S W.	18	2354
" Ibex Island			15	—
" Goodriches Island			9	2378
" Windsers Creek	30	N E	7	2385
" Elk rapid (Swift water)			15	2400
" Thompsons Creek	28	N E	27½	2427½
" Judieths River[3]	100	S W	11½	2439
" Ash rapid (Swift water)			4	—
" Slaughter River	40	S W.	11	2454
To the Stone wall Creek above those emence natural walls	30	N E	26	2480
" Maria's River	186	N E	41	2521
" Snow River	50	S W	19	—
" Shields River	35	S W	28	2568
" the foot of the enterance of portage River 5 Miles below the Great falls	45	S W	7	2575

Leaveing the Missouri below the Falls and passing by Land to the navagable waters of the Columbia River

Names of remarkable places	width of the rivers & Creeks	Distance from one place to another	Distance from the falls of Missouri	Distance from the Mississippi
	yds.	Ms.	Ms.	Miles
To the enterance of Medicine River ⟨passed 1st pitch of 87 feet, 2d of 19 feet, 3d of 47 feet 8 inches, and 4th of 26 feet 5 inches added to the rapids makes a fall of 362 feet⟩	137	18	18	2593

To fort Mountain passing through the plains between Medicine river and the Missouri near the Missouri	—	15	33	2608
To the Rocky Mountains at a Gap on the ridge which divites the waters of the Missouri from those of the Columbia passing the N pt. of a mtn. and then Crossing Dearborns river	—	35	68	2643
To a fork of Cohahlarishkit river from the N. passed 4 Creeks from N.	45	40	108	2683
To Seamans Creek from the N	20	7	115	
" Werners ⟨River⟩ Creek N	35	10	125	2700
" the East fork of Clarks river at the enterance of Cohahlarishkit R	120	30	155	2730
" Clarks River below the forks	150	12	167	2742
[*word crossed out, illegible*]				
" Travellers rest Creek on the west Side of Clarks river above the forks	25	5	172	2747
" the forks of Travellers rest Creek at a right hand road	—[4]	18	190	
" " Hote Springs, on the Creek	—	13	203	2778[5]
" " quawmash glades passing the head of the Creek to a branch of Kooskooske river		7	210	
To the North branch of Kooskooske river, a left hand road leads off at 5 ms.		7[6]	217	
To the junction of the roads on the top of a Snowey Mountain[7] the left hand road passing by a fishery		10	227	2802
To Hungary Creek from the right ⟨of⟩ passing on a Deviding mounteing [*crossed out, illegible*] Covered with deep Snow except on two places which are open with a South exposure at 8 & 36 miles		54	281	2856

To a Glade up Hungary Creek		6	287
To a Glade on a Small branch of do		8	295
" a Glade on Fish Creek	10	9	304
" Collins's Creek	25	13	317
" quawmash flatts		11	328	2903
" Kooskooske or Flat head River in a pine Country—	120	12	340	2915

Note in passing from the falls of Missouri across the Rocky Mountains to the navagable waters of the Columbia you have 200 miles of Good road, 140 miles of high Steep ruged Mountain 60 miles of which is Covered from 2 to 8 feet deep with Snow in the last of June.

remarkable places decending the Columbia &c. &c.	width of the rivers and Creeks	the Side on which they are situated	Distance from one place to an other	Distance Decending the Columbia	Distance from the Mississippi
	yds.		Ms	Ms.	Miles
To the enterance of Rock dam Creek	20	N.	8	8	2923
" " Chopunnish River	120	N.	5	13	2928
" " Colters Creek	35	N.	37	50	2978
" Lewis's River at the enteranc of the Kooskooske River	200	S	23	73	2988
" the Swet house Village & run	—	S	7	80	
" " pilots village	—	N.	11	91	3006
" " *Ke-moo-e-nimm* Creek	20	S	48	139	
" Drewyers river below the the narrows of Lewiss R	30	N.	5	144	3059
" " Cave rapid (Canoe sunk)	—	—	28	172	
" " Bason rapid (bad)	—	—	34	206	3121
To the Discharge Rapid (bad)	—	—	14	220	3135

" Columbia at the Mouth of Lewiss river from the East		S E	7	227	3142
" *Wal lar wal lars* River passd. 11 large Mat Lodges of that nation	40	S E	16	243	3158
" Museleshell Rapid (bad)[8] passed 33 mat lodges of the Wallar wallers	—	—	25	268	3183
" Pillacon Rapid passed 48 lodges of the Pishquit-pahs nation		N.	22	290	3205
" 21 Lodges of the wahhawpum nation residing on three Islands at the commencement the high country—	—	N.	18	308	3223
" 8 Lodges of the wahhawpums at short rapid	—	N	27	335	3250
" Rocky Rapid. 9 lodges of the same nation	—	N	13	348	3263
" River LaPage, bad rapid	40	S	9	357	3272
" 27 lodges of the Enesher nation at fishstack rapid	—	N	10	367	3282
" Towannahiooks River	180	S	8	375	3290
" The Great Falls of the Columbia river of 37 ft. 8 Ins. near which there are 40 Mat Lodges of the Enesher Nation		N	4	379	3294
The short narrows 45 yds. wide	—	—	2	381	3296
" Skillute Village of 21 large-wood houses at the long narrows from 50 to 100 yds. wide		N.	4	385	3300

" Chilluckitequaw Village of 8 large wood houses		N	14	399	3314
" Cataract river a few miles below a Village of 7 houses and immediately above one of 11 Houses of the Chilluckittequaw nation	60	N	10	409	3324
" Sepulcher Rock, opposite to a Village of Hs. of Chilluckittqs	—	N	4	413	3328
River Labeich opposite to 26 houses of the Smackshop Nation, Houses scattered on the N. side	46	S	9	422	3337
" Little Lake Creek 3 houses of the Smackshop nation	28	N	10	432	3347
" Cruzatt's River	60	N	12	444	3359
" The Grand Rapid just below the village of the Yehuh tribe of the Shahala Nation of 14 wood houses	—	—	6	450	3365
" Clahclellah Village of the Shahala nation, near the foot of the rapids. 7 houses	—	N	6	456	3371
" Wahclellar Village of the Shahala nation 23 houses just below the entrance of the beacon rock creek	—	N	6	462	3377
Tide Water.					
" Phoca Rock in the river 60 feet above water—	—	—	11	473	3388
" Quicksand River	120	S	9	482	3397
" Seal River	80	N	3	485	
" Nechacomee village opposite to the dimond Island	—	S	4	489	

" Shahala Village of 25 temperary houses	—	S	12	501	3416
" Multnomah River	500	S	14	515	3430
" Multnomah Village	—	S	6	522	
" Quathlahpahtle Village	—	N	8	529	
" Cahwahnahiooks River	200	N	1	530	3445
" Cathlahaws Creek and Village	18	N	10	540	3455
" Lower extremity of Elallah or deer Island	—	S	6	546	
" Coweliske River about the entrance and up this river the Skillute nation reside	150	N	3	559	3474
To Fannys Island & bottom	—	S	16	575	3490
" the Sea otter Island	—	—	12	587	3502
" " Upper Village of the Warkiacums Nation	—	N	6	593	3508
" " Cath lâh mâhs Village of 9 large wood houses S. Seal Isds.	—	S	14	607	3522
Point William opsd. Shallow Bay		S	10	617	3532
" Point Meriwether above Meriwethers Bay	—	S	9	626	3541
" *Clat-Sop* Village below Meriwether Bay and 7 miles N W of *Fort Clatsop*		S	8	634	3549
" Point Adams at the enterance of Columbia into the pacific Ocean or Great South Sea in Latitude 46° 15′ and Longtd. 124° 57′ West from Green witch.		S	6	640	*3555*

[X: *See Book No 9*][9]

Note   Fort Clatsop is Situated on the West Side of an three miles up the Netul River from Meriwethers bay and Seven miles East from the nearest part of the Sea Coast.   at this fork Capt. M. Lewis and Capt. Wm. Clark wintered in the winter 1805 & 6—.

The rout by which we went out by the way of the Missouri to it's head 3096 miles thence by land, by way of Lewis'es River over to Clarks river and down that to the enterance of travellers rest Creek where all the roads from different routs Come together thence across the ruged part of the rocky Mountains to the navagable branches of the Columbia 398 Miles.   thence down that river 640 miles to the pacific Ocian makeing a Total distance of 4134 miles—. On our return in 1806 from Travellers rest Creek directly to the *falls* of the Missouri River Shortins the distance about 579 miles, and a much better rout, reduceing the distance from Mississippi to the Pacific Ocean to <u>3555</u> Miles, 2575 miles of this distance is up the Missouri to the *Falls* of that river— from thence passing through the plains and across the Rocky mountain to the navagable part of Koos-kooske river a branch of the columbia <u>340</u> miles, 200 miles of which is a good road, 140 miles over a tremendious Mountain Steep and broken, 60 miles of which is covered Several feet deep with Snow on which we passed the last of June; from the navagable part of the Kooskooske we decended that rapid river 73 miles to its enterance into Lewis's river and down that river 154 miles to the Columbia and down that river 413 Miles to enter-ance into the Pacific Ocian, about 180 miles of this distance is tide water. passed Several bad rapids and narrows and one Considerable fall 268 miles above the enterance of this river of 37 feet 8 inches—   the Total distance decending the Columbian waters 640 miles making a total of 3555 miles on the most direct rout from the Mississippi at the mouth of the Missouri to the pacific Ocian

The fur trade may be carried on from the heads of the Missouri to the mouth of Columbia much cheaper than by any rout be which it Can be Conveyed to the East indias.   ⟨you⟩ form an establishment on the River Rochejhone for the reception of the furs of that river & South and one at Marias river below the great falls of Missouri.   the Shoshones within the rocky mountains the Tushepaws on Clarks river and maney nations west of the Rocky mountains would visit those establishments from whome horses might be got on the most reasonable termes for the purpose of packing the furs across those mountains which may be passed from the 20th of June untill the last of September.[10]

You may leave those establishments on the Missouri 15 or 20 of June and arive on the Kooskooske river between the 1s & 5th of July. from that time you have untill the middle of September to decend the River and return to the mountains in time to pass them before the Snow becomes too Deep to Cross them.

A Summary Statement of the Rivers, Creeks, and the most remarkable places assending the *River Rochejhone*, their distances from each other, and from the Missouri as estimated by me in 1806 also the Total distances from the Mississippi.

Names of Places &c.	The side on which they are situated	width of the rivers & Creeks in yards	Distance from one place to another in miles	Distance from the Missouri assending	Computed distances from the Mississippi assending
Latd.	Side	yds	Ms.	Ms.	Total Ms.
from Missouri up the River Rochejhone					1888
To the enterance of Jos. Fields River	S. E	35	8	8	1896
" " yallow rock (river narrow)—	S E	—	6	14	
" " Buffalow Crossings a low plain each side			33	47	
" " Ibex River	S. E.	30	31	78	1966
" " Samuels Creek	N W	30	12	90	
" " Buffalow Creek	N W	30	18	108	
" " Pine Brook	S. E.	20	29	137	
" " Cat fish Creek	S. E.	20	10	147	
" " Gibsons River	S. E	60	8	155	2043

" " Oak-tar-pon-er Stone Coal River	S E	40	18	173	2061
" " Shabonos River	N W	100	7	188	2068
" " Wolf rapid (not bad)			12	192	2080
" " Wah-har-sop, red-stone River	S. E.	100	3	195	2083
" " Yorks dry river	N W	88	7	202	2090
" " Yellow Bear rapids (not bad)			1	203	2091
" " Buffalow Shoals (not bad[)]			20	223	2111
" " Dry River	N W	100	9	232	
" Lezeka or Tongue River	S. E.	150	11	243	2131
" " Turtle Creek	S E	40	20	263	
" " *Mar-Shas-kap* River	S E	25	22	285	2173
" " Wood Brook	S E	30	16	301	
" " upper *Stone Coal* Bluffs	S E		6	307	2195
" " Little Horn River	S E	100	11	318	2206
" " Table River	N W	70	2	320	
" " Little Wolf River	N W	80	30	350	
" " Chimney Bluffs	N W		18	368	
" " White Creek	N W	30	17	385	
" " Laabeech's River	S E	60	7	392	2281
" " Windsers River	N W	50	26	418	2307
" " Elk River	N W	40	4	422	
" Big horn River	S E	220	15	437	2326
" " Island Brook	N W		16	453	
" " White Clifts (below the pine hills)	N W	—	27	480	
" " Halls River	N W	40	9	489	2378

" Shannons river from which place party decended in Buffalow Skin Canoes	S E	22	10	499	2388
" " pompeys Tower 200 feet high & 400 yds. around in an open bottom	S E		9	508	2397
" " Tumbling Bluff	N W	—	12	520	
" " Big Dry brook	N W	60	16	536	
" " Pryors Creek in the big bend	S E	25	10	546	2435
" " Rock Creek	N W	18	5	551	
" " Pryors River	S E	35	6	557	2446
" " Yellow Clifts	S E	—	9	566	
" " Horse Creek	S E	20	10	576	
" Clarks Fork (The lodge where all dance)	S E	150	23	599	2487
" " Black bluffs opposit ☞ to the place Capt. C. built 2 Canoes to dcd.	S E		27	626	2514
" " Bluffs above the extencive open bottoms on the N W side	N W		26	652	
" " Rose Bud river	S E	40	6	658	2546
" " Dry Creek	N W	20	19	677	
" " Muddy Creek	N W	15	16	693	
" " Weasel Creek	S E	10	16	709	
" " Brattens River	S E	25	10	719	2607
" " Otter River	N W	30	12	731	2638
" " Beaver river	S E	30	1/4	731 1/4	
" " Thy Snaged Creek	S E	20	5 3/4	737	
" " Rivers a Cross	both	28	10	747	2635
" a Small rapid not bad			24	771	
" Stinking Cabin Creek	S E	20	14	785	

" Shield River boald	N W	35	16	805	
" the foot of the Rocky Mountains covered with snow 15 of July in Latd. *45° 22' 34"* North	}	—	—	16	817	2905

Note   the distance by land from Clarks fork to the mountain is only 120 miles.   all the Streams falling in above Clarks fork are boald

Portage from the River Rochejhone to the Head of the Missouri at the *three* forks.

	Miles	Miles across from the Rochejhone
From the Rochejhone 2 miles below the Rocky Mountain on a Course nearly S 75° W. to the top of the deviding ridge which divides the water of the rochejhone from those of the Missouri, passing up on the N. Side of portage run to the forks of the road the Country open, ascent gentle	9	
To the middle branch of the East fork of Galletins River takeing the left hand road, this Stream running to the left	½	9½
To a Gap in the mountain passing up a Small branch on it's N. Side with a gradual ascent Country open and the course nearly west	2½	12
To the middle branch of the east fork of Galletins River passing down on the N. Side of a branch Crouded with beaver dams	3	15
To the three forks of the East fork of Gallitins river passing on the S side	3	18
To the main fork of Gallitins river passing through a leavel plain N 78° W.	12	30
To the arm of the river which forms beaver Island, passing through the island a leavel open plain on a course N 70° W. an emensity of Beaver dams &c. on each side.	6	36

To Galletins River below the forks passing through an open leavel place on a course N. 78° W. on the S. Side of the R.	6	42
To the Missouri imediately below the three forks. Jeffersons, Madisons and Galletins Rivers on a Course N 85° W. through an open plain passing over 2 Small hills after Crossing the river on its N. Side	6	48

Rout from the head of Jeffersons River at the place we left the Canoes to the mouth of Travillers rest on Clarks river on my rout in July 1806

From the forks where our Canoes were left in 1805 up the west branch on an Old Shoshone road about nine miles	9
To a Gap in the mountains which divides Willards Creek waters from those of the Wisdom river on a course N 30° West	15
To the boiling Hot Spring in a vally near the 3 forks of Wisdom river, crossed 2 forks of wisdom river from the right hand	9
To Glade Creek passing Wisdom river and 6 large Creeks from a Snow toped mountain to the West, passing a Spur of the mountain after Crossing the last Creek on a Course N. 56° W.	22
To the head of Glade Creek keeping on an old roade which passes up on the N. Side	11
To Oatlashoot vally leaving Glade Creek an heading to our right and passing over a dividing mountain which Seperates the waters of the Missouri from those of Clarks river	5
To the Middle fork of Clarks river from the left hand in Oatlashshoot Vally	8
	79
To flour Camp Creek from the S E.	10
To the West fork of Clarks river from the W.	10
To Scattered Creek from the East	38

To Travellers rest Creek from the west where the different roads meet before the mountain is assended } 23   <u>81</u>

160

Note this rout is generally leavel and firm and every par of it will afford a very good waggon road by removing a fiew logs and Cutting a little on hill Side.

Note The Indians inform us that there is an excellent road from the 3 forks of the Missouri through a low gap in the mountains to the East fork of Clarks river which passes down that fork to its junction and up on the West Side of the main fork to Travellers rest Creek which they travel with their families in 6 days the distance must be about 150 miles, that added to 48 which is the portage from the River Rochejhone is 198 miles which is 26 miles further than the rout by the way of the falls of the Missouri—.

One other rout from the River Rochejhone which is also a good one but Something further is from the head of the east fork of Galletins River on a direct course to the mouth of Wisdom River and up that river and Glade Creek and across to Clarks river in the Oatlashshoot Valley and from thence down that river to the Travellers rest Creek, at which point all the roads in this quarter of the appear to Center at the foot of those tremendious mountains— the best and most direct rout is by way of the falls of the Missouri and Travelers rest— Several roads pass from the Missouri above the falls to Travellrs rest Creek.—

refur to Book No. 9— from the 19 Novr. to 29 of January 1806, for a Statement of the River Rochejhone & that part of our rout from the Falls of Missouri across the Mountains on our outward bound journey, all of which is estimated.[11]

LEWIS AND CLARK'S POINTS FROM ST. CHARLES
TO THE PACIFIC COAST AND RETURN

Lewis and Clark's Name	*Present Name and Location*
St. Charles	St. Charles, St. Charles County, Missouri
Osage Womans River	Femme Osage River, St. Charles County

Chauretts Creek	Charette Creek, Warren County, Missouri
Shepherds Creek	Big Berger Creek, Franklin County, Missouri
Gasconnade River	Gasconade River, Gasconade County, Missouri
Muddy River	Auxvasse River, Callaway County, Missouri
Grand Osage River	Osage River, Osage-Cole county line, Missouri
Murrow Creek	Moreau River, Cole County
Cedar Creek	Cedar Creek, Callaway County, Missouri
Lead Mine Hill	Cole County (see "Mine Hill" at entry of June 4, 1804)
Manitou Creek	Moniteau Creek, Cole County
Split Rock Creek	Perchee Creek, Boone County, Missouri
Saline or Salt River	Petite Saline Creek, Moniteau County, Missouri
Manitou River	Moniteau Creek, Howard-Boone county line, Missouri
Good Womans River	Bonne Femme Creek, Howard County
Mine River	Lamine River, Cooper County, Missouri
Arrow Prarie	Vicinity of Arrow Rock State Park, Saline County, Missouri (see entry of June 9, 1804)
Two Charliton Rivers	Little Chariton and Chariton rivers, Chariton County, Missouri
antient village of the Missouri Nation	Carroll and Chariton counties, Missouri (see entries of June 13, 15, and 16, 1804)
Grand River	Grand River, Carroll-Chariton county line
Snake Creek	Wakenda Creek, Carroll County
Antient village of the little Osage	Saline County, Missouri (see entry of June 15, 1804)
Tigers Creek	Crooked River, Ray County, Missouri
Eueberts Creek	Sniabar River, Lafayette County, Missouri (see entry of June 21, 1804)

Fire prarie Creek	Near Jackson-Lafayette county line, Missouri (see entry of June 22, 1804)
Fort point	Near Ray-Clay county line, Missouri
Hay Cabin Creek	Little Blue River, Jackson County
Coal bank	Jackson County (see entry of June 25, 1804)
Blue water River	Big Blue River, Jackson County
Kanzas River	Kansas (Kaw) River, Wyandotte County, Kansas
Little River Platt	Platte (Little Platte) River, Platte County, Missouri
1st Old Kanzas Village	Leavenworth County, Kansas (see entry of July 2, 1804)
Independance Creek	Independence Creek, Atchison-Doniphan county line, Kansas
St. Michaels prarie	Vicnity of St. Joseph, Buchanan County, Missouri (see entry of July 7, 1804)
Nodawa River	Nodaway River, Holt-Andrew county line, Missouri
Wolf or Loup River	Wolf Creek, Doniphan County, Kansas
Big Ne-me-hur River	Big Nemaha River, Richardson County, Nebraska
Tar-ki-o Creek	Tarkio River (Big Tarkio Creek), Holt County, Missouri (see entry of July 13, 1804)
Neesh-nah-ba-to-no River	Nishnabotna River, Atchison County, Missouri (see entries of July 14 and 17, 1804)
Little Nemahar River	Little Nemaha River, Nemaha County, Nebraska
Bald pated prarie	Vicinity of Waubonsie State Park, Fremont County, Iowa (see entry of July 16, 1804)
Weeping water Creek	Weeping Water Creek, Otoe County, Nebraska
River Platt	Platte River, Cass-Sarpy county line, Nebraska

Butterfly or papelion Creek	Papillion (Big Papillion) Creek, Sarpy County
Musquetor Creek	Mosquito Creek, Pottawattamie County, Iowa (see entry of July 22, 1804)
Antiant Village of the Ottoes	Omaha, Douglas County, Nebraska (see entries for July 27 and 28, 1804)
antient Ayauways village	North of Council Bluffs, Pottawattamie County (see entry of July 28, 1804)
Bowyers river	Boyer River, Pottawattamie County
Councill Bluffs	Vicinity of Fort Calhoun, Washington County, Nebraska (see entry of July 30, 1804; *Atlas* map 13)
Soldiers River	Soldier River, Harrison County, Iowa
Ea-neah, Wau-de-pon (Little Sioux R.)	Little Sioux River, Harrison County, Iowa
Wau-car-de or bad Spirit Creek	Blackbird (South Blackbird) Creek, or North Blackbird Creek, Thurston County, Nebraska (see entry of August 11, 1804)
Island 3 miles N E of the Mahar vilg.	In either Dakota County, Nebraska, or Woodbury County, Iowa (see entry of August 13, 1804; *Atlas* map 16)
Floyds River	Floyd River, Sioux City, Woodbury County
Big Sieoux River	Big Sioux River, South Dakota-Iowa state line
Copperas . . . bluffs	Dakota County, Nebraska (see entry of August 22, 1804; *Atlas* maps 16, 17)
Hot or burning Bluffs	Dixon County, Nebraska (see entry of August 24, 1804; *Atlas* map 17)
White Stone River	Vermillion River, Clay County, South Dakota
little bow Creek	Bow Creek, Cedar County, Nebraska
River Jacque or James River	James River, Yankton County, South Dakota
Calumet Bluff	Near Gavins Point Dam, Cedar County, Nebraska

Good Mans Isd.	Between Bonhomme County, South Dakota, and Knox County, Nebraska (see entries of September 1 and 2, 1804; *Atlas* map 18)
Plumb Creek	Emanuel Creek, Bonhomme County
White paint Creek	Bazile Creek, Knox County (see entry of September 4, 1804)
Quicurre or rapid River	Niobrara River, Knox County
poncar River	Ponca Creek, Knox County
Dome	Old Baldy, Boyd County, Nebraska (see entries of September 7, 1804, and August 31, 1806; *Atlas* map 19)
Island of Cedar	Little Cedar Island, between Gregory and Charles Mix counties, South Dakota (see entry of September 10, 1804; *Atlas* map 20)
White River	White River, Lyman County, South Dakota
three Rivers of the Sieoux pass	Crow Creek, Elm (Wolf) Creek, and Campbell Creek, Buffalo County, South Dakota
big bend	Big Bend of the Missouri River, Lyman, Hughes, and Buffalo counties, South Dakota (see entry of September 20, 1804; *Atlas* map 22)
Tylors River	Medicine River (Creek), Lyman County
Fort on Cedar island	Dorion Island No. 2 (now submerged), between Hughes and Lyman Counties, South Dakota (see entry of September 22, 1804; *Atlas* map 22)
Teton River	Bad River, Stanley County, South Dakota
upper . . . Ricara villages	Stanley County (see entry of October 1, 1804; *Atlas* map 23)
Chyenne River	Cheyenne River, Stanley-Dewey county line, South Dakota
La-hoo-catts Island	Dolphees (Lafferty) Island, between Dewey and Potter counties, South Dakota (see entry of October 4, 1804; *Atlas* map 24)

Sar-war-kar-na River	Moreau River, Dewey County
We-tar-hoo River	Grand River, Corson County, South Dakota
1st Ricaras Village	Ashley Island, between Corson and Campbell counties, South Dakota (see entry of October 8, 1804; *Atlas* map 25)
2d Ricaras 3 Villages	Corson and Campbell counties (see entry of October 9, 1804; *Atlas* map 25)
Stone Idol Creek	Spring (Hermaphrodite) Creek, Campbell County
War-re-con-ne River	Beaver Creek, Emmons County, North Dakota
Cannon Ball River	Cannonball River, Sioux-Morton county line, North Dakota
Chesschetar River	Heart River, Morton County
Old Ricara & Mandan Villages	Mercer County, North Dakota (see entries of October 19–25, 1804; *Atlas* maps 28, 29)
Fort Mandan	McLean County, North Dakota, probably under Missouri River (see *Atlas* map 29)
Mandan Villages	Mercer County (see entries of October 26 and 27, 1804; *Atlas* map 29)
Knife River	Knife River, Mercer County
Minetarre [*Hidatsa*] villages	Mercer County (see entry of October 27, 1804; *Atlas* map 29)
Island	McLean County (see entries of October 30, 1804, and April 8, 1805; *Atlas* map 46)
Miry River	Snake Creek, McLean County
Island in the little bason	McLean County (see entry of April 10, 1805; *Atlas* map 46)
Little Missouri River	Little Missouri River, Dunn County, North Dakota
Wild Onion Creek	Deepwater Creek, McLean County
Goose egg Lake	Shell Creek, Mountrail County, North Dakota

Shabonos [*Charbonneau's*] Creek	Bear Den Creek, Dunn-McKenzie county line, North Dakota
Goat pen Creek	Little Knife River, Mountrail County
Halls Strand Lake & Creek	Tobacco Creek, Williams County, North Dakota
White earth River	Little Muddy River, Williams County
Rochejhone or Yellow Stone River	Yellowstone River, McKenzie County
Marthys River	Big Muddy Creek, Roosevelt County, Montana
Porcupine River	Poplar River, Roosevelt County
little Dry Creek	Spring Creek, McCone County, Montana
Big Dry Creek	Sand Creek, McCone County
Little Dry River	Prairie Elk Creek, McCone County
Gulf	Valley County, Montana (see *Atlas* maps 49, 58)
Milk River	Milk River, Valley County
Big Dry River	Big Dry Creek, McCone-Garfield county line, Montana
Werners Run	Duck Creek, Valley County
Pine Creek	Seventh Point Coulee, Valley County
Gibsons River	Sutherland Creek, Valley County
Brown Bear defeeted Creek	Snow Creek, Garfield County
Brattens River	Timber Creek, Phillips County, Montana
Burnt Lodge Creek	Seven Blackfoot Creek, Garfield County
Wisers [*Weiser's*] Creek	Fourchette Creek, Phillips County
Muscle Shell River	Musselshell River, Garfield-Petroleum county line, Montana
Growse Creek	Beauchamp Creek, Phillips County
North Mountain Creek	Rock Creek, Phillips County
South Mountain Creek	South Mountain, or Armells, Creek, Fergus County, Montana

Ibex Island	Grand Island, Phillips-Fergus county line (see *Atlas* maps 51, 60)
Goodriches Island	Dry Island, Fergus County (see *Atlas* maps 52, 60)
Windsers [*Windsor's*] Creek	Cow Creek, Blaine County, Montana
Elk rapid	Bird Rapids, Blaine-Fergus county line (see entry of May 26, 1805; *Atlas* maps 52, 60)
Thompson's Creek	Birch Creek, Chouteau-Blaine county line, Montana
Judieths River	Judith River, Fergus County
Ash Rapid	Deadman Rapids, Fergus-Chouteau county line (see entry of May 29, 1805; *Atlas* maps 52, 60)
Slaughter River	Arrow Creek, Fergus-Chouteau county line
Stone wall Creek	Eagle Creek, Chouteau County
Maria's River	Marias River, Chouteau County
Snow River	Shonkin Creek, Chouteau County
Shields River	Highwood Creek, Chouteau County
portage River	Belt Creek, Cascade-Chouteau county line
Medicine River	Sun River, Lewis and Clark, and Cascade counties, Montana
fort Mountain	Square Butte, Cascade County, Montana (see entry of July 15, 1805; *Atlas* map 54)
Gap on the ridge [of the Rocky Mountains]	Lewis and Clark Pass, Lewis and Clark County (see entry of July 7, 1806)
Dearborns river	Dearborn River, Cascade-Lewis and Clark county line, Montana
Cohahlarishkit river	North Fork Blackfoot River, Powell County, Montana
Seamans Creek	Monture Creek, Powell County
Werners Creek	Clearwater River, Missoula County, Montana
East fork of Clarks river	Blackfoot River, Missoula County
Clarks River	Clark Fork River, Missoula County

Travelers Rest Creek	Lolo Creek, Missoula County
forks of Travelers rest creek	Grave Creek, Missoula County
Hote Springs	Lolo Hot Springs, Missoula County (see entry of September 13, 1805; *Atlas* map 69)
quawmash glades	Vicinity of Packer Meadows, Idaho County, Idaho (see entry of September 13, 1805; *Atlas* maps 69, 70)
North branch of Kooskooske river	Crooked Fork, Idaho County
Snowey Mountain	Wendover Ridge, Idaho County (see entry of September 15, 1805; *Atlas* map 70)
Hungary Creek	Hungery Creek, Idaho County
Glade up Hungary Creek	On Hungery Creek, Idaho County (see entries of September 19 and 20, 1805; *Atlas* map 70, "Small Prarie")
Glade on a Small branch	On Fish Creek, Idaho County (see entry of September 19, 1805; *Atlas* map 70)
Glade on Fish Creek	On Eldorado Creek, Idaho County
Collins's Creek	Lolo Creek, Clearwater and Idaho counties, Idaho
quawmash flatts	Weippe Prairie, Clearwater County (see Clark's entry of September 20, 1805; *Atlas* map 71)
Kooskooske or Flathead River	Clearwater River, Clearwater County
Rock dam Creek	Orofino Creek, Clearwater County
Chopunnish River	North Fork Clearwater River, Clearwater County
Colters Creek	Potlatch River, Nez Perce County, Idaho
Lewis's River	Snake River, at mouth of Clearwater River, Nez Perce County, Idaho-Asotin County, Washington border
Swet house Village	Mouth of Alpowa Creek, Asotin County (see entry of October 11, 1805; *Atlas* map 73)

pilots Village	Vicinity of present Wawawai, Whitman County, Washington (see entry of October 11, 1805; *Atlas* map 73)
Ki-moo-e-nimm Creek	Tucannon River, Columbia County, Washington
Drewyers [*Drouillard's*] river	Palouse River, Franklin-Whitman county line, Washington
Cave rapid	Pine Tree Rapids (now under Lake Sacajawea), Franklin–Walla Walla county line, Washington (see entry of October 14, 1805; *Atlas* map 74)
Bason rapid	Fishhook Rapids, Franklin–Walla Walla county line (see entry of October 15, 1805; *Atlas* map 75)
Discharge Rapid	Five-Mile Rapids, Franklin–Walla Walla county line (see entry of October 16, 1805; *Atlas* map 75)
Columbia at the mouth of Lewiss river	Columbia River, at the mouth of the Snake River, Franklin, Walla Walla, and Benton counties, Washington
Wallar wallars River	Walla Walla River, Walla Walla County
Museleshell Rapid	Vicinity of present McNary Dam, Benton County, Washington-Umatilla County, Oregon border (see entry of October 19, 1805; *Atlas* map 75)
Pillacon Rapid	Vicinity of Crow Butte State Park, Benton County (see entry of October 20, 1805; *Atlas* map 76)
wahhawpum nation	Klickitat County, Washington (see entry of October 20, 1805; *Atlas* map 76)
short rapid	Klickitat County, Washington-Gilliam County, Oregon border, now under Lake Umatilla (see *Atlas* map 77)
Rocky Rapid	Klickitat County, below Rock Creek (see *Atlas* map 77)

River LaPage [*Lepage*]	John Day River, Gilliam-Sherman county line, Oregon
fishstack rapid	Klickitat County, above Miller Island (see entry of October 22, 1805; *Atlas* map 77)
Towannahiooks River	Deschutes River, Wasco-Sherman county line, Oregon
Great Falls of the Columbia river	Celilo Falls, Klickitat County, Washington-Wasco County, Oregon border
short narrows	The Dalles of the Columbia River, Klickitat County, Washington-Wasco County, Oregon border
long narrows	The Dalles of the Columbia River, Klickitat County, Washington-Wasco County, Oregon border
Chilluckitequaw Village	Klickitat County, opposite the vicinity of Crates Point (see entry of October 27, 1805; *Atlas* map 78)
Cataract river	Klickitat River, Klickitat County
Sepulcher Rock	Lower Memaloose Island, Hood River County, Oregon (see entries of October 29, 1805, and April 14, 1806; *Atlas* map 78)
River Labeich [*Labiche*]	Hood River, Hood River County
Little Lake Creek	Little White Salmon River, Skamania County, Washington
Cruzatt's [*Cruzatte's*] River	Wind River, Skamania County
Grand Rapid	Cascades of the Columbia River, Skamania County, Washington, Hood River and Multnomah counties, Oregon
Clahclellah Village	Skamania County (see entries of October 31, 1805, and April 9, 1806; *Atlas* map 79)
Wahclellar Village	Skamania County (see entry of November 2, 1805; *Atlas* map 79)
beacon rock creek	Perhaps Woodward Creek, Skamania County

Phoca Rock	Phoca Rock, Multnomah County (see entry of November 2, 1805; *Atlas* map 79)
Quicksand River	Sandy River, Multnomah County
Seal River	Washougal River, Skamania County
diamond Island	Government and McGuire islands, opposite Portland, Multnomah County (see entry of November 3, 1805; *Atlas* map 79)
Shahala Village	Portland, Multnomah County (see entry of November 4, 1805; *Atlas* map 79)
Multnomah River	Willamette River, Multnomah County
Multnomah Village	Sauvie Island, Multnomah County (see entry of November 4, 1805; *Atlas* map 80)
Quathlahpahtle Village	Clark County, Washington, just above Lewis River (see entry of November 5, 1805; *Atlas* maps 79, 80)
Cahwahnahiooks River	Lewis River, Clark-Cowlitz county line, Washington
Cathlahaws Creek	Kalama River, Cowlitz County
Elallah or deer Island	Deer Island, Columbia County, Oregon (see *Atlas* map 80)
Coweliske River	Cowlitz River, Cowlitz County
Fannys Island & Bottom	Crims Island and Bradbury Slough, Columbia County (see entry of November 6, 1805; *Atlas* map 81)
Sea otter Island	Perhaps Puget Island, Wahkiakum County, Washington (see entry of November 7, 1805; *Atlas* map 81)
Upper Village of the Warkiacums	Vicinity of Cathlamet, Wahkiakum County (see entry of November 7, 1805; *Atlas* map 81)
Cathlâhmâhs Village	Clatsop County, behind Karlson Island (see entries of November 11 and 26, 1805; *Atlas* map 82)
Point William	Tongue Point, Clatsop County (see entry of November 27, 1805; *Atlas* map 82)

405

Point Meriwether	Astoria and Youngs Bay, Clatsop County (see entry of November 29, 1805; *Atlas* map 82)
Clat-Sop Village	Point Adams, Clatsop County (see entry of November 21, 1805; *Atlas* map 82)
Fort Clatsop	Fort Clatsop National Memorial, on Lewis and Clark River, Clatsop County (see entry of December 7, 1805; *Atlas* map 84)
Point Adams	Point Adams, Clatsop County (see *Atlas* map 82)
River Rochejhone	Yellowstone River, Mackenzie County, North Dakota
Jos. Fields River	Charbonneau Creek, Mackenzie County
yallow rock	Mouth of Horse Creek, Yellowstone River, Mackenzie County (see Clark's entry of August 2, 1806)
Buffalow Crossings	On Yellowstone River below Sagebrush Creek, Richland County, Montana (see Clark's entry of August 2, 1806; *Atlas* maps 112, 122)
Ibex River	Smith Creek, Richland County (see Clark's entry of August 2, 1806; *Atlas* maps 112, 122)
Samuels Creek	Burns Creek, Richland County
Buffalow Creek	Thirteenmile Creek, Dawson County, Montana
Pine Brook	Sand Creek, Dawson County
Catfish Creek	Cedar Creek, Dawson County
Gibsons River	Cabin Creek, Prairie County, Montana
Oak-tar-pon-er Stone Coal River	O'Fallon Creek, Prairie County
Shabonos [*Charbonneau's*] River	Cherry Creek, Prairie County
Wolf rapid	On Yellowstone River below Powder River,

	Prairie County (see Clark's entry of July 31, 1806; *Atlas* map 121)
Wah-har-sop, redstone River	Powder River, Prairie County
Yorks dry river	Custer Creek, Prairie County
Yellow Bear rapids	Mouth of Camp Creek, Prairie County (see Clark's entry of July 30, 1806; *Atlas* map 121)
Buffalow Shoals	On Yellowstone River below Sand Creek, Custer County, Montana (see Clark's entry of July 30, 1806; *Atlas* map 120)
Dry River	Sunday Creek, Custer County
Lezeka or Tongue River	Tongue River, Custer County
Turtle Creek	Moon Creek, Custer County (see Clark's entry of July 29, 1806; *Atlas* map 120)
Mar-Shas-kap River	Graveyard Creek, Rosebud County, Montana
Wood Brook	Sweeney Creek, Rosebud County
upper Stone Coal Bluffs	On Yellowstone River above Sweeney Creek, Rosebud County (see Clark's entry of July 28, 1806)
Little Horn River	Rosebud Creek, Rosebud County
Table River	Horse Creek, Rosebud County
Little Wolf River	Big Porcupine Creek, Rosebud County
Chimney Bluffs	On Yellowstone River, opposite Reservation Creek, Rosebud County (see Clark's entry of July 27, 1806, *Atlas* maps 111, 119)
White Creek	Starved to Death Creek, Treasure County, Montana
Laabeech's [*Labiche's*] River	Sarpy Creek, Treasure County
Windsers [*Windsor's*] River	Muggins Creek, Treasure County
Elk River	Alkali Creek, Treasure County
Big horn River	Bighorn River, Treasure and Yellowstone counties, Montana
Island Brook	Buffalo Creek, Yellowstone County

White Clifts	On Yellowstone River below Cow Gulch, Yellowstone County (see Clark's entry of July 26, 1806; *Atlas* maps 110, 117)
Halls River	Cow Gulch, Yellowstone County
Shannons river	Fly Creek, Yellowstone County
pompeys Tower	Pompeys Pillar, Yellowstone County (see Clark's entry of July 25, 1806; *Atlas* maps 110, 116)
Tumbling Bluff	On Yellowstone River, between Rock and Pompeys Pillar creeks, Yellowstone County
Big Dry Brook	Crooked Creek, Yellowstone County
Pryors Creek	Pryor Creek, Yellowstone County
Rock Creek	Five Mile Creek, Yellowstone County
Pryors River	Dry Creek, Yellowstone County
Yellow Clifts	Sacrifice Cliff, Yellowstone County (see Clark's entry of July 24, 1806; *Atlas* maps 108, 116)
Horse Creek	Blue Creek, Yellowstone County
Clarks Fork	Clarks Fork Yellowstone River, Yellowstone County
Black bluffs opposit [Canoe Camp]	On Yellowstone River below Bullion Creek, Carbon County, Montana
Bluffs . . . N W side	Vicinity of Youngs Point, Carbon County
Rose Bud river	Stillwater River, Stillwater County, Montana
Dry Creek	Berry Creek, Stillwater County (see Clark's entry of July 18, 1806; *Atlas* maps 107, 115)
Muddy Creek	White Beaver Creek, Stillwater County
Weasel Creek	Hump Creek, Sweet Grass County, Montana
Brattens [*Bratton's*] River	Bridger Creek, Sweet Grass County
Otter River	Sweet Grass Creek, Sweet Grass County
Beaver river	Lower Deer Creek, Sweet Grass County

Thy Snaged Creek	Upper Deer Creek, Sweet Grass County (see Clark's entry of July 17, 1806; *Atlas* maps 107, 114)
Rivers a Cross	Big Timber Creek (north) and Boulder River (south), Sweet Grass County
Small rapid	On Yellowstone River below Jarrett Creek, Sweet Grass County (see Clark's entry of July 16, 1806; *Atlas* map 107)
Stinking Cabin Creek	Mission Creek or Locke Creek, Park County, Montana (see Clark's entry of July 16, 1806; *Atlas* maps 107, 114)
Shield River	Shields River, Park County (see Clark's entry of July 15, 1806; *Atlas* maps 106, 107, 113)
foot of the Rocky Mountains	Bridger Range, Park County
dividing ridge	Bozeman Pass, Bridger Range, Gallatin County, Montana (see Clark's entries of July 13 and 15, 1806; *Atlas* maps 106, 113)
middle branch of the East fork of Galletins River	Jackson Creek, Gallatin County (see Clark's entry of July 15, 1806; *Atlas* maps 106, 113)
middle branch of the east fork of Galletins River passing down . . . a branch	East Gallatin River (coming down Kelly Creek), Gallatin County (see Clark's entry of July 14, 1806; *Atlas* maps 106, 113)
three forks of East fork of Gallitins river	Bridger, Rocky, and Bozeman creeks, Gallatin County (see Clark's entry of July 14, 1806; *Atlas* maps 106, 113)
main fork of Gallitins river	Gallatin River, Gallatin County
Galletins River	Gallatin River
forks where our Canoes were left	Camp Fortunate, forks of the Beaverhead River, Beaverhead County, Montana (see entry of August 17, 1805, and Clark's entry of July 8, 1806; *Atlas* map 66)
Gap in the mountains	Big Hole Pass, Beaverhead County (see Clark's entry of July 7, 1806; *Atlas* maps 67, 103, 104)

Willards Creek	Divide Creek, Beaverhead County (see Clark's entry of July 7, 1806; *Atlas* maps 67, 103, 104)
Wisdom River	Big Hole River
boiling Hot Spring	Jackson Hot Spring, Beaverhead County (see Clark's entry of July 7, 1806; *Atlas* maps 103, 104)
Glade Creek	Trail Creek, Beaverhead County, passing Big Hole River (see Clark's entry of July 6, 1806; *Atlas* maps 68, 103)
head of Glade Creek	Gibbons Pass, head of Trail Creek, Continental Divide, Beaverhead and Ravalli counties, Montana (see Clark's entry of July 6, 1806; *Atlas* maps 68, 103)
Oatlashoot vally	Ross's Hole, Ravalli County (see entry of September 4, 1805, and Clark's entry of July 5, 1806; *Atlas* maps 68, 103)
Middle fork of Clarks river	East Fork Bitterroot River, Ravalli County
flour Camp Creek	Warm Springs Creek, Ravalli County (see Clark's entry of July 5, 1806; *Atlas* map 68)
West fork of Clarks river	West Fork Bitterroot River, Ravalli County (see entry of September 7, 1805; *Atlas* map 68)
Scattered Creek	Mill, North Spring, and Burnt Fork creeks, Ravalli County (see entry of September 8, 1805; *Atlas* map 68)
Travellers rest Creek	Lolo Creek, Missoula County, Montana

1. The figures for this column do not appear in many instances in Voorhis No. 4.

2. Unnamed in Voorhis No. 4.

3. Given as "Big Horn River" in Voorhis No. 4.

4. Given as "10" in Voorhis No. 4.

5. The figures under the respective columns are given as "3, 10, 200, and 2775" in Voorhis No. 4.

6. This figure is given as "5" in Voorhis No. 4 and no other figures appear under this entry.

7. The Voorhis No. 4 version reads: "To the Junction of the roads on the tope of the

highest mountain crossed a fork at Flathead R. at 2 ms." The figure under column two is given as "15." After this entry the Voorhis No. 4 version differs considerably with the co-dex journal. In the Voorhis notebook Clark condensed the remaining entries to a single page, mentioning only the major points from "Hungary Creek" to the coast.

8. With this entry it appears that Lewis begins writing and seems to do so intermit-tantly until the entry for "Fannys Island" at mileage 3490. It is not certain whether he also entered the mileage figures.

9. This phrase in red ink appears to be in Clark's handwriting. Book no. 9 refers to Codex I which was notebook number nine in Biddle's numbering system. The emenda-tion, therefore, must have been written about 1810 when Clark and Biddle were confer-ring on the latter's work on the history of the expedition. A similar reference occurs at the end of this section of Codex N, again written in red and again apparently in Clark's hand.

10. This paragraph and the next one are crossed out with a heavy diagonal line.

11. This paragraph, apparently in Clark's hand, is written in red ink; see a note above in reference to "Book No. 9."

Part 2: Miscellany

The following miscellaneous items do not fit into other sections of this chapter. These notes were apparently made after the party left Fort Clatsop in March 1806 or are related to the period after that time, perhaps being written as late as after the return to St. Louis in September 1806.

[Clark]   [*undated*][1]

The navagation of the Missouri to the neighbourhood of the falls is only obstructed by a regularly Swift Current, Sand bars, & trees un-beaded in the bottom   no rapids or falls of any Consequence and [in?] The 2575 miles.

The large Rivers which fall into the Missouri are

1st   Osage on S. Side   navagable a long way
2   Kanzas S. S.   do   in Canoes long way
3   R. Plate not nav: one inch
Little & Big R. Scioux & R. Jacque nav: a Short Dists. on N. S.
R. Quecurre not navagbe. one inch
⟨Teton River Nav for Ca⟩
White River Nav. for Canoes Som Distance S. Side

Teton R.   do   do   do   S. Sd.

Chyenne large & nav. for boats Some Way S. S.

Cannon Ball & 2 other on S. Side for Cans a Short dists.

Little Missouri abov Mandans Nav. a ⟨Short⟩ long Dis for Cans S. Side

White Earth River Small Nav. for Cans Sht Dist. N. Sd.

Rochejhon (or Yellow rock R.) Navg a long ways   Capt. Clark decended this
    river 818 miles in Cans.

Porcupine River high up on N. Side   Nav. Short dists.

Marias River near the falls   navg for boats a Short distance & for Canoes to
    near the mountains   on the N. Side of the Missouri

Medicine Ri. 35 abov the falls navigable a few Miles N. Side

The 3 forks Jefferson Madisins & Galitin Rivers are all navgable for Small
    Canoes to their Source ⟨plenty beaver⟩

☞ The rout which I should propose to carry on this trade across the
Continant is from St Louis by the Missouri to the Falls of that river 2575
Miles ⟨in Balluax of [*blank*] Weight roaling requiring 8 men⟩ then by land
on horses to the Forks of Kooskooske West of the Great rocky mountains
340 Miles thence Down Lewis River & the Columbia 640 Miles to the Pacific Ocian. The best Situation for a Tradeing Establishment on that River
is 125 miles above it's ⟨mouth⟩ Enterance at the ⟨Enterance⟩ confluence of
Multnomah River from the South   here vestles of any Size may ride in
Safty

The winter Establishments of Lewis & Clark in 1804 & 5 was at Mandans Nation 1600 miles up the Mandan Misouri in Latd. 47° 21′ 47″
North and within 150 miles of the British Tradeing Establishments on
the waters of Lake Winnipic & Hudsons Bay—   in the Spring of 1805
the party proceded on in large pereogus & Canoes to the falls of the Missouri 966 Miles in Latd. 47° 8 4 N. *Current rapid & muddy*   here the party
left the large perogue, and hauled the Canoes acrossed a portage of 18
miles, through an open plain.   here the Missouri has a fall within 17 m
of about 362 feet in which there are Several pitches are perpendiclr. and
fall ⟨to an imenc hight⟩ one of 97 feet, 19 feet & 47 & 26 feet 5 Inches.
⟨above those falls⟩ from those falls we view the range of Rocky Mountains
(so Called) to a great Distance to N W. & South— above those falls the
cors Missouri is more South   in assending we penetrate the 1st range of

Rocky Mountains at about 30 Miles on a Direct line, then with the Derection of the Mountains to the East of S. 181 Miles to the 3 forks Jefferson Madson's & Galitines River in Lat. 45° 22′ 34″ N— we Proceeded up Jeffersons River in a S Westely Direction 276 miles by water to its Source or head Spring in Lat. 44° 33′ 22″ North— from thence across to Lewis River a Branch of the Columbia is 10 mile west (here the *Shoshone* or Snake Indians reside) this river is not navagable & no road in this Direction across to the W. of those Emenc mountains. ⟨our Cours⟩ we hired a guide and proceded on over Emenc mountains on which there was Snow Augt. & Septr. to Clarks River a Branch of the Columbia, about 100 miles where we met with the *Tushepaws* or flat head Inds. then Down that river in a vally about 200 Miles Travelers rest Creek Latd. 46 48 26 at a road which passes from the plains East of the Mountains near the falls of Missouri across those Mountains to the plains of Columbia West of those mountains (and the rout proposed to Carry on the Trade) here Commences the rugid part of those Emenc Mountains, after resting a few Days on Clarks River at this Road where we found a fiew deer, we proceded on over those emenc rugid Mountains of Snow (in which the party were Compelled to live on horse flesh) to the Forks Kooskooske 183 miles 140 miles of which distance was over emenc Mountains 60 ms. of Snow here Canoes were built & decended the Kooskooske ⟨73⟩ to Lewis's river from the South down that river to the main Columbia from the N. in Latd. 46° 15′ 13″ and down the Columbia to its enterance in Lat. 46 19 11 N. and Longt. 124° 57′ W. of Greenwich being 640 miles by Water and nearly a West Course. The party arived on the pacific Coast 17 Nov. & built a fort in which they Continued untill the 23 of March following & then Set out on their return by water as far as the Great falls of the Columbia 268 where Some hors were precured to Carry ⟨bagga⟩ Some Currents passes ⟨3 involands⟩ & then on foot through an open Country for [*blank*] miles to the foot of the Mtn.

[*blank*] miles to the foot of the mountain where the party were obliged to delay from the 9th of May untill the 24th of June for the Snows of the mountain to Subside Sufficient to Cross, and then pased over Snow for 60 ms generally from 3 to 6 or 8 feet deep quit ⟨firm &⟩ Consolidated, or Sufficiently So to bear a hors at the Enterance of Travelers rest on

Clarks river Capt Lewis & Clark Seperated. Lewis passed imedeately to the falls of the Missouri on an old indian parth of good road　left a party at that place to prepar ⟨Geer & Wheels &c⟩ and proceded with 3 men to Explore a large N. fork of the Missouri Called *Marias* River and met with a party of Indians & was Compelled to kill 2 of them. Clark with [*blank*] men passed up Clarks river and across the heads of Several branches of the Missouri to the place the Canoes had been left on his outward bound journey at the head of Jeffersons river, ⟨Sent down⟩ decended Jeffersons river to the 3 forks, and Sent on the Canoes down the Missouri under the derection of a Sergt. and proceded himself up Galitines River and passed over to the River Rochejhon or Yellow rock river from the South in Latd. 45° 22 N. and ⟨built⟩ made Canoes of wood & Buffalow Canoes & decended that river 818 miles to its junction with the Missouri 1880 Miles from St. Louis.

The Streams of the Missouri near & within those mountains abound in beaver & otter.

The Muddiness of the Missouri is Caused by the Washing in of it's banks— within the rocky mountains the Water is Clear

The Pumies Stone which is found as low as the Illinois Country is formd by the banks or Stratums of Coal taking fire and burning the earth imedeately above it into either pumies Stone or Lavia, this Coal Country is principly above the Mandans—

The Country from the Mississippi to the River Plate 630 Miles ⟨will afford of a good⟩ furnishes a Sufficient qty of Wood for Settlements— above that River the ⟨wood⟩ Country becoms more open, and wood principally Confined to river & Creek bottoms.　the uplands furtile and open, with Some exceptions　on the Rochejhone R. Capt Clark Saw Some Pine Country and the ranges of low Black mountains are Covered with wood.　most of the large Rivers fall in on the South side of the Missouri.

1. This brief summary of the expedition's route and its major features may have been started at Fort Clatsop but includes discussions of terrain that was explored after that time. It may have been a preliminary draft for the descriptions of the party's trip that the captains sent to Jefferson and others in September 1806; see Jackson (LLC), 1:317–43. The document as printed here is a combination of two items at the American Philosophical Society. The first part is from the little field book containing Clark's draft of his side

trip from Fort Clatsop to the coast, January 6–10, 1806, and other miscellaneous items such as this one. The second part is from Codex T, beginning with the paragraph "[*blank*] miles to the foot of the mountain." The first words of Codex T repeat the last words from this section of the field draft and the two clearly belong together. See Appendices B and C, vol. 2; Moulton (SJ), 198–99.

[Clark]   [*undated*] [1]

Cowe[lis]kee River

Chah nwah na hi oos River, alter to quathlah potte r.

add Several on Wappato Island

The Multnomah

The Skillute Nation on The Coweleske River

Multnomah River and the tribes on Wappato Island

Seal & Quicksand Rivers

add Several nations and their names on the Columbia

Mt. Jefferson & Clarkamos River &c.

add the *Skaddatts*—   and other nations

a large Creek above River la page on North Side

alter the Towarnahiooks River

add a River below the Mucle Shele rapid on South Side *You-ma-lol-am*

Walllah wallah River & the road by land

South fork of Louises River & the Stream & Nations

Clarks River & the Streams & Nations. Lake &c.

The East and West fork of Clarks River &c. &c.

Wisdom River and hot Spring Vally. Willards Creek & &c.

Galletins River and the portage of 48 miles & mountains

River Rochejhone and it's waters

1. This document is a loose sheet in the Voorhis collection, written by Clark some time after he completed his exploration of the Yellowstone River. This list of Indian tribes and locations was apparently intended as an aid in the creation of a map of the explorers' route and the placement of Indian tribes.

[Clark]   [*undated*] [1]

Note. The *Iynn* commence about the Calumet Bluffs and downwards.—

    950 Ms. up the Missouri

The Prarie Fowl common to the Illinois are found as high up as the River Jacque above which the Sharpe tailed Grows commence   950 Ms.

The Black Walnut is found as high up as ⟨Floyds⟩ White Stone river and from thence down on the high rich lands.   900 Ms.

Mulberry is found as high up as Grand River de Sieoux.   858

Prickly pear is not Common below the Queequerre   1000 ms

Hickory is to be found below the Mahars and black birch in the Same Country, also the *horn beem*   (830 ms.)

Racoons is found from the Calumet Bluffs downwards & on the Pacific Coast also the *honey locus* and *Coffee nut*   650

Indian Hen & Small Species of Kildee which frequent drift is found as high up as the Entrance of the Little Sieux river   733 ms.

The large *Black* and *Brindle Wolf* is found as high up as the Mahars Village—   the Small burrowing wolf of the prarie is found as low as the Mahars & some fiew near the Missippi   836 Ms.

The *Black Bear* is found in abundance as high as the little Sioux river, and the are found much higher but scerce. The *Ass smart* is also found in the Same neighbourhood.   733 ms.

Parotqueet is Seen as high as the Mahar Village   836 ms.

Opossum is found as high as the River platt.   600 ms.

Grey Squrils are found as high up as little Sieux R   733

Hack berry and Hasel bushes are found as high up as the Council bluff   also red oake and *Sycamore* several species of oake Iron wood   650 mes.

Papaws arrow wood and [*letters crossed out, illegible*] elder are found as high as the little Nemahaw, also Sugar tree   480 mil

Buckeye & ⟨Sugartree⟩ is found as high up as the old Kanzas village above Independance Creek   285 ms

Green Bryar found as high up as [*blank*]

Pacans are found as high up ⟨as Osarge River⟩[2]   400

In decending the Missouri & Rochejhone

The *Grapes* of the Small kind first appear on the River Rochejhone near it's enterance into the Rocky mountains   2700 mils   but are not abundant on that river, the grape are abundant below cannon ball rivers

1500 ms up   and from thence down to the enterance of the river into the Mississippi.   no grapes of the large kind

Wild plumbs first appear at the cut off or Mandan Isld.   below the mandans tho' they are Scerce and Small   they becom abundant and fine in the neighbourhood of the enterance of White River.   1580 ms

white oake first appear 60 miles below the Ricaras Vilg. and are found in considerable quantity in the river bottoms just above the enterance of Corvus Creek.   1370 mes up

white ash at ash rapid on the Missouri up and on the River rochejhone 60 miles above it's enterance.   2443 ms. up

Elm is found Something higher up the rivers than the ash   2500

Prickly ash first appears a fiew miles above Bull Island in the river bottoms. Shoemate commences—   2500

Turkeys first appear at the enterance of Tylors Rivr above the big bend 1200 miles up this ⟨river⟩ Missouri   1206

The pointed tail Prarie fowl are found above the Big bend upwards.   1200 ms. up   box elder as high as the Mandans   1600

The party coloured Corvus or *Magpy* Commence at or about Corvus Creek and from thence upwards.   1130

The Fox Squirel first appear a fiew miles above the Dome where we first met with the *burrowing or Barking Squirels*   1030 Mils. up the [Missouri] Missouri whipperwill is the common attendant of those squirels.

The Big horn animal is found as low as the Beaver bend a fiew miles below the enterance of the rochejhone.   1800 ms. up

The Antilope or Cabra are found in great abundance as low as the Chyenne River, and are seen scattering as low down as the neighbourhood of the Mahar village.   or 800 ms up

Mule or Black tail Deer is met with ⟨at⟩ on the Snowey mts. up and are found as low down the Missouri as the antient fortification & on Boon homm Island or good mans Island   1000 m

Brarow are found as low as Council Bluff   650 ms. up

Yellow Oker above the upper old Kanzas Village in a ben on the S side

Chock Cherry found between the 2 Nemahars Rivers 500 miles up the Missouri also another species of Cherry

Sycamore is found at Ball pated prarie

417

1. This document is found in Codex N, pp. 153–54 (reading backwards). The last three entries (yellow oker, chock cherry, and sycamore) are found only in another copy, in the notebook Voorhis No. 4; it also contains other slight variations that are omitted here. The species may be identified as: lynn, American linden; prairie fowl common to the Illinois, greater prairie-chicken; sharp-tailed grouse; black walnut; red mulberry; prickly pear; hickory, either bitternut hickory or shagbark hickory; black birch, perhaps river birch, *Betula nigra* L.; American hornbeam; raccoon; honey locust, *Gleditsia triancanthos* L.; coffeenut, Kentucky coffee-tree, *Gymnocladus dioica* (L.) K. Koch; Indian hen, greater prairie-chicken; killdeer, *Charadrius vociferus* [AOU, 273]; black wolf, gray wolf; small wolf, coyote; black bear; ass smart, perhaps smartweed, *Polygonum* sp.; parroquet, Carolina parakeet, *Conuropsis carolinensis* [AOU, 382]; opossum, *Didelphis virginiana;* gray squirrel; hackberry, *Celtis occidentalis* L.; hazelnut, *Corylus americana* Walt.; red oak, *Quercus borealis* Michx.; sycamore; iron wood, hop-hornbeam, *Ostrya virginiana* (Mill.) K. Koch; pawpaw; arrowwood, black haw; elder, common elderberry; sugar tree, sugar maple, *Acer saccharum* Marsh.; western buckeye, *Aesculus glabra* Willd.; green briar, probably bristly greenbriar, *Smilax hispida* Muhl.; pecan, *Carya illinoensis* (Wang.) K. Koch; small grape, probably river-bank grape, *Vitis riparia* Michx.; large grape, *Vitis* sp.; wild plum; white oak, probably bur oak (see September 2, 1806); white ash, probably green ash (see September 2, 1806); American elm; prickly ash; shoemate, perhaps smooth sumac (see June 10, 1806); turkey; pointed tail prairie fowl, sharp-tailed grouse; boxelder, *Acer negundo* L.; black-billed magpie; fox squirrel; barking squirrel, prairie dog; Missouri whip-poor-will, common poorwill; bighorn sheep; antelope, pronghorn; mule deer; brarow, badger; yellow ocher, the mineral limonite (see July 5, 1804); choke cherry.

2. Another word was substituted for these crossed out ones but is not legible. The Voorhis version is no help. The word begins with "N" and both the Nemaha and Nodaway rivers are in the area of four hundred miles up the Missouri by Clark's calculations, but the letters do not appear to form those words.

[Clark]   From St. Louis 1806[1]

Memorandum of articles fowarded to Louisville by Capt. Clark in care of Mr. Wolpards[2] 1s.

one large Box Containing

4   large Horns of the Bighorn animal
2   Sceletens   do   do   do
2   Skins horns & bons of   do
4   Mandan Robes of Buffalow
1   Indian Blanket of the Sheep
1   Sheep Skin of the rocky mountains
1   Brarow Skin
3   Bear Skins of the White Speces

3 barking Squirls
2 Skins of the big horn
1 Mule or black tail Deer Skin
1 Hat made by the Clatsops Indians
2 Indian Baskets
4 buffalow horns
1 Tigor Cat Skin Coat
1 long box of sundery articles
1 Tin box containing Medicine &c &c. &c.

a Small Box of papers

Books and Sundery Small articles

a Hat Box containing the 4 vols. of the Deckinsery of arts an ciences[3]   two Indian wallets a tale of the black taile Deer of the Ocean & a Vulters quill with a buffalow Coat.

Capt. Lewis forward to Washington by Lieut. Peters[4] in

Box No. 1

6 Skins and Sceletens complete of the mountain ram, three male and 3 female
1 Blacktail Deer Skin
1 Sheep Skin
4 Barking Squirels
3 Bear Skins
1 White Wolf
3 beaver tales

No. 2

2 Boxes Containing Various articles
1 Tin Case   do   do
1 air gun
4 Robins
1 Clat sop hat

    1. This list appears in Codex N, pp. 1–2. A dark vertical line runs the length of the text.

    2. Probably Adam Woolford, or Woodford, who operated a boat between St. Louis and Louisville; see April 15, 1804.

    3. Jackson (SBLC), 11–13, discusses what these volumes may be. One possibility is Ephraim Chambers' *Cyclopedia: or, An Universal Dictionary of Arts and Sciences.* Another is Owen's *Dictionary,* so called after the publisher.

    4. George Peter; see September 22, 1806.

Sources Cited

Allen (PG)　　　　　　　Allen, John Logan. *Passage through the Garden: Lewis and Clark and the Image of the American Northwest*. Urbana: University of Illinois Press, 1975.

AOU　　　　　　　　　American Ornithologists' Union. *Check-list of North American Birds*. 6th ed. Baltimore, Md.: American Ornithologists' Union, 1983. [AOU] in brackets with numbers refers to a species item number in the book.

Appleman (LC)　　　　Appleman, Roy E. *Lewis and Clark: Historic Places Associated with Their Transcontinental Exploration (1804–1806)*. Washington, D.C.: United States Department of the Interior, National Park Service, 1975.

Atlas　　　　　　　　Moulton, Gary E., ed. *Atlas of the Lewis and Clark Expedition*. Lincoln: University of Nebraska Press, 1983.

Bailey　　　　　　　　Bailey, L. H. *Manual of Cultivated Plants*. Rev. ed. New York: Macmillan, 1949.

Baldwin (KA)　　　　Baldwin, Leland D. *The Keelboat Age on Western Waters*. Pittsburgh: University of Pittsburgh Press, 1941.

Barkley　　　　　　　Barkley, T. M., ed. *Atlas of the Flora of the Great Plains*. Ames: Iowa State University Press, 1977.

Benson (HLCE)　　　Benson, Keith R. "Herpetology on the Lewis and Clark Expedition: 1804–1806." *Herpetological Review* 3 (September 1978): 87–91.

Bergantino　　　　　Bergantino, Robert N. "Lewis's Fight with the Blackfeet: A Re-evaluation of the Site." Butte, Montana, 1990.

Berry   Berry, Don. *A Majority of Scoundrels: An Informal History of the Rocky Mountain Fur Company.* New York: Harper, 1961.

Boivin & Lôve   Boivin, Bernard, and D. Lôve. "*Poa agassizensis,* a New Prairie Bluegrass." *Le Naturaliste Canadien* 87 (June–July 1960): 173–80.

Booth & Wright   Booth, W. E., and J. C. Wright. *Flora of Montana, Part II.* Bozeman: Montana State University, 1959.

Brackenridge   Brackenridge, Henry M. *Journal of a Voyage up the River Missouri Performed in Eighteen Hundred and Eleven.* In Thwaites (EWT), 6:23–166.

Bradbury   Bradbury, John. *Travels in the Interior of America, in the Years 1809, 1810, and 1811.* . . . In Thwaites (EWT), 5:25–320.

Bradley (MS)   Bradley, James H. "The Bradley Manuscript, Book 2." *Contributions to the Historical Society of Montana* 8 (1917): 126–96.

Bradley (MMC)   ———. *The March of the Montana Column: A Prelude to the Custer Disaster.* Edited by Edgar I. Stewart. Norman: University of Oklahoma Press, 1961.

Brown   Brown, Lloyd A. *The Story of Maps.* Boston: Little, Brown, 1949.

Burroughs   Burroughs, Raymond Darwin. *The Natural History of the Lewis and Clark Expedition.* East Lansing: Michigan State University Press, 1961.

Carter (RC)   Carter, Harvey L. "Ramsay Crooks." In Hafen, 9:125–31.

Carter (RM)   ———. "Robert McClellan." In Hafen, 8:221–28.

Chittenden   Chittenden, Hiram M. *The American Fur Trade of the Far West.* 2 vols. New York: Harper, 1902.

Christman   Christman, Gene M. "The Mountain Bison." *American West* 8 (May 1971): 44–47.

Chuinard (OOMD)   Chuinard, Eldon G. *Only One Man Died: The Medical Aspects of the Lewis and Clark Expedition.* Glendale, Calif.: Arthur H. Clark, 1979.

Cook   Cook, Warren L. *Flood Tide of Empire: Spain and the Pacific Northwest, 1543–1819.* New Haven: Yale University Press, 1973.

Coues (HLC) Coues, Elliott, ed. *History of the Expedition under the Command of Lewis and Clark.* . . . 1893. Reprint. 3 vols. New York: Dover Publications, 1965.

Coues (NLEH) ———, ed. *New Light on the Early History of the Greater Northwest.* 3 vols. New York: Harper, 1897.

Criswell Criswell, Elijah Harry. *Lewis and Clark: Linguistic Pioneers.* University of Missouri Studies, vol. 15, no. 2. Columbia: University of Missouri Press, 1940.

Cruikshank Cruikshank, Ernest Alexander. "Robert Dickson, the Indian Trader." *Collections of the State Historical Society of Wisconsin,* 12 : 133–53. Madison, Wis.: Democrat Publishing Company, 1892.

Cutright (LCPN) Cutright, Paul Russell. *Lewis and Clark: Pioneering Naturalists.* Urbana: University of Illinois Press, 1969.

Dickson (HH) Dickson, Frank H. "Hard on the Heels of Lewis and Clark." *Montana, the Magazine of Western History* 26 (Winter 1976): 14–25.

Dickson (JD) ———. "Joseph Dickson." In Hafen, 3 : 71–79.

Dorn Dorn, Robert D. *Vascular Plants of Montana.* Cheyenne, Wyo.: Mountain West Publishing, 1984.

Ehrenberg Ehrenberg, Ralph. "Our Heritage in Maps: 'Sketch of Part of the Missouri & Yellowstone Rivers with a Description of the Country &c.'" *Prologue, the Journal of the National Archives* 3 (Fall 1971): 73–78.

Ewers (BRNP) Ewers, John C. *The Blackfeet: Raiders on the Northwestern Plains.* Norman: University of Oklahoma Press, 1958.

Ewers (ILUM) ———. *Indian Life on the Upper Missouri.* Norman: University of Oklahoma Press, 1968.

Fahey Fahey, John. *The Flathead Indians.* Norman: University of Oklahoma Press, 1974.

Fernald Fernald, Merritt Lyndon. *Gray's Manual of Botany.* 8th ed. New York: D. Van Nostrand, 1950.

Foley Foley, William E. *The Genesis of Missouri: From*

Wilderness Outpost to Statehood. Columbia: University of Missouri Press, 1989.

Foley & Rice Foley, William E., and C. David Rice. *The First Chouteaus: River Barons of Early St. Louis.* Urbana: University of Illinois Press, 1983.

Frazer Frazer, Robert W. *Forts of the West: Military Forts and Presidios and Posts Commonly Called Forts West of the Mississippi River to 1898.* Norman: University of Oklahoma Press, 1965.

Frey Frey, Rodney. *The World of the Crow Indians: As Driftwood Lodges.* Norman: University of Oklahoma Press, 1987.

Glover Glover, Richard, ed. *David Thompson's Narrative, 1784–1812.* Toronto: Champlain Society, 1962.

Hafen Hafen, LeRoy E., ed. *The Mountain Men and the Fur Trade of the Far West.* 10 vols. Glendale, Calif.: Arthur H. Clark, 1965.

Hagan Hagan, William T. *The Sac and Fox Indians.* Norman: University of Oklahoma Press, 1958.

Hahn Hahn, Barton E. *Flora of Montana: Conifers and Monocots.* Bozeman: Montana State University, 1977.

Hanson Hanson, Charles E. *The Northwest Gun.* Lincoln: Nebraska State Historical Society, 1955.

Harris Harris, Burton. *John Colter: His Years in the Rockies.* New York: Charles Scribner's Sons, 1952.

Hassrick Hassrick, Royal B. *The Sioux: Life and Customs of a Warrior Society.* Norman: University of Oklahoma Press, 1964.

Hay & Werner Hay, Thomas Robson, and M. R. Werner. *The Admirable Trumpeter: A Biography of General James Wilkinson.* New York: Doubleday, Doran, and Company, 1941.

Heitman Heitman, Francis B. *Historical Register of the United States Army, from Its Organization, September 29, 1789, to September 29, 1889.* Washington, D.C.: National Tribune, 1890.

Hitchcock & Chase Hitchcock, A. S. *Manual of the Grasses of the United*

	States. Revised by Agnes Chase. 2d ed. 2 vols. New York: Dover Publications, 1971.
Hitchcock et al.	Hitchcock, C. Leo, Arthur Cronquist, Marion Ownbey, and J. W. Thompson. *Vascular Plants of the Pacific Northwest.* 5 vols. Seattle: University of Washington Press, 1955–69.
Hodge	Hodge, Frederick Webb, ed. *Handbook of American Indians North of Mexico.* 1912. Reprint. 2 vols. St. Clair Shores, Mich.: Scholarly Press, 1968.
Hollon	Hollon, W. Eugene. *The Lost Pathfinder: Zebulon Montgomery Pike.* Norman: University of Oklahoma Press, 1949.
Holmgren	Holmgren, Virginia C. "A Glossary of Bird Names Cited by Lewis and Clark." *We Proceeded On* 10 (May 1984): 28–34.
Houck	Houck, Louis. *A History of Missouri from the Earliest Explorations and Settlements until the Admission of the State into the Union.* 3 vols. Chicago: R. R. Donnelley and Sons, 1908.
Hyde (IHP)	Hyde, George E. *Indians of the High Plains: From the Prehistoric Period to the Coming of the Europeans.* Norman: University of Oklahoma Press, 1959.
Innis	Innis, Harold A. *The Fur Trade in Canada: An Introduction to Canadian Economic History.* 1930. Reprint. Toronto: University of Toronto Press, 1970.
Irving (Astor)	Irving, Washington. *Astoria.* 1836. Reprint. Portland, Oreg.: Binfords and Mort, 1967.
Jackson (DS)	Jackson, Donald. "Call Him a Good Old Dog, But Don't Call Him Scannon." *We Proceeded On* 11 (August 1985): 5–8.
Jackson (SBLC)	———. "Some Books Carried by Lewis and Clark." *Bulletin of the Missouri Historical Society* 16 (October 1959): 3–13.
Jackson (JP)	———, ed. *The Journals of Zebulon Montgomery Pike with Letters and Related Documents.* 2 vols. Norman: University of Oklahoma Press, 1966.
Jackson (LLC)	———, ed. *Letters of the Lewis and Clark Expedition*

	with Related Documents, 1783–1854. 2d ed. 2 vols. Urbana: University of Illinois Press, 1978.
James	James, Thomas. *Three Years Among the Indians and Mexicans.* Edited by Milo M. Quaife. New York: Citadel Press, 1967.
Josephy	Josephy, Alvin M., Jr. *The Nez Perce Indians and the Opening of the Northwest.* New Haven: Yale University Press, 1965.
Lamb	Lamb, W. Kaye, ed. *The Journals and Letters of Sir Alexander Mackenzie.* Cambridge: Cambridge University Press, 1970.
Lavender (FW)	Lavender, David. *The Fist in the Wilderness.* New York: Doubleday, 1964.
Little (CIH)	Little, Elbert L., Jr. *Atlas of United States Trees.* Vol. 1, *Conifers and Important Hardwoods.* Washington, D.C.: United States Department of Agriculture, Forest Service, 1971.
Little (MWH)	———. *Atlas of United States Trees.* Vol. 3, *Minor Western Hardwoods.* Washington, D.C.: United States Department of Agriculture, Forest Service, 1976.
Long	Long, John. *Voyages and Travels of an Indian Interpreter and Trader. . . .* In Thwaites (EWT), 2:21–329.
Loomis & Nasatir	Loomis, Noel M., and Abraham P. Nasatir. *Pedro Vial and the Roads to Santa Fe.* Norman: University of Oklahoma Press, 1967.
McDermott (GMVF)	McDermott, John Francis. *A Glossary of Mississippi Valley French, 1673–1850.* St. Louis: Washington University, 1941.
Majors	Majors, Harry M. "John McClellan in the Montana Rockies, 1807: The First Americans after Lewis and Clark." *Northwest Discovery* 2 (November–December 1981): 554–630.
Mattes (JR)	Mattes, Merrill J. "Joseph Robidoux." In Hafen, 8:287–314.
Mattes (FR)	———. "Report on Historic Sites in the Fort Randall Reservoir Area, Missouri River, South

Dakota." *South Dakota Historical Collections* 24 (1949): 470–577.

Mattison (OR)   Mattison, Ray H. "Report on Historical Aspects of the Oahe Reservoir Area, Missouri River, South and North Dakota." *South Dakota Historical Collections* 27 (1943): 1–159.

Mattison (GP)   ———. "Report on Historic Sites Adjacent to the Missouri River, Between the Big Sioux River and Fort Randall Dam, Including Those in the Gavins Point Reservoir Area." *South Dakota Historical Collections* 28 (1956): 22–98.

Mattison (GR)   ———. "Report on Historic Sites in the Garrison Reservoir Area, Missouri River." *North Dakota History* 22 (January–April 1955): 5–73.

Mattison (BB)   ———. "Report on the Historic Sites in the Big Bend Reservoir Area, South Dakota." *South Dakota Historical Collections* 31 (1962): 243–86.

Meyer   Meyer, Roy W. *The Village Indians of the Upper Missouri: The Mandans, Hidatsas, and Arikaras.* Lincoln: University of Nebraska Press, 1977.

Miller (MNA)   Miller, Orson K., Jr. *Mushrooms of North America.* New York: E. P. Dutton, 1972.

MRC   Missouri River Commission. *Map of the Missouri River from Its Mouth to Three Forks, Montana, in Eighty-four Sheets.* Washington, D.C.: Missouri River Commission, 1892–95.

MRY   *Missouri River: Gavins Point Near Yankton, South Dakota to Stanton, North Dakota.* Omaha, Nebr.: Corps of Engineers, 1949.

MRM   *Missouri River: Mouth to Rulo.* Kansas City, Mo.: Corps of Engineers, 1947–49.

MRR   *Missouri River: Rulo, Nebraska, to Yankton, South Dakota.* Omaha, Nebr.: Corps of Engineers, 1947–49.

Morgan   Morgan, Dale L., ed. *The West of William H. Ashley, 1822–1838.* Denver: Old West Publishing Company, 1964.

Mueggler & Stewart   Mueggler, Walter F., and William L. Stewart. "Grassland and Shrubland Habitat Types of

	Western Montana." United States Department of Agriculture, Forest Service, General Technical Report INT-66. Ogden, Utah, 1980.
Munnick (PD)	Munnick, Harriet D. "Pierre Dorion." In Hafen, 8:107–12.
Nasatir (BR)	Nasatir, Abraham P. *Borderland in Retreat: From Spanish Louisiana to the Far Southwest.* Albuquerque: University of New Mexico Press, 1976.
Ney	Ney, Virgil. *Fort on the Prairie: Fort Atkinson on the Council Bluff, 1819–1827.* Washington, D.C.: Command Publications, 1978.
Oglesby	Oglesby, Richard Edward. *Manuel Lisa and the Opening of the Missouri Fur Trade.* Norman: University of Oklahoma Press, 1963.
Osgood (ODS)	Osgood, Ernest S. "Our Dog Scannon—Partner in Discovery." *Montana, the Magazine of Western History* 26 (Summer 1976): 8–17.
Osgood (FN)	———, ed. *The Field Notes of Captain William Clark, 1803–1805.* New Haven: Yale University Press, 1964.
Peebles (LT)	Peebles, John J. "On the Lolo Trail: Route and Campsites of Lewis and Clark." *Idaho Yesterdays* 9 (Winter 1965–66): 2–15.
Peebles (RLC)	———. "The Return of Lewis and Clark." *Idaho Yesterdays* 10 (Summer 1966): 16–27.
Peterson	Peterson, Harold L. *The Book of the Continental Soldier.* Harrisburg, Pa.: Stackpole Company, 1968.
Quaife (MLJO)	Quaife, Milo Milton, ed. *The Journals of Captain Meriwether Lewis and Sergeant John Ordway Kept on the Expedition of Western Exploration, 1803–1806.* Madison: State Historical Society of Wisconsin, 1916.
Rees	Rees, John E. "The Shoshoni Contribution to Lewis and Clark." *Idaho Yesterdays* 2 (Summer 1958): 2–13.
Rogers	Rogers, Ann. "Was it the Pawpaws?" *We Proceeded On* 13 (February 1987): 17–18.
Ronda (AE)	Ronda, James P. *Astoria and Empire.* Lincoln: University of Nebraska Press, 1990.

Ronda (LCAI)   ———. *Lewis and Clark among the Indians*. Lincoln: University of Nebraska Press, 1984.

Ronda (SLW)   ———. "St. Louis Welcomes and Toasts the Lewis and Clark Expedition." *We Proceeded On* 13 (February 1987): 19–20.

Russell (FTT)   Russell, Carl P. *Firearms, Traps, and Tools of the Mountain Men*. New York: Knopf, 1967.

Russell (GEF)   ———. *Guns on the Early Frontiers: A History of Firearms from Colonial Times through the Years of the Western Fur Trade*. Berkeley: University of California Press, 1962.

Space   Space, Ralph S. *The Lolo Trail: A History of Events Connected with the Lolo Trail Since Lewis and Clark*. Lewiston, Idaho: Printcraft Printing, 1970.

Speck   Speck, Gordon. *Breeds and Half-Breeds*. New York: Clarkson N. Potter, 1969.

Sprague (GG)   Sprague, Marshall. *The Great Gates: The Story of the Rocky Mountain Passes*. Boston: Little, Brown, 1964.

Stoddard   Stoddard, Amos. *Sketches, Historical and Descriptive, Of Louisiana*. Philadelphia: Mathew Carey, 1812.

Thwaites (EWT)   Thwaites, Reuben Gold, ed. *Early Western Travels*. 32 vols. Cleveland: Arthur H. Clark, 1904–7.

Thwaites (LC)   ———, ed. *Original Journals of the Lewis and Clark Expedition, 1804–1806*. 8 vols. New York: Dodd, Mead, 1904–5.

Uphof   Uphof, J. C. Th. *Dictionary of Economic Plants*. New York: Verlag von J. Cramer, 1968.

Voget   Voget, Fred W. *The Shoshoni-Crow Sun Dance*. Norman: University of Oklahoma Press, 1984.

Wedel (NPT)   Wedel, Waldo R. "Notes on the Prairie Turnip (*Psoralea esculenta*) Among the Plains Indians." *Nebraska History* 59 (Summer 1978): 154–79.

Weems   Weems, John Edward. *Men Without Countries: Three Adventurers of the Early Southwest*. Boston: Houghton Mifflin, 1969.

Welsh et al.   Welsh, S. L., N. D. Atwood, L. C. Higgins, and S. Goodrich. *A Utah Flora*. Great Basin Naturalist Memoir No. 9. Provo: Brigham Young University, 1987.

West   West, Helen B. "Meriwether Lewis in Blackfeet Country." Museum of the Plains Indian, Browning, Montana, 1964.

Wheeler   Wheeler, Olin D. *The Trail of Lewis and Clark, 1804–1806.* 2 vols. New York: G. P. Putnam's Sons, 1904.

Wood & Moulton   Wood, W. Raymond, and Gary E. Moulton. "Prince Maximilian and New Maps of the Missouri and Yellowstone Rivers." *Western Historical Quarterly* 12 (October 1981): 373–86.

Wood & Thiessen   Wood, W. Raymond, and Thomas D. Thiessen, eds. *Early Fur Trade on the Northern Plains: Canadian Traders among the Mandan and Hidatsa Indians, 1738–1818.* Norman: University of Oklahoma Press, 1985.

Index

Medical problems (*continued*)
smallpox, 308–9; malaria,
346; dermatitis, 366n;
sunburn, 365–66; infec-
tious conjunctivitis, 366n;
illness, 45–46, 57–58,
59n, 79, 162, 204–5, 209,
255, 281, 365; injury, 3,
35–36, 138, 200, 202–3,
285, 286n

Medicine: cleaning and dressing, 35; poultices, 46, 57,
58, 59n, 158, 205; mer-
cury, 79; laudanum, 107;
lint, 156, 157n; tents, 156,
157n, 324; opium, 162;
litters, 204–5; chocolate,
359; mentioned, 164, 419.
See also Bark, Peruvian

Medicine Rock Coulee, 120n

Medicine (Tylor's) River,
324–25, 324–25n, 335,
380, 398, 417

Mediterranean Sea, 346

Melanerpes erythrocephalus,
144n. *See also* Wood-
pecker, red-headed

Melanerpes lewis, 78n

Melanoplus saguinipes, 208n

Melanoplus spretus, 208n

Meleagris gallopavo, 325n

Melgares, Facundo, 364n

Members of party: hunting,
46–47, 74, 77, 85, 93,
104, 106, 163, 286, 309,
321, 325, 327, 329, 351;
duties, 77, 283; return,
106–7; sent out, 111, 169;
morale, 137; rations, 146;
and tobacco, 172

Menetarra village, 305n

Mercury. *See* Medicine

Mertensia paniculata, 30n

Metaharta village, 298, 303,
303n

Meteorology. *See* Weather
observations

Mexico, 356n

Milk River, 120n, 123, 123n,
147, 148n, 150, 151n,
381, 400

Milkvetch, 193n

Miller Creek, 85, 86n, 100

Mill (Scattered) Creek, 393,
410

Miner Creek, 183, 186, 188n

Mission (Stinking Cabin)
Creek, 189, 192, 192n,
391, 409. *See also* Locke
Creek

Mississippian Madison
Group, 180n

Mississippi River: conditions,
374; distances on, 377,
388–89, 414; animals on,
416; mentioned, 79, 347n,
355, 355n, 370, 370n, 417

Missouri, camps in: Atchi-
son County, 355n; Holt
County, 356n; Andrew
County, 357n; Buchanan
County, 357n, 358n,
359n; Jackson County,
361n; Clay County, 361n;
Carroll County, 362n;
Saline County, 365n;
Cooper County, 365n;
Cole County, 366n; War-
ren County, 368n; St.
Charles County, 369n;
St. Louis County, 370n

Missouri Fur Company,
198n, 279n, 316n

Missouri Indians, 354n, 378,
395

Missouri River: Indians on,
52, 74, 88, 157, 213–14,
278, 280, 289, 291, 301,
314, 323, 360, 362, 412;
conditions, 71, 140–41,
146, 298, 354, 414; de-
scribed, 79, 111–12, 114,
118, 140, 147, 183, 186,
191, 248, 277, 310, 322,
343, 353, 365; animals on,
97, 106, 125, 128, 139,
141, 276, 278, 321, 374,
414; arrive at, 106, 334;
characteristics, 112, 114,
238; hunting on, 146,
157, 276, 280, 290, 322,
356; distances on, 277,
291, 359, 377, 388, 412;
navigational problems on,
278, 411; mentioned,
1–4, 43n, 85, 87n, 93, 95,
96n, 98n, 102, 104, 106n
107, 107n, 108n, 111n,
112n, 120n, 137, 139n,
140n, 147n, 148n, 151n,

154, 157–58, 158n, 162n,
180n, 183n, 188n, 252,
275, 279n, 280n, 281n,
282n, 286, 287n, 289n,
303n, 316n, 323n, 328n,
343n, 345n, 346, 347n,
349n, 350n, 352, 352n,
353n, 354, 355n, 357n,
358n, 359n, 361, 361n,
362n, 364n, 365n, 367n,
368n, 370, 376, 378, 382,
389, 392–93, 415–17,
418n

Missouri River. *See also* Big
Bend of the Missouri
River; Great Falls of the
Missouri River; Stone
Walls of the Missouri
River; Three Forks of the
Missouri River; White
Cliffs of the Missouri

Mitutanka village, 305n, 307n

Moccasins. *See* Clothes

Mock orange, Lewis's, 13n

Molothrus ater, 108n

Moniteau Creek, 377, 395

Montagne à la Bosse, 212n

Montana, camps in: Missoula
County, 65n, 69n, 86n,
90n; Powell County, 92n;
Lewis and Clark County,
95n, 96n, 98n; Cascade
County, 98n, 99n, 100n,
106n, 107n, 108n, 122n;
Chouteau County, 111n,
115n, 137n, 139n, 140n;
Liberty County, 116n;
Toole County, 117n,
120n; Glacier County,
122n, 124n; Pondera
County, 133n; Blaine
County, 141n; Fergus
County, 142n; Phillips
County, 142n, 145n; Pe-
troleum County, 145n;
Valley County, 147n,
148n; McCone County,
148n; Richland County,
149n; Ravalli County,
162n, 164n, 166n;
Beaverhead County,
169n, 171n, 173n, 176n,
177n; Jefferson County,
178n; Madison County,
178n; Gallatin County,

Pronghorn (antelope, cabri,
goat) (*continued*)
232, 259, 326, 417; described, 112; habits, 112;
scarcity, 238; mentioned,
92n, 115, 179, 210, 237,
245, 255, 327n, 328, 418n
Proulx, Basil, 369–70, 369n
Prunus americana, 324n. *See
also* Plum, wild
Prunus pensylvanica, 159n. *See
also* Cherry, pin
Prunus serotina, 159n
Prunus virginiana, 12n. *See
also* Cherry, choke
Pryor, Nathaniel: sent out, 3,
205, 208, 211–12,
218–19, 222n, 265, 303,
326; duties, 74, 77, 170,
175, 209–10; separated,
156, 285n; listed, 162n,
179; hunting, 182; returns, 206, 218, 283–85,
334; journal, 212n, 286n;
creek named for, 219,
222n, 229n, 286n; injured, 285, 286n; route,
285n, 286n; mission
(1807), 316n; mentioned,
176–77, 332
Pryor Creek, 223, 227, 229n,
285, 286n, 391, 408
Pryor Mountains, 198, 203n,
205, 208n, 228n, 286n
Pseudotsuga menziesii, 12n. *See
also* Fir, Douglas
Psoralea esculenta, 283n. *See
also* Breadroot
Puget (Sea Otter) Island, 387,
405
Pumice, 414
Pumpkin Creek, 248, 250n
Pumpkins, 350
Pursh, Frederick, 13n, 21n,
80n
Purshia tridentata, 94n
Pyrite, 379

Quarie, 369
Quartzite, 124n
Quawmash (and similar spellings). *See* Camas
Quercus alba, 345n
Quercus borealis, 418n

Quercus macrocarpa, 345n. *See
also* Oak, bur
Quinn Creek, 186, 188n
Quivers, 135

Raccoon, 355, 356n, 416,
418n
Rafts, 82–83, 86n, 137, 323
Rain. *See* Weather conditions
Rainbow Falls, 111, 112n
Rampart Creek (Marapa
River), 318, 319n
Rattlesnake, prairie, 147,
148n, 266, 267n
Rattlesnake Cliffs, 175–76,
176n, 299n
Rattlesnake Creek
(Beaverhead County),
175, 176n
Rattlesnake Creek (Missoula
County), 86–87, 87n,
89n, 100
Rattlesnakes, 176, 238
Raven, common, 75, 78n, 93,
117, 210
Razor Creek, 223, 227, 229n
Recurvirostra americana, 114n
Redcedar, western, 25, 26n,
28
Red River, 355n
Redroot, 7, 11, 12n
Reed, 367, 368n
Reservation Creek (Custer
County, Mont.), 248,
249–50n
Reservation Creek (Rosebud
County, Mont.), 240,
241n, 407
Revolutionary War, 370n
Rhamnus purshiana, 12n. *See
also* Cascara
Rhus aromatica, 240n
Rhus glabra, 12n. *See also*
Sumac, smooth
Rhus radicans, 12n. *See also*
Ivy, poison
Ribbons, 78, 314, 338
Ribes americanum, 203n. *See
also* Currant, wild black
Ribes aureum, 107n. *See also*
Currant, golden
Ribes inerme, 100n
Ribes irriguum, 13n
Ribes niveum, 13n

Ribes oxyacanthoides, 287n
Ribes setosum, 100n, 287n
Ricara (and similar spellings)
Indians. *See* Arikara
(Ricara) Indians
Richard, 348n
Richweed, 338, 344n
Rifle, Model 1803, 156, 157n
Rifles, 27, 29, 34, 36, 80,
137n, 138, 155–56, 289n.
See also specific weapons;
Arms and ammunition
Rings, 318
Rio Grande del Norte, 277,
279n
Riparia riparia, 210n
Rivet, François, 311, 316n
Roaring Lion Creek, 163,
164n
Robes, 288, 302, 314, 318
Robidoux, Joseph, 362, 362n
Robin, American, 75, 78n,
93, 419
Rochejhone (and similar
spellings). *See* Yellowstone
(Rochejhone) River
Rock Creek (Beaverhead
County, Mont.), 171n
Rock Creek (Klickitat
County, Wash.), 403
Rock Creek (Ravalli County,
Mont.), 163, 164n
Rock Creek (Yellowstone
County, Mont.), 408
Rock (North Mountain)
Creek (Phillips County,
Mont.), 142, 142n, 382,
400
Rocky Creek, 181–82, 183n,
185, 392, 409
Rocky Mountain House,
133n
Rocky Mountains: Indians,
14, 18, 131, 388; observed, 26, 201, 205, 217,
224–25, 227; plants, 30n,
126n, 132n, 270n, 416;
route through, 88, 377,
384; animals, 89, 145,
238; birds, 112, 112n; described, 122–23, 392;
Colter in, 303n; conditions, 414; mentioned, 23,
73n, 87, 96n, 97, 103,